CUSTOM AS A SOURCE OF LAW

A central puzzle in jurisprudence has been the role of custom in law. Custom is simply the practices and usages of distinctive communities. But are such customs legally binding? Can custom be law, even before it is recognized by authoritative legislation or precedent? And, assuming that custom is a source of law, what are its constituent elements? Is proof of a consistent and long-standing practice sufficient, or must there be an extra ingredient – that the usage is pursued out of a sense of legal obligation, or, at least, that the custom is reasonable and efficacious? And, most tantalizing of all, is custom a source of law that we should embrace in modern, sophisticated legal systems, or is the notion of law from below outdated, or even dangerous, today? This volume answers these questions through a rigorous multidisciplinary, historical, and comparative approach, offering a fresh perspective on custom's enduring place in both domestic and international law.

David J. Bederman is K. H. Gyr Professor in Private International Law at Emory University. Professor Bederman has published extensively on diverse legal topics, including legal history, constitutional law, and international legal theory and practice. In addition to a number of books and dozens of articles and essays, his major publications include *Globalization and International Law* (2008), *The Classical Foundations of the American Constitution* (2008), *The Spirit of International Law* (2002), *International Law in Antiquity* (2001), and *International Law Frameworks* (2001).

D1569205

CUSTOM AS A SOURCE OF LAW

DAVID J. BEDERMAN

Emory University School of Law

CAMBRIDGE
UNIVERSITY PRESS

CAMBRIDGE UNIVERSITY PRESS
Cambridge, New York, Melbourne, Madrid, Cape Town, Singapore,
São Paulo, Delhi, Dubai, Tokyo, Mexico City

Cambridge University Press
32 Avenue of the Americas, New York, NY 10013-2473, USA

www.cambridge.org
Information on this title: www.cambridge.org/9780521721820

First published 2010

Printed in the United States of America

A catalog record for this publication is available from the British Library.

Library of Congress Cataloging in Publication data
Bederman, David J.
Custom as a source of law / David J. Bederman.
p.   cm.
Includes bibliographical references and index.
ISBN 978-0-521-89704-4 (hardback) – ISBN 978-0-521-72182-0 (pbk.)
1. Customary law.   2. Law – Sources.   I. Title.
K282.B43 2010   340.5–dc22
2010022750

ISBN 978-0-521-89704-4 Hardback
ISBN 978-0-521-72182-0 Paperback

In Memory of Harold J. Berman
Colleague, Mentor, and Friend

Contents

Preface

Few people today are likely to concur with the classical Greek poet Pindar's maxim, "Custom is the king of all."[1] Nevertheless, the thrust of this book is that custom – the unofficial and unenacted practices of communities – lives as a source of obligation in contemporary legal cultures and remains a potent jurisprudential force, for both domestic polities and international law.

A central puzzle in jurisprudence has been the role of custom in law. Custom is simply the practices and usages of distinctive communities. But are such customs legally binding? Can custom be law, even before it is recognized by authoritative legislation or precedent? Assuming that custom is a source of law, what are the elements of custom? Is proof of a consistent and long-standing practice sufficient, or must there be an extra ingredient that the practice is pursued out of a sense of legal obligation or, at least, that the custom is reasonable and efficacious? How does one actually prove a custom? Most tantalizing of all, is custom a source of law that we should recognize in modern, sophisticated legal systems, or is the notion of "law from below" outdated, or even dangerous, today?

I came to write this book as a consequence of my friendship and collaboration with the late Harold J. Berman, my colleague at Emory Law School. We co-taught a one-credit-hour course on customary law on four occasions during the late 1990s and drew a packed audience of students. The course unfolded over seven two-hour lectures and tried to answer a deceptively simple question: Is all law ultimately derived from legislation or administration or adjudication, or is it also formed from the informal usages and understandings that are considered legally binding by those who practice or share them?

Traditionally, such binding usages and practices have been called "customary law." One peculiarity of the modern law school curriculum is that we do not give much reflection now to the sources of law in contemporary legal culture, and law students reflexively assume that all law must be derived from a legislature passing statutes or judges deciding cases. In short, we implicitly train law students from virtually their very first day of studies that law is a "top-down" social construct, an Austinian vision of authoritative commands. Harold Berman's insight for a course on customary law was to serve as an antidote to this assumption, to remind law students (as future lawyers and leaders) that law is as much made from the "bottom up" by relevant communities.

The course that Hal Berman and I taught together surveyed – like this book – the topic historically and comparatively, with material derived from anthropology and sociology (such as the law used by preliterate peoples) and legal history (especially the origins and evolution of the Western legal tradition and the English common law). The parts of the course that drew the most excitement (and epiphanies) from the students were the discussions of the use of custom in contemporary tort, property, commercial, and even constitutional law. When students realized that custom was all around us as lawyers (whether trade usages in the Uniform Commercial Code,[2] or industry practices as establishing a standard of care,[3] or in separation-of-powers disputes[4]), it became easier to accept its role in today's legal practice. This was especially so after Hal's set of lectures on international commercial custom – the *lex mercatoria* – for millennia used by global communities of merchants to regulate such aspects of trade as the content of bills of lading and cargo insurance (for ocean transport), letters of credit, and other forms of international documentary transactions.

There is a central set of paradoxes for customary law, and students were quick to recognize and exploit these in their questions and discussion: Isn't there something more that makes a community practice into a binding custom? Customs can be both good and evil; how does one distinguish between them? Is a custom binding even before it has been recognized by a court or legislature?

In response, Hal told a simple story, one that says much about him as a clever teacher, an insightful scholar, and a devoted family man. Hal was married to his wife, Ruth, for sixty-six years before he passed away in 2007. According to Hal, every Sunday for those sixty-six years, he would prepare a brunch for Ruth (provided they weren't traveling away from home). By any measure of consistency ("every Sunday") and duration ("sixty-six years"), this was an established usage and practice of a particular community – the Berman household. But, Hal asked the class (with an inevitable grin and accompanying laughter from the students), is this a binding custom? What if, Hal mused, one Sunday morning he just didn't feel like making brunch, or (in a fit of pique) he was angry with Ruth and wanted to withhold a meal? Could Ruth sue him for specific performance? Had an informal usage ripened into a binding custom?

Had the extra ingredient been added that converted a "mere" practice into a "legal" custom?[5]

Never in the course of our teaching did Hal and I reach a resolution on this simple example, freighted with great wisdom. This book reflects my humble attempt to provide a comprehensive survey of customary law. At the same time, I essay here a broad jurisprudential explanation for custom as a source of law, even though this subject has seemed to be impervious to previous attempts at consistent theorization.[6]

The narrative here unfolds in three steps. In Part One of this book, I survey the broad and rich interdisciplinary literature of customary law, focusing on ethnography and anthropology, cultural and legal history, sociology, psychology, and economics. The intellectual history of customary law that I trace in Part One has broad implications for the rest of the volume. It is indispensable in establishing the discussion in Part Two, which is a review of the role of customary norms in a variety of contemporary domestic jurisdictions, with examples drawn from European, North American, African, and Pacific Basin polities. Here, the narrative is organized around discrete realms of legal doctrine within which custom remains influential. These include family law, property, contracts, torts, and even constitutional law. This analysis naturally segues into Part Three of the book, in which the current role of custom in international law (both private and public) is assessed. While disputes about the relevance of customary norms in their transnational settings have been quite contentious – especially as to trade usages in the "new" law merchant and with regard to customary international law – these species of custom share many characteristics with those in domestic law contexts.

When viewed all together, I try to propose here an integrated (although not completely unified or complete) theory of custom. I argue that custom's jurisprudential foundations are strong and deep. They are premised on such diverse justifications as the functional reciprocity of obligations, the rationality and utility of customary rules, and the positive act of law-making by a community of legal actors. Also characteristic of customary legal systems is an acceptance and recognition of pluralism for norms, a robust mechanism for signaling the acceptance or rejection of new rules, and a general struggle for law. All of these attributes give customs their legitimacy and durability.

As for the elements of custom, I contend that the best algorithm for the creation of customary norms is the traditional notion that there must be *both* proof of an objective practice within a relevant community *and* a subjective determination of the value of the norm, whether expressed as a sense of legal obligation or the reasonableness of the rule. Lastly, I contend here that custom has a rightful place as a source of legal obligation in mature and sophisticated legal cultures such as our own. More than that, custom is all around us. It is followed in a multiplicity of communities, recognized in a variety of jurisdictions, and enforced in many different doctrinal situations. Custom is alive and well, so it would be wise to grant it the jurisprudential respect it deserves.

I incurred many obligations in writing this book, the gestation of which took more than fifteen years. I have already acknowledged the intellectual debt I owe to my departed colleague, Professor Harold J. Berman. This project was nurtured through workshops at Emory Law School and completed during a sabbatical leave from my home institution. Superb research assistance was provided by reference librarians at Emory University and the University of Virginia School of Law (where I held a visiting appointment in 1996–97). I also profited from scores of conversations with colleagues, particularly through the American Society of International Law and its committees on International Law in Domestic Courts and International Legal Theory. Short passages in this book have previously appeared in print, including material in Chapters 3, 6, and 11.[7]

Particular thanks go to my editor at Cambridge University Press, John Berger, who encouraged this project at every step. As always, without the love and support of my family, this book would not have been possible.

Abbreviations

AJCL	American Journal of Comparative Law
AJIL	American Journal of International Law
AJJ	American Journal of Jurisprudence
Ann. Dig.	Annual Digest of Public International Law Cases
Blackstone	William Blackstone, *Commentaries on the Laws of England* (1765–69)
BYBIL	British Year Book of International Law
CLR	Columbia Law Review
Eng. Rep.	Reports of English Cases (1094–1873)
F. Cas.	Federal Cases (U.S.) (1789–1880)
F.2d & F.3d	Federal Reporter (U.S. appeals) (1880-)
F. Supp.	Federal Supplement (U.S. districts) (1932-)
HLR	Harvard Law Review
I.C.J.	International Court of Justice
ICLQ	International and Comparative Law Quarterly
I.L.M.	International Legal Materials
I.L.R.	International Law Reports
JAL	Journal of African Law
JLE	Journal of Law and Economics
JLS	Journal of Legal Studies
LSI	Law and Social Inquiry
P.C.I.J.	Permanent Court for International Justice
RCADI	Recueils des Cours de l'Academie de Droit International de la Haye
Stat.	U.S. Statues at Large
UCLR	University of Chicago Law Review
U.N.T.S.	United Nations Treaty Series
U.N. Doc.	United Nations Document

U.S.	United States Supreme Court Reporter (when used in the Notes)
U.S.C.	United States Code
VCLT	Vienna Convention on the Law of Treaties
VJIL	Virginia Journal of International Law
VLR	Virginia Law Review
Y.B. Int'l L. Comm'n	Yearbook of the U.N. International Law Commission
YLJ	Yale Law Journal

CUSTOM AS A SOURCE OF LAW

PART ONE

Customary Law in Perspective

1

Anthropology
Custom in Preliterate Societies

All law begins with custom. Anthropologists know this, and see the role of custom in law as part of a larger phenomenon of the law of primitive peoples, or even more simply "primitive law."[1] While that label for this subject is admittedly preferable to older references to the "law of savages,"[2] it is not the terminology adopted here because of the value judgments and moral freighting of distinguishing between human societies that are "primitive" and "modern." For the purposes of considering this topic, it seems unnecessary to denominate any jurisprudence as "primitive," and it also deflects focus from the real attributes of these societies: the nonliterate or preliterate character of their material and legal culture. This is not just "political correctness"; it is a search for an accurate and neutral term-of-art. So, to the extent that anthropological and ethnographic scholarship has informed our understanding of custom's role in law, it seems best to describe this subject as part of the law of preliterate societies. This is so, irrespective of whether such groups ultimately make the transition and reach a level of literate legal culture, are nomadic or sedentary in character, or are tribal or semipermanent in structure.

Presumably all law in preliterate culture is custom. But, as a matter of ethnographic study, that may not always be the case, and it leads to a central quandary explored in this volume: Is custom always unwritten or unenacted law? A related question to be addressed in this chapter is whether customary norms of behavior should be a more important source of law in preliterate societies, as opposed to those with a vibrant, literate legal culture.

Another significant aspect of an anthropological view of custom is that it should help discern the strengths and weaknesses of the use of custom in preliterate societies. After all, custom should reinforce what people really *do*, rather than what they *say* they do. If a society's law is based nearly exclusively on custom, it should, at least notionally, succeed in perfectly tracking human behavior or, at least, social expectations of proper social norms. The problem is distinguishing between binding customs and mere habits of a group (or subgroup) in a particular culture. A theme that runs throughout this volume is to identify what I have already called the "extra ingredient" that converts a helpful or gracious usage or practice into a binding norm of customary law.[3] In preliterate cultures, it might be especially daunting to identify a social or psychological element of coercion in behavior that accounts for this transformation, but that has been a major task for ethnographers working in the field.

If there are signal strengths in the use of custom by preliterate societies, so, too, must there be substantial weaknesses, and these observations have come to dominate the ethnographic literature on this subject. Custom, one might presume, cannot easily change to meet new social patterns or challenges. Custom can become hardened into formalism and ritual, empty of meaning and divorced from social context. A related concern is that custom that is appropriate for one type of social behavior is incorrectly applied (by analogy or other means) to an unrelated social situation. In such a manner reasonable usages can become unreasonable customs.[4] Finally, custom can be used as a method of social control by elites. Since customary law in preliterate cultures is definitionally unwritten, it falls to "keepers" of custom to maintain its integrity and substance – and to apply and enforce it. Whether these are aristocracies or sacerdotal colleges, as Sir Henry Maine described in his 1861 volume *Ancient Law*,[5] they effectively exercise monopolies on legal knowledge and can be responsible for the maladministration of justice or, even worse, corruption of the entire legal system. In short, if customary law is unwritten and unenacted, how can it be consistently and fairly administered across a wide population over a long period?

To grasp the vast anthropological literature on sources of law in preliterate societies, it makes sense to start with the theories of custom on this subject as they have evolved over the past century or so. My goal here is not so much to chart an intellectual history of custom in "primitive law," but rather to stake out the main contours of the debate that has defined what legal custom really is in these societies. That should allow a fresh look at how ethnographers have understood the proof, applications, and evolutions of custom in a variety of preliterate societies. Lastly, we can see how many preliterate societies made the transition to literate legal cultures and the consequent effects this has had on the role of custom as a source of law in their jurisprudence.

THEORIES OF CUSTOM IN THE LAW OF PRELITERATE SOCIETIES

For anthropologists and ethnographers, developing a working theory of custom in preliterate societies has been mostly a matter of a preoccupation with, and a struggle over, definition. As one might expect, H. L. A. Hart, in his magisterial *The Concept of Law*, captured the wide nuances of the debate in a few well-chosen words:

> It is, of course, possible to imagine a society without a legislature, courts or officials of any kind. Indeed, there are many studies of primitive communities which not only claim this possibility but depict in detail the life of a society where the only means of social control is that general attitude of the group towards its own standard modes of behaviour in terms of which we have characterized rules of obligation. A social structure of this kind is often referred to as one of "custom": but we shall not use that term because it often implies that the customary rules are very old and supported with less social pressure than other rules. To avoid these implications we shall refer to such a social structure as one of primary rules of obligation. If a society is to live by such primary rules alone, there are certain conditions which ... must clearly be satisfied. The first of these conditions is that the rules must contain in some form restrictions on the free use of violence, theft, and deception.... Such rules are in fact always found in primitive societies.... Second, though such a society may exhibit the tension ... between those who accept the rules and those who reject the rules except where fear or social pressure induces them to conform, it is plain that the latter cannot be more than a minority ... for otherwise those who reject the rules would have too little social pressure to fear. This too is confirmed by what we know of primitive communities where, though there are dissidents, the majority live by the rules seen from the internal point of view.
>
> ... It is plain that only a small community closely knit by ties of kinship, common sentiment, and belief, and placed in a stable environment, could live successfully by such a régime of unofficial rules. In any other conditions such a simple form of social control must prove defective and will require supplementation in different ways.[6]

In Hart's conception, societies employing custom – or only "primary rules of obligation" – are "primitive" and merely a "simple form of social control." In such societies, custom "arises," whereas in more complex polities, law is "made."[7] Such primitive communities can only subsist within a small, "stable" ambit, where custom is sanctioned by ties of "kinship, common sentiment, and belief." Moreover, the primary norms of obligation must be kept limited – literally to the prohibition of lying, cheating, stealing, and killing – and there is always a subversive challenge to these customary norms by a large part of the community, who may only observe them out of a sense of "fear or social pressure" but not actual obligation or approval. Hart believed that custom was inflexible because it was not under anyone's rational control, and that without a prescribed procedure for changing custom, reform would be frustrated.[8]

Hart's standard critique of primitive custom was a caricature when initially written in 1961, and certainly completely outmoded when revised a decade later. And yet it continues to exert a substantial influence on the subject, far out of proportion to its limited engagement with anthropological and ethnographic empiricism. Despite his invoking[9] the great writers in this area – Bronislaw Malinowski, A. S. Diamond, Karl Llewellyn, and E. Adamson Hoebel – Hart does not appear to have read these works in any great depth. Had he done so, he would have discovered both methodological and substantive divisions in authority on the underlying question he was essaying: Can custom endure as a significant aspect of any legal system, whether "primitive" or "modern"?

Indeed, the debate goes back as far as Sir Henry Maine's 1861 treatise, which is only tangentially related to matters of custom and the preliterate legal cultures of ancient Greek, Roman, and Hindu societies. Maine does offer a distinction between "made" and "implicit" law,[10] and from this legal writers turned their attention to the problems posed by the use of custom in preliterate societies.[11] It was only with Bronislaw Malinowski's slim, provocative, and utterly subversive 1926 volume, *Crime and Custom in Savage Society*, that this subject came, finally and at long last, into ethnographic focus.[12] The reason is that Malinowski took sharp aim at previous scholars' critiques of primitive custom (later adopted by Hart), and did so through the lens of empiric observation of the Trobriand Islanders of New Guinea.[13]

Rather than viewing custom in preliterate societies as some sort of automatic and reflexive submission to immutable and outdated modes of behavior or social expectations,[14] Malinowski saw customary rules as the fulfillment of reciprocal social relationships. The intricate trade patterns between coastal and upland Trobriands were premised on the notion that "[e]ach community has … a weapon for the enforcement of its rights: reciprocity."[15] This, in turn, affected all customary obligations of the Trobriands, leading to "rules [that are] essentially elastic and adjustable, leaving a considerable latitude within which their fulfillment is regarded as satisfactory."[16] This principle of "give and take" in reciprocal customary relationships was enforced through sanctions of ostracism and removal from the community.[17]

"If we designate," Malinowski wrote,

> the sum total of rules, conventions, and patterns of behaviour as the body of custom, there is no doubt that a native feels a strong respect for all of them.... The force of habit, the awe of traditional command and a sentimental attachment to it, the desire to satisfy public opinion – all combine to make custom be obeyed for its own sake. In this the "savages" do not differ from the members of any self-contained community of a limited horizon, whether

this be an Eastern European ghetto, an Oxford college, or a Fundamentalist Middle West community.[18]

Malinowski believed that "the main factors in the binding machinery of primitive law" were "reciprocity, systematic incidence, [and the] publicity and ambition" of the participants in the customary social system.[19] Far from seeing law as a unitary phenomenon, Malinowski saw the law of preliterate societies as "not a homogeneous, perfectly unified body of rules, based upon one principle developed into a consistent system. [Rather,] the law of these natives consists … of more or less independent systems, only partially adjusted to one another."[20]

In short, Malinowski's ethnography of the Trobriands – developed through two years of continuous field study – culminated in three main empiric observations: that Trobriand society was generally orderly, that such order was not derived from such Western "trappings as police and courts," and that "despite the general prevalence of order, [Trobriands] regularly tested its limits by self-interested acts of deviance and resistance."[21] The Trobriands were, according to one set of later commentators, neither "primitive communists [nor] 'slaves to custom'."[22]

Although Malinowski's rudimentary methodologies for legal ethnography have been criticized,[23] along with his emphasis on "structural-functionalism" of reciprocal relations,[24] he reached some crucial conclusions about custom in preliterate societies. The first of these was that custom is a source of positive law, imposed not from the "top down" in an Austinian sense, but from the "bottom up" in the unique context of tribal cultures and values. In making this observation, Malinowski was marking a deep departure from the writings of earlier scholars such as Sidney Hartland.[25] Second, Malinowski acknowledged that custom requires obligation to be enforceable as law – whether as reflected in reciprocity, publicity, or ostracism as the sources of sanction. So, in this respect, he was the first to articulate a theory of custom in preliterate societies that distinguishes it from "mere" usages or practices,[26] and comes close to an *opinio juris* requirement that we will see in other customary law contexts. The chief problem of custom was, as Malinoswki saw it, to distinguish between "rules implicitly followed and rules formulated."[27] Lastly, Malinowski reminded his audience that customary law patterns of organization were hardly unique to preliterate societies, although he spoke chiefly of "the members of any self-contained community of a limited horizon."[28]

Malinowski's open-textured theory of custom in preliterate societies would not go unchallenged, however, and in 1941, Karl N. Llewellyn and E. Adamson Hoebel published *The Cheyenne Way: Conflict and Case Law in Primitive*

Jurisprudence, which would set in motion a disciplinary revolution in legal ethnography and also a new perspective on the role of custom in tribal cultures. That this volume was issued by one of the then-leading American philosophers of the legal realism school (as well as an authoritative law reformer)[29] and by a young fieldworker who would later become the preeminent legal anthropologist of his generation[30] only magnified its subsequent influence.[31]

It is no surprise that *The Cheyenne Way*'s primary contribution to the literature was methodological, insofar as the book's exposition emphasized a "realistic sociology" presented through "cases of trouble and how they were resolved" in Cheyenne society.[32] Based on fieldwork conducted over two summers in the Cheyenne country,[33] and the taking of oral histories of "trouble cases" from the past decades of Cheyenne Indian experience,

> the manner of interpretation rests in the first instance on the technique of the American case lawyer, save that each case is viewed not lopsidedly and solely as creator and establisher of correct legal doctrine, but is viewed even more as a study of men in conflict, institutions in tension, and laymen or craftsmen at work on resolution of tension. Law-stuff, seen thus, is seen more deeply and more sharply, simply as law-stuff. It is our firm conviction that to see it thus is to see it also in its working relation to social science at large. Modern American jurisprudence can thus enrich, and be enriched by, the study of non-literate legal cultures.[34]

The "trouble case" methodology, replete with a Case-Finder thoughtfully provided in the book's index,[35] was fully consistent with Llewellyn's legal realist bent and his emphasis on how particular legal cultures actually resolve disputes among their constituents.[36] It also reflected the prevailing tendencies of such ethnographers as Franz Boas, Llewellyn's and Hoebel's colleague at Columbia.[37] But Llewellyn and Hoebel's volume also exposed fatal flaws in their scholarly method. Not the least of these was the failure to fully capture the provenance and context of the "law stories" they collected through their oral histories (what they called "memory cases").[38] Many of these anecdotes ranged from the Cheyenne experience between 1820 and 1880, even before sustained contact with European intruders, and so may have reflected a Cheyenne way of life that was long gone by the time Llewellyn and Hoebel visited the reservation in 1935 and 1936.[39]

Qualms of methodology aside, the authors of *The Cheyenne Way* acknowledged their intellectual debt to Malinowski,[40] even as they aggressively contested his views on custom. The reason for this schism was apparent. It was essential for Llewellyn's jurisprudence to draw a sharp distinction between law and custom, between what participants in a legal culture *sense* are their rights and obligations and what they *know* for certain are.[41] Llewellyn and Hoebel thus sought to disprove a role of custom in Cheyenne folkways. By implication, they viewed Malinowski's theories of reciprocity with distrust since, they asserted, such theories depended on a clear expression of interests and persons involved in a customary usage that are notably absent in Cheyenne legal culture. Far from such usages being a "neutral custom" (as Llewellyn and Hoebel characterized Malinowski's theory[42]), there was no evidence of the validity of customs being reflected in the Cheyenne cases.[43]

Llewellyn and Hoebel's book is as flat a renunciation of the idea of customary practices in preliterate societies as any anthropologist could aspire to. "Custom" is a "slippery" "concept," they concluded.[44] For starters, custom is "ambiguous" – it *"fuse[s]* and *confuse[s]* the notion of 'practice' (say, a moderately discernible line of actual behavior) with the notion of 'standard' (say, an actually held idea of what the proper line of actual behavior should be).'[45] Second, "such terms as 'custom' ... lack edges. They *diffuse* their reference gently and indiscriminately over the whole of relevant society.... [T]hese concepts obscure that great range of trouble in which practices ... plus their appropriate standards ... can conflict within a [complex] society.'[46] Llewellyn and Hoebel went on to observe that

> such terms as "custom" ... have come to lend a seeming solidity to any supposed lines of behavior to which they are applied, and a seeming uniformity to phenomena which range in fact from the barely emergent hit-or-miss, wobbly groping which *may* some day find following enough to become a practice, on through to an established and nearly undeviating manner in which all but idiots behave.[47]

And so, if it were not enough that the concept of custom in preliterate societies was ambiguous, ill-defined, and both over- and underinclusive in content, it also "lead[s] attention and emphasis away from the fact that the firmest and clearest practice or standard operates only upon and through the minds of persons. Nowhere is the fact more basic to understanding than in regard to law-stuff.'[48]

Of course, the metaphysical language employed by Karl Llewellyn, as principal investigator of *The Cheyenne Way*, became the gist of jurisprudential legend – and the butt of criticism. Nowhere defined or otherwise explained in the book was the meaning of his curious phraseologies of "law-ways" or "law-stuff," which Llewellyn gleefully used to debunk Malinowski.[49] And while these circumlocutions may have been intended to blur the edges between "complex" and "primitive" legal cultures and demonstrate a common set of sociological values among various legal rules, norms, and institutions,[50] the result is a pervading sense of ethnographic imprecision in the book.[51] Even more damning, in their pursuit of a neoevolutionary view of culture, Llewellyn and Hoebel may have raised a romantic vision of the "noble savage," praising Cheyenne law-ways in a manner not supported by the empiric evidence or truly deserving of such jurisprudential favor.[52]

The last half-century has seen notable advances in methodologies for legal ethnography, including further refinements on "case studies" for the transcription of tribal legal usages and practices.[53] It would be difficult to say that much has been added to the Malinowski-Llewellyn-Hoebel debate on the general role of custom. Indeed, R. F. Barton in his 1949 volume, *The Kalingas: Their Institutions and Custom Law*, seemed to disclaim that there could even be a coherent theory of custom for preliterate societies.[54] Other writers tended to align themselves with Malinowski's reciprocity views,[55] and A. S. Diamond in the 1971 revision of his book, *Primitive Law Past and Present*, indicated that custom only matters if "there are breaches and sanctions follow breaches."[56]

Perhaps the fullest view of customary norms in the legal cultures of preliterate societies can be found in the work of Max Gluckman, including his *Politics, Law and Ritual in Tribal Society* (1965) and *The Judicial Process Among the Barotse* (2nd ed., 1967). Like Llewellyn and Hoebel, Gluckman was also jurisprudentially aligned with the legal realism school, in the wing led by Benjamin Cardozo. Gluckman embraced Cardozo's notion of "the creative energy of custom" and that "[i]t is ... not so much in the making of new rules as in the application of old ones that the creative energy of custom manifests itself today. General standards of right and duty are established. Custom must determine whether there has been adherence or departure."[57] For these reasons, Gluckman decried the false distinction between law and custom drawn by Llewellyn and Hoebel, "as if they are in some sense antithetical concepts.... Custom has the regularity of law but is a different kind of social fact."[58] But Gluckman took seriously the idea of legal man as a social animal – a reasonable person, unlike Malinowski's atomistic and autonomous creature who followed custom out of a reciprocal need for material necessities. Custom thus has an obligatory character of legal sanction, even though it is unenacted and not necessarily "court-enforced."[59] "'[L]aw'," according to Gluckman, "is a body of binding rules and includes 'custom'."[60]

This intellectual history sketch of custom's legal ethnography has a point: arriving at a working definition of custom in preliterate legal cultures. If law is not, as Harold Berman has forcefully argued, "a body of rules imposed on high[,] but ... rather an integral part of the common consciousness, the 'common conscience' of the community,"[61] then custom can have a notable resilience in societies facing profound change, not the least of which is transition to literate material culture.[62] The balance of this chapter explores both the strengths and weaknesses of custom in these contexts.

PROOF, APPLICATIONS, AND EVOLUTIONS OF PRELITERATE CUSTOM

Preliterate legal cultures all evinced similar responses to common challenges: organizing family structures, allocating communal property, ensuring respect for authority, and suppressing crime (especially homicide). These themes can be traced back to the early twentieth-century ethnography of Bronislaw Malinowski, who studied the Trobriand Islanders, a Melanesian society living off the northeast coast of New Guinea. The Trobriands recognized no political overlordship and instead were organized into distinct tribes and subtribes with a matrilineal organization of family units within tribes.[63] There was a strict hierarchy of relations within tribes (led by a chieftain), and low-grade disputes between villages of the same tribal organization were generally resolved amicably by procedures that we would recognize today as being a form of ritualized arbitration. Likewise, in the writings of Max Gluckman, who observed the customary law practices of the Barotse and Tiv peoples of what was then northern Rhodesia (now Zimbabwe) and the Tswana tribes of Bechuanaland (today's Botswana), he found common patterns of property rights and economic entitlements, order-maintenance strategies, and dispute settlement devices.[64]

For example, a crucial part of Trobriand family and property law was customs enforcing matrilineal authority and prohibiting incest among individuals in the same extended family unit. Indeed, both of these were subjects of the three customary case studies recounted by Malinowski, the first such attempt in legal ethnography. Prohibitions against incest are a feature of virtually every human community, and the Trobriands' absolute taboo on such conduct appeared to be vigorously enforced. But appearances were deceiving, and an apparent toleration for incest was found by Malinowski in the case of Kima'i, who had sexual relations within his exogamous unit (with the daughter of his mother's sister). "This had been known but generally disapproved of," according to Malinowski, but nothing was done until the maternal cousin's jilted lover publicly denounced Kima'i.[65] In response, Kima'i "put on festive attire and ornamentation, climbed a coconut palm and addressed the community," and after "launch[ing] forth a veiled accusation against the man [and invoking] the duty of his clansmen to avenge him," he flung himself sixty feet to his death.[66] Kima'i's rival was then repeatedly assaulted, seriously wounded, and then ostracized from the community.[67]

From this Malinowski could conclude that "[t]his is the ideal of native law, and in moral matters it is easy and pleasant to adhere to the ideal.... [but] [w]hen it comes to the application of morality and ideals to real life ... things take on a different complexion. ... [This] could be called a well-established system of evasion ... of one of the most fundamental laws of the tribe."[68] Or, put another way, this illustrates the tension in customary law between what is *said* and what is *done* in the enforcement of a social norm. But in other cases, Malinowski observed a high degree of compliance with custom among the Trobriands. In maintaining family order (which was the basis for all property law), they were especially uncompromising. In a matrilineal system of authority, this meant that a maternal uncle (not the father) is the head of a clan unit and a father must favor a nephew, not his own son. A prominent chief allowed his son, Namwana Guya'u, to remain at home and advanced him over his nephew and legitimate heir, Mitakata. After months of festering rivalry, Guya'u was ritually and permanently exiled (*yoba*) from the village.[69]

From Trobriand family and property law came important customary principles of status and intervillage relations. The Trobriands were very sensitive to gradations of hierarchy and status; certain kinds of affronts could not be tolerated (as witnessed in the Kima'i affair). Malinowski narrated the story of Si'ulobubu, a commoner who offered a choice insult to a rival chief, To'uluwa, during a long conflict between two tribes.[70] Even when the tribal war was resolved, Si'ulobubu's offense could not be forgiven and he was speared by To'uluwa's men. The victim's family acknowledged that he was deserving of that sanction and sought neither to initiate a vendetta (*lugwa*) nor to seek compensation (*mapula*).[71] For the resolution of disputes between ostensibly friendly tribes, a ritualized form of food challenge (*potlatch* in Pacific Northwest terminology, or *buritila'ulo* for the Trobriands) was adopted in which feasts of yams were exchanged between the contesting groups.[72]

Preliterate peoples understood that a practice might be observed in a community, but still did not rise to the level of a binding and obligatory custom. Gluckman noted among the Tswana that a usage unaccompanied by that extra ingredient of obligatory sanction was given one term (*mokgwa*), while a binding custom was denominated with a different label (*molao*).[73] Indeed, among the African tribes that Gluckman observed there was a fairly sophisticated jurisprudence to distinguish these two sources of law. To be a binding custom, a norm has to be (1) "certain and definite and established," (2) applicable to the parties, (3) not contrary to statute or another source of positive law, (4) "be reasonable and moral," and (5) "graced with antiquity" or at least respected as venerable.[74] Elders and judges were expected to know tribal customs; there was no need for a special proof that a custom at least existed.[75]

Gluckman's formulation of the proof and elements of preliterate custom illustrates a significant tension with other legal ethnographers.[76] While Malinowski certainly did not go so far as Llewellyn and Hoebel's view that the only customs that mattered were those norms, the violation of which were met by sanctioned force or coercion,[77] for the Polish ethnographer and his followers a customary norm is one that draws its sanction from reciprocal obligation. If one social segment no longer cared to follow a custom (or did not need to do so for purposes of serving some material advantage), the custom would wither away and die.[78] What Gluckman found among the Tswana and Barotse was that tribal elders and judges looked at all the relevant conduct of the parties to test conformance with both "mere" usage or practice and with obligatory custom. After all, an individual's violation of a minor usage (*mokgwa*) could still be evidence of greater wrongdoing or culpability; observance would demonstrate a party's *bona fides*.[79] Many African preliterate legal systems worked because they fundamentally assessed the reasonableness of conduct in light of custom.[80] In these two anthropological views we have a central dilemma for the legal character of custom. Is the "extra ingredient" that catalyzes a "mere" usage into a binding custom a sense of obligation (based on reciprocity), or is it the reasonable character of the norm?

If preliterate legal cultures can show us much about the formation and birth of customs, they also can illustrate how customs become obsolescent and die. Gluckman was especially mindful in his research of how African tribal systems attempted to reconcile sometimes apparently contradictory customs.[81] Even more pertinently, he showed these cultures could adjust to changing social conditions and decide that former customs were in desuetude, and thus had no further legal effect. In what Gluckman called "The Case of the Father and [H]is Son's Cattle," a tribal court held that a custom (one that allowed a father to claim right to his son's property disposable to third parties) was "unreasonable in the circumstances of modern life."[82]

One consistent theme among the ethnographic scholarship of custom in preliterate societies is the extent to which practices from "immemorial antiquity"[83] are transformed over time. In one particular doctrinal field, common to virtually all preliterate cultures – the law of homicide – this has especially been true. Whether among the Kalingas of Luzon Island,[84] the pre-removal Cherokee Nation,[85] the Cheyenne tribe,[86] various neolithic cultures,[87] or the medieval Germanic and Nordic peoples,[88] the cultural response to homicide evolved from sanctioned revenge killings (blood feud) to the payment of monetary penalties or exactment of symbolic penalties (*weregild* or composition). The customary response to murder thus was transformed from the realm of a private (or, at least, clan or tribal) offense, expiated by a retributive act, to a crime against the peace of the community at large, met by public sanctions. Similar trends have been observed in the transformation of preliterate cultures' customary norms of family, property, and delictual relations.

TRANSITIONS FROM PRELITERATE TO LITERATE LEGAL CULTURES

Indeed, the very process of converting a body of unwritten customs into the fabric of a literate legal culture has been a central dynamic for jurisprudential change, one that will be recounted in the following chapters. As an oral legal tradition is being transcribed, it is important to understand whether, and to what extent, older customs are being merely codified into written laws or are being "progressive[ly] develop[ed]"[89] in a more ambitious law-reform effort. Even more significantly, one might wonder whether, in making the transition to literacy, customary norms are even being recognized in such cultures as a legitimate source of law.

Sir Henry Maine was the first to raise these issues in his discussion of archaic Greek law emerging from the Homeric oral tradition. As he wrote:

> Even in the Homeric poems ... we have the germ or rudiment of a Custom, a conception posterior to that of Themistes or judgments. However strongly we, with our modern associations, may be inclined to lay down a priori that the notion of a Custom must precede that of a judicial sentence, and that a judgment must affirm a Custom or punish its breach, it seems quite certain that the historical order of the ideas is that in which I have placed them. The Homeric word for a custom in the embryo is sometimes "Themis" in the singular – more often "Dike," the meaning of which visibly fluctuates between a "judgment" and a "custom" or "usage." Νόμος [nomos], a Law, so great and famous a term in the political vocabulary of the later Greek society, does not occur in Homer.[90]

In preliterate societies, according to Maine's theory, a custom need not necessarily be "affirm[ed]" by a court ruling, or even a statutory enactment [*nomos*, in the sense that Maine (but not Pindar) described], in order to be valid and binding.[91]

This hypothesis has been empirically confirmed in the legal ethnography of several societies just on the cusp of transformation into literate material and legal cultures. Among the Tswana and Barotse, in Gluckman's narration, African tribal cultures retained custom as an essential source of law, even as they moved toward a virtual "common law" system of precedent or *stare decisis* borrowed from their British colonial masters.[92] Exactly the same phenomenon could be seen in the jurisprudence of the early nineteenth-century Cherokee nation[93] or those of twentieth-century North American tribal units,[94] all under pressure from the dominant legal culture of the United States.

For the purposes of the chapters that follow, and especially what Harold J. Berman described as the formation of the Western legal tradition, the crucial evolution was the passing of the legal folk culture of Germanic and Scandinavian peoples in northern Europe after the fall of the Roman Empire and before the High Middle Ages (approximately 500–1150 CE). Berman, as a contemporary adherent of the German Historical School,[95] placed in context the view that "all law is essentially the product of natural forces associated with the *Geist* of each particular people, and nothing is more representative of these evolutionary processes than the autochthonous customs which are found to exist in each community."[96] Stripped of any national romanticism (or even any fascist or atavistic overtones),[97] it seems beyond doubt that Germanic folk law (*volkrecht*) was particularly grounded in customary norms.[98] For Berman, there was a "sanctity [to] custom. Custom is sacred and its norms are sacred.... Yet the German folklaw does not fit easily into the model or archetype of Customary Law – ... including Archaic Law and primitive law – if only for the reason that it came under the influence of Christianity."[99] While one can certainly contest the spiritual impulses of early medieval folk custom in transition – and some scholars have done so[100] – that does not detract from Berman's wider point that custom can remain an enduring source of legal obligation even as societies move toward a firmer jurisprudential footing of legal rules and institutions. In short, custom can be a signal strength for any legal system – preliterate or literate, primitive or modern.[101]

Taken together, these are an especially important set of reflections in this book. That is why they are explored at the outset. Insofar as contemporary areas of law (including public international law and international commercial law) have been characterized as "primitive" in their fundamental character, it is necessary to understand this ostensible linkage between custom as an important source of law in those legal cultures and traditions that are, somehow and in some way, not recognized as fully "modern" or "fully-matured."[102] As H. L. A. Hart noted, "[c]ustom is not in the modern world a very important 'source' of law. It is usually a subordinate one...."[103] In such terms was custom condemned as not only being primitive, but not really positive, as a source of law. So, far from being an anachronistic beginning to this volume, problems raised by the "primitive" character of custom in all legal cultures shall be a recurring theme here.

2

Culture

The Western Legal Tradition of Positivism

If anthropology and ethnography have conditioned our understanding of the law of preliterate peoples and nonstate societies, cultural traditions have formed our judgments about the role of customary norms in "sophisticated" legal systems. In large measure, these cultural and social values have been transmitted to us today through the medium of the Western legal tradition. And although the very concept of a distinctive Western jurisprudential approach is a morally freighted idea and heavily contested in the literature,[1] it remains a useful point of reference for any discussion about the role of custom in law. As a matter of necessity, the Western customary law tradition is a cultural and historical construct that begins with Roman law, continues with its first reception in medieval Europe, and then climaxes with its later intellectual revival and transformation in the nineteenth century.

Given custom's cultural milieu, the central problem is appreciating whether custom is a species of natural law or positive law. This goes to such questions as whether a practice can displace a contrary statute (or other form of positive law-making authority) or can be in conflict with right reason. Can custom subsist in both local and general forms or just apply to particular groups or institutions within a polity? And (reverting to a matter raised in the last chapter) what exactly converts an informal usage into a binding custom? Framing these inquiries in this manner does not necessarily presume whether unenacted legal norms practiced by a community and respected as law are a form of positive law (and thus directly linked to the assent of the individuals following them) or of natural law (and so independently based on the exogenous morals and values of the relevant community without reference to consent).

CUSTOM IN ROMAN LAW

Our knowledge of the role of custom in Roman law – that body of jurisprudence that applied within the Roman Republic and the Western and Eastern
Empires (c. 700 BCE- 700 CE) – is based on a handful of legal writings. It was
these texts that were transmitted into various iterations of European civil law
as part of the Western legal tradition. From the Emperor Justinian's compilation of texts – the *Institutes, Digest,* and *Code* – some conclusions can be
readily drawn, and these reflect directly on the main inquiry of the status of
customary law as a positive source of legal obligation.

For example, in Justinian's *Institutes,* it is flatly stated that "the unwritten law
is that which usage has established; for ancient customs, being sanctioned by
the consent of those who adopt them, are like laws."[2] Custom was thus seen as
part of the "unwritten law" (*ius non scriptum*), and this is consistent with early
Roman Republican jurisprudence, derived from Greek philosophical sources,[3]
which allowed that binding legal sources were derived from "statutes, resolutions
of the senate, authority of the learned in the law, edicts of the magistrates, custom
and equity."[4] So even in early Roman jurisprudence, custom was seen as part of
the positive, affirmative law of a people (*nomos eggraphos* in Greek), not as a
form of natural law (*nomos agraphos* in Greek, or the *ius naturale* in Latin).[5] The
Institutes also make clear that custom is created by "usage" (*usus*) of "ancient custom" (*mores*) "sanctioned by the consent (*consensu*) of those who adopt them."[6]

Despite this strong endorsement for the positive roots of custom in Roman
law, there remains a significant linguistic problem derived from these ancient
juristic texts. The Justinianic materials refer to custom by a variety of terms.
Usus was a descriptive term for a practice or usage.[7] *Mos* and *mores* were
seemingly intended to reflect "general habits of life, that disposition towards
certain institutions ... which reside in the genius of the Roman people."[8]
Roman Republican sources often referred to the *mos maiorum* as the "custom
of our ancestors." Lastly, the phrase *consuetudo* was meant to reflect a usage
or practice that was accepted as law, either through an act of consent by the
people (tacit or express) or by other means of adoption.[9] Although contemporary scholars of Roman legal history have concluded that "too many different
things are included by the different expressions which we translate 'custom' ...
and too little distinction is drawn between them for us to formulate rules with
any certainty,"[10] nevertheless "custom is clearly accepted as a source in the law
of Justinian, and the rules which modern systems have evolved for testing the
validity of an alleged custom are taken partly from Roman texts."[11]

Part of the confusion over the nomenclature of custom in Roman law arises from the fact that it evolved over a millennia. In archaic Roman law, first established in the XII Tables, many customary norms were codified.[12] During the Roman Republic (c. 500 BCE – 30 BCE), the role of custom may have been limited in private law. Indeed, there appears to be only a handful of examples of private law duties (whether in family law, property, contracts, or delicts) that were derived from customary sources. One of these was the prohibition of marriage between closely related persons, a rule of incest that (as we have seen from the previous chapter) was common for all preliterate societies.[13] Likewise, the patrilineal principle of Roman family and society was enshrined in custom's rule of *patria potestas*, the right of the father (*paterfamilias*) over the lives of every member of his family.[14] In a related fashion, there was a customary norm against legally cognizable gifts between spouses, even though such donations were notionally allowed by statute, the *lex Cincia* of 204 BCE.[15] Custom also provided the basis for the rule of allowing minor children to substitute in an inheritance (pupillary inheritance, *substitutio pupillaris*).[16] In the law of contract, there was also a customary requirement for the approval of a tutor for the obligations of his ward,[17] and the complete and several liability of bankers in the transaction of *expensiliatio* (solidary liability for literal contracts of entries in account books).[18] In the area of delict, for one cause of action, the *legis actio per pignoris capionem*, we know that it was employed to enforce some claims in accordance with statute and others by custom.[19]

Roman law was more than the *ius civile*, or private law between citizens. It also included the *ius gentium* (in this sense, the law between foreigners and Roman citizens), the *ius honorarium* (those actions annually decreed by the urban praetor, the Roman official charged with the administration of justice), the *ius sacrum* (official religious practices),[20] and the *ius publicum* (that body of enacted statutory law).[21] Some of the *Digest* extracts clearly indicate such a result. For example, in Julian's statement (the remainder of which is heavily contested in the literature and will be explored below), "in those cases where we have no applicable written law [what is applied] is the practice established by customs and usage. And if this is in some way deficient, we should hold to what is most nearly analogical to and entailed by such a practice."[22]

In any event, by 212 CE and the *constitutio Antoniniana* – in which Roman citizenship was extended to all free inhabitants of the Empire – any distinction between *ius civile* and *ius gentium* was swept away, and, at the same time, local or provincial customs were recognized as binding in the legal practice of the Dominate and later Empire. This made sense since the universalization of Roman law over the entire vastness of the Empire had to be balanced with local interests and traditional customs.[23] Indeed, Justinian's *Digest* records extracts reflecting these developments towards a "vulgarized" Roman law that combined simplified Roman law procedures and customary norms.[24] Ulpian thus speaks of parties "relying upon a custom either of a *civitas* or of a province,"[25] and Modestinus cites a juristic opinion involving a peculiar local custom for the owners of estates, and not their tenants, to be responsible for grain rations and seasonal distributions.[26]

Analytically distinct from local or regional usages in Roman law were the practices of tribunals in various provinces – the custom of the courts (*mos iudiciorum*).[27] Sometimes these were pegged at high levels of abstraction, as in the rescript of the Emperor Severus, recorded by Callistratus in the *Digest*: "in cases of ambiguity arising from statute law, statutory force ought to be ascribed to custom or to the authority of an unbroken line of similar judicial decisions."[28] On other occasions, these court customs were highly technical, as in the amount of fees charged by advocates.[29] This ambiguity in the character of regional customs in Roman law – as reflecting either local popular usage or simply the outcomes of provincial tribunal rulings – has bedeviled the wider debate as to whether a custom can be truly binding except with a statutory recognition or a court ruling.[30] In writing his *Duties of a Proconsul*, Ulpian seemed to suggest just such a result: "When it appears that somebody is relying upon a custom either of a *civitas* or of a province, the very first issue which ought to be explored ... is whether the custom has ever been upheld in contentious proceedings."[31]

Roman law thus bears on three central questions about the role of custom in law. The first is what does it take to prove a custom? Second, what converts an informal usage into a binding practice? And, third, can a custom stand against a contrary statute or in the face of reason? Of these inquiries, the classical Roman law sources are most unsatisfying as to the first – what proves (as opposed to what confirms) a custom? As already noted, the key element of proof for Roman jurists was popular consent (*consensus omnium*) to a practice. While Julian wrote of "[a]ge-encrusted custom ... established by use and wont,"[32] and Hermogenian of "long custom ... observed over many years,"[33] the emphasis in the juristic sources is not on the proof of the antiquity, or even the longevity, of the usage. Rather, it is on the "accept[ance] by the judgment of the populace ... [through] the very substance of [their] actions,"[34] or "sanctioned ... by the tacit agreement of the citizen."[35] This accords with the general precept undergirding all Roman law, that "every rule of *jus* is either made by agreement or established by necessity or built up by custom."[36] So, at most, one can conclude that proof of a practice in Roman law depended upon a showing of its longevity, consistency, and widespread observance.

That begs the question, though, of what converted a practice, consistently and conscientiously observed by a populace, into a legally binding, cognizable, and enforceable custom. The traditional view of legal historians is that Roman law provided an answer.[37] The "extra ingredient" that catalyzed a mere usage into a binding custom was the sense of legal obligation on the part of the communities or individuals following the practice, or what was known in Latin as *opinio juris sive necessitatis*, or simply *opinio necessitatis*.[38] Although this doctrine was not expressed in the juristic sources, it is at least implicit in Julian's comment that custom is what "the populace has approved without any writing [and] shall be binding upon everyone. What does it matter whether the people declares its will by voting or by the very substance of its actions?"[39]

Of course, the defects of *opinio necessitatis* as an authoritative doctrine as to the formation (or transformation) of custom were as well known to the Romans as they are today. The first of these is the paradox that the birth of a custom is always premised on error.[40] If we believe that *opinio necessitatis* correctly describes the psychological condition of the first party to observe a custom as binding, then we would also have to agree that that "first-mover" of a custom was acting mistakenly. As Celsus suggested, "[a] proposition does not hold good in analogical cases if it was not originally brought in on a rational ground, but adhered to in the first place in error and thereafter by custom."[41] "Consequently," as Alan Watson has observed in relation to this paradox, "the first behavior rested on an error because the behavior was not accompanied by *opinio necessitatis* and should not be counted towards the creation of the customary law."[42] Taken to its logical extreme, no custom can ever be created unilaterally because every "first-mover" was acting erroneously as to the "binding" character or "sense of legal obligation" of the practice.

To answer this paradox in the formation of custom, such analytic jurisprudes or "high positivists" as John Austin announced that customary law was essentially a nullity – the "extra ingredient" that converted a usage into a custom was either statutory codification or judicial decree.[43] It is perfectly possible to reject Austin's extreme view that the relevant sources of law are reduced to the commands of the sovereign as reflected in the acts of its legislature and judiciary.[44] That does not necessarily resolve custom's formation paradox or its implicit challenge to a coherent view that custom is a form of positive law but different in character from traditional sources of legal obligation. The answer from Roman law is that custom is, indeed, a positive source of obligation, more akin to statute than some inchoate natural-law sense of morality or right or innate practices. As Gaius in his *Institutes* noted: "All people who are governed under laws and customs observe in part their own special law and in part a law common to all men."[45]

If Roman law's *opinio necessitatis* doctrine creates an incongruity at the birth of a customary norm, so, too, does it present a contradiction when a custom is in its death-embrace with a statute or its own obsolescence. A traditional critique of *opinio necessitatis* is that once a custom is established, it cannot be abandoned.[46] The processes of customary law formation are reversible: a practice develops contrary to a previous usage, with a growing sense that the previous custom is not binding. The real problem is what to do with a statutory rule that is contradicted by a later, emerging practice.

For this problem, classical Roman law provided two very different solutions. From the constitution of Constantine of 319 CE, as extracted in Justinian's *Code*, we have a proto-Austinian answer that "[t]he authority of custom and long-continuing usage is not to be taken lightly, but it is not to prevail to the extent of overcoming either reason or statute."[47] But from a controversial – and perhaps also interpolated or corrupted[48] – passage from Julian, as extracted in the *Digest*, there is this:

> Age-encrusted custom is not undeservedly cherished as having almost statutory force.... For given that statutes themselves are binding upon us for no other reason that they have been accepted by the judgment of the populace, certainly it is fitting that what the populace has approved without any writing shall be binding upon everyone.... [S]tatutes may be repealed not only by vote of the legislature but also by the silent agreement of everyone expressed through desuetude.[49]

Likewise, a passage from Justinian's *Institutes* says that "the laws which every state has enacted, undergo frequent changes, either by the tacit consent of the people or by a new law being subsequently passed."[50]

Consistent with this second set of sources there are examples of Roman statutes entering desuetude (literally and semantically the opposite of *consuetudo*) by reason of customary nonuse, including the second chapter of the *lex Aquilia*[51] and the statute barring the succession of *gentiles* (foreigners) to a Roman inheritance.[52] We also have some nonjuristic sources,[53] including the correspondence between the Emperor Trajan and the scholar-official Pliny the Younger concerning the continued validity of the *lex Pompeia municipalis Bithyniae data* (concerning the qualifications of provincial senators from the Bithynian city-states). The Emperor wrote: "[T]he authority of the statute (on the one hand) and long-continuing custom contrary to the statute (on the other) might place you in a quandary.... [W]e should make no change to what is past [and observe the custom] ... but in the future the *lex Pompeia* is to be observed; [but] if we wish to extend its force retroactively, this must need result in great confusion."[54] From this exchange we know that the idea of statutes (whether enacted by the old popular assemblies or by imperial decree) simply being abrogated by contrary customs did not sit well with Roman authorities, but it nevertheless occurred.[55]

That leaves the ultimate question of whether Roman law could contemplate the possibility of an unreasonable custom, and thus place in true tension *consuetudo* as *lex* (and thus positive law), but in violation of right reason (a natural law principle). The answer seems to be "no"; custom was viewed by the Romans as naturally capturing reasonable social necessity.[56] This is at least implicit with Celsus's principle that all law derives from a "rational ground," and no error should be confirmed or perpetuated by mere custom.[57]

CUSTOM IN THE MEDIEVAL *IUS COMMUNE*

Roman law provided a rich set of materials for future legal generations concerning custom as a source of law – its formation, character, and relative normative authority. After the rediscovery of Roman law as a source of study by law faculties of the medieval European universities at Bologna, Padua, Paris, Salamanca, Heidelberg, Cracow, Oxford, and Cambridge,[58] a bold effort was made to intellectually integrate Roman law principles with the bodies of law created by the Roman Catholic Church (the canon law) and the indigenous bodies of customary law regimes created (over the last half-millennium) for feudal and manorial,[59] commercial,[60] urban,[61] and royal[62] constituencies. The *ius commune* was this pan-European amalgam of inherited Roman law, the emerging canon law of the Church, and preexisting customary regimes.[63] The evolution of the *ius commune* – in the words of Richard Helmholz, neither "a code in the modern sense ... [nor] like the English common law"[64] – was largely driven by the interactions between legal scholars and officials (whether acting as judges or legislators) and constituent communities. The medieval *ius commune* was the cultural bridge of the Western legal tradition, with Roman law at one temporal post and early modern nation-state legal systems at the other.[65]

While obviously there were differences and variations in the *ius commune* among European polities (particularly as between England and the continent, more on which in the next chapter), there was also a surprising degree of commonality.[66] One of these was in respect to the nature of custom as a source of law. This was a natural development because customary law was competing for authority with no less than two legal juggernauts: the canon law of the Church and the centralized legal authority of such emerging national entities as Norman Sicily and Italy, Plantagenet England, the France of Philip II Augustus, and the Holy Roman Empire in Germany.[67]

The canon law developed a highly systematized approach to legal problems, including the hierarchy of sources within a religious polity that notionally observed divine scripture and natural rights as the highest law. Beginning with Gratian's *Decretum* (or, more accurately, the *Concordance of Discordant Canons*) of c. 1140 CE, which was likened to Justinian's *Digest* as a compilation and commentary on juristic writings, the canon law also developed through legislation: papal bulls or the decrees of church councils. The issues subsumed within canon law, and thus part of the legal jurisdiction of the Church (as distinct from secular polities), included not only internal Church administration and property, but also the personal status of all clergy (whether pastoral or in orders), as well as all family law (and attendant matters) for Church members.[68] The systematization of the canon law was largely seen as a reaction to the untoward dependence of the Church and its constituents on local customs in the resolution of disputes, as was common from 800 to 1200 CE.[69]

Using the Roman sources, canon law distinguished between mere practices (*mos* or *mores*) and binding custom (*consuetudo*).[70] And, like Roman law, the canonists saw custom as a species of positive, manmade law. Somewhat confusingly, Gratian articulated a wider notion of natural law that included not only the Gospels, but also any universally valid and reasonable legal principle.[71] In Gratian's hierarchy of legal authority, no human law – whether written or unwritten,[72] statutory or customary – could violate natural right and reason.[73] He elaborated on this point in an opening passage of the *Decretum*: "Custom is a sort of law established by usages and recognized as ordinance when ordinance is lacking. It does not matter whether it is confirmed by writing or by reason, since reason also supports ordinances.... Custom is so called because it is in common use."[74] If custom is subordinate to natural right, it must also give way to conflicting statutes or regulations,[75] although Gratian advised against promulgating laws at odds with the customs of the constituency for which the statute or regulation was intended.[76]

According to Gratian, the basis of custom (as opposed to a mere practice) is its long-standing observance,[77] the approbation of the relevant community in adopting the usage,[78] and its congruence with natural right and reason. The revolutionary move for Gratian and the canonists was to impose an anterior requirement of reasonableness for all customs as a condition for their recognition and enforcement. In a rhetorical flourish that would resonate throughout the legal history of the Middle Ages,[79] Gratian quoted Pope Gregory the Great's recast of the patristic remark that "Jesus did not say, 'I am the custom', but [rather], 'I am the truth'."[80] The totality of Gratian's and the canon law's treatment of customary law reflects, in the views of modern scholars, an intent to centralize legal authority within the Church and to suppress dangerous or irrational customs. The easiest way to accomplish this was to establish a metanorm that any challenged custom must be deemed rational and necessary by the relevant Church authority to which a dispute was addressed.[81] So, while Gratian said he would defer to the customs of the universal Church and a long-standing (and thus, perhaps, unassailable) local custom, newer practices should be abrogated if changing circumstances require this in order to protect the freedom of individual Christians.[82]

The wider *ius commune* came to adopt many of the modalities of custom from the canon law and Roman law. From the thirteenth and fourteenth centuries CE in Europe, local and regional customs were increasingly the subjects of written compilations, and although they ceased to be (strictly speaking) *ius non scriptum*, they were hardly enacted through affirmative legislative acts of codification.[83] Likewise, a harder distinction arose between the customary practices of a defined community (whether local or occupational in character) and the custom of the courts (the old Roman *mos iudiciorum*).[84] Nevertheless, the Roman law's and canon law's emphasis on antiquity and public consent as being necessary for the formation of a custom persisted.[85] Admittedly, antiquity was often converted into a period of years, usually no less than a decade or generation (20 years) or a comparable period from the Roman law of prescription.[86] One ambivalence that was removed from the preexisting Romanist and canonist sources was the relative place of custom in the hierarchy of legal authority, and the Middle Ages saw, for the first time, a clear notion that statutes preempted contrary custom.[87]

Another major innovation of the medieval *ius commune* was in how a disputed custom was to be shown in legal proceedings.[88] For Bartolus, a custom had to be proven on the competent testimony of two witnesses from the relevant community or be so notorious as to be the legitimate subject of judicial notice.[89] In actual practice in France, Germany, and the Low Countries, lay assessors were often employed for this purpose, joining judges for the proceeding.[90] Custom could also be determined by an inquisitorial process, *enquête par turbe*, by which a council of respectable citizens would give their opinion as to the content and scope of a customary practice.[91] Finally, a handful of medieval European jurisdictions (including the Outremer and Castille) took the position that a practice could only be formalized into a binding custom if it had been confirmed by at least one or two court judgments.[92] However ascertained, customs were then recorded in either juristic compilations or royal compendia (as with the French royal *bien commun de tous* described by Philippe de Beaumanoir in the thirteenth century[93]) that served as a future reference.

The medieval *ius commune* thus extended and enriched the classical, Roman law tradition for custom as a source of law. Aside from making definitive improvements in understanding how a community usage had to be proven in actual practice,[94] medieval European law also sought a reconciliation of the relative place of customary norms in a matrix that included other positive law-making (statutes, especially those of royal institutions) and natural-law values (including the holy scripture of the Church and essential community standards). This concordance of discordant doctrine was incomplete, however, and it would take nearly another half-millennia to attempt a reconciliation.

CUSTOM AND THE HISTORICAL SCHOOL

As has already been considered in the previous chapter,[95] a people's (whether pre- or postliterate) customary law has been regarded as the main pillar of their legal identity. This was a central tenet of what came to be called the Historical School of Jurisprudence, founded by Edmund Burke, Carl Friedrich von Savigny,[96] and Sir Henry Maine, and which has offered a "third-way" between the Scylla of positivism and the Charybdis of natural law. As primarily espoused by such writers as Savigny and Georg Friedrich Puchta,[97] custom was a species of positive law, but special and distinct as reflecting the "common consciousness of the people.... Custom therefore is the indicator (*kennzeichen*) and not a ground of origin (*enstehunsgrund*) of positive law."[98] The German historicists' conception of custom as something inchoate and almost mystical – premised on the will of the *Volk* – was, of course, an ontology, and not even very historical. While Roman law emphasized the *consensus omnium* in the formation of a customary rule, this was a matter of proof, not principle.[99] Nevertheless, the Historical School tended to exalt custom as a source of law, even ahead of the *ius scriptum* of statute.[100]

The historicist view of custom was, not surprisingly, assaulted on all fronts. There was, as always, the traditional high-positivist critique of Austin: custom had to be subordinate to affirmative legislation and could only be binding with judicial recognition or legislative codification. Even on its own terms, the historicist belief in a necessary link between custom and a nationalist *volkgeist* was savaged by a more internationalist and cosmopolitan vision of custom, tracing its intellectual lineage through the Romanist tradition of *ius gentium* and the medieval European *ius commune*. Insofar as the historicists ignored international customs (whether reflected in the *lex mercatoria* or public international law), their theory was regarded as practically deficient.[101] In addition, the German Historical School theory of custom was also in tension with Otto von Gierke's corporatist vision of society – with its emphasis on practical rationality and cooperative conduct between various social cohorts – inasmuch as historicists could embrace irrational or unnecessary customs.[102] Moreover, nothing in Savigny's or Puchta's theories actually explained what made a custom legally binding. This exposed the historicists to criticisms, derived from interpretations of Roman law, that a legal usage owed its force only to judicial pronouncements as merely the "custom of the courts."[103]

Lastly, from a sociological perspective, the German historicists' characterization of custom as *volkgeist* may have mischaracterized the elite nature of the processes of customary law formation. As Carleton Kemp Allen wrote,

> [c]ustoms are often the product not of a widespread conviction but of the convenience or interest of a ruling class which imposes its will on a majority of society. Many customs … are purely local in origin, and many are the result of mingled influences which cannot be called peculiarly popular or national.… Law is here a fact rather than an idea.… [C]ustom grows by the force of practical example far more than by the impulse of reasoned conviction.[104]

This flies in the face of custom being a "bottom-up" phenomenon, or, in the words of Harold J. Berman:

> [T]he Western legal tradition grew – in part – out of the structure of social and economic relationships within and among groups on the ground. Behavioral patterns of interrelationships acquired a normative dimension: usages were transformed into custom. Eventually custom was transformed into law. [L]aw … is custom transformed, and not merely the will or reason of the lawmaker. Law spreads upward from the bottom and not only downward from the top.[105]

Custom's cultural paradox – as an elite or popular institution, as a token of nationalism or of group identity, and as reflecting positive commands or natural values – remains as much a conundrum today as throughout the past two millennia.

3

History

The Common Law and Custom

If custom was largely perceived as a cultural phenomenon for medieval Continental jurists, it took on a decidedly historical cast in England. This would have a profound effect on attitudes towards custom in the Anglo-American common-law tradition, particularly with the normative hierarchy of custom in relation to other law sources, the requisite proofs of custom, and other restraints on evolving customary norms. In England, these transformations in the roles of custom took place over three broad periods. In what I refer to here as the "pre-Blackstonian epoch," two distinctive ideas of customary law emerged from the *ius commune* (considered in the last chapter). One of these was the idea that the judge-made common law was itself a customary regime. The other was the continuation of a more traditional notion of local or special systems of legal practices being recognized in derogation of the common law.

These two strands of English legal thought were woven together in the writings of Coke, Selden, and Hale as part of the English constitutional struggles of the sixteenth and seventeenth centuries, but were only finally fully synthesized and digested in William Blackstone's *Commentaries on the Laws of England* (1765). Blackstone's work was immensely influential for what would follow in British jurisprudence, but also for developments in the United States and other common-law jurisdictions,[1] and the full scope of his doctrine is recounted at length here. Post-Blackstonian intellectual currents – particularly Jeremy Bentham's writing, but also late-nineteenth- and early-twentieth-century debates in U.S. legal circles – will also be considered in order to give a full *tour d'horizon* of the common-law tradition's historic engagement with the role of custom in law.

THE PRE-BLACKSTONIAN EPOCH

As has already been discussed, the *ius commune* in England managed to combine elements of canon law, the law of the newly emerging royal courts, and preexisting customary regimes (especially in manorial and urban contexts). For certain matters – such as sanctuary on church grounds, secular jurisdiction over church officials, and mortuary fees for parishioner burial[2] – customary norms were typically followed by English tribunals, even though with the significant caveat that the practices had to be ruled as reasonable (and in accordance with other natural principles) in order to be found binding.[3] From these modest beginnings, customary practices in English law came to be more regularly and systematically observed. One of the first acts of William the Conqueror was, for example, to inquire of English nobility from all the counties their particular customs.[4]

At the same time, confusion arose as to whether the practice being referred to was a local or particular custom (for a specific community or trade), or, instead, the "general custom of the realm (*consuetudo regni*)."[5] Glanvill's volume *On the Leges and Consuetudines of England* (c. 1190) seemed to treat all the laws of England as unwritten, including not only customs but charters "promulgated about problems settled in council on the advice of the magnates and with the supporting authority of the prince."[6] The treatise writer known as Bracton (?1225–60), took a similar view of kingly authority to create a general custom of the realm, but also (at variance with Azo's *Summa Codicis*, of which it was quite derivative[7]) referred to "many *consuetudines*, varying from place to place, for the English have many things by *consuetudo* which they do not have by *lex*, as in the various counties, cities, boroughs, and vills."[8] Bracton elsewhere observed that "*consuetudo*, in truth, in regions where it is approved by the practice of those who use it, is sometimes observed as and takes the place of *lex*. For the authority of *consuetudo* and long use is not slight."[9] Indeed, Bracton discusses many examples of such particular customs running contrary to the general law of the realm.[10] Some of these variant customary regimes encompassed entire counties, as with the Kentist practice of *gavelkind*, which suspended the formal common-law rule of primogeniture for inheritance of real property.[11] And, most importantly of all, Bracton seemed to follow Roman juristic sources in not necessarily insisting on antiquity, or even a long temporal pedigree, in order for a putative practice to be confirmed as a binding custom.[12]

As English law developed during the Year Book period, the Janus-faced nature of custom persisted. John Fortescue in his mid-fifteenth-century pamphlet, *De Laudibus Legum Anglie*, suggested that English common law was derivative of customary practices of the English people, and not just necessarily the practices and precedents of the English royal courts.[13] Christopher St. German's volume, *Doctor and Student* (1528), went further to examine the essential "presuppositions" of the common law.[14] In speaking of the *consuetudo regni* – "divers[e] general customs of old time used throughout the realm: which have been accepted and approved by our sovereign lord the king and his progenitors and all their subjects"[15] – his views were populist and historical. "These be the customs," he concluded, "that properly be called the common law."[16] St. German's vision of the common law is an admixture of royal justice (kings and judges) and the collective historical wisdom of the English people.[17] He also recognized the continued vitality of local and particular customs, indicating that juries could decide on the existence of a practice, but the judges would decide if the alleged custom was against the laws of reason or God, "though they might be against the general customs or maxims of the law."[18]

In actual practice during the Year Book period of the sixteenth century, and just prior to the Stuart constitutional crises, customary norms were widely being applied at variance with the common law. This was largely because rural constituencies were pressing for greater rights against manorial holdings (through the expansion of customary rights of copyhold) and those vested interests were resisting (through efforts at enclosure).[19] A similar process of transformation was occurring in cities, especially in London and other major trade centers, where greater freedoms were being sought using the vehicles of commercial custom and town-rights.[20] All of this resulted in increased vigilance being exercised by royal courts in the acceptance of local or particular customs. Putative customs were sometimes rejected as unreasonable, although rarely because of a lack of age or antiquity.[21] As T. F. T. Plucknett observed of this period,

> the remarkable feature of custom was its flexibility and adaptability. In modern times we hear a lot too much of the phrase 'immemorial custom'. In so far as this phrase implies that custom is or ought to be immemorially old it is historically inaccurate. In an age when custom was an active living factor of society, there was much less insistence upon actual or fictitious antiquity.[22]

It was during Sir Edward Coke's tenure on the royal courts of Common Pleas and King's Bench that English understandings of the limits and extent of local or particular customs came to be fundamentally modified. In his juristic writings, Coke emphasized "of every custom there shall be two essential parts, time and usage; Time out of mind ... and continual and peaceable usage without lawful interruption."[23] In *Gateward's Case* of 1607, the Court of King's Bench struck down a local custom to rights in common as being insufficiently certain as being applied to all the "inhabitants" of a district, and not a particular estate.[24] The following year, in the *Case of Tanistry*,[25] a court effectively demolished Ireland's customary land-tenure regime by holding that while the relevant practices had been observed "by the frequent iteration and multiplication of this act,"[26] the customs were nonetheless unreasonable and "encounter to the Commonwealth."[27] So, even while juries remained involved in the determination of the existence of particular customs (and so maintained their roles not only as "fact-finders" but as "law-finders"), royal judges increased their ability to negate a finding that a custom was lawful.[28]

And even as Stuart-era judges were narrowing the scope of local or special customs in derogation of the common law, they were exalting the common law as a customary regime. But this system was of a particular character: reflecting the "artificial reason" of the profession of English judges and lawyers.[29] This "custom of the courts" conception, likening back to the Roman *mos iudiciorum*, stood in sharp contrast to a vision of the common law as populist and deeply rooted in the practices of the English people-at-large, and not just the legal intelligentsia or political elite.[30] Sir Matthew Hale's *The History of the Common Law of England* (written c. 1670, but only published in 1713) arguably took this tack, although he acknowledged parliamentary supremacy over the content of both the judge-made common law and customary regimes.[31] Thomas Hobbes went further and espoused a naturalist rejection of customary regimes, "den[ying] that any Custom of its own Nature, can amount to the Authority of a Law: For if the Custom be unreasonable ... it ought to be abolished; and if the Custom be reasonable, it is not the Custom, but the Equity [its being in accord with natural reason] that makes it Law."[32]

So, on the eve of William Blackstone's systematization of the English common law through his *Commentaries*, there were many divergent strands of thought in relation to customary norms and regimes. These reflected both a single thrust for uniform law for the entire realm (under principles of artificial reason) and a continued recognition that local or particular usages could derogate from the common law, and yet enhance it.

BLACKSTONE'S CUSTOMARY MOMENT

A useful way to consider the history of the English[33] common-law doctrine of custom is to give a critical reading to William Blackstone's discussion of the subject, which appears in the Introduction to the first volume of his work on the sources of law in England. After considering the *leges scriptae*, the Acts of Parliament, Blackstone turned his attention to the "unwritten laws of England," including the idea of the common law as an expression of the "general customs" of the entire people of the country.[34]

Despite the vociferous criticism this characterization has been subjected to from all scholarly and jurisprudential quarters,[35] Blackstone sought to justify his conclusion from the historical sources of compilations of customary practices in England, including those of Saxon Kings Alfred, Edgar, and Edward the Confessor.[36] It was these recordings that provided the basis of the essential "maxims and customs"[37] of common law that Blackstone so reverently referred to:

> But though this is the most likely foundation of this collection of maxims and customs, yet the maxims and customs, so collected, are of higher antiquity than memory or history can reach: nothing being more difficult than to ascertain the precise beginning and first spring of an ancient and long established custom. Whence it is that in our law the goodness of a custom depends upon its having been used time out of mind; or, in the solemnity of our legal phrase, time whereof the memory of man runneth not to the contrary. This it is that gives it its weight and authority; and of this nature are the maxims and custom[s] which compose the common law, or *lex non scripta*, of the kingdom.[38]

Indeed, Blackstone sought to compare the English law of custom with that of Rome:

> The Roman law, as practiced in the times of its liberty, paid also a great regard to custom; but not so much as our law: it only then adopting it, when the written law is deficient. Though the reasons alleged in the Digest will fully justify our practice, in making it of equal authority with, when it is not contradicted by, the written law. "For since," says Julianus, the "written law binds us for no other reason but because it is approved by the judgment of the people, therefore those laws which the people hath approved without writing ought also to bind every body. For where is the difference, whether the people declare their assent to a law by suffrage, or by a uniform course of acting accordingly?" Thus did they reason while Rome had some remains of her freedom.... [I]t is one of the characteristic marks of English liberty, that our common law depends upon custom; which carries this internal evidence of freedom along with it, that it probably was introduced by the voluntary consent of the people.[39]

For Blackstone, "general usage" and "universal reception" were the hallmarks of the English common law as a customary regime, verging on a sociological compact and set of reciprocal obligations between the rulers and people.[40]

Despite all this fairly abstract discussion of the common law as the quintessentially English custom of the realm, Blackstone took pains in his

Commentaries to differentiate a second form of custom, "particular customs, or laws, which affect only the inhabitants of particular districts."[41] "[F]or reasons that have now been long forgotten," Blackstone wrote, "particular counties, cities, towns, manors, and lordships, were very early indulged with the privilege of abiding by their own customs, in contradistinction to the rest of the nation at large."[42]

Blackstone's subsequent discussion of the medieval origins of certain customs – such as the Kentish practice of gravelkind, the establishment of urban courts without royal grant,[43] and the usages of various classes of merchants – was summary and intended (obviously) to be illustrative only.[44] The point that he proceeded to was that "[t]he rules relating to particular customs regard either the proof of their existence; their legality when proved; or their usual method of allowance."[45] As to proof, Blackstone noted that, with the exception of the custom of gravelkind in Kent,

> [a]ll other private customs must be particularly pleaded, and as well the existence of such customs must be shewn, as that the thing in dispute is within the custom alleged. The trial in both cases (both to shew the existence of the custom, [such] as, "that in the manor of Dale[,] lands shall descend only to the heirs male, and never to the heirs female;" and also to shew "that the lands in question are within that manor") is by a jury of twelve men, and not by the judges; except the same particular custom has been before tried, determined, and recorded in the same court.[46]

This was an immensely significant observation: proof of a local[47] custom was made as a matter of fact, upon oath of witnesses before a jury.[48] It was only after a jury had found both that the custom obtained and that the relevant property, relationship, or transaction was situated within the ambit of the custom, did some sort of legal force attach to that fact. And, most particularly of all, the legal finding of a custom applied only to that court; it did not operate as precedent within a conception of *stare decisis*.[49]

But "[w]hen a custom is actually proved to exist," Blackstone went on, "the next inquiry is into the *legality* of it; for, if it is not a good custom, it ought to be no longer used. To make a particular custom good, the following are necessary requisites."[50] What follows is Blackstone's[51] now-famous checklist of the elements making a custom legally valid: long, continued, and peaceable usages that are reasonable, certain, compulsory, and consistent. What must be emphasized is that he was describing a process of ascertaining custom in which the fact of the custom was proved first before a jury, and only then was the validity and scope[52] of the custom tested as a matter of law by the judges.[53]

The first element mentioned by Blackstone is also the most characteristic feature of custom and the most problematic. A custom, he wrote,

> must have been used so long, that the memory of man runneth not to the contrary. So that, if any one can shew the beginning of it, it is no good custom. For which reason no custom can prevail against an express act of [P]arliament, since the statute is a proof of a time when such a custom did not exist.[54]

The most striking thing about this passage is its oblique reference to the doctrine of legal memory.[55] In England, legal memory has come to be regarded as running from the coronation of King Richard I on September 3, 1189. "From time immemorial" meant anything originating before that date.[56] "The difficulty of bringing evidence to show the existence of a custom from time immemorial," one writer has noted, "is made easier by an evidentiary presumption that, if regular usage can be shown, and there is no other contrary evidence ... then the court can assume that the custom had existed from the accession of Richard I in 1189."[57]

Closely allied to the requirement of antiquity is that a custom must have been, according to Blackstone, observed continuously. Blackstone was very precise about what legal events would, or would not, interrupt a custom:

> Any interruption would cause a temporary ceasing: the revival gives it a new beginning, which will be within time of memory, and thereupon the custom will be void. But this must be understood with regard to an interruption of the *right*; for an interruption of the *possession* only... will not destroy the custom. As if the inhabitants of a parish have a customary right of watering their cattle at a certain pool, the custom is not destroyed, though they do not use it for ten years; it only becomes more difficult to prove: but if the *right* be any how discontinued for a day, the custom is quite at an end.[58]

As with much of his jurisprudence, Blackstone is making exceedingly fine distinctions here.[59] He correctly notes that the lack of exercise of a customary right clouds its validity in two ways. First, it surely will make the proof before the jury more difficult.[60] Second, it may suggest to a judge that, as a matter of law, the right itself has been extinguished.[61] In truth, English courts were fairly liberal about validating customary rights that had not been exercised for substantial periods of time, including, in one case, a lapse of one hundred and fifty years.[62]

So much for the temporal aspects of custom's validity. Next to be considered by Blackstone were three elements that had to do with the manner in which the custom was enjoyed since "time immemorial." The first of these was that the custom "must have been *peaceable,* and acquiesced in; not subject to contention and dispute. For as customs owe their origin[] to common consent, their being immemorially disputed, either at law or otherwise, is a proof that such consent was wanting."[63] Some scholars[64] have read this as being a warning that custom cannot be procured by stealth or fraud, or, in other words, that consent must manifest an open and notorious claim of right. Blackstone's requirement of peaceableness was probably his own invention; earlier descriptions of the doctrine of custom preferred to itemize certainty as being essential.[65] As to that requirement of certainty, Blackstone's *Commentaries* merely listed kinds of customs that a court would be obliged to find as too vague. "A custom that lands shall descend to the most worthy of the owner's blood is void; for how shall this worth be determined? [B]ut a custom to descend to the next male of the blood, exclusive of females, is certain, and therefore good."[66] This could be taken too far, and Blackstone noted that in the case of a custom that prescribed that a fine worth a year's improved value on a piece of land was still certain, inasmuch as that value could be readily ascertained.[67]

The requirement of certainty already had been extensively considered by English judges well before the publication of Blackstone's treatise.[68] As already noted, in the 1608 decision of the Court of King's Bench in *Gateward's Case,*[69] it was ruled that particular[70] rights of common in manor land could not be held by the "inhabitants" of the district. That class was too vague and uncertain.[71] Instead, they could be customarily acquired by the "copyholders," or tenants, on the lord's estate. Chief Justice Willes, in *Broadbent v. Wilks,*[72] said that a custom must be certain "because, if it be not certain, it cannot be proved to have been time out of mind, for how can anything be said to have been time out of mind when it is not certain what it is?"[73] Clearly, the requirement of legal certainty was a way that judges could second-guess the proofs made before a jury that the custom had actually existed.[74]

Indeed, in the period when Blackstone was writing, many customs got invalidated as being uncertain. In one case, a custom that applied to the "poor householders" of a town was struck as being insufficiently definite.[75] In another case, the custom was alleged that the townspeople could enter a private estate in order to play "rural games."[76] This, too, was rejected. The key point made in all of these cases is that the custom had to be fairly exact as to the class it benefitted, as well as the rights it conferred. Many decisions used, therefore, the discussion of legal certainty as a vehicle to repeat the essential point that a custom was, fundamentally, local. As Judge Buller noted in a 1795 case:[77]

A custom for all the inhabitants of a parish to play at all kinds of lawful games, sports[,] and pastimes in the close of "A," at all seasonable times of the year, at their free will and pleasure, is good. But a similar custom, for all persons for the time being, being in the parish, is bad.

How that which may be claimed by all the inhabitants of England can be the subject of a custom, I cannot conceive. Customs must in their nature be confined to individuals of a particular description, and what is common to all mankind can never be claimed as a custom.[78]

Customs were thus usually limited to the confines of the relevant county, parish, manor, or estate.[79]

Consistency was the last of Blackstone's three elements having to do with the manner in which the custom was practiced. "One custom cannot be set up in opposition to another. For if both are really customs then both are of equal antiquity, and both established by mutual consent: which to say of contradictory customs is absurd."[80] As Carleton Kemp Allen has written, though, "[t]here does not seem to be much substance in this rule beyond the unquestionable truth that if two customs ... are manifestly incompatible, then one or the other is incorrectly called a custom."[81]

Very closely connected to these factors going to the nature of a custom is the inquiry of why those who practice the custom do so. As already noted, Blackstone considered consent as being a key ingredient of custom. He made this point even more sharply in his consideration of the legal force of custom:

Customs, though established by consent, must be (when established) *compulsory*; and not left to the option of every man, whether he will use them or no. Therefore a custom, that all the inhabitants shall be rated toward the maintenance of a bridge, will be good; but a custom, that every man is to contribute thereto at his own pleasure, is idle and absurd, and in deed no custom at all.[82]

This passage admits to many different nuances – quite too many, in fact.

Carleton Kemp Allen suggested that Blackstone meant that for a custom to be valid as law (and not merely followed as some sort of habit), the people practicing it must do so out of an actual sense of legal obligation, *opinio juris sive necessitatis*.[83] There is, however, no historical support for this extreme, positivist notion of consent in making customary rights, at least not in England.[84] Later judges interpreted Blackstone merely to mean that the custom being claimed was of right and not by "leave asked from time to time."[85]

"Customs must be *reasonable*," Blackstone said for his concluding, legal element of the doctrine, "or rather, taken negatively, they must not be unreasonable."[86] This invocation of legal reasonableness was intended as the ultimate trump card for the judges' review of the validity of custom. The kind of unreasonableness that would render a custom bad was "not always, as Sir

Edward Coke says, to be understood of every unlearned man's reason, but of artificial and legal reason, warranted by authority of law."[87] The "artificial" reason that Coke and Blackstone referred to meant that judges could uphold a custom, "though the particular reason of it cannot be assigned; for it sufficeth, if no good legal reason can be assigned against it."[88]

It also meant that judges could use their legal reason to strike down a custom. Such applications of artificial reason sometimes took the form of judges holding, on largely evidentiary grounds,[89] that no reasonable jury could have found that a particular custom had existed.[90] This arguably occurred in *Wilson v. Willes*,[91] where the court rejected another copyholder custom in a manor estate, this one supposedly allowing the tenants to carry away anything they wanted to from the manorial wasteland, "as hath been fit and proper to be so used and spent every year, at all times in the year, as often and in such quantity as occasion" may require.[92] Lord Chancellor Ellenborough wrote that the custom was "indefinite and uncertain," and that

> [t]here is nothing to restrain the tenants from taking the whole of the turbary of the common, and destroying the pasture altogether. A custom of this description ought to have some limit but here there is no limitation to the custom as laid but fancy and caprice.[93]

And although Ellenborough spoke to the definiteness of the custom, he was really ruling as to its unreasonableness.

A discussion of reason was occasionally used as a surrogate for a holding that the custom conflicted with an Act of Parliament or a fundamental rule of the common law.[94] The best example of this occurred in the *Case of Tanistry*,[95] where at issue was the validity of the Irish Brehon customary law of succession, which (like the Kentish gavelkind) deviated from the common-law rule of primogeniture. Unlike their homegrown custom, English judges showed little solicitude to the Irish usage, assuming they even understood it.[96] In ruling that the custom was "encounter to the Commonwealth,"[97] the English court was acting in the belief that "they were substituting a civilized institution for a set of mischievous usages proper only for barbarians."[98]

Blackstone's understanding of these cases clearly implied that he approved of judges exercising broad discretion in striking customs as unreasonable.[99] To the extent that the unreasonableness of custom is a legal question, the standard used by judges in England has been summarized as whether the custom is "fair and proper, and such as reasonable, honest and fair-minded men would adopt."[100] Or, as Lord Justice Brett put it, invoking natural justice,[101] "[w]hether it is in accordance with fundamental principles of right and wrong."[102] Finally, utilitarian concerns were periodically enunciated as the reasonable basis of a custom.[103] As a consequence, English courts have struck customs as unreasonable where they had the effect of being "to the general prejudice, for the advantage of any particular person,"[104] or where the effects of a custom fell unevenly on a class of people.[105]

BLACKSTONE'S INFLUENCE: BENTHAM AND
AMERICAN COMMON LAW

Blackstone's *Commentaries* ostensibly offered a complete theory of custom as an integral part of English law. This was not only in regard to its general aspect as the incarnation of the common law of the realm or the custom of the courts (depending on one's perspective), but also as a set of local or particular usages in derogation of the common law. His views would resonate in Anglo-American jurisprudence – and in the decisions of courts from common-law jurisdictions – for much of the next two centuries.

The first milestone of Blackstone's influence was antithetical, beginning with the philosophical writings of David Hume, for whom custom was more a sociological phenomenon than an historical truth. Although Hume saw custom as "the great guide of life"[106] and "the governing principle of mankind,"[107] he was skeptical of its legal relevance.[108] Jeremy Bentham, in his 1776 gloss on Blackstone, *A Comment on the Commentaries*, went much further in his critique, almost (but not quite) anticipating the high positivism of John Austin. For starters, Bentham distinguished what he called custom *in pays* (local customs or usages of an industry) from custom *in foro* (the custom of the judges). Custom *in pays* is the behavior of a distinct segment of society (whether geographically or occupationally defined) arising "originally [and] spontaneous[ly]" or from sort of legal compulsion or obligation manifesting consent to be bound.[109] Consistent with the rest of his jurisprudence, Bentham was utterly dismissive of the idea that English common law was a custom *in foro*, derived (as Blackstone asserted) from ancient usages. Sharing Hobbes' general disdain for arguments based on the putative antiquity of a legal norm, he asserted that "I know not that we owe any ... deference to former times,"[110] and, as an empirical matter, Bentham could show that many practices (including much of commercial custom) were hardly supported by ancient usage.[111] For Bentham, it was not antiquity that made the custom, but, rather, the idea that its nonobservance would be legally sanctioned. Likewise, it was absurd (according to Bentham) that judges were merely "discovering" the essential postulates and maxims of the common law through the device of unearthing immemorial custom.

Despite his harsh treatment of custom *in foro*, a careful reading of Bentham reveals some solicitude for custom *in pays*. Bentham first distinguished between customs that are "legalized" and those that are not. A "legalized" custom, according to Bentham, was a practice or usage declared as binding by a court or actually codified by a legislature.[112] A single judicial act of punishing the nonobservance of a supposed customary norm was thus sufficient to render that behavior legally binding, provided it is in the context of generally enforcing customs of that type.[113] As an example of such a dynamic, Bentham described the commercial custom of common carriers being liable for damage to goods in their possession. This usage began as "reasonable" and an "expectation of the parties," based on principles of "good will" and "justice," and which later hardened through iterations of judicial recognition and enforcement in the resolution of actual disputes among merchants.[114]

To his credit – and in stark contrast with Austin's later writings – Bentham imagined that a nonlegalized custom could still have prescriptive weight by at least raising expectations of compliance among constituents of the communities observing them.[115] "The ground for all legal decisions," Bentham wrote, "is expediency, real or supposed. One ground of expediency is popular expectation: one ground of expectation is past usage."[116] Anticipating later sociological, psychological, and economic insights (for more on which see the next chapter), Bentham viewed the practical enforcement of custom as a "habit" of compliance.[117] In a sense, Bentham was the intellectual progenitor of both Malinowski's "reciprocity" ethnography of custom,[118] as well as Hart's neo-positivist jurisprudence.[119] As with the rest of his moral philosophy, Bentham saw a custom's reason as being based in its utility – its ability to track the actual behavior of social cohorts.[120]

English law quickly responded to the Blackstone-Bentham debate. In 1832, Parliament adopted the Prescription Act.[121] Passed on the initiative of the Chief Justice of King's Bench, it was intended to remedy the "[i]nconvenience and [i]njustice" resulting from the common-law requirement (as enunciated by none other than Blackstone) that a local custom had to be proven to have originated before 1189 (the commencement of "legal memory").[122] By its terms, the Prescription Act made it easier to prove copyhold custom for easements and servitudes in real property,[123] but it had an even broader impact on the proof of other customs in England during the nineteenth century, resulting in a renaissance in the enforcement of all sorts of customs.[124] English law, on the eve of its great transplantation to the colonies (especially Canada, South Africa, Australia, and New Zealand) was thus quite accommodating to the use of local or particular customs, even as the notion of the common law as itself a customary regime was no longer viewed with favor.

Because jurisdictions in the United States received English common law contemporaneous with Blackstone's thesis on custom, and not at the time of Bentham's antithesis (as reflected in the Prescription Act), American jurisprudence had a different take on the "problem" of custom. Earlier writers, such as John Milton Goodenow, were avowedly hostile to Blackstone's formal treatment of local customs and were virtually dismissive of their relevance in the new, enlightened American legal context. "But in a government like ours," Goodenow wrote, "whose foundation is in written and positive law; untrammeled by custom or tradition ... what is not written or published is not law...."[125] Justice Joseph Story, in his contribution to Francis Lieber's *Encyclopedia Americana*, echoed these same sentiments: "The common law consists only of [general customs] and [ecclesiastical and admiralty] kinds of customary law..., there being no local or provincial law existing in any particular country or district of any state, as contradistinguished from that which prevails in the state at large."[126] In another entry, Story wrote that "in some of the states, there are some customs and peculiarities which grew up in early times. But they are few, and, in a general sense, unimportant."[127] As Virginia's Supreme Court noted in a case decided on the eve of the American Civil War, "at this day and in this age, in a government like ours, there can be little need of a resort to such a source as custom for legal sanction."[128]

As in England during the early part of the nineteenth century, custom enjoyed a doctrinal revival in the United States during the latter part of that century and in the first decades of the twentieth. A large part of these jurisprudential debates took place in the context of the codification movement that was prevalent in many states (particularly New York and California) and the inevitable intellectual backlash to the idea that the common law could be enshrined in that matter. James Coolidge Carter was the nation's leading opponent to David Dudley Field's civil law codification movement.[129] One line of his attack on codification was to assert that legislation had relatively little impact on legal developments. While this seems a quaint notion for today's legisprudence of statutes, Carter supported his theory by asserting that "[w]hat has governed the conduct of men from the beginning of time will continue to govern it to the end of time.... [T]hat to which we give the name of Law always has been, still is, and will forever [ ] be Custom."[130] Carter was careful to qualify his views and point out that "while all Law is Custom, all Custom is not necessarily Law.... There is a large range of human conduct of which the law takes no notice, even though it is under the control of custom quite as much as the part which the law assumes to regulate."[131] Carter recognized, however, that his theory of *über*-custom – strangely redolent of Savigny and Puchta – was legal apostasy from a positivist perspective:

> Legal writers have at all times allowed much weight to custom, viewing it as one, but only one, of the sources of law, as if there were some governmental power standing above custom, the function of which was to pronounce judgment on the wisdom of custom, and select from it the rules it would enforce and reject the rest.[132]

Carter thus expressed an American reimagination of the German historicist view on custom. It fell to other American writers, most notably Oliver Wendell Holmes, John Chipman Gray, and Karl Llewellyn, to modernize that theory and put it on a firmer jurisprudential footing. Holmes made the tantalizing assertion that the common law was a customary regime, developed flexibly and consonant with reason, and in accordance with the "felt necessities" of the community of people that observed it.[133] Stripped of its super-majoritarian implications, Holmes's jurisprudence seemed to merge the common law as both *made* by judges, but *formed* by community expectations.[134]

John Chipman Gray's *The Nature and Sources of the Law* (1909) essentially agreed with Holmes' view that custom was made by judges.[135] He also took direct aim at Carter's expansive sentiments of custom and the invocations of *volkgeist* from the German Historical School, even as he took pains not to verge on the strict positivisim of Austin.[136] While acknowledging that Carter's theory was superior to Blackstone's, insofar as Carter rejected the necessity of antiquity and consistency in the proof of a custom,[137] Gray still critiqued Carter's assertion that custom was the font of all law. "Now custom is not *opinion*," Gray wrote, "it is practice.... Custom is what men *do*, not what they *think*."[138] Gray thus conceded that "custom ... is undoubtedly one of the sources, and a very important source, of part of the Law,"[139] particularly in the areas of civil procedure, contract interpretation, and the rule of negligence in torts.[140] In a bit of legal sociology, Gray discussed the claims practices of miners, developed in the turbulent years of the California Gold Rush, as indicative of an effective customary regime outside a contractual context, so deft that California law adopted these practices as the rule of decision in litigation.[141]

For writers after Blackstone, the real issue, the fundamental objection to custom, was its very nature as a source of law. Customary law is unwritten and unenacted. Some might argue that it lacks the very essence of positive law. Particularly in a democratic society that embraces the rule of law, many would consider the doctrine of custom a dangerous anachronism. The nub of this theoretical challenge to custom was that the unformed, inchoate expectations and usages of a community can have no binding force as law until they are recognized by the positive instruments of law in a democratic society: the legislature or the courts.

Jeremy Bentham, in his gloss on Blackstone's *Commentaries*, made precisely this point, and it has been repeated in much of the legal literature of the nineteenth and twentieth centuries. For modern jurisprudes such as Hans Kelsen, in order for custom to be valid, it must be endowed as a "law-creating fact" and have some sovereign imprimatur.[142] For legal realists like Karl Llewellyn (a voice heard from Chapter 1), a coherent theory of customary law was impossible, a project to be eschewed in favor of simply recognizing the practices of a relevant community. For Llewellyn, "usages of trade" were the embodiment of "business-stuff,"[143] just as "law-ways" captured the "law-stuff" of the Cheyenne Indians.

These are extreme forms of positivism that reduce to the claim that individuals and communities cannot make law; only judges and legislatures can. This intensely positivistic character of modern American law is captured in this passage from the Supreme Court's iconic 1938 decision in *Erie Railroad Co. v. Tompkins*, derived from Justice Holmes: "'[B]ut law in the sense in which courts speak of it today does not exist without some definite authority behind it.... [T]he authority and only authority is the State.'"[144]

To embrace this proposition is to deny the very idea of custom. The solution to this immodest problem is to identify what must be the extra ingredient that transforms the identified, consistent, and long-standing practices of a community into binding law. If one admits that practice alone is insufficient to make a custom, what more is needed? There are several contenders. Some have suggested that the actors observing the usage must do so out of a sense of legal obligation. In short, it is not enough that an individual or community observe a custom; they must really believe that the custom is law. This is simply a restatement of *opinio juris sive necessitatis*.

This intensely positivistic and circular notion of custom – usages are only binding when they are recognized by the users as binding law – may well be unnecessary doctrinally, because the English common law of custom embodied an alternative to *opinio juris*. Blackstone called it compulsion, the idea that "[c]ustoms, though established by consent, must be (when established) compulsory; and not left to the option of every man, whether he will use them or no."[145] Blackstone regarded compulsion as very different from the notion that people observed a custom out of a sense of legal obligation. He believed that consent to a custom could be manifested in the form of acquiescence. And as long as the custom comported with artificial reason – the right reason of the judges – custom could be made by tacit consent of those who were to be governed by it. The debate begun by Blackstone, which was itself derivative of earlier deliberations within the common-law tradition, continues to this day.

4

Economics, Sociobiology, and Psychology:
The Human Impulse of Custom

Ethnography, cultural studies, and legal history have shaped our understandings of custom. To complete the picture, one also needs to look at the intersection of economics, sociobiology, and psychology. This literature is fairly recent (arising over the last century), combining elements of evolutionary psychology, moral conventionalism, and the study of social norms. Many of these writers see custom as counterpoised with law, as almost an alternative paradigm for resolving disputes. Others see custom as evil, particularly targeting vulnerable populations as victims of outmoded usages, and argue that there must be doctrinal safeguards to prevent particularistic customary norms in preempting generally adopted social values. Yet other scholars question whether custom is inimical to modern legal cultures characterized by a large, diffuse, mobile, technologically sophisticated, and diverse society. The ultimate question raised by these disciplines is whether custom is reflected in basic human nature (self-interest or reciprocal altruism) or is it also an impulse based upon efficiency and rationality?

CUSTOM AS FUNCTIONAL

As was recounted in Chapter 1, legal ethnographers such as Bronislaw Malinowski tended to emphasize the fact that customary norms enabled reciprocal relations between sometimes disparate groups within a society.[1] Custom was thus seen as a structural and functional component of social relations, and customary norms were primarily intended to promote a social group's survival and prosperity.[2] Crude forms of this theory can be traced back in intellectual history to the work of Social Darwinists, such as Walter Bagheot and William Sumner, of the late nineteenth and early twentieth centuries.[3]

But a more promising *locus classicus* for this notion of custom as a functional phenomenon in human societies is the work of such legal sociologists as Gabriel de Tarde,[4] Emile Durkheim,[5] and Eugen Ehrlich.[6] In Tarde's psychological construct, custom was seen as a manifestation of a human impulse to imitate and model behavior and the ultimate stabilizing force in a society.[7] Ehrlich expanded on this, while, at the same time, distinguishing sociological accounts of custom from those provided by such legal historians as Puchta and Savigny. Reduced to its essence, Ehrlich's argument criticized the German Historical School of Jurisprudence[8] for failing to acknowledge that customs could evolve over time, and (as an evolutionary phenomenon) were largely extralegal in character.[9]

Ehrlich also distinguished between rules of custom (as reflected in the actual practices of social cohorts) and the legal institutions that enforce those rules:

> It is not these legal propositions that live and have their being within the consciousness of the people, but the legal institutions and the norms of law of corporations and other communities, of property, and of contract, upon which the institutions are based, and from which the legal propositions are deduced.... [L]egal institutions and norms appertaining to them continue to rise among the people themselves, e.g., ... the bill of exchange among the bankers, the demarcation of boundaries, and the servitude of pasture among the peasants; only the legal propositions are being formulated by the jurists in their teachings and writings and in statutes.[10]

Ehrlich essentially believed that law was relatively unimportant for constraining human behavior – social forces tended to produce the same norms in all human societies. His distinction between customs and the legal institutions that apply them has had significant doctrinal consequences. He pointed out that there were some usages that were of such long standing and importance that judges could not ignore them, and (perhaps) that statutes could enter into desuetude by customary deviance.[11]

While the psychological literature for the internalization of norms is a rich one,[12] and inclines in support of the notion that customs are designed to enhance a society's health, there are a number of powerful critiques for this structural-functionalist approach to customary law. There is a methodological problem – common to all sociological and ethnographic observations[13] – of how to distinguish those usages that truly do promote social cohesion from those that privilege certain segments of society (at the expense of others) or are atavistic, anachronistic, or worse. Inherent in a structural view of custom is the equitable problem of a norm that may be functional to some, but not all, members of a relevant community.

Another danger inherent in the functionalist take on custom is an artifact of the theory's origins in Social Darwinism. To the extent a custom is validated by whether it promotes a society's survival and prosperity, it really turns on the conceit that a society is a collective, living organism. But can the wisdom of a usage adopted by particular members or cohorts of a society be aggregated and attributed to the whole? As Robert Ellickson has observed, "[t]he difficulty with this sort of organic analysis is that evolutionary processes, as most biologists understand them, select either genes or individual organisms, not groups, for survival."[14] It is for this reason that in order for a functionalist account to make much sense it must be accompanied by either rigorous, empirical sociobiological research, which can demonstrate that certain norms are genetically "hard-wired,"[15] or – at the opposite extreme – an acceptance that, within any given society, groups will compete for the imposition of norms that best serve their selfish interests.[16] At present, sociobiological empirics of custom are weak and unproven. So, if a rule of customary law is to be validated by its functional utility for a society in aggregate, it must be shown – whether in the idiom of social control or economic efficiency – to be a structural feature for that culture or community.

CUSTOM AS SOCIAL CONTROL

There is another intellectual lineage explaining the dynamics of custom, very different in tone and texture from the Social Darwinists and their sociobiological successors. Max Weber viewed customary norms as a form of social control instrument, and connected the enforcement of those rules with established legal bureaucracies.[17] The Legal Realist school of American jurisprudence, led by such figures as Karl Llewellyn[18] and Lon Fuller[19] (both of whom were introduced in Chapter 1), certainly saw that while law was a positive act of will, legal norms need not invariably "spring from the barrel of a gun or from the mind of a law-giver, ... [but could] evolve from the actions and expectations – the customs – of ordinary people going about their daily business."[20] And there has also been a libertarian branch of moral philosophy and political economy, foreseen by David Hume and Jeremy Bentham,[21] and culminating in the work of Friedrich Hayek, that has sought to create a unified theory of customary law as central to the "spontaneous order" of all human societies.[22]

Hayek's moral philosophy turned on the observation that human societies, at all levels of development, will seek to impose order on their constituents:

> that rules ... exist and operate without being explicitly known to those who obey them applies also to many of the rules which govern the actions of man and thereby determine a spontaneous social order. Man certainly does not know all the rules which guide his actions in the sense that he is able to state them in words. At least in primitive human society, scarcely less than in

animal societies, the structure of social life is determined by rules of conduct which manifest themselves only by being in fact observed. Only when individual intellects begin to differ to a significant degree will it become necessary to express these rules in a form in which they can be communicated and explicitly taught, deviant behavior corrected, and differences of opinion about appropriate behavior decided.[23]

This handy definition of custom was accompanied by an important caveat: just because human practices may be evidence of a spontaneous order, custommaking may reflect deliberate action by a society.[24] For Hayek, custom is "grown" law, not imposed from an established political order.[25]

Borrowing from Rawls' distinction between *rules* ("a propensity or disposition to act or not act in a certain manner") and *practices* (as synonymous with "custom"),[26] Hayek offered two vignettes of customary law at work in different societies. The first is among what he called "primitive" peoples. Because Hayek's appreciation of legal ethnography was very limited,[27] he drew the surprising conclusion that in preliterate societies, "the earliest deliberate efforts of headmen or chiefs of a tribe to maintain social order must ... be seen as taking place inside a given framework of rules, although they were rules which existed only as a 'knowledge how' to act and not as 'knowledge that' they could be expressed in such and such terms."[28] Hayek thus saw the process of custom creation in primitive societies as a "top-down" exercise: a leader would seek to "teach or enforce rules of conduct which he regards as established," and, as part of this process, would "obtain consent" or "legitimacy" for the recognition of a practice.[29] Hayek's model for custom-generation, in all but the most "modern" or sophisticated of societies, was as the product of social elites (whether village headmen, sacerdotal colleges, or trade guilds) seeking to project their control over other groups.

Hayek's modeling of primitive legal custom has applications far beyond the field of legal anthropology and the law of preliterate peoples. It applies equally to any legal culture that is small, discrete, or insular, based on the character of its constituents. Most famously, John Chipman Gray's analysis of customary norms among California Gold Rush mining communities[30] can be viewed as a Hayekian primitive and spontaneous order.[31] So, too, can the usages of cowboys in the old West[32] and of New England whaling vessels.[33] A consistent theme of these customary regimes is the decentralized allocation of property rights – and attendant contractual duties – in what might otherwise be considered commonage.[34] However, it is highly doubtful that Hayekian primitive custom is likely to be of much significance in large-scale contemporary cultures characterized by high degrees of mobility (geographic and social), and a diversity of constituents, interests, and values.[35]

Counterpoised with primitive custom, Hayek pointed to the English common law as a paradigmatically modern approach to social control – balancing elements of liberty and order. Hayek's first jurisprudential move was to distinguish law consciously created through political processes (what he called "legislation"), from the spontaneous law that evolves out of daily affairs (what he called the "law of liberty").[36] Hayek's gloss on the notion of the common law as a customary regime (explored in the previous chapter) has been immensely controversial. For starters, he arguably confuses a norm that is the product of a customary usage with one that is created by judicial precedent:

> The important insight to which an understanding of the process of evolution of law leads is that the rules which will emerge from it will of necessity possess certain attributes which laws invented or designed by a ruler may but need not possess, and are likely to possess only if they are modelled after the kind of rules which spring from the articulation of previously existing practices.[37]

"Previously existing practices" is Hayek's synonym for "custom," but his reference to "laws invented or designed by a ruler" seems to be limited to the realm of statutory law. What role, then, is there for the common-law judge in Hayek's jurisprudence? "The task of the judge," he responded,

> will be to tell [the parties to a dispute] what ought to have guided their expectations, not because anyone had told them before that this was the rule, but because this was the established custom they ought to have known. The question for the judge here can never be whether the action in fact taken was expedient from some higher point of view, or served a particular result desired by authority, but only whether the conduct under dispute conformed to recognized rules.[38]

Not all customs are to be judicially enforced, however. According to Hayek, only those that are general or "abstract" should receive that sanction.[39] It is only in instances that "there exists genuine doubt about what is required by established custom, and where in consequence the litigants may differ in good faith,"[40] that the common-law judge is at liberty to fashion a new rule, and only if the judge "is charged with the task of finding a rule which after being stated is recognized as appropriate."[41]

Not surprisingly, the Hayekian caricature of the emasculated judge – limited in private law disputes to applying only existing customary norms – has not found favor among public intellectuals on the bench, even those otherwise disposed to favor his libertarian leanings. As Judge Richard Posner has written, Hayek "is insufficiently critical of the limitations of custom as a normative order. He puts too much weight on evolution, neglecting the fact that, lacking a teleology, evolution cannot be assumed to lead to normatively attractive results."[42] Posner observes that customary regimes, as acephalous, sometimes only evolve with glacial speed.[43] Even more disturbingly, "some customs often support cooperative activities that are harmful to society as a whole."[44] Not only are customary regimes institutionally inefficient, so, too, many customary norms embed values or outcomes that are contrary to public welfare.

Hayek's conflation of custom and common law may also be quite ahistorical.[45] His is no Blackstonian account. While English common law recognized and applied "immemorial usages," Hayek saw custom, rather, as something almost primeval and inchoate: "law that existed for ages before it occurred to man that he could make or alter it."[46] As was discussed in the previous chapter, English common-law judges were often cast in the role of restraining what they regarded as unreasonable indigenous customary regimes, especially in the area of property rights.[47] Hayek's lack of recognition[48] of these aspects of the English legal history handicapped his analysis.[49]

The critiques of Hayekian custom as spontaneous order have thus become legion. Richard Posner has not only defended the prerogatives of common-law judges, but also raised a claxon of concern that customary regimes can sometimes seek to legitimate insidious practices. In regard to certain domains of property-rights allocations, he pointed out that "manufacturers could be expected to evolve a custom of ignoring the pollution they create; that custom could not be made the basis of environmental law."[50] In the realm of contracts, Posner has observed that "competing firms might evolve a custom that price cutting is []ethical; that custom, encouraging an unwholesome degree of cooperation, obviously could not be made the basis of antitrust law – in fact, it has to be forbidden by that law."[51] Much of the impetus for the modern, regulatory state thus seems to be focused on eradicating or correcting what might otherwise be acceptable "usages of trade" or practices of distinct communities.

There is even sharp disagreement among scholars as to whether customs – at least in the sense that Hayek employed the term – even exist. Some writers suggest that Hayek believed that custom was some form of natural law, and was not even positive in content.[52] Others, such as Richard Craswell and Lisa Bernstein, discriminate between "weak-form customs" ("understanding[s] gleaned from the rough aggregation of practices in the market as a whole"[53]) from "strong-form Hayekian customs," which are supposed to "gradually emerg[e] over time from transactors' independent choices."[54] Posner rejects this skepticism as to the very existence of customs, but otherwise agrees with the larger problems inherent in Hayek's analysis:

Sometimes it makes sense for law to follow custom because custom may indeed impound the information relevant to the activity that the custom concerns. The set of customs known as the "law merchant" provided, and rightly so, the foundation of modern Anglo-American contract law. But often it makes no sense to base law on custom because a custom may reflect conditions that have changed – lacking central direction, custom tends to lag behind social and economic change – or may be the product of incentives that diverge from the socially desirable.... Customs may in short be vestigial and dysfunctional. And again, on the crucial question of when law should reject custom, Hayek casts no light.[55]

This debate thus brings into sharper focus the wider question of the continued relevance of the Burkean notion that decentralized social forces contribute vitally to social order.[56] Hayek's theory of custom as spontaneous order – despite its methodological, empirical, and jurisprudential flaws – continues to exert a strong influence over the field.

CUSTOM AS EFFICIENT

The ultimate criticism of Hayekian custom may be, however, that it does not promote outcomes that maximize public or private welfare. The idea that "efficient custom should evolve through the natural selection of rules and practices"[57] is not one that Hayek would likely have embraced.[58] Rather, the qualification that a custom should be efficient in order to be judicially enforced is a principle that has arisen in the dynamic literature of law and economics over the course of the past half-century.[59]

This perspective on custom began with Ronald Coase's Nobel Prize-winning work at the intersection of law and economics, property and contract. In a 1960 article, "The Problem of Social Cost,"[60] Coase theorized that when trade in an externality is possible and there are no transaction costs, bargaining will lead to an efficient outcome regardless of the initial allocation of property rights. As Coase famously observed, however, transaction costs could not be ignored, and, therefore, the initial allocation of property rights often did matter. One normative conclusion sometimes drawn from the Coase theorem is that property rights should initially be assigned to the actors gaining the most utility from them.[61]

The implications of Coase's theorem on the function and utility of customary regimes was first explored by William M. Landes and Richard A. Posner in their 1987 volume *The Economic Structure of Tort Law*. Using an example drawn from the fields of products liability, they questioned whether an industry standard for safety – essentially an industry custom – could serve as a conclusive defense against a charge of negligence in designing a product. Without anticipating too much of the discussion in Chapter 8, it is worth noting Landes' and Posner's conclusion that

> [i]f transaction costs are low, an optimal allocation of resources to safety as to other activities will be achieved by negotiation regardless of the liability rule in force. In these circumstances whatever is customary is, at least prima facie, optimal.... This conclusion assumes, however, that consumers have adequate information about the safety characteristics of the products they buy. If they do not, transaction costs may be high.... We are led to predict that compliance with custom will not be a defense in accident cases where transaction costs are high but will be where those costs are low.[62]

In an additional move, Landes and Posner also hypothesized that the same considerations that would make adherence to custom a defense in a tort case would also be applicable in bilateral contractual relations.[63]

Under an economic view, customary regimes are a form of communication between social or market participants. Norms are bid and accepted between actors in a community, seeking equipoise in a rule of behavior that maximizes wealth or happiness, welfare or utility. In the context of the bundle of rules that we call private law – property, torts, and contracts – "market forces internalize all costs, regardless of the rule of liability."[64] A well-functioning system of customary law reduces transaction costs; a dysfunctional regime raises them.

As with much of law and economics literature, this perspective on custom has both descriptive and prescriptive aspects. Insofar as courts will actually enforce contested trade usages or other practices, and so accurately predict the outcomes of disputes involving custom, economic theories may well have substantial traction. This will be explored in much greater detail in Chapters 6, 7, and 8 in this volume. For present purposes, though, the real question is whether, as a normative matter, it is desirable that a community enforce customs that are economically efficient.

Going beyond the descriptive theories of Coase, Landes, and Posner, other scholars have vigorously maintained that

> custom should be followed in those cases in which there are repeat and reciprocal interactions between the same parties, for then their incentives to reach the correct rule are exceedingly powerful. Because the parties operate perforce under a veil of ignorance, they will have every incentive incrementally to find the best set of accommodations to advance their joint welfare. So long as general constraints, such as the credible threat of retaliation for opportunistic conduct, are imposed upon future behavior, the only way that

the individual can maximize his own self-interest is to seek the rule that advances the interest of the group as a whole. In a word, custom works well for direct competition, but not so well for follow-on cases.[65]

In this passage by Richard Epstein, the emphasis is on stable custom – "repeat and reciprocal interactions" leading to a "correct," and, presumably, efficient rule that maximizes "joint welfare."[66]

So, as Richard Craswell has observed, "customs are most likely to be efficient in communities whose members interact frequently and are well informed about the matters governed by the custom, and when the costs and benefits of the custom are felt primarily by the members of the community themselves rather than being externalized to outsiders."[67] As a normative matter then, judges and legislators can adopt efficient legal rules simply by "identify[ing] those communities whose customs are likely to be efficient ... without having to analyze the efficiency of the resulting rules."[68] That is the strongest articulation of an economic theory of custom based on efficiency.

But this notion of custom as a surrogate for the most efficient legal rule has been by no means fully embraced in the law and economics literature. Drawing on theories of cultural evolution in law,[69] Jody Kraus has asserted that the norms recommended by commercial actors actually tend to be suboptimal.[70] Or, put another way, the practices that survive to become trade usages may not always be the fittest or most robust. Processes of natural selection, guided variation, and biased transmission may actually distort customary regimes.[71] And so, Kraus concludes:

> most commercial actors intend their practices to maximize profit. But the claim that actors seek to maximize profit cannot suffice to demonstrate that their practices will be optimal. A rational, profit-maximizing merchant will invest in the development of more efficient commercial practices until the marginal cost of such investments equals the marginal gain in expected increased efficiency. Merchants therefore will cease investments in developing more efficient commercial practices long before they develop optimal practices. Further increases in efficiency will almost invariably be available, although the cost to individual merchants of discovering how to achieve those increases will outweigh their benefits. Cost-effective investments in acquiring commercial practices are unlikely to lead to optimal commercial practices. Optimality is a luxury that merchants cannot afford.[72]

The idea that custom is efficient actually captures a number of very different concepts. In one sense, it harkens back to the Blackstonian condition that a custom, in order to be judicially enforced, had to be reasonable.[73] Instead of a common-law judge's "right reason," efficiency may seek to expand broader notions of social welfare. Likewise, an efficient custom may really be evidence of market effects, or the extent of transaction costs in communications between community members.[74] Custom can also be a descriptive statement of what practices are generally observed in a relevant society. Finally, an efficient custom can stand as a proxy for an ideal legal rule.

The ultimate problem in seeing custom as the reification of economic efficiency is the perennial one of confusing cause with effect. If customary usages are the product of "bottom-up, optimal private ordering,"[75] then they may well exhibit an exogenous form of efficiency, as well as a Hayekian "spontaneous order." But what if customary regimes "simply reflect and amplify questionable court decisions" in a weird "lock-in effect" or "doctrinal feedback" loop?[76] In short, what we might recognize as customs may be nothing more than false signals that "exacerbate[] herd behavior"[77] – proverbial lemmings racing for the edge of the cliff.

CUSTOM AS ANTILAW

A final methodological take on custom is not even a legal one. Indeed, it might properly be regarded as the antithesis of law. As Robert Ellickson has observed "law-and-economics scholars and other legal instrumentalists have tended to underappreciate the role that [nonlegal] systems play in achieving social order,"[78] a point echoed in the work of James Coolidge Carter, Karl Llewellyn, E. Adamson Hoebel, and Lon Fuller.[79] Just as efficiency explanations of custom fail for lack of empirical proof or public policy justifications, law-and-society accounts of custom (whether framed in the idiom of structural-functionalism, psychological imperative, or social control) do not satisfy for the want of a unifying theory.[80] If, as Arthur Leff famously quipped, economics is a desert, then sociology is a swamp.[81]

One way to drink in the desert, or not to drown in the swamp, is to recognize that customary regimes may actually reflect an alternative to legal rules, institutions, and processes. Judge Richard Posner's taxonomy of *laws* (promulgated by an official authority and enforced by legal sanctions) and *norms* (which are not)[82] is one useful way to make this recognition, although it comes dangerously close to raising the heresy (dispelled in Chapter 2) that custom is some form of protonatural source of obligation. Norms, in Posner's conception, can be actuated and enforced through a variety of human feelings and interactions: shame, guilt, and humiliation.[83] The danger, Posner points out, of norms being internalized is that "the norms may be bad ones.... they may be dysfunctional for society as a whole."[84] In addition, widespread internalization of norms reduces human freedom when freedom is viewed functionally in terms of scope of choice rather than formalistically as freedom from legal constraints. When norms are enforced by external sanctions, the individual balances the benefits of violation against the costs. When norms are internalized, he does not make a choice – it has been made for him, by his parents, teachers, or peers.[85]

Customs may thus have to be cabined, not only to weed out bad norms, but also to maximize human freedom. Far from Hayek's utopian vision, customary regimes may be the most visible edge of a particular, and peculiar, totalitarianism.

Posner also makes a "related but subtler point … that because norms, once created, are difficult to uncreate, the stock of norms may be large even though the flow is small."[86] Norm-creation is thus a public good, which the state and legal institutions may take a legitimate interest in, including the supplemental legal enforcement of norms, regulating and protecting private sanctions for norm violations, and suppressing bad norms.[87] Implicit in Posner's analysis is that the world of law (its processes and forms) is distinct from the domain of custom.

Robert Ellickson, in his appropriately titled volume, *Order Without Law: How Neighbors Settle Disputes* – a qualitatively empirical and jurisprudential study of cattle ranching in Shasta County, California – implicitly adopts the distinction between laws and norms. He is highly skeptical that legal or political oversight of customary regimes is likely to be successful. Quite the contrary, he posited that most landowners and herders in the region resolved disputes as to wandering cattle (a paradigmatic Coasean problem of social cost reflected in property-right allocations[88]) by informal settlement using customary usages. This community's "live and let live" attitude, as actuated in dispute resolution "beyond the shadow of the law,"[89] was tantamount to establishing a customary alternative to formal legal systems.[90]

There are thus limits to law, and customary regimes typically mark the boundaries of law's domain. That is not to say, of course, that in Ellickson's and Posner's world of custom as "antilaw," that "bottom-up" usages do not also have their limitations. Quite apart from the problem of atavistic practices or those norms reflecting community interests at the expense of outsiders, there is also the concern that customs may lag and not be as responsive to social dynamics as one might hope.[91] The important point raised by these scholars is that customary regimes may, if properly configured, allow social groups a high degree of liberty, even in highly structured and sophisticated legal cultures.

* * *

Whatever trope is chosen to gauge a customary regime – functionalism, social control, efficiency, or liberty – these idioms stand in sharp contrast to more conventional values for measuring the worth of customs. These other qualities are articulated in legal ethnography, history, and jurisprudence, and tend to emphasize a usage's tradition, certainty, and justice. The debate about the role and status of custom in law dates back over three millennia, transcends many cultural divides, and has preoccupied the attentions of scholars from many different academic fields. These two broad streams of intellectual history for customary law have now reached a confluence of perspectives on the role of custom in law.

We may legitimately differ as to the motivations for following custom, but it seems inescapable that there is a documented phenomenon of rules being made by constituent members of recognized communities. Whether we call these informal law, *consuetudo*, ancient usages, spontaneous order, or efficient norms really does not matter. What does signify is how these standards of conduct are actually interpreted and enforced within and outside the relevant communities of adherents. How do customs interact with other sources of law (particularly statutes and judicial decisions)? And then there is that most beguiling question of all: what transforms a mere practice into a binding custom?

These connections between law and custom can today be seen at two jurisdictional levels, both positive constructs: domestic legal systems and international law. For each of these domains, law has both a private and public character, and custom figures into both. Indeed, to a surprising degree, customary norms remain a potent and robust form of positive law-making. The balance of this book explores the role of custom in many distinctive areas of contemporary legal doctrine and discourse.

PART TWO

Custom in Domestic Legal Systems

5

Family Law

Custom continues to permeate almost all realms of contemporary law. This may seem a highly surprising and counterintuitive proposition. The anthropological, cultural, sociological, and economic perspectives revealed earlier might lead to a conclusion that customary law is a historic relic, an artifact of primitive law that has no place in modern, highly sophisticated legal systems. But this would be a profoundly mistaken position to embrace. Rather, customary norms continue to exist side by side with other mechanisms of positive law-making: constitutions as fundamental law, statutes adopted by legislatures, and case precedents decided by judges. More than merely subsisting within established legal orders, customary law regimes reinforce and strengthen existing systems of rules by anchoring them to the experiences and legal judgments of the relevant communities that follow those rules. In short, custom is no mere souvenir of bygone law; it is an integral and coherent part of any healthy, functioning contemporary legal system.

This part unfolds by examining five distinct realms of domestic legal regimes: family law, property, contracts, torts, and constitutional law. This sequence is by no means serendipitous. One possible critique of the continued relevance of customary law is to confine its applicability to purely "private law" topics. For sure, custom in domestic legal orders often has its greatest impact on norms related to the ownership and transmission of property, the enforcement of promises, and redress for civil wrongs. One of the central propositions of this volume is that custom remains a potent force in such purely public law domains as constitutional law and the law of nations. Indeed, custom may have especial force in those legal systems where determinations of status (especially family status), which combine both public and private law elements, are at issue. Within each of these five fields of domestic law, problems of the recognition and application of customary norms will be broadly reviewed in a comparative context. While the focus of the narrative will largely be devoted to the role of custom in common-law systems, in general (and in United States law, in particular), this will not invariably be the case in all instances. The goal here is to provide as wide a conspectus as possible of the character of customary law regimes as a part of the "living law" of contemporary domestic orders.

CUSTOMARY FAMILY LAW AS "INVENTED TRADITION"

Family law describes the set of norms that determine the status of relationships within family units (including the institutions of marriage and child-rearing) and attendant rights to property. In most civil law jurisdictions, these familial status relationships are the subject of civil codes distilled from essential principles of Roman law (some of which were discussed in Chapter 2). As narrated in Chapter 3, in common-law traditions, family relationships were an essential subject of judicial decisions in England (deriving their force from both canon law and custom), as later modified by Acts of Parliament. This divide between common and civil law traditions for familial statuses is largely misleading because both flowed from the common font of Roman law and canon law. Inasmuch as there is a Western legal tradition of the family – premised on individual autonomy, monogamy, and certainty in transmission of property rights – it would be fanciful to ascribe variations in the content of family law norms between jurisdictions to customary influences.

The best legal laboratory for assessing the continued role and function of customary family law are those jurisdictions where the great Western legal traditions collided with well-developed, indigenous systems of norms, at sharp variance with European values. The most spectacular examples of this confluence of legal traditions, and the resulting pluralism of family law rules and systems, was in Africa and the South Pacific. This was an inevitable consequence of the dynamics of European (and especially British) colonialism that occurred in these regions. This began in the middle to late nineteenth century, culminated in the processes of decolonization in the second half of the twentieth century, and continues today in postindependence legal evolutions in these countries.

A consistent aspect of British colonial rule was the adoption, for at least some purposes, of indigenous customary law, particularly as regards family relationships and attendant property rights. Whether in western or southern Africa,[1] Hong Kong,[2] or the South Pacific islands,[3] British colonial authorities routinely gave legal recognition to local customs as applied to statuses and relationships among native peoples (less frequently as between native peoples and colonizers). Indigenous courts – presided over by tribal chiefs or elders and not by colonial officials – were authorized to dispense justice in accordance with customary norms, at least for disputes within their jurisdiction (as determined by the identity of the parties or the issues in dispute).[4]

Make no mistake: the willingness of British colonial authorities to accept the application of indigenous customary family law was heavily qualified by views of white European superiority and the civilizing mission of colonialism. But no less an authority than the Privy Council – the final arbiter of colonial appeals in the British Empire – could make this statement about the nature of African customary law in 1919:

> Some tribes are so low in the scale of social organisation that their usages and conception of rights and duties are not to be reconciled with the institutions or the legal rights of civilised society.... On the other hand, there are indigenous peoples whose legal conceptions, though differently developed, are hardly less precise than our own. When once they have been studied and understood they are no less enforceable than rights arising under English law.[5]

Recognition and application of customary family law by colonial authorities was not just a matter of common-law comity; it was also accomplished by statute. A number of colonial governments adopted laws giving legal recognition to native marriages concluded under local custom.[6]

The main trends of African customary family law during the British colonial period have been well documented in the literature, whether through ethnographic studies or legal treatises.[7] The first, and perhaps overriding, principle was support for indigenous leadership systems (kinship, tribal, and chieftaincy structures), which were co-opted by the instruments of British colonial rule. This necessarily meant legal recognition of customary law regimes that were overseen by those local indigenous leaders.[8] In southern Africa, these leadership institutions could be quite elaborate, with local units of organization recognized at the levels of clans, villages, wards, tribes, and kingdoms.[9] The essential basis of legitimacy for all these institutions were kinship and extended family structures. The regulation of the status of family groupings was thus a crucial objective of customary law regimes.[10]

Because of the strong corporatist objectives of the British colonial embrace of customary family law norms, it was sometimes assumed (both in the anthropological and legal literature) that Africans had no real conception of individual status. All family relationships were, according to this theory, communal. Marriage, for example, was the merger of two families in a ritual exchange, not the union of a man and a woman exercising individual autonomy. This fallacy of the negation of individual status in African customary family law at times verged on the espousal of principles of primitive communism and collective responsibility in legal relationships.[11] The reality, of course, is far more complex. As T. Olawale Elias noted in his 1954 volume, *The Nature of African Customary Law*, African family custom is every bit as preoccupied with individual status and rights as any Western legal system.[12] Far from being static institutions, customary regimes have evolved in Africa through mechanisms that would be evident in other legal traditions: supplanting customs with new norms, or avoiding inconvenient usages by adopting legal fictions.[13]

These jurisprudential and ethnographic views of custom were bound to be the subject of a backlash. It is perhaps not surprising that customary law in the developing world – especially customary family law – came to be viewed in the 1970s and 1980s as a purely capitalist and colonialist construct.[14] Customary legal regimes were an "invented tradition" by colonial masters, seeking to preserve a compliant population and existing social structures.[15] Far from faithfully applying an organic, "living" body of customs, native courts under colonial regimes created an "official" version of custom that often bore little resemblance to real customary norms practiced "on the ground."[16] Even more insidiously, this "official custom" was a "tendentious montage with slender links to the past, supportive of the project of colonial rule, and entrenching the position of elders over juniors, men over women."[17] In short, according to the views of such writers as Martin Chanock, Francis Snyder, and Peter Fitzpatrick, traditional family law norms that existed in precolonization Africa and the Pacific were so distorted and perverted as part of the colonial enterprise as to utterly deny them any legitimacy as customary law.[18]

Even after stripping the "invented tradition" theory of custom of its neo-Marxist, deconstructionist, and postcolonial ideologies,[19] there might still be something left to commend it. To lay at the feet of colonialism the blame for all customary regimes that are elitist, patriarchal, sexist, and ageist is revisionism and anachronism of the worst sort. Many of these features of customary family law (in both Africa and the Pacific) preexisted the colonial period and have persisted afterwards. One should, however, be rightfully skeptical of the purported origins of any ostensible customary norm, especially in the area of family law. It is especially problematic where customs are codified by political agencies that may not truly reflect or represent the legitimate aspirations of the communities affected. That applies equally to British colonial institutions, the white apartheid regime in South Africa, or despotic postcolonial governments. Even more pertinently, one must be wary to distinguish the "living law" of communities from what may be an ossified "official law" of an earlier time and polity.[20]

CUSTOMARY FAMILY LAW IN PLURALISTIC LEGAL SYSTEMS

A common feature of postcolonial societies in the developing world, especially those that had been under British colonial government, is that their legal systems are pluralistic. This was partly a tradition of British imperial policy, where colonies that had been under previous French or Dutch rule (such as Québec, Ceylon, and the Cape Colony) had their previous civil law traditions left intact. Even more pertinently, in west Africa (especially Sierra Leone,[21] Ghana, and Nigeria), east Africa (particularly Kenya), southern Africa (South Africa, Botswana,[22] and Zimbabwe), and the South Pacific (Papua New Guinea,[23] Fiji, and the Solomon Islands[24]), common-law jurisprudence and institutions lived side by side with customary regimes. In all of these jurisdictions, customary law remains an especially potent force in shaping the contours of family law and relations.

Even among these widely dispersed locales, common themes of legal order emerge concerning the relationship between custom and common law. Each of these jurisdictions has confronted questions as to the application and ascertainment of custom, the resolution of conflicts between customary regimes, the potential repugnancy of customary norms with common law or constitutional principles, and the dynamic of codification of custom and the role of courts in that process. In almost all instances, the primary substantive issues implicating custom have been in the realm of family status and its consequent effects on property rights.

One of the first challenges for customary family law regimes is how to prove the existence of particular norms. The key dilemma is whether a customary rule should be treated as a matter of law for sole determination by a judge, or, rather, as a question of fact that must be pleaded and proven by the parties and (where appropriate) submitted to a jury. Some postcolonial statutes, enacted in compliance with constitutional provisions notionally recognizing indigenous customary law,[25] have indicated that custom should be plead and proven as fact.[26] In Nigeria, however, this general handling of custom as a fact to be proven[27] has been slightly modified by statute to allow for situations where

> a custom may be judicially noticed by the court if it has been acted upon by a court of superior or coordinate jurisdiction in the same area to an extent which justifies the court asked to apply [the custom] in assuming that the persons or the class of persons concerned in the area look upon the [custom] as binding in relation to circumstances similar to those under consideration.[28]

This provision has been construed by the Nigerian Supreme Court to mean that judges have the discretion to accept the existence of a customary norm on notice, without proof, provided that the purported rule has the "reputation" required.[29] During the colonial and apartheid periods of South Africa, the same approach was adopted: custom was a matter of fact to be proved, unless it was so notorious as to be subject to judicial notice.[30] By statute today in South Africa, a customary norm is subject to judicial notice, provided that "such law can be ascertained readily and with sufficient certainty."[31] Absent that, the custom may be proven by the parties to a case by competent evidence.[32] Postcolonial courts have been broadly eclectic in their selection of evidence for proof of custom, relying on sources as varied as that provided by ethnographers, local elders, chiefs or other assessors, or the testimony of the parties themselves.[33]

That leads to the problem of what to do when a purported norm of customary law conflicts with a rule from another legal system. In cases where there might be two incompatible customary regimes for family law, a choice of law would have to be made by a court. In Nigeria, this has become an exceedingly complex matter because family status and rights might be determined under English common law, under Sharia law (in force in the north of the country),[34] or under any number of distinct regional customary regimes.[35] In cases of conflict between customs, courts are obliged to choose the one that truly is applicable between the parties.[36] In cases involving individuals with different tribal, linguistic, or religious affiliations, Nigerian[37] and South African[38] courts have sought to use conflicts-of-law principles to divine the body of personal law that was intended by the parties to govern the relevant transaction, whether the intent of the celebrants of a marriage or that of an individual dying intestate. Such intent could be inferred from the nature of the transaction, the previous conduct of the parties, or even generalized evidence as to the way of living of the individuals concerned. For some jurisdictions, such as Zimbabwe and Lesotho,[39] the cultural orientation of the parties is the decisive element of the analysis of which body of family law is to be applied.

Quite apart from conflicts issues, what is to be done when a rule of custom allegedly contradicts a fundamental legal principle? Putting aside the constitutional and human rights dimensions of this question (which will be considered presently), this is typically referred to as repugnancy. In British colonial practice, customs at variance with English common law were permissible, but would be stricken if deemed to be contrary to natural justice, equity, good conscience, or public policy.[40] Despite this wide formulation, only those "customs as inherently impress[ed] [a court] with some abhorrence or are obviously immoral in their incidence"[41] were struck as repugnant. In apartheid South Africa, at least, customary law was declared repugnant in only a handful of cases.[42]

This rule was continued in postcolonial practice, with the important proviso, of course, that customary norms were to be viewed in totality and in the context of the justice, equity, conscience, and public policy of the African country concerned.[43] In *Onkonkwo v. Okagbue*,[44] the Nigerian Supreme Court applied these standards and nevertheless concluded that an Onitsha custom that allowed a woman to be "married" to a man already deceased was repugnant. The Nigerian Supreme Court gave broad ambit to principles of equity and natural justice in reaching its conclusion, and held that once a custom was declared repugnant as a matter of law, Nigerian courts would no longer enforce it. In South Africa, repugnancy has been statutorily narrowed to situations where "indigenous law [is] opposed to the principles of public policy or natural justice."[45] Interestingly, this same statute confirmed that the practice of *lobola* or *bogadi* – the payment of brideprice for the conclusion of customary marriages – was definitionally *not* repugnant to South African law.[46] The repugnancy doctrine has thus remained a check on what a polity might regard as atavistic customs, although increasingly, such determinations will be made in the context of entrenched or constitutional values.

Aside from the constitutional transformation of customary family law (which will be considered in more detail below), the other way that custom can be altered is more straightforward: through legislative codification or judicial pronouncement. In most of the pluralistic legal systems of Africa and the Pacific that have recognized custom, statutes are increasingly being employed to codify the substantive norms of customary family law or, at a minimum, to establish the boundaries and limits of its recognition. During the British colonial period, it was understood that the act of codification transmuted a body of "living" custom into an "official" code, very much the same way that a bug is frozen in time in a block of amber.[47] In some jurisdictions, this process of codification was fairly limited. In Nigeria, for example, the rule was long established that statutes in derogation of custom (as with the common law) must be expressly drafted.[48] Even more pertinently, Nigeria's 1990 Marriage Act allows for marriages to be concluded under either customary law or the provisions of the statute.[49] This was the template also for much marriage legislation in the South Pacific.[50]

In South Africa, especially under the white apartheid regime, the codification dynamic was anything but benign. The 1927 Native Administration Act was an early lynchpin of the apartheid legal structure, since it created a separate justice system to administer customary law among the black population of the country.[51] Under this statute, a broad body of case law was developed by native commissioners (overseen by a Native Appeal Court), that, over time, managed to create an official body of customary family law.[52] If that was not enough, South African regimes sanctioned the promulgation of codes for Natal and Zululand as part of the infamous homeland or Bantustan initiatives, and these enactments covered family law norms in the form of a restatement.[53] Today, this edifice of "official" customary law has been partially demolished by the 1998 Recognition of Customary Marriages Act (RCMA),[54] which repealed the Native Administration Act and the Natal and Zulu codes.[55] The RCMA has substantive provisions on the formalities, requirements, and consequences of customary marriages,[56] as well as granting the South African Minister of Justice the power to issue further regulations,[57] but it does not purport to articulate every aspect of the customary laws of marriage in the country.

TRANSFORMING CUSTOMARY FAMILY LAW

If codification has not been a serious challenge to the future of customary family law, what role is there for common-law judges ruling on its content? For almost all of the African and Pacific jurisdictions discussed here, judges have taken an active role in shaping customary family law rules, whether through the process of ascertaining the content and scope of those norms or (in exceptional instances) striking them for repugnancy or unconstitutionality.[58] Against the backdrop of extraordinary social changes in these nations and emerging principles of constitutional order (including gender equality), customary family law is bound to change. It has, especially with regard to four common – and crucial – institutions of most customary family law regimes: bridewealth, family property, primogeniture, and polygyny.

In African customary family law, a traditional aspect of marriage has been the payment of bridewealth – the transfer by the groom (or his family) to the wife's family of an amount of wealth (usually livestock) reflecting the reproductive capacity of the woman over her lifetime.[59] For some scholars, brideprice really reflects the value of male children to be born to a marriage and represents an interfamilial transfer of wealth.[60] As already noted, at least in South Africa, the marriage practice of brideprice (there known as *lobolo, rovoro,* or *bogadi*) has been statutorily recognized as a nonrepugnant custom.[61] Where marriages are contracted only upon partial payment of brideprice (with the rest to be paid over time), South African courts have enforced those subsequent payments by effectuating customary remedies of dissolution of the marriage or the forced return of the wife and her children.[62] Even though South Africa's RCMA does not expressly make the payment of brideprice an element for a valid customary marriage, refunds of *lobolo* are often the most contentious issue in customary divorces. The amount of a refund will often depend on the number of children produced from the marriage (the more procreation, the less the refund) and the conduct of the parties in the marriage (the less creditable the conduct of the wife, the greater the refund).[63]

Closely allied with the institution of brideprice is the nature of family property in African customary law. As already mentioned, the metaphor of the corporate character of family property can be taken too far so as to abnegate the very notion of individual property.[64] Nevertheless, customary regimes for titling property (both land and chattels) in the name of a family, and not in individual constituents of the family unit, persist in many African nations. In Ghana, for example, the chief of an extended family structure (known as a "stool") controls as trustee that stool property, separate and apart from what may be his or her own property.[65] Stool lands cannot be alienated except with the consent of the chief and his councillors, and members of the stool may have usufructuary rights to particular lands.[66] In Nigeria there has evolved a very sophisticated jurisprudence for the regulation of family property – its acquisition, governance, use, and sale.[67] In South Africa, customary rules of family and house property have been reformed by the 1998 RCMA. Under that statute, the default regime for all future customary monogamous marriages will be that marital estates will be in community of property for purposes of profit and loss.[68] Prospective spouses may contract around the community property default by prenuptial agreements, but the RCMA was recognized as a major reform, as it placed wives in a position of equality with husbands as to property rights in marriage.

Indeed, the primary motivating force for reform of customary marriages in Africa has been the perception that traditional institutions discriminate against women in all stages of their lives (whether as girls about to enter into matrimony, as wives managing within a family property regime, or as widows after the loss of a husband). While brideprice institutions have generally evaded challenge under the new constitutional or human rights standards of gender equality (despite the appearance that women are "commodified" by such payments),[69] restrictive rules of family property and primogeniture have not. In Nigeria, though, customary rules by which a wife is barred from inheritance of her husband's property (such rights going to the eldest son or to all children in equal shares) have been upheld as not repugnant to English common law and not in any express derogation of any constitutional principle of gender equality.[70]

In South Africa, however, constitutional values of gender equality have prevailed over any ostensible rights claimed under customary law. The South Africa Constitution of 1996 enshrined a right to culture[71] that has been generally construed to extend to claims existing under customary law.[72] Such rights, according to the Constitution, "may not be exercised in any manner inconsistent with any [other] provision of the Bill of Rights."[73] As has been noted by the South Africa Constitutional Court, "customary law should be accommodated, not merely tolerated, as part of South African law, provided the particular rules or provisions are not in conflict with the Constitution."[74] After some fits and starts,[75] South African courts have limited the application of customary family law regimes where they clearly infringed on the equality rights of women, whether under the Constitution or by statute.[76] In *Bhe v. Magistrate, Khayelitsha*,[77] the Constitutional Court struck down the Native Administration Act inasmuch as it countenanced a custom by which a deceased man's estate (having no male issue) devolved to his father or nearest male relative, and not his spouse or daughters. The Court found that the primogeniture custom – with the concomitant obligation upon a male heir to support the decedent's wife (or wives) and daughter(s) – was being undermined by modern living conditions in South Africa, especially the trend towards urbanization and nuclear families.[78]

Quite significantly, the Court split as to the appropriate remedy for an unconstitutional custom. The majority, pending further legislation, chose to apply the Intestate Succession Act to allow the wife in *Bhe* to inherit, even though that Act is notionally inapplicable to customary marriages.[79] A dissenting justice would have had the Court modify the offending custom to make it constitutionally sound, perhaps by allowing the firstborn child (whether son or daughter) to inherit.[80] This approach, Justice Ngcobo argued, was consistent with the South Africa Constitution's command for courts to "apply customary law when that law is applicable"[81] and that "when developing the common law or customary law, every court, tribunal[,] or forum must promote the spirit, purport[,] and objects of the Bill of Rights."[82]

Although not directly implicated in the *Bhe* case, the thorniest issue of customary family law was nevertheless present. Polygyny, and the analogous institution of concubinage,[83] is a consistent feature of most customary family law regimes in Africa and the Pacific basin. It has been in partial decline since the mid-twentieth century, largely because of the depopulation of rural areas and the emergence of economic conditions that preclude husbands from being able to properly support multiple wives and families.[84] Nevertheless, it remains a possibility under customary family regimes in Africa, including Nigeria[85] and South Africa. In southern African custom, the legal effect of polygynous marriages was to create distinct household units ("houses") within a larger family. A husband was obliged to treat all his spouses with equal respect due to their rank (based on the seniority of the marriage).[86] In contemporary South

Africa, polygyny remains a robust institution, especially with male migrant workers having, simultaneously, both rural and urban spouses.[87]

After a great deal of debate by South Africa's Law Commission,[88] polygyny was recommended as not being an atavistic custom that should be abrogated by statute. The 1998 RCMA accepted this position by statutorily recognizing preexisting polygynous marriages under customary law,[89] and by permitting subsequent polygynous marriages, provided they complied with the terms of the Act.[90] The most important of these conditions was that if a husband wished, after his first marriage, to contract subsequent marriages, it required a court order approving a marital property system for all the wives and houses involved. Such an order must take into account the circumstances of all the family groups affected by the new marriage and ensure an equitable distribution of the estate.[91] If such cannot be safeguarded, the court can refuse to allow the subsequent marriage. The RCMA does not, however, provide whether a polygynous marriage concluded in contravention of its terms is void *ab initio* or merely voidable.[92]

The Law Commission and RCMA did not, however, answer the fundamental concern as to whether polygyny inherently discriminated against women, and was, thereby, in violation of the South Africa Constitution's gender equality guarantee. The *Bhe* Court studiously left open the question of the constitutionality of customary practices of polygyny, even as it sought to craft a statutory interpretation of successions to property in polygynous marriages.[93] In subsequent debates in the Law Commission and South African civil society, strong arguments have been advanced that polygynous marriages may, in certain circumstances, benefit rural women, so long as their property rights (in the event of divorce or the spouse's death) are safeguarded.[94]

In the South Africa Constitutional Court's *Bhe* opinions, we have the full range of contemporary legal responses to traditional custom: accommodation and transformation, codification and precedent. Far from withering away, customary family law regimes and institutions appear to be thriving in a handful of pluralistic legal cultures, where they were acquiesced in during the colonial period and not suppressed in an urge towards legal modernization. In societies as diverse as Nigeria, South Africa, Papua New Guinea, and the Solomon Islands, customary law will remain an essential source for substantive rules of marriage, divorce, child custody, succession, and traditional governance. Custom has resisted what would otherwise be strong impulses towards codification and harmonization of essential rules of family status, relationships, and transactions. So even in a legal domain as freighted with public law (and even constitutional) dimensions as family law, in those cultures where customary regimes have taken root, they are likely to flourish.

6

Property

As already suggested in the last chapter, the canonical divide between private and public law subjects has always bedeviled much thinking about customary law. As a set of doctrines, family law combines elements of both, and, as just discussed, customary regimes can continue to exert a powerful pull in those jurisdictions where indigenous marital and succession practices were recognized and accepted. So, too, with property law. Very sophisticated contemporary legal systems – most notably those of Australia and the United States – have embraced group title to property, premised on ostensibly indigenous practices, institutions, and procedures. In this respect, common-law systems have sometimes been more receptive of property rights based on indigenous custom, than they have with family statuses and relationships grounded on the same source of law.

Unlike in family law, common law has, since medieval times (see Chapter 3), incorporated local customs as an element affecting property use, particularly of commonages.[1] Unwritten and unrecorded customary servitudes continue to exist and be judicially enforced, even in U.S. jurisdictions. Perhaps as an unintended effect of jurisprudence construing the United States Constitution's property rights and due process guarantees, customary land rights have emerged as a divisive issue. At stake is nothing less than the essential character of customary norms: though inchoate, are they binding from the moment of their adoption by the relevant community concerned, or must they be statutorily codified or judicially recognized before being constitutionally enforced?

Aside from the point that property law often does mix idioms of public and private rights, there may be something even more fundamental about the interaction of customary norms in this field. It has been intimated, by no less authorities than James Coolidge Carter[2] and T. F. T. Plucknett[3] (both introduced in Chapter 3), that legislation can only really preempt custom in private law fields, not in the realm of public law. The contours of customary property law readily test that hypothesis, and probably disprove it. While customary norms can still subsist in developed property regimes – at least within narrow doctrinal niches – they are less subject to statutory correction than one might think. More likely (and as was seen with South Africa in the last chapter), they are transformed by constitutional means.

INDIGENOUS CUSTOM AND PROPERTY RIGHTS

Whereas Africa was the locus of the greatest interaction of custom and common law in the field of family norms, the Pacific basin has seen the widest diversity of approaches in the realm of property law. Common to most societies of Australasia or Oceania, land was sacred, noncommodified, collectively held, and essential to indigenous power structures. (The culture of the Trobriand Islanders, introduced in Chapter 1, comes readily to mind.) Grafting common-law doctrines onto these customary land regimes has been problematic, but some legal trends are readily discerned.

In some Pacific island jurisdictions – most notably mid-ocean jurisdictions such as the Marshall Islands and Federated States of Micronesia – traditional and collective customary land-tenure systems have been inexorably supplanted by notions of individual ownership, fee simple title, and exclusivity of use.[4] Other legal systems – particularly those formerly under British dominion – have adopted a position that uneasily recognizes indigenous customary land tenure in a context of English common-law property rights.[5]

In Australia, the High Court's landmark 1992 decision in *Mabo v. Queensland (No. 2)*[6] accepted the concept of native title in common law, premised on indigenous groups' connection or occupation of land under traditional customs. Australia's 1993 Native Title Act[7] substantively codified the subject of customary property practices (especially the extinction of native titles), established a comprehensive statutory scheme for the registration of indigenous land titles and access rights, and provided for the adjudication of all disputes.[8] Essentially, the Australian approach has been to completely merge indigenous customary property rights into a common-law property system,[9] with consequent limitations on the scope of those native rights.[10]

At least in jurisdictions subject to United States' sovereignty,[11] the best example of the process of incorporation and transformation of indigenous property customs has been in Hawaii.[12] In order to appreciate these developments, one must recall the unique political history of the Hawaiian Islands. By the 1820s, a strong, centralized indigenous government was in place, ruled by a hereditary kingship.[13] As outside influences (particularly British and American) began to grow, Anglo-American law came to be used more and more in resolving disputes between native islanders and outsiders.[14] In 1840, Kamehameha III drafted the first constitution of the kingdom, which was henceforth a constitutional monarchy. In 1893, a cabal of American-led colonists overthrew the monarch, and in 1894, the Republic of Hawaii was declared, which persisted until 1897, when Hawaii was annexed as a territory to the United States. Hawaii became a state of the United States in 1959.[15]

In Hawaiian law, unlike any other jurisdiction in the United States, there is a clear tension between two different forms of the customary regimes. The first is the one considered earlier in Chapter 3, the English doctrine enunciated by Blackstone, applied sporadically in American jurisdictions,[16] and given recognition in early Hawaiian cases.[17] There is also a native Hawaiian doctrine of customary, indigenous rights. The possible divergence of these two strands of the doctrine can be seen in Hawaii's statute receiving the common law:

> The common law of England, as ascertained by English and American decisions, is declared to be the common law of the State of Hawaii in all cases, except as otherwise expressly provided by the Constitution or laws of the United States, or by the laws of the State, or fixed by Hawaiian judicial precedent, *or established by Hawaiian national usage*....[18]

This statute – now known as section 1–1 – was adopted by the Hawaiian constitutional monarchy on November 25, 1892. Its provision regarding "Hawaiian national usage" has been construed to give recognition to any custom that arose before that date.[19] As a corollary, the English common law was only selectively incorporated into Hawaiian law.[20] What this meant, in the words of one court, was that "the question here, unlike that in the United States, was not whether the court should decline to follow [an English common law] rule, but whether it should adopt a rule," particularly in view of indigenous customs.[21] Unlike any other U.S. jurisdiction, Hawaiian custom (as explained by Hawaiian judicial precedents) actually preempts the common law.[22]

One example of a Hawaiian usage arose in *Application of Ashford*,[23] an action to register title to land. The real estate in controversy was beach property located between the high-tide mark and the vegetation line, what was called *ma ke kai* in Hawaiian. The owners wished a judicial recognition of their title in the dry-sand beach. The state opposed and proved at trial, by the testimony of indigenous elder *kamaaina* witnesses,[24] that the proper boundary was at the vegetation line and not at high tide. The Hawaii Supreme Court agreed, and held that the boundary was set "in accordance with tradition, custom[,] and usage in old Hawaii."[25] This drew a sharp dissent from Justice Marumoto of the Court, who described the custom validated by the decision as "primitive in concept and haphazard in application."[26] In a 1970 case, *State v. Zimring*, the Hawaii Supreme Court seemed to agree with Justice Marumoto's concerns by rejecting the testimony of a *kamaaina* witness who purported to describe a custom in which landowners acquired property created by volcanic eruptions.[27] The court held that the affidavit of the *kamaaina* had to be struck since it was hearsay and could not speak to a material fact in the case: whether such a custom had existed before 1892.[28]

Read together, *Zimring* and *Ashford* produce a distinctively Hawaiian gloss on the doctrine of custom. Hawaii has adopted the equivalent of a statute establishing legal memory. But instead of dating legal memory to the coronation of King Richard I, Hawaii statute settled it at 1892, a date beginning the political transition of the islands from constitutional monarchy to independent republic and United States territory.[29] Hawaiian proof of local customs was somewhat at variance with English models. Instead of a jury serving as the fact-finder of the existence of customs, Hawaiian law privileged the role of native witnesses, who offered direct testimony to the court on the timing and extent of the custom.

All of this reception-statute jurisprudence must be read alongside a provision from the current Hawaiian Constitution (drafted in 1978):

> The State reaffirms and shall protect all rights, customarily and traditionally exercised for subsistence, cultural[,] and religious purposes and possessed by *ahupua`a* tenants who are descendants of native Hawaiians who inhabited the Hawaiian Islands prior to 1778, subject to the right of the State to regulate such rights.[30]

The first occasion in which this provision was construed was in *Kalipi v. Hawaiian Trust Co.*,[31] where at issue was a claim by native Hawaiians[32] to enter a landowner's undeveloped property in exercise of their customary gathering rights, rights that were not only recognized by the Hawaii Constitution, but for many years also in statute.[33] The key point made by the *Kalipi* court was that the provision of the Hawaii Constitution and the gathering-rights statute both limit their application to the inhabitants of the particular *ahupua`a*, a land division running from the mountains down to the coast.[34] In this case, the Hawaii Supreme Court held that native Hawaiian gathering rights did not preclude a landowner from developing his property in a way that might later interfere with those rights.[35]

The critical language of the *Kalipi* case was in reference to the interrelation of custom under Hawaii statute section 1–1 and the reservation of gathering rights under section 7–1:

> We perceive the Hawaii usage exception to the adoption of the English common law to represent an attempt on the part of the framers of the statute

to avoid results inappropriate to the isles' inhabitants by permitting the con-
tinuance of native understandings and practices which did not unreasonably interfere with the spirit of the common law. The statutory exception
to the common law is thus akin to the English doctrine of custom whereby
practices and privileges unique to particular districts continued to apply to
the residents of those districts even though in contravention of the common
law. See, 1 W. Blackstone, Commentaries *74.... This, however, is not to say
that we find that all the requisite elements of the doctrine of custom were
necessarily incorporated in § 1–1. Rather, we believe that the retention of
a Hawaiian tradition should in each case be determined by balancing the
respective interests and harm once it is established that the application of the
custom has continued in a particular area.[36]

This passage could be read as a definitive attempt to restrain a doctrine of
Hawaiian custom that would unduly interfere with established, Anglo-
American notions of exclusivity in landownership. The Court was careful to
give credence only to those "native understandings and practices which did
not unreasonably interfere with the spirit of the common law."[37] Moreover,
"the Hawaiian usage exception in § 1–1 may be used as a vehicle for the continued existence of those customary rights which continued to be practiced
and which worked no actual harm upon the recognized interests of others."[38]

This carefully wrought compromise started to unravel in *Pele Defense Fund
v. Paty*,[39] where at issue were gathering rights that were held not as part of an
ahupua`a, but rather were more generally held by all native peoples on an
island.[40] Here we have the difference in what the English cases perceived was
a custom held by an inchoate community and those exercised by the holders
of a definite estate (really, a prescriptive right). In *Pele Defense Fund*, a Hawaii
court had (for the first time) to consider a true customary right that was in the
character of a *profit à prendre*, extractive rights held by an indefinite class of
people. The Hawaii Supreme Court concluded that such rights were permissible under the statutory recognition of custom.[41] Once again, though, the
Pele court affirmed that extra-*ahupua`a* gathering rights could not abridge a
landowner's right to improve and develop his property.[42]

In the Hawaii Supreme Court's 1995 decision in *Public Access Shoreline
Hawai`i v. Hawai`i County Planning Commission* ("PASH"),[43] the disavowal
of the rules against profits by custom was made express.[44] Much more than
that, this opinion ended the two-faced nature of custom in Hawaii. The *PASH*
decision accomplished what nearly 150 years of Hawaiian jurisprudence had
failed to do: the repudiation of the English common law of custom in favor
of an entirely indigenous construction of the doctrine. The *PASH* opinion
performed this transformation on two levels.

The first was to simply remake the Blackstonian legal requisites of customary rights in the image of a native Hawaiian law. Having already refashioned the requirement of antiquity and certainty, there remained other difficult features of the English doctrine to overcome. The Hawaii Supreme Court's point of departure was its 1858 characterization of the doctrine in *Oni v. Meek*. In response, the *PASH* court noted:

> The court in *Oni* also appears to have misconstrued other elements of the doctrine of custom by concluding that the custom urged in that case was "so unreasonable, so uncertain, and so repugnant to the spirit of the present laws[.]" 2 Haw. at 90. Contrary to the apparent understanding of the *Oni* court: (1) "consistency" is properly measured against other customs, not the spirit of the present laws; (2) a particular custom is "certain" if it is objectively defined and applied; certainty is not subjectively determined; and (3) "reasonableness" concerns the manner in which an otherwise valid customary right is exercised – in other words, even if an acceptable rationale cannot be assigned, the custom is still recognized as long as there is no "good legal reason" against it. See Blackstone's Commentaries at 76–78.[45]

This refashioning of some of Blackstone's elements for custom were certainly welcome. The *PASH* court was correct to return the inquiry of reasonableness to its original footing of being an inquiry to see whether a custom actually offended reason. Likewise, its emphasis on "objective" certainty is unexceptional.[46] The problem is with the Hawaii court's refashioning of consistency. It is true, as Blackstone said, that consistency would be measured as against other customs. But the Hawaii Supreme Court seems to be saying that a Hawaiian custom's consistency with the common-law principles of property law simply does not matter. This would be in line with how the Hawaiian doctrine of custom, as recognized in statute section 1–1, has been interpreted. Of course, it is not what Blackstone had in mind, since he presumed that "[c]ustoms, in derogation of the common law, must be construed narrowly."[47]

The Hawaii Supreme Court was not content to replace the classic, Blackstonian elements of custom to suit the needs of Hawaii's particular vision of the doctrine. The court used the *PASH* opinion as a vehicle to challenge traditional Anglo-American notions of property law. This was the second means of transforming custom in Hawaii. In particular, the court took aim at the concept of exclusivity, that the key strand in the landowner's bundle of rights was the ability to exclude others from the property: "Our examination of the relevant legal developments in Hawaiian history leads us to the conclusion that the western concept of exclusivity is not universally applicable in Hawai`i.[48] Gone was the cautionary language of *Kalipi* that only those "native understandings and practices which did not unreasonably interfere with the spirit of the common law" would be allowed.[49]

Even more ominously, the Hawaii Supreme Court indicated in *PASH* that native Hawaiian gathering rights, to the extent that they were to be protected by the state (as commanded under the state constitution), could result in land-owners being prevented from developing or improving their property:

> [W]e refuse the temptation to place undue emphasis on non-Hawaiian principles of land ownership in the context of evaluating deliberations on development permit applications. Such an approach would reflect an unjustifiable lack of respect for gathering activities as an acceptable cultural usage in pre-modern Hawai`i, which can also be successfully incorporated in the context of our current culture. Contrary to the suggestion in *Kalipi* that there would be nothing to prevent the unreasonable exercise of these rights, [Hawaii Constitution] article XII, section 7 accords an ample legal basis for regulatory efforts by the State.... In other words, the State is authorized to impose appropriate regulations to govern the exercise of native Hawaiian rights in conjunction with permits issued for the development of land previously undeveloped or not yet fully developed.[50]

Here, at last, is the policy crux of this extraordinary transmutation of the Hawaiian doctrine of custom: giving life to customary practices that may "be successfully incorporated in the context of our current culture."[51] The legal authority for this policy preference was to be found in a 1986 Hawaii law, defining the "Aloha Spirit"[52] that the *PASH* court embraced:

> In accordance with HRS § 5–7.5(b), we are authorized to "give consideration to the 'Aloha Spirit'." The Aloha Spirit "was the working philosophy of native Hawaiians[;] ... 'Aloha' is the essence of relationships in which each person is important to every other person for collective existence."[53]

Collective existence and community are thus at the heart of Hawaii's revolutionary doctrine of customary property rights. The relationship between the English and Hawaiian versions of the doctrine partly accounted for this. Blackstone's formulation of the English doctrine was intended to constrain its willful use by juries. As elements of the English doctrine were discarded or modified in Hawaii decisions, the brakes on its extended application were released. In one respect, of course, the activism of Hawaiian judges in embracing custom seems quite defensible: after all, the native Hawaiian people *did* have a highly developed system of customary property rights that existed before colonial contact. Hawaii has thus witnessed the moderation of a property regime characterized by strongly individualistic rights (an artifact of common law introduced in the colonial period), through the articulation of group ownership principles.[54]

CUSTOMARY EASEMENTS AND THE PARADOX
OF JUDICIAL TAKINGS

These conflicting models for the interaction between customary and common-law property regimes assume (as they must) that traditional land tenure and access rights remain robust in many contemporary legal systems. Traditional norms may include what were referred to by Blackstone as "local customs," servitudes over land that were held by an inchoate group of residents of the locality.[55] The recognition and application of such customary easements leads to an even more fundamental problem: what transforms a property usage into a binding rule of customary law?

This issue is magnified in legal cultures, such as the United States, where there is a constitutionally entrenched guarantee to property rights.[56] A key question for "takings" jurisprudence is whether an essential property right has been confiscated by the government or regulated in such a way as to deny the property owner all use of his property.[57] As the U.S. Supreme Court observed in the 1992 landmark decision in *Lucas v. South Carolina Coastal Council*:

> Where the State seeks to sustain regulation that deprives land of all eco-nomically beneficial use, we think it may resist compensation only if the logically antecedent inquiry into the nature of the owner's estate shows that the proscribed use interests were not part of his title to begin with…. [A] [state] must identify background principles of nuisance and property law that prohibit the [landowner's] uses.[58]

So here we have the nub of the problem: does a public easement, created by custom of (assumptively) long-standing character, but only first recognized by a court much more recently, become part of the state's "background principles of … property law"? If the custom has merged with those principles, a prop-erty owner never had the right to build on their land in a way that interfered with the public's rights. In short, the state took nothing when it regulated consistent with the custom. But if the custom only adheres at the time it is first positively recognized in the public law – through a judicial precedent or statute[59] – then the owner's right to build had vested, and they should be entitled to just compensation if the state purports to later bar improvement of their property.

U.S. courts have tended to hold that a customary easement over prop-erty is valid from the time of the custom's formation, and not just when it is statutorily codified or judicially recognized.[60] For example, the Hawaiian custom of allowing beach access was challenged as a regulatory taking of property, an argument that was brushed aside by the Hawaiian Supreme Court in the *PASH* decision:

> In the instant case, Nansay [the landowner] argues that the recognition of traditional Hawaiian rights beyond those established in *Kalipi* and *Pele* would fundamentally alter its property rights. However, Nansay's argument places undue reliance on western understandings of property law that are not universally applicable in Hawai`i. Moreover, Hawaiian custom and usage have always been a part of the laws of this State. Therefore, our recognition of customary and traditional Hawaiian rights, … does not constitute a judicial taking.[61]

Hawaiian exceptionalism – based on indigenous land practices – was thus in tension with common-law "western understandings" of property rights.

Even more extraordinarily, courts in Oregon have radically transformed the common-law doctrine of local custom. Unlike Hawaii's experience – which mixed English common law with indigenous land practices – Oregon's jurisprudence was a bold, instrumental move to create a public recreational easement over the entirety of the state's ocean beaches. This customary servitude was announced for the first time in the 1969 decision of *State ex rel. Thornton v. Hay*.[62] The Oregon Supreme Court, in delocalizing customary easements, was obliged to reformulate the Blackstonian doctrinal elements, particularly to overcome the limiting factors of antiquity, certainty, and reasonableness.[63] That Court offered this paean to custom:

> Because so much of our law is the product of legislation, we sometimes lose sight of the importance of custom as a source of law in our society. It seems particularly appropriate in the case at bar to look to an ancient and accepted custom in this state as the source of a rule of law. The rule in this case, based upon custom, is salutary in confirming a public right, and at the same time it takes from no man anything which he has had a legitimate reason to regard as exclusively his.[64]

It was inevitable that Oregon's custom of public beach access would be challenged as a "judicial taking," an unexpected pronouncement of a rule of property law that had been hitherto unknown in the jurisdiction.[65] As in Hawaii, Oregon courts deflected that assertion. In *McDonald v. Halvorson*, the Oregon Court of Appeals considered such an argument and simply ruled that:

> In *Thornton*, the Supreme Court merely confirmed the public's right of use in the "dry-sand area" of Oregon's beach land, which the public has always

assumed to be a part of the public beach. Although the "dry-sand area" belongs to the property owners, it has always been subject to the public's recreational easement.... State law is the source of the sticks that constitute a property owner's bundle of rights.... Thus, the court in *Thornton* merely declared a right of use which the public always had.... Defendants have no protected property interest in the public's easement over the "dry-sand area," and therefore there can be no "taking."[66]

In subsequent cases, culminating in *Stevens v. City of Cannon Beach*,[67] this logic was repeated: *Thornton* merely declared a preexisting custom; there was no change in Oregon property law; no taking was effected. *Thornton* was only "an expression of state law that the purportedly taken property interest was not part of the plaintiffs' estate to begin with. Accordingly, there was no taking within the meaning of the Oregon or United States constitutions."[68]

The Oregon Supreme Court put an even finer point on this rejection of judicial takings in *Stevens*. It did not matter, the Court said, that the landowners had acquired their property before the decision in *Thornton* was handed down; rather, "the question is when, under *Thornton*'s reasoning, *the public rights came into being*. The answer is that they came into being long before plaintiffs acquired any interests in their land."[69] The Oregon Supreme Court then used the idiom of the decision of the U.S. Supreme Court in *Lucas v. South Carolina Coastal Council*,[70] and noted that "*Thornton* merely enunciated one of Oregon's 'background principles of ... the law of property'."[71] The custom declared in *Thornton* was not, according to the *Stevens* court,[72] an unconstitutional judicial taking because the custom was not, again in the words of *Lucas*, "newly legislated or decreed," but rather, "inheres in the title itself, in the restrictions that the background principles of the State's law of property and nuisance already placed upon ownership."[73]

Despite the takings concerns implicated in the Oregon Supreme Court's decision, the U.S. Supreme Court denied certiorari in the *Stevens* case.[74] Justice Scalia (joined by Justice O'Connor) penned a vigorous dissent from denial of review, concluding that "[t]o say that this case raises a serious Fifth Amendment takings issue is an understatement."[75] Justice Scalia began his analysis with a review of Oregon custom jurisprudence after *Thornton*, and was forced to conclude that Oregon's "new-found 'doctrine of custom' is a fiction."[76] "[T]he Supreme Court of Oregon's vacillation on the scope of the doctrine of custom.... reinforce[s] a sense that the court is creating the doctrine rather than describing it."[77] The dissent noted that

[J]ust as a State may not deny rights protected under the Federal Constitution through pretextual procedural rulings ..., neither may it do so by making nonexistent rules of state substantive law. Our opinion in *Lucas* ... would be a nullity if anything that a State court chooses to denominate "background law" – regardless of whether it is really such – could eliminate property rights.[78]

Justices Scalia and O'Connor would have had the Court grant review in order to consider

> [p]articularly in light of the utter absence of record support for the crucial factual determinations in that case, whether the Oregon Supreme Court chooses to treat it as having established a "custom" applicable to Cannon Beach alone, or one applicable to all "dry-sand" beach in the State, petitioners must be afforded an opportunity to make out their constitutional claim by demonstrating that the asserted custom is pretextual. If we were to find for petitioners on this point, we would not only set right a procedural injustice, but would hasten the clarification of Oregon substantive law that casts a shifting shadow upon federal constitutional rights the length of the State.[79]

There seems to be no doubt that customary claims to public rights will increase in the coming years,[80] especially as governments discover the benefits of the approach. Custom is a cheap and easy solution to the nagging problem of public rights in private property. Custom is ancient. Custom extols community. Custom makes us feel good. What could possibly be wrong with a doctrine like this?

Custom's bright and cheery demeanor has been forcefully espoused by many legal writers "support[ing] government regulations restricting" property rights and advancing communal interests in property.[81] And one would have to be a bit of a boor not to feel some favor for a doctrine that allows the rustic villagers to dance around the maypole on the manor lawn,[82] that permits hardy fishermen to dry their nets on the shore as they have from time immemorial,[83] and, yes, that gives you and your loved one the right to take a midnight stroll on a windswept beach. All this, one might suppose, is precisely the evil of custom. Custom can be a blunt instrument against the property rights of the minority, a sharp sanction against economic hold-outs and political dissidents.

In the face of various critiques of the application of customary norms in advanced property regimes – and they are legion and of long standing[84] – the historical notion of custom has become the darling of both communitarian philosophers and land-use regulators. At the same time that both of these groups have wielded instrumental thinking in support of the doctrine of custom, it is important also to value historical fidelity in understanding the origins and evolution of the doctrine. If custom is really about shared values and expectations – a wider embodiment of Hawaii's "Aloha Spirit" – it seems unreasonable to apply purely utilitarian principles in its pursuit. It is also what Lord Justice Brett meant when he said that the ultimate test of a custom is "[w]hether it is in accordance with fundamental principles of right and wrong."[85] Some public goods come at just too high a cost to individual liberty and property.

7

Contracts

Exchanges of promises – the essence of contract – often occur in a group context. When they do, should the mutual expectations of the contracting parties, especially as conditioned by the business practices of the relevant commercial community, have a bearing on the legal enforcement of their contractual rights and obligations? Hitherto in this discussion of custom's contemporary relevance, the community aspect of custom has been tied (at least implicitly) to place, whether for purposes of establishing family relationships or property claims. But a sense of community can be fashioned also by shared interests: a common profession, business, craft, or trade. Traced to antiquity's *collegia opificum* and medieval guilds, customary practices have always been a singular feature of commercial communities.

Today in sophisticated legal cultures (particularly Anglo-American jurisdictions), unofficial business norms can be enforced legally as trade customs and usages in two ostensibly different fashions. The first is through the common law of merchant custom, very distinct in scope and effect from the English doctrine of local custom affecting property servitudes. Merchant custom was introduced in Chapter 3 (in the context of the evolution of English common law) and elaborated upon in Chapter 4 (as an economic phenomenon), but here the objective is to elucidate the legal elements for the proof, application, and enforcement of customary norms in commercial situations. Common-law merchant custom remains a robust form of interstitial norm-making for a variety of business communities.

This is despite the fact that the second mechanism by which contemporary legal systems have recognized and enforced trade usages is through statutes. Custom's uneasy courtship with codification has been discussed previously (see Chapter 5's discussion of South African customary family law), but here it is particularly evident. Karl Llewellyn – who was introduced in Chapter 1 as a leading ethnographer of customary law for preliterate peoples – was also the chief architect of the Uniform Commercial Code (UCC), which has become a template for business law codification not only in the United States, but around the world.[1] The UCC's provisions[2] on the law merchant and trade usages certainly gave official sanction to commercial custom, but the real question (considered here) is whether it truly altered the contours of the common-law doctrine.

THE COMMON LAW OF COMMERCIAL CUSTOM

As suggested in Chapter 3, what distinguished merchant from local customs under English common law was that commercial usages were not tied to a locality and there was no requirement that they be proven to have existed from "time immemorial."[3] In England, trade usages were proven as fact before a jury, unless they were so notorious (by way of earlier precedents recognizing the custom) as to be subject to judicial notice.[4] Trade usages were regarded as a norm of trade, adopted by persons engaged in a particular kind of business, which were so well known that persons contracting in matters relating to that business were presumed to do so on the understanding that such rules were followed unless expressly or impliedly excluded. A trade usage was thus evidence of an agreement to deal upon particular terms.[5]

As with local customs affecting landed property interests, English jurists expressed reservations about extending "the office of a usage or custom."[6] Lord Denman in the 1840 case of *Trueman v. Loder*, observed that

> [W]hat can be more difficult than to ascertain, as a matter of fact, such a prevalence of what is called a custom of trade, as to justify a verdict that it form a part of every contract? Debate may also be fairly raised as to the right of binding strangers by customs probably unknown to them; a conflict may exist between the customs of two different places; and supposing all these difficulties removed, and the custom fully proved, still it will almost always remain doubtful whether the parties to the individual contract really meant that it should include the custom.[7]

This sentiment was echoed by no less an authority than U.S. Supreme Court Justice Joseph Story, who was instrumental in fashioning an American federal general common law of commerce, which reached its pinnacle in the landmark 1842 decision in *Swift v. Tyson*.[8] His views are worth setting out at length:

> I own myself no friend to the almost indiscriminate habit of late years, of setting up particular usages or customs in almost all kinds of business and trade, to control, vary, or annul the general liabilities of parties under the common

law, as well as under the commercial law. It has long appeared to me, that there is no small danger in admitting such loose and inconclusive usages and customs, often unknown to particular parties, and always liable to great misunderstandings and misinterpretations and abuses, to outweigh the well-known and well-settled principles of law.... The true and appropriate office of a usage or custom is, to interpret the otherwise indeterminable intentions of parties, and to ascertain the nature and extent of their contracts, arising not from express stipulations, but from mere implications and presumptions, and acts of a doubtful or equivocal character. It may also be admitted to ascertain the true meaning of a particular word, or of particular words in a given instrument, when the word or words have various senses, some common, some qualified, and some technical, according to the subject-matter, to which they are applied. But I apprehend, that it can never be proper to resort to any usage or custom to control or vary the positive stipulations in a written contract, and, à fortiori, not in order to contradict them. An express contract of the parties is always admissible to supersede, or vary, or control, a usage or custom; for the latter may always be waived at the will of the parties. But a written and express contract cannot be controlled, or varied, or contradicted by a usage or custom; for that would not only be to admit parol evidence to control, vary, or contradict written contracts; but it would be to allow mere presumptions and implications, properly arising in the absence of any positive expressions of intention, to control, vary, or contradict the most formal and deliberate written declarations of the parties.[9]

Despite the cogent critiques of Lord Denman and Justice Story (which are as relevant today as they were in the early 1800s), trade usages retained their vitality and utility for one simple reason: people in business tolerate ambiguity to a much higher degree than lawyers do.[10] Moreover, members of a trade community tend to be "repeat" players in business, and the accretive process of assimilating practices and norms would be expected in such circumstances.

Once the notion of commercial customs was embraced in principle, that left substantial contention as to the elements needed to be satisfied in order to prove, apply, and enforce such norms. On this score, Blackstone was of little help. While, as narrated in Chapters 3 and 6, his etiology of local customs as property servitudes was both immensely influential and problematic, he gave no similar attention to the essentials of merchant custom, except to intimate that they were different from local ones. Without such a handy restatement,[11] Anglo-American common law was compelled to muddle through layerings of judicial precedents with decidedly mixed results.

The first – and perhaps essential – predicate for a commercial custom is proof of its notoriety within the relevant business community such that the participants to a contract or transaction can be charged with its knowledge or appreciation. A usage's notoriety is often conflated by judges as inquiries into the custom's generality, certainty, and uniformity – but not necessarily any great antiquity.[12] This is often established by proving numerous instances of the actual practice,[13] although such evidence is often adduced through expert testimony as to the nature and extent of the usage.[14] Once the general status of the custom is established, courts have often had to wrestle with a more difficult question: what level of knowledge of the usage is required for the contracting party the practice is to be enforced against? Courts have rarely required proof of actual knowledge.[15] Rather, so long as the contracting parties are participants in the same trade or business,[16] if a usage is sufficiently notorious, there is a rebuttable presumption that the contracting parties were knowledgeable of it or should have been aware of it.[17]

But there is a deep ambiguity in the Anglo-American jurisprudence of commercial custom: whether a practice, in order to be enforced as against contracting parties, must be regarded as compulsory by those people in business. Many precedents are clear that a "loose and variable" practice, one that leaves some material element to individual discretion, is not enforceable.[18] Some cases appear to emphasize that a practice that arises from "mere acts of courtesy or accommodation" will not be sufficiently compulsory and binding to be enforceable,[19] a commercial restatement of the *opinio juris sive necessitatis* requirement from Roman law (see Chapter 2).

Whether a trade practice requires proof that it is followed out of a sense of legal obligation in order to be enforceable is at the root of the semantic distinction between "customs" and "usages," at least in commercial law. It has been held by a number of courts,[20] and in a number of statutory codifications,[21] that while all commercial customs must be shown to be compulsory, trade usages need not to nevertheless be enforced as against contracting parties that are aware of them. This goes well beyond the oft-repeated maxim that a "usage is no more than a fact, custom is a law; there may be usage without custom, but there can be no custom without usage to accompany or precede it: usage consists in the repetition of acts, and custom arises out of this repetition."[22] Indeed, it suggests that in the unique context of commercial law – whether domestic (considered in this chapter) or international (see Chapter 10) – customary norms have a fundamentally different character than they might in other private law contexts.

In many of the commercial custom cases, one has the impression that if a practice is deemed reasonable, such will often serve as a surrogate or proxy for its binding character.[23] In short, a practice's "right reason" or just plain "common sense"[24] is the missing ingredient that transforms a trade usage into an enforceable custom. In the U.S. Court of Appeals for the Second Circuit's 1944 decision in *Dixon, Irmaos & Cia. v. Chase National Bank*, the court studiously avoided imposing a requirement of compulsion in order to render enforceable a usage in the New York banking industry (concerning documentary letters of credit) and, instead, emphasized the practice's "reasonableness and utility."[25] This ruling was to have immense influence on the drafting of the Uniform Commercial Code (discussed below).[26] Other judicial decisions have used the argot of shared risk and reward among contracting parties, and have enforced customs, even those inconvenient in application,[27] provided they were not "calculated to throw disproportionate burdens on either party."[28] As with the English property cases of the enclosure period (discussed in Chapter 3), judges have routinely accepted proof that certain commercial customs exist (at least as to their notoriety), and even accepted that proven customs are entitled to a presumption of reasonability,[29] but, nevertheless, have still legally disqualified them as being unreasonable[30] or as against public policy.[31]

Of course, in today's world of "legisprudence,"[32] perhaps the most effective check on the uncontrolled growth and influence of commercial customs is that none may conflict with a statute. Although some authorities[33] expand this rule to mean that custom can never abrogate any "positive law" – forgetting that customary norms are, themselves, positive law-making[34] – this is perhaps the most oft-repeated axiom in customary law jurisprudence.[35] It has not gone unquestioned, however. Lord Justice Bowen in the 1885 case of *Perry v. Barnett*,[36] was willing to accept a custom on the London Stock Exchange that would have made enforceable an order to sell bank shares that was in contravention of an Act of Parliament, provided that all parties concerned were cognizant of the practice. Moreover, while virtually all authorities agree that a custom cannot trump a statute, many also accept that vague legislative acts can be construed by custom and usage.[37]

LLEWELLYN'S MOMENT: THE UCC'S CODIFICATION OF TRADE CUSTOM

Attempts to codify the elements of commercial custom, and so to place them on a firmer doctrinal footing and to distinguish them from local customs, were a relatively new phenomenon.[38] For U.S. jurisdictions at least, that such was attempted at all was the result of one man's vision. Karl Llewellyn's unique role as a legal ethnographer and sociologist has been considered before in this volume (see Chapters 1 and 4). As a leading exponent of Legal Realism, he was as perplexed as the rest of his colleagues by the notion that law need not be a "top-down" construct, and he sought throughout his career to explore the ways that relevant communities made law through their practice. This was part of his instrumental approach (with all of its methodological limitations) towards the Cheyenne Indians.

It was also key to his twenty-year experience as the lead drafter of the restatement effort that came to be known as Article 2 (Sales) of the UCC, what some scholars have acclaimed as "the most successful codification in American law."[39] Throughout the project, conducted by the Conference of Commissioners on Uniform State Laws (CCUSL) and American Law Institute (ALI), Llewellyn sought to "codify the common practices and understandings of the marketplace."[40] Apparently, Llewellyn conducted qualitative empirical research with interviews of merchants in various trades,[41] in much the same fashion as he spent the summer of 1935 in the Cheyenne country collecting anecdotal case histories.[42] In addition, Llewellyn was heavily influenced by earlier German commercial codifications, which had expressly recognized the role of trade usages in fashioning commercial norms.[43] By late 1940, Llewellyn had a complete draft of UCC Articles 1 and 2 prepared.

Llewellyn's objective was the immodest goal of distancing usages of trade from the preexisting common law of merchant custom and to revolutionize its acceptance as a way to ground law in commercial realities.[44] Llewellyn saw usages of trade as the controlling concept of UCC Article 2: adding, subtracting, supplementing, and modifying contractual terms, while filling gaps in incomplete or incoherent contracts.[45] Indeed, it might also be suggested that Llewellyn's view of an overarching role for trade usages was part-and-parcel of a project that heavily emphasized merchants in sales transactions, and tended to minimize (or ignore altogether) the role of consumers.[46] As some scholars have observed, in Llewellyn's mind, merchant custom was the equivalent of Cheyenne "law-ways."[47]

The result of Llewellyn's efforts – with substantial compromises within the CCUSL and ALI review processes – were two key provisions on merchant practices. UCC section 1–103 provides simply that "[u]nless displaced by the particular provisions of this Act, the principles of law and equity, including the law merchant … shall supplement its provisions."[48] With even greater elaboration, UCC section 1–205, entitled "Course of Dealing and Usage of Trade," sets out these relevant provisions on commercial practices:

(2) A usage of trade is any practice or method of dealing having such regularity of observance in a place, vocation or trade as to justify an expectation that it will be observed with respect to the transaction in question. The existence and scope of such a usage are to be proved as facts. If it is established that such a usage is embodied in a written trade code or similar writing the interpretation of the writing is for the court.

(3) A course of dealing between parties and any usage of trade in the vocation or trade in which they are engaged or of which they are or should be aware give particular meaning to and supplement or qualify terms of an agreement.

(4) The express terms of an agreement and an applicable course of dealing or usage of trade shall be construed wherever reasonable as consistent with each other; but when such construction is unreasonable express terms control both course of dealing and usage of trade and course of dealing controls usage of trade.

(5) An applicable usage of trade in the place where any part of performance is to occur shall be used in interpreting the agreement as to that part of the performance.

(6) Evidence of a relevant usage of trade offered by one party is not admissible unless and until he has given the other party such notice as the court finds sufficient to prevent unfair surprise to the latter.[49]

Even a cursory review of this provision would reveal its many revolutionary aspects. For starters, commercial practices (whether denominated as "custom" or "usage") are to be seen as consistent with "established rules of law," not in opposition to them.[50] According to section 1–205(4), a strict hierarchy of sources is apparently established: the "express terms of an agreement" prevail over the parties' "course of dealing,"[51] and course of dealing trumps usages of trade.[52] Section 1–205(5) recognizes a conflict-of-laws rule in which the place of performance determines the relevant locality for a usage of trade. As for pleading and proof, section 1–205(6) requires that proof of a usage of trade be noticed to an opposing litigant, in much the same way as proof of foreign law is.[53]

Where Llewellyn's provision on trade usage really marks a departure from common-law templates is in its implied transformation of the elements that transform a commercial practice into a binding rule for purposes of contract construction. As the official commentary to section 1–205 (largely drafted by Llewellyn) notes:

A usage of trade under subsection (2) must have the "regularity of observance" specified. The ancient English tests for "custom" are abandoned in this connection. Therefore, it is not required that a usage of trade be "ancient or immemorial", "universal" or the like. Under the requirement of subsection (2) full recognition is thus available for new usages and for usages currently observed by the great majority of decent dealers, even though dissidents ready to cut corners do not agree. There is room also for proper recognition of usage agreed upon by merchants in trade codes.... Subsection (3), giving the prescribed effect to usages of which the parties "are or should be aware", reinforces the provision of subsection (2) requiring not universality but only the described "regularity of observance" of the practice or method. This subsection also reinforces the point of subsection (2) that such usages may be either general to trade or particular to a special branch of trade.[54]

Some have suggested that Llewellyn's emphasis on "regularity of observance" and "justify[ing] ... expectation[s] [of] observ[ance]" placed the proof of a trade usage on an objective basis and eliminated the encrusted formalities of Blackstone's version of local custom.[55] The elimination of the antiquity standard and any vestige of an *opinio juris* requirement were particularly significant.[56] At the same time, Llewellyn understood:

> the ancient requirement that a custom or usage must be "reasonable." However, the emphasis is shifted. The very fact of commercial acceptance makes out a prima facie case that the usage is reasonable, and the burden is no longer on the usage to establish itself as being reasonable. But the anciently established policing of usage by the courts is continued to the extent necessary to cope with the situation arising if an unconscionable or dishonest practice should become standard.[57]

The Uniform Commercial Code thus fundamentally reshuffled the elements of commercial custom.

There is some truth to all of this, but there remain doubts whether judicial interpretations of UCC section 1–205 have actually lived up to Llewellyn's vision of a robust role for merchant custom in the making of contemporary commercial law. A handful of courts have appeared to assume that the UCC worked no material changes on the common-law doctrine of merchant custom.[58] While other decisions have recognized section 1–205's relaxation of the requirement that parties actually be aware of a trade usage,[59] others have imposed a high evidentiary standard for proof of commercial customs.[60] Despite the UCC rhetoric of "decent dealers"[61] and "policing" against "unconscionable or dishonest practices,"[62] no usage (validated as such) has ever been struck as unreasonable.[63] There is a real risk that Llewellyn's vision of merchant custom is nothing more than a fig leaf for marketplace morality.[64]

By far and away, the most contentious issue in the post-UCC decisions on trade usages is the extent to which commercial customs can be employed to interpret contracts, even those agreements that would not otherwise be considered ambiguous or incomplete. As noted above, this was precisely the issue in the Second Circuit's *Dixon, Irmaos* ruling, which sparked a firestorm of scholarly debate about the propriety of trade usages modifying what would otherwise seem to be the clear provisions of contracts (in that case, the terms of documentary letters of credit).[65] Llewellyn sided, in section 1–205(4), with the view that commercial custom could add, modify, or elucidate terms of a contract but could not outright contradict an express agreement.

Some parol evidence applications of UCC section 1–205 are hardly objectionable, such as to employ a trade usage to give meaning to a contractual term (especially a term-of-art) for which there is no definition provided in the agreement.[66] Other uses are far more controversial. Some post-UCC cases, including the 1971 Fourth Circuit decision in *Nitrogen Corp. v. Royster Co.*,[67] gave wide latitude to courts to allow the introduction of trade usages as a way to subvert bargained-for contractual expectations. Some courts have gone further and allowed trade usages to modify contracts that have been deemed to be unambiguous.[68] The Fourth Circuit actually had qualified its holding by ruling, based on the language of UCC section 1–205(4), that "evidence of usage of trade … should be excluded whenever it cannot be reasonably construed as consistent with the terms of the contract."[69] Other courts grasped this language, resisted the employment of trade usages, and held that "extrinsic evidence [such as commercial custom] might jeopardize the certainty of … contractual duties" and "contracts would lose their utility as a means of assigning the risks of the market."[70] These precedents have motivated some drafters of transaction documents to include clauses that prohibit any recourse to trade usages as background rules for contract construction.[71]

THE POST-LLEWELLYN REACTION

The contemporary law of commercial custom thus remains a muddle in most Anglo-American common-law jurisdictions. Traces of the Blackstonian version of merchant custom persist, albeit with substantial alteration of certain elements of proof and application. The UCC has codified an objective and flexible formulation of trade usages into many U.S. jurisdictions (and, through analogous enactments,[72] other legal systems). Yet judges routinely confound Llewellyn's vision with Blackstone's formalism.

This is especially evident in disputes where one contracting party relies on (what they view, at least as) the unambiguous terms of a bargained-for exchange, while the other seeks to employ a trade usage to substantially modify the terms of performance to their advantage. When such disputes are truly between sophisticated merchants "in the trade," courts appear willing to truly delve into the details of the alleged commercial custom, to weigh its costs and benefits, and to appropriately apply it.[73] Where there is any hint that a trade usage is being used to bludgeon or ensnare an unsuspecting party (especially a consumer), courts are justified in quickly dispatching the alleged trade usage as either factually unproven in application or legally invalid as unreasonable, or void as against public policy.

Aside from these doctrinal quibbles, there has been a backlash against the entire Llewellyn premise of the UCC: "to permit the continued expansion of commercial practices through custom, usage and agreement of the parties...."[74] Why, some scholars have wondered, should courts be effectuating "immanent business norms" and use them to decide cases?[75] Lisa Bernstein's 1996 path-breaking research engaged in an empirical exercise that Karl Llewellyn would have admired: she carefully examined the private arbitral dispute settlement system used by the National Grain and Feed Association (NGFA) and concluded that even trade associations of merchants[76] were reluctant to apply established trade usages as against their own members, who ought to know them and contract in their shadow.[77] Bernstein concluded that modern merchants prefer the certainty of express contractual terms to the flexibility of trade usages, which may (at a judge's or arbitrator's whim) be incorporated by reference, or not.[78] Moreover, Bernstein also suggested that reliance on trade usages may well benefit bigger "players" in the relevant industry, parties that can most directly influence the formation and acceptance of new practices, which will (inevitably) be in their business interests.[79]

As was discussed in Chapter 4, there may be sociological and economic explanations for the phenomenon that trade usages may not perfectly capture the most efficient commercial norms, and, indeed, in many circumstances, may be deliberately designed to be suboptimal.[80] Some scholars have observed this trend in the case law of commercial custom.[81] More significantly, some contemporary judges appear to be applying a yardstick of utility and efficiency as a surrogate for "reasonability." Judge Richard Posner, echoing the Second Circuit's move in *Dixon, Irmaos*, explicitly applied economic analysis in order to qualify a trade usage as reasonable.[82] This is not consistent with the UCC's admonition that trade usages ought to be accorded a robust presumption of being reasonable.[83]

Despite these scholarly protestations, commercial custom continues to permeate many forms of business dealings. No attempt by lawyers to completely "paper" every transaction, to incorporate by reference all extrinsic norms, is likely to be achievable – or desirable – for the parties involved. Ambiguous or incomplete contracts will continue to be drafted, and dispute settlers (whether judges or arbitrators) will sometimes be compelled to consult extrinsic evidence of the parties' intent in order to properly construe agreements. Whether it is Blackstone's idiom of merchant custom or Llewellyn's vision of trade usage, commerce remains a significant ambit for customary law.

More importantly, the political economies of group identity will often coun-sel like-minded individuals in common lines of business to prescribe their own rules of conduct, if for no other reason than to avoid having unwanted norms thrust upon them by outsiders. Contractual relations and transactions – unlike those seen within family structures or relevant to property rights – strongly lend themselves to private ordering. In many communities, a single transac-tion between two parties may have broad network effects. This demands that there be common (and tailor-made) rules for the formation, construction, and enforcement of particular contracts. Custom provides a realistic, although certainly not frictionless or costless, mechanism for matching commercial expectations with commercial realities.

8

Torts

Torts are definitionally nonconsensual civil wrongs. Because there is no consent, the actors in a tort or delict – victim and perpetrator – usually have no shared community relationship.[1] So, unlike any of the legal realms in which custom figures prominently (and which have been considered so far in this part), the law of torts and negligence is typically one where common community values do not count. In the drama that is each instance of a delictual wrong, the players are usually strangers to one another. But does that necessarily mean that they should be estranged from the communities of expectations and norms that each may individually embrace?

In the continuum of private-public law relations and disputes, torts (like criminal law, with which it is always compared) has strong public law overtones. Custom, as a consequence, is often viewed skeptically as a source of legal norms in tort. Yet, ironically enough, it is in the law of negligence or fault that custom-based standards of care find their greatest fulfillment in the law. We take it as an article of faith that community standards establish the relevant duties of care, whether we employ one English judge's quaint idiom of the "man on the Clapham omnibus,"[2] or simply the "reasonable person." As one court elegantly put the matter, the customary manner of doing something "would presumably represent the standard of ordinary prudent" people.[3]

As Roscoe Pound conceptualized it, proof of a common practice aids in "formulat[ing] the general expectation of society as to how individuals will act in the course of their undertakings, and thus to guide the common sense or expert intuition of a jury or commission when called on to judge ... particular conduct under particular circumstances."[4] Torts treatises have accepted the probative power of proof of custom and usage. "Chief among the rationales offered is," according to one such authority, "the fact that it reflects the judgment and experience and conduct of many."[5] Inherent for the relevancy and reliability of customary norms is the feasibility of safety precautions, their practicality in actual operation, and the readiness with which they can be adopted by participants in an industry or trade.[6]

Customary norms of behavior thus implicate a central puzzle in the law of negligence, one that has been observed by courts and commentators for centuries: Is negligence the departure from actual standards of care (what people *really* do in certain situations) or from an idealized vision of conduct (what they *ought* to do)?[7] As Justice Oliver Wendell Holmes noted: "What usually is done may be evidence of what ought to be done, but what ought to be done is fixed by the standard of reasonable prudence, whether it is usually complied with or not."[8] This observation leads to problems and perplexities with the doctrinal contours of applying customary norms in tort, as well as significant public policy questions. These will be addressed in turn in this chapter.

CUSTOM AS A SWORD AND SHIELD IN TORT

Custom has a Janus-faced nature in contemporary tort law. It can be a sword wielded by a victim: A tortfeasor's failure to observe customary behavior (however determined) may be prima facie proof of negligence. But it can also be a powerful shield in the hands of an actor: Proof of conformance with custom might be a conclusive defense to a charge of negligence. Both of these applications of custom can apparently coexist quite comfortably in any sophisticated legal system of compensation for accidents. Understanding both aspects of the role of custom in tort law is essential to appreciating its contemporary relevance.[9]

Custom as a sword is – despite its natural appeal as an intuitive proof of a defendant's standard of care – the less documented and less understood of these applications. One reason for this may be that it really is applied almost subliminally by judges and juries to reach negligence determinations. There is the concern that "the jury will define negligence simply by a departure from custom."[10] While plaintiffs have been generally permitted to present evidence that a defendant's methods of conducting its affairs are more dangerous than those customarily used in that trade or sector,[11] it is not enough to show that a tortfeasor's conduct merely departed from industry practice. In short, as Professor Morris observed over a half-century ago, *non*conformity with custom is not the same as *sub*conformity.[12] Or, put another way, "evidence should not be admitted on behalf of the plaintiff unless it tends to show that the method pursued was not only unusual, but more dangerous in itself than the ordinary one."[13] Even when such an enhanced showing is made, usually it is not dispositive of the ultimate determination of negligence. Proof of subconformity with custom, in short, helps a plaintiff get a case to a jury, but does not guarantee victory.[14]

A particularly tricky problem arises when a business adopts especially stringent industry practices as "private rules" of conduct.[15] One court criticized such evidence in the strongest possible terms:

> But a person cannot, by the adoption of private rules, fix the standard of his duty to others. That is fixed by law, either statutory or common. Such rules may require more, or they may require less, than the law requires; and whether a certain course of conduct is negligent, or the exercise of reasonable care, must be determined by the standard fixed by law, without regard to any private rules of the party.... [T]he more cautious and careful a man is in the adoption of rules in the management of his business in order to protect others, the worse he is off, and the higher the degree of care he is bound to exercise. A person may, out of abundant caution, adopt rules requiring of his employés a much higher degree of care than the law imposes. This is a practice that ought to be encouraged, and not discouraged. But, if the adoption of such a course is to be used against him as an admission, he would naturally find it to his interest not to adopt any rules at all.[16]

This court distinguished "private rules" of conduct from those generated by statute or common law, but left unstated how customary norms – those adopted by a larger community – were to be treated. Later courts have, in any event, recognized that a defendant's own internal rules of conduct – whether or not compliant with a larger industry custom – could be relevant to the question of negligence.[17]

The use of custom as a putative shield by defendants in tort has an even longer and more-checkered jurisprudence.[18] There are certainly cases that have decided that conformance with custom can be a conclusive riposte to a charge of negligence. In *Steggall v. W. T. Knepp & Co.*, the plaintiff was injured in a store when a roll of linoleum fell on her. The defendant proved that the linoleum had been displayed in the customary manner: by standing the rolls on end. Several qualified witnesses testified that linoleum rolls so handled will not fall unless pushed over. The trial judge directed a verdict for the defendant, and this was affirmed on appeal.[19] In this case, there was thus not only evidence of conformity with custom but also that abidance with such a practice was exceptionally safe. But some courts have directed verdicts for defendants on mere proof of conformance to custom, irrespective of the reasonableness of the usage, its cost effectiveness, or its safety record.

The most infamous example of this was in the 1890 case of *Titus v. Bradford, B. & K. R. Co.*, where the court held that a business owner

> is not bound to use the newest and best appliances. He performs his duty when he furnishes those of ordinary character and reasonable safety, and

the former is the test of the latter, for, in regard to the style of implement, or nature of the mode of performance of any work, "reasonably safe" means safe according to the usages, habits, and ordinary risks of the business.... No man is held by law to a higher degree of skill than the fair average of his profession or trade, and the standard of due care is the conduct of the average prudent man. The test of negligence in employers is the same, and however strongly they may be convinced that there is a better or less dangerous way, no jury can be permitted to say that the usual and ordinary way, commonly adopted by those in the same business, is a negligent way for which liability shall be imposed. Juries must necessarily determine the responsibility of individual conduct, but they cannot be allowed to set up a standard which shall, in effect, dictate the customs, or control the business, of the community.[20]

Although most courts have rejected this categorical version of custom as a shield, many will still instruct jurors that compliance with custom may be evidence of due care.[21]

Of the greatest interest, though, are those cases in which a defendant has offered strong proof of an industry custom, but a court nevertheless does not allow a jury to hear of it. There may be many reasons for this. In some instances, judges may hold that the custom is "violative of law and good faith, and could not receive judicial sanction."[22] In the same vein, there may be an express holding that the custom is contrary to a statutory standard of care.[23] Some courts have determined that because the plaintiff was a stranger to the defendant and could not have been aware of the tortfeasor's community practice, evidence of the practice would be inadmissible.[24]

Other judges have simply made a ruling that the custom could not be evidence of a safe practice. In an 1884 decision from Maine, the court was considering an ostensible practice among mine operators to cut unguarded ladder-holes in platforms in the excavations and whether the operator was responsible for the plaintiff's 35-foot fall:

> If the defendants had proved that in every mining establishment that has existed since the days of Tubal-Cain, it has been the practice to cut ladder-holes in their platforms, situated as this was while in daily use for mining operations, without guarding or lighting them, and without notice to contractors or workmen, it would have no tendency to show that the act was consistent with ordinary prudence, or a due regard for the safety of those who were using their premises by their invitation. The gross carelessness of the act appears conclusively upon its recital. Defendants' counsel argue that "if it should appear that they rarely had railings, then it tends to show no want of ordinary care in that respect," that "if one conforms to custom he is so far exercising average ordinary care." The argument proceeds upon an

erroneous idea of what constitutes ordinary care. "Custom" and "average" have no proper place in its definition.[25]

As one Minnesota court put the matter evocatively: "Local usage and general custom, either singly or in combination, will not justify or excuse negligence. They are merely foxholes in one of the battlefields of law, providing shelter but not complete protection against charges of negligence."[26]

So, what evidence of a custom of care would be probative in a negligence case? What makes custom dispositive in tort? The tort cases complete the trajectory begun by the trade usage decisions (discussed in the last chapter) and mark a complete departure from a Blackstonian vision of custom in Anglo-American common law. For those parties wishing to set up an industry practice as either a sword or shield, there is no requirement that a custom of care be supported by great antiquity or be followed obligatorily out of a sense of legal obligation (our old doctrinal companion, *opinio juris sive necessitatis*).

In order to be probative of a standard of care, evidence of a custom must include proof of widespread usage.[27] As the New York Court of Appeals held in the 1982 *Trimarco v. Klein* decision, "it is not to be assumed [that] customary practice and usage need be universal. It suffices that it be fairly well defined and in the same calling or business so that 'the actor may be charged with knowledge of it or negligent ignorance'."[28] As a practical matter, as with trade usages, proof of a custom of care is established "by opinion testimony of a person with personal knowledge or by the specific introduction of instances of conduct sufficient in number to support a finding of routine practice."[29]

The judicial decision that speaks most directly to the essential requisites of custom in tort is *The T.J. HOOPER*,[30] a canonical case in the American law of negligence from the early 1930s. The facts were simple: The plaintiffs owned barges that were being hauled by defendants' tugs. While in transit, a storm blew in. Those tugs in the convoy that had working radios heard of the impending storm and successfully sought shelter. Defendants' tugs had no radios, could not hear the warning, and so did not take cover; and the barges foundered. The plaintiffs charged the defendants with negligence for not having radios on board. The plaintiffs argued, as a sword, that an industry custom existed and that defendants' subconformance was conclusive as to the unseaworthiness of the tugs and the tug owners' negligence. The defendants denied that an industry practice existed.[31]

The trial court, presided over by Judge Coxe, held that the plaintiffs had successfully proven that there was an industry custom to equip tugs with radios in order to receive twice-daily weather broadcasts, and that the defendants had a duty to provide tugs so equipped. Failing in that duty, they were negligent.

Judge Coxe found that ninety percent of the coastwise tugs in the region were
so equipped, although the radio sets were typically the property of the tug
master, and not supplied by the tug owner.[32] On appeal, Judge Learned Hand
reversed this finding: "It is not fair to say that there was a general custom
among coastwise carriers so to equip their tugs. One line alone did it; as for
the rest, they relied upon their crews, so far as they can be said to have relied
at all."[33] Judge Hand's analytical distinction between radios being the personal property of tug masters – as opposed to installed and maintained by
the tug owners – has been criticized in the literature as being economically
irrelevant[34] and plainly contrary to the factual record of the case.[35] But that
hardly matters.

The T.J. HOOPER's true significance for recognition of customary norms of
negligence is with Judge Learned Hand's next move. Having found no industry custom for tug owners to provide vessels with radios, he nevertheless ruled
that such was the standard of care:

> Is it then a final answer that the business had not yet generally adopted receiv-
> ing sets? There are, no doubt, cases where courts seem to make the general
> practice of the calling the standard of proper diligence; we have indeed given
> some currency to the notion ourselves. Indeed in most cases reasonable pru-
> dence is in fact common prudence; but strictly it is never its measure; a whole
> calling may have unduly lagged in the adoption of new and available devices.
> It never may set its own tests, however persuasive be its usages. Courts must
> in the end say what is required; there are precautions so imperative that even
> their universal disregard will not excuse their omission. But here there was
> no custom at all as to receiving sets; some had them, some did not; the most
> that can be urged is that they had not yet become general. Certainly in such a
> case we need not pause; when some have thought a device necessary, at least
> we may say that they were right, and the others too slack.[36]

This passage as much as rules that even if the tug owners had proven the
obverse custom – that there was *no* practice to carry radios – such would be
unreasonable and could not be a defense.[37]

In short, *The T.J. HOOPER* stands for the proposition that, irrespective of
whether a custom is being used as a sword or shield, it must be shown to be
reasonable, and this has become the touchstone for later decisions.[38] As the
Trimarco Court observed:

> once its existence is credited, a common practice or usage is still not neces-
> sarily a conclusive or even a compelling test of negligence. Before it can be,
> the jury must be satisfied with its reasonableness, just as the jury must be sat-
> isfied with the reasonableness of the behavior which adhered to the custom

or the unreasonableness of that which did not. After all, customs and usages run the gamut of merit like everything else. That is why the question in each instance is whether it meets the test of reasonableness.[39]

As we have seen in the context of custom in defining property rights (in Chapters 3 and 6), or in fixing the scope of contractual obligations (Chapter 7), imposing a test of reasonableness is the last recourse of the common-law judge to cabin the effect of community-based norms.

CUSTOM AND NEGLIGENCE, EFFICIENCY AND PUBLIC POLICY

The T.J. HOOPER and *Trimarco* thus reflect a modern trend that appears to favor the instrumental use of custom as a sword in the hands of tort plaintiffs, rather than as a shield defending tortfeasors. This has not been without criticism. Some of these have been rooted in tort doctrine.[40] Others have been premised on economic concerns of efficiency (introduced in Chapter 4) and the demands of effective public policy. In no other doctrinal realm could customary norms have broader implications, and it is worth addressing these here.

The fundamental economic question posed by custom in tort is whether the application of industry practices is an efficient way to peg the appropriate standard of care. Despite the very contemporary phenomenon – in both common law and civil law jurisdictions – for statutes and regulations to establish the standard of care in many situations where accidents can occur, there are certainly limits to this process. Legislators and government regulators cannot contemplate every circumstance in which torts are likely to arise and definitively prescribe norms of behavior for every such combination of conditions. So, recourse to "private rules of conduct" seems inevitable in the absence of statutory command or regulatory guidance, something that has been recognized in the cases. In *The T. J. HOOPER*, Judge Coxe observed that no federal law or regulation affirmatively imposed a requirement for small tugs to carry radios, hence his recourse to industry custom.[41] In *Trimarco*, the New York statute that required the use of tempered glass in bathroom shower enclosures was only applicable to those installed after an effective date, and the plaintiff's fixture was not covered.[42]

A powerful economic argument for the use of industry custom as a proxy for an appropriate standard of care is that it reflects many iterations of cost-benefit analysis by participants in that relevant community. Putting aside the problem that this analysis is engaged in only by the class of putative tortfeasors (without regard for the potential victims of a particular practice), one can legitimately wonder whether this can be empirically shown. Some cases appear to acknowledge that actors in a trade or business will seek the most cost-effective safety precautions.[43] Counterpoised with these judicial observations are other cases where courts have been expressly critical of an industry safety record, as reflected through its customary practices. Judge Hand in *The T.J. HOOPER* extolled the benefits of radio sets (and their relatively cheap cost) in his repudiation of industry custom. In another admiralty case, the court criticized a shipping practice that probably was consistent with cost-benefit analysis:

> The slogan that "time is money" may have its place in business but is unacceptable where human safety is involved.... The tanker industry cannot hoist itself by its own boot straps through the device of setting up standards of conduct amounting to something less than reasonable care under all the circumstances and then predicate a defense on such substandards.[44]

These custom-of-care cases can thus boil down to what Professor (now Judge) Guido Calabresi described as the Hobson's choice "between the costs of accidents and the cost of limiting ourselves ... to less desirable (because more expensive or less pleasant) but safer activities."[45]

As was considered in Chapter 4,[46] the conditions under which a custom of care is likely to successfully and efficiently emerge from a set of industry practices may well be different in the respective realms of contract and tort. In contractual relations, we can readily accept the fiction of trade usages as a form of implicit communication between market actors. But for torts – unless one had reason to suspect that both victim and tortfeasor were part of the same community and the plaintiff was no stranger to the defendant's custom – we must be more circumspect that custom can efficiently serve this information-exchange function as to cost-effective safety measures.[47]

Ironically, *The T.J. HOOPER* may present just such a caveat, if we are to believe that the barge owner got what he bargained for by selecting a tug without a working radio.[48] When Landes and Posner predicted that "compliance with custom will not be a defense in accident cases where transaction costs are high but will be where the costs are low,"[49] they were quick to point out that "the most famous case that rejects custom as a defense was a case of low transactions costs, *The T.J. HOOPER*."[50] Judge Hand's opinion was the ultimate repudiation of the Coase Theorem and, implicitly at least, his own formula for negligence in *Carroll Towing*.[51] There is thus no simple economic explanation as to when an efficient safety practice will arise.

In Richard Epstein's construct, custom is most likely to emerge as a proxy for efficient behavior and the true standard of care in situations where the frequency of the problem is high and the amount at stake is low. The high-frequency level means that the parties are likely to have a lot of experience or instances on which to test and retest the judgment of custom. Since the stakes involved in each individual case are small, the tendency to deviate from the successful equilibrium on either side will be low.... [52]

According to Epstein, low frequency/low severity and low frequency/high severity situations are unlikely to produce reliable customs.[53] The tricky situation is with high frequency/high severity scenarios, where resolutions based on customary norms might be useful, but simply too much is at stake. "The legal system," as reflected in the positions of lawyers and the rulings of judges, "may therefore disrupt customary practices."[54]

Seen in this light, Judge Learned Hand's *T.J. HOOPER* opinion was truly revolutionary, and not just owing to its repudiation of industry practices reflecting ostensible cost-efficiencies. What was really subversive was that instead of recognizing market actors as the motive force for appropriate standards of care, Judge Hand substituted a common-law judge's "right reason" of safety as the controlling element in contemporary tort law.[55] Borrowing from the tradition of English judges overruling local land customs (see Chapter 3), judges are now cast in the decisive role as the arbiters for customs of care. This is particularly so in the realms of professional malpractice. Lawyers have certainly accepted this for cases involving their own professional misconduct.[56] This move has had surprising, and, perhaps, unintended, consequences for medical malpractice and prospects for health care reform.

The *locus classicus* for medical customs of care is the Washington Supreme Court's 1974 decision in *Helling v. Carey*.[57] The issue in that case was whether an ophthalmologist was negligent in failing to diagnose glaucoma in a patient under 40 years of age. There was substantial evidence in the record, and the court apparently agreed, that the customary standard of medical care was such that glaucoma tests were not administered to younger patients because the incidence of the disease was so statistically low in that age cohort.[58] Nevertheless, the court held:

> The defendants argue that the standard of the profession, which does not require the giving of a routine pressure test to persons under the age of 40, is adequate to insulate the defendants from liability for negligence because the risk of glaucoma is so rare in this age group.... The incidence of glaucoma in one out of 25,000 persons under the age of 40 may appear quite minimal. However, that one person, the plaintiff in this instance, is entitled to the same protection, as afforded persons over 40, essential for timely detection of the evidence of glaucoma where it can be arrested to avoid the grave and devastating result of this disease. The test is a simple pressure test, relatively

inexpensive.... Under the facts of this case reasonable prudence required the timely giving of the pressure test to this plaintiff. The precaution of giving this test to detect the incidence of glaucoma to patients under 40 years of age is so imperative that irrespective of its disregard by the standards of the ophthalmology profession, it is the duty of the courts to say what is required to protect patients under 40 from the damaging results of glaucoma.[59]

Similar holdings from other U.S. jurisdictions summarily rejected customary standards of medical care in favor of court-imposed benchmarks.[60]

Helling's cost-benefit analysis, at least as recounted by the court (relatively cheap and uninvasive diagnostic tests, as opposed to the risks of blindness caused by glaucoma), seemed quite sensible. Some writers have questioned (as with *The T.J. HOOPER*) whether the court got the facts of the custom correctly,[61] and other opinions have outright rejected the economic assumptions of the *Helling* decision.[62] Washington's legislature even sought to later supersede the holding by statute.[63] But the damage was done. In the wake of *Helling*, doctors began to practice what was soon called "defensive medicine," not knowing when their customary standards of medical care would be summarily rejected by a court in a subsequent tort action. The result has been spiraling costs of health care, especially related to diagnostic testing in situations where the cost-benefits and risk-rewards may not necessarily weigh in favor of extra safety precautions.

Attempts to revitalize customary standards of medical care have been much discussed in the literature[64] and in public policy debates about health care reform. Likewise, one possible thrust of tort reform might be to redress the balance between customs of care being employed as shields, and not just as swords, essentially reversing the trend begun with Judge Learned Hand's decision in *The T.J. HOOPER*. So there is a delicate balance yet to be struck in the effect of customary norms of negligence. It is an equilibrium that judges, legislatures, and (most importantly of all) communities of care practitioners will all have to strive to achieve.

9

Constitutional Law

Constitutional law is the most public of domestic public-law topics. Indeed, the entire notion of a polity's fundamental law would seem to be the ultimate exemplar of a legal domain that should, in the construct of writers such as James Coolidge Carter, H. L. A. Hart and T. F. T. Plucknett,[1] be utterly immune from customary influences. Inasmuch as constitutions are a *lex scriptum*, custom should, under this theory, play no role in their construction, application, or interpretation.

The reality is that customary regimes have not only been a historical feature of English constitutional governance from the Middle Ages, but also have contemporary relevance in separation-of-powers debates within the tradition of U.S. constitutionalism. So, even in this most public of legal arenas, customary regimes can survive and flourish. Any explanation for this ostensible paradox must account not only for the historic origins of custom and the common law (narrated in Chapter 3), but also the continued relevance of the practices of political branches in the resolution of structural or institutional disputes within domestic polities. Constitutional custom is not only a historical construct; it is a phenomenon associated with the common law of government officerial prerogatives, as well as a pragmatic approach to the resolution of separation-of-powers disputes.

ENGLISH CONSTITUTIONAL CUSTOM

English constitutional history arguably had two decisive moments, both born of rebellion: the events leading to King John's consent at Runnymede to the Magna Carta in 1215, and those leading to King Charles I's adoption of the Petition of Right (1628) and William III's proclamation of the Bill of Rights (1689) during the long course of the English Civil War and its aftermath. A significant aspect of these constitutional conflicts was the preservation of the customs of the realm – the medieval *consuetudo regni* discussed in Chapter 3[2] – against the encroachments of royal power (occasionally verging on absolutism). At stake in England was nothing less than the constitutional custom of power divided between the crown and other constituencies, whether the feudal nobility, or, later, the parliamentary commons.

The mythology of English constitutional custom reaches back to Anglo-Saxon times,[3] in which elected kings were bound to enforce a tribal law, and they were severely limited in their ability even to codify that custom, much less to propound new laws.[4] In prefeudal and preconquest England, freemen notionally had substantial rights of equality, due process, and access to justice.[5] The imposition of Norman rule after 1066 obviously changed those constitutional conditions, visiting not only an alien class of noble overrulers, but also a harsher and more rigid form of feudal obligations than had hitherto existed in England. Even so, the old Anglo-Saxon customs existed, not only those of local character, but also the "ancient liberties" of the realm. The key difference was that these customs came to be adopted by Norman nobility (and their Anglo-Saxon collaborators in the occupation) as an instrument to resist and defy efforts at the increasing centralization of the royal administration and courts, especially royal collections of taxes and service obligations.[6]

One of the first major invocations of custom in a foundational English constitutional instrument was Henry I's Coronation Charter of 1100. Henry I was the fourth and youngest of William the Conqueror's sons. The Charter was issued in response to the perceived abuses of Henry's brother, William Rufus, especially his creative (and ruthless) taxation of the nobility. The Coronation Charter begins with the preamble that Henry shall "henceforth remove all the bad customs through which the kingdom of England has been unjustly oppressed," and then proceeds to itemize those "bad customs."[7] To remedy these evil practices, the Coronation Charter (sometimes called the "Charter of Liberties") refers to "just and legitimate reliefs" available during the reign of William the Conqueror.[8] Despite these protestations of fidelity to immemorial custom and liberties of the land, Henry I's charter was forgotten in the quest by later Angevin kings' (especially Henry II's) drive to greater royal centralization of power.[9]

Over a century later, though, the Coronation Charter's provisions on customary liberties were invoked in many pleas made to the crown, then held by King John.[10] Ironically enough, given his reputation as a protoautocratic tyrant, John's writs often invoked "the custom of England," even going so far as to direct that custom could prevail over earlier, written decrees.[11] Custom was often seen as the traditional modes of justice and court procedure,[12] the English equivalent of Roman law's *mos iudiciorum* (discussed in Chapter 2).[13]

By the later stages of the rebellion against King John (led by the nobles, but also supported by the Church, the city interests, and the old class of Anglo-Saxon freemen),[14] custom had been co-opted by all relevant legal regimes arrayed against royal power: feudal and manorial law, canon law, and urban law.[15]

The text of the Magna Carta is thus a potpourri of references to customs. Mentioned are feudal obligations and privileges, especially rights of descent and inheritance.[16] Royal exactions of feudal services were likewise constrained by customary usages.[17] Urban customs were recognized in these magisterial tones: "And the city of London shall have all its ancient liberties and free customs, both by land and by water. Besides we will and grant that all the other cities, boroughs, towns, and ports shall have all their liberties and free customs."[18] Merchant customs were also accepted,[19] as were preexisting procedures for county court sessions.[20] Even more extraordinary, the Angevin kings' penchant for enclosing properties within the domains of royal forests, and imposing bizarre and novel laws for their administration, was attacked in these terms:

> Concerning all bad customs of forest and warrens, of foresters and warreners, of sheriffs and their officers, and of river-banks and their wardens, inquisition shall at once be made in each county through twelve knights of that same county placed under oath, who ought to be elected by the good men of the same county. And within forty days after the inquisition has been made, they [the bad customs] shall be utterly abolished by the same [knights], so that they shall never be restored....[21]

Recognizing the reciprocity of customary usages, one of the concluding passages of the Great Charter proclaims: "Now all these aforesaid customs and liberties, which we [the King] have granted, in so far as concerns us, to be observed in our kingdom toward our men, all men of our kingdom, both clergy and laity, shall, in so far as concerns them, observe toward their men."[22]

The next transformative moment for English constitutional custom was in the seventeenth century. The Tudor monarchy's (particularly Henry VIII's and Elizabeth I's) concentration of royal power saw a confluence of Roman law concepts combined with absolutist principles of kingly governance. This "encouraged the idea that the will of the sovereign was law, to the detriment of the old Germanic notion of the supremacy of an impersonal customary law."[23] In reaction to the Stuart kings' tyrannical tendencies, legal thinkers such as Sir John Davies and Sir Edward Coke (both introduced in Chapter 3) propounded a return to "ancient custom," with regard for constitutional liberties and restraints on kingly power.[24] The primary exhibits of customary constitutionalism enlisted in this resistance were the relevant provisions of Henry I's Coronation Charter and the Magna Carta.

The historic connection with medieval constitutional custom was high-lighted in the 1627 *Case of the Five Knights*. The imprisonment of individuals charged with violating Charles I's dubious exactment of a forced loan from his subjects was challenged in that case, and the writ of habeas corpus was claimed as a customary right of Englishmen.[25] Chief Justice Hyde of the Court of King's Bench, although allowing the continued detention of the prisoners, held that "the common custom of the law is the common law of the land, and that hath been the continual common custom of the law, to which we are to submit; for we come not to change the law, but to submit to it...."[26]

Parliament responded to this equivocal pronouncement on customary constitutional norms by the adoption, in 1628, of the Petition of Right.[27] The essential provision of the Petition, aside from its entreaty that detentions be justified under writs of habeas corpus with an express determination of the legal grounds for the imprisonment, was a restatement of chapter 39 of the Magna Carta: "no freeman may be taken or imprisoned, or be disseised of his freehold or liberties or his free customs, or be outlawed or exiled or in any manner destroyed, but by the lawful judgment of his peers or by the law of the land."[28] King Charles replied to the petition in these terms:

> The king willeth that right be done according to the laws and customs of the realm; and that the statutes be put in due execution, that his subjects may have no cause to complain of any wrongs or oppressions, contrary to their just rights and liberties, to the preservation whereof he holds himself ... as well obliged as of his prerogative.... [29]

Charles's failure to abide by this promise was one of the precipitating causes of the English Civil War, the Commonwealth of the Interregnum, and – after James II's deposition – the Glorious Revolution and the proclamation of the 1689 Bill of Rights. In all of these transitions, the customs of the "ancient constitution" was constantly invoked.[30]

The contemporary relevance of English constitutional custom is, of course, not so much rooted today in cabining the prerogatives of the Crown, even though British monarchs continue to swear as part of their coronation oath that they will govern their peoples "according to their respective laws and customs."[31] Instead, the focus of governance has shifted to the accommodation of parliamentary supremacy in the context of cabinet government. Made famous by Walter Bagheot's 1867 volume, *The English Constitution*, the fighting question was "checks and balances" of parliamentary democracies and the challenges of effective and collegial government.[32] British constitutionalism today is customary not because the fundamental law is unwritten, but, rather, because the essential sources still remain unconsolidated.[33]

"UNDER COLOR OF ... CUSTOM" AND OFFICIAL AUTHORITY

It would be easy to assume that constitutional customary norms today are solely relevant in the separation-of-powers context of competing branches of government (cabinet and Parliament in Britain; Congress and the presidency in the United States). While this remains a robust area of jurisprudence (as will be considered presently), there does remain scope for customary assertions of individual liberties as a restraint on the power of government officials.[34] George Rutherglen's distinction as to various constitutional uses of custom is relevant here:

> On the modern view, custom influences the content of the law at two different points: either in determining what the law should be as it is officially promulgated or, after it has been adopted, in determining how it is enforced. The official sources of law – statutes, judicial decisions, and regulations – are plainly affected by custom, and may explicitly refer to it, as in the Uniform Commercial Code. These forms of positive law, however, supersede the customs on which they are based; all of the force of law results from the official decision adopting custom as law. Custom in the administration of the law operates entirely differently, without the need for any formal endorsement by the state. Its effects on the operation of state law are less obvious, but just as consequential.[35]

This volume has taken issue with the Austinian, "modern view" that custom can only be derivative of other sources of positive law (legislation, regulation, and precedent). Even if that position is correct – and the canonical sources of U.S. jurisprudence are certainly ambivalent on that score[36] – that still leaves constitutional dimensions for the enforcement and administration of justice, especially in the realm of civil liberties.

Here, there are two forces at work: custom can provide no defense to official action contrary to statute; nor can deprivations of constitutional rights be justified by "bad customs," to use the evocative language of Henry I's Coronation Charter. As to the first point, in U.S. jurisdictions at least, it has been long established that "[i]f an act is not an official duty, private custom, no matter how long continued, cannot make it such."[37] Likewise, where a government officer's duties are prescribed by statute, usage or custom will not excuse the discharge of such responsibilities in a different manner.[38] In a similar vein, a private party may not rely on the practice of an administrative agency in construing a statutory command, contrary to its clear language.[39] Despite occasional invocations of "historical custom"[40] as a means of ascertaining the extent of governmental authority, this has been vigorously criticized by judges.[41]

Even more controversial in the United States is the notion that certain governmental practices – not contained in a statute or regulation but still rising to the level of a consistent usage – could be actionable if they deprive an individual of a federal constitutional right. The key mechanism for the enforcement of such constitutional rights remains a provision of the Civil Rights Act of 1871,[42] which was intended by Congress to remedy the depredations of the Ku Klux Klan against the just-freed African American slaves in the reconstructed South in violation of the guarantees of the Thirteenth and Fourteenth Amendments to the Constitution, which abolished slavery and ensured due process as against state action.[43] The private right of action provision – now known simply as "section 1983" – is triggered whenever there is a deprivation of a federal right "under color of any statute, ordinance, regulation, custom, or usage of any State."[44] A burning constitutional question in the United States has been the extent to which the Fourteenth Amendment's due process and equal protection guarantees can be enforced through section 1983 as against private actors or in resistance to "informal" or "unofficial" government discrimination. Put another way, is section 1983's reference to a "custom or usage" being "under color of" state authority really an oxymoron?

One way to reconcile this language, suggested by some commentators,[45] is that the 1871 Act's reference to "customs and usages" was confined to Blackstone's construct of "local customs" at variance with the common law. With the constitutional abolition of slavery and indentured servitude, and the preemption of contrary Southern state statutes, the only way that vestiges of slavery could persist in law would be through custom or usage, and one might suppose that section 1983 was intended to close this jurisprudential loophole. As convenient as this explanation might be, it suffers from one disability: It appears to have been expressly rejected by the U.S. Supreme Court in the late 1890s, albeit in very different – and notorious – contexts. In *Robertson v. Baldwin*,[46] the Court upheld laws that made it a crime for seamen to desert their vessels against a Thirteenth Amendment involuntary servitude challenge on the ground that such services by mariners "have from time immemorial been treated as exceptional."[47] Justice Harlan, writing in dissent, protested that "immemorial usage" could not possibly derogate from a constitutional liberty,[48] but the majority apparently disagreed. Even more shockingly – in a decision that marked one of the Supreme Court's jurisprudential nadirs – in *Plessy v. Ferguson*, it held that a state's "separate-but-equal" policy of discrimination against blacks in public accommodations (and, by implication, public education) was justified because a state legislature was "at liberty to act with reference to the established usages, customs and traditions of the people."[49] That these decisions have been rightfully and utterly repudiated does not detract from the point that when the drafters of the 1871 Act invoked "custom and usage," they probably did not mean it in the narrow, technical, and local sense that Blackstone employed.

An alternative account of section 1983's "custom and usage" provision would be to suggest that it is entirely consistent with the congressional intent to extend maximum constitutional protections against informal government practices. After all, the "under color of" language suggests that resistance to discriminatory state actions should not be rendered unenforceable merely because that conduct is not justified by the actual authority of the state. Were it otherwise, discriminatory regimes could persist, even though the government asserted they were "unofficial" or "unsanctioned." The problem, of course, is that such an interpretation of section 1983 would create a broad class of constitutional tort litigation in the federal courts and subvert state remedies and proceedings. Even more than that, it might blur the line between state-supported (if not officially sanctioned) discrimination, as opposed to purely private conduct, which is notionally beyond constitutional redress in section 1983.

Not surprisingly, no resolution has been reached on whether (or when) a custom and usage is "under color of" state action for purposes of constitutional litigation. Justice Frankfurter in his dissent in *Monroe v. Pape*,[50] although disagreeing with the majority's extension of the ambit of section 1983, nevertheless believed that it did make actionable instances where state officials received immunity from liability for their violation of federal rights by virtue of state practice (say, consistent failures to prosecute), as opposed to the explicit provisions of state law.[51]

This was confirmed in the Court's 1970 decision in *Adickes v. S. H. Kress & Co.*, holding that the practice of local police in enforcing the discriminatory decisions of white restauranteurs in excluding black diners from their premises satisfied the "under color of" requirement of section 1983.[52] Even so, there was a jurisprudential division in this opinion. The majority insisted that custom or usage can only have "the force of law"[53] by virtue of persistent endorsement of state officials and "command[ing]"[54] (in almost an Austinian idiom) compliance with that custom.

In contrast, Justice Brennan endorsed a somewhat wider vision of custom, one resonant with Justice Benjamin Cardozo's[55] notion of "the creative energy of custom":

> I read "custom, or usage" in § 1983 to mean what it has usually meant at common law – a widespread and longstanding practice, commonly regarded as prescribing norms for conduct, and backed by sanctions. The sanctions need not be imposed by the State. A custom can have the effect or force of law even where it is not backed by the force of the State. The power of custom to

generate and impose rules of conduct, even without the support of the State, has long been recognized.[56]

Justice Douglas, in his partial dissent, went even further and, expressly invoking the writings of Bronislaw Malinowski,[57] rejected a narrow, hyperpositivist, "Hamiltonian" (or Austinian) idea that custom can never be law.[58] For Justice Douglas, custom "include[s] the predominant attitude backed by some direct or indirect sanctions inscribed in law books,"[59] "includ[ing] the unwritten commitment[s], stronger than ordinances, statutes, and regulations, by which men live and arrange their lives."[60] Whether Justice Douglas would have extended section 1983 litigation to counter *any* social practice established independently of the law, as some commentators have suggested,[61] is certainly a possibility. In any event, the perfect equilibrium for custom and usage in section 1983 constitutional litigation has not yet been calibrated. That it ever will be is unlikely, since that would require a high degree of jurisprudential consensus as to custom's proper place as a source of law in American jurisprudence.

"PRACTICAL CONSTRUCTION" AND SEPARATION-OF-POWERS DISPUTES

A much more modest – and resolvable – question of constitutional interpretation is whether the actual practices of governmental branches can be reliable evidence for resolution of separation-of-powers controversies. In other words, can a governmental practice, one "deeply embedded in the history and tradition of th[e] country,"[62] legitimize it as constitutional, even if that authority is exercised by the "wrong" branch of government in a way that violates the textual constitutional command of separate powers? It appears from the U.S. Supreme Court's jurisprudence that evidence of the "practical exposition"[63] or "practical construction"[64] of powers granted under the constitution by the respective branches can be dispositive of separation-of-powers disputes.

Indeed, as early as 1803 in *Stuart v. Laird*, the Supreme Court indicated that

> Another reason [suggested] for reversal is, that the judges of the [S]upreme [C]ourt have no right to sit as circuit judges, not being appointed as such, or in other words, that they ought to have distinct commissions for that purpose. To this objection, which is of recent date, it is sufficient to observe, that practice and acquiescence under it for a period of several years, commencing with the organization of the judicial system, affords an irresistible answer, and has indeed fixed the construction. It is a contemporary interpretation of

the most forcible nature. This practical exposition is too strong and obstinate to be shaken or controlled. Of course, the question is at rest, and ought not now to be disturbed.[65]

This language has been revisited by later Supreme Courts in a variety of separation-of-powers contexts,[66] and has been recognized by a number of commentators.[67] While the idea of "practical construction" of the Constitution's separation-of-powers provisions would seem most often to implicate the balance of authority between the political branches (Congress and the executive), that is not invariably so. *Stuart*, after all, involved the power of Supreme Court justices to "ride circuit" and sit on lower courts created by Congress.[68]

At the outset it is important, though, to distinguish the various techniques for employing custom in constitutional interpretation. One of these is to use evidence of the "practical construction" of a constitutional provision by the political branches from the early years of the Republic (before 1820) as a proxy for the views of the founders in constitutional interpretation.[69] This is just another form of originalism – the school of constitutional interpretation that seeks to recapture the understandings of the Constitution's drafters and ratifiers and so to anchor the application of those provisions. When used in this way, constitutional customary norms are not based on usage and practice at all: They are merely an embodiment of original understanding. If constitutional custom has any real meaning, though, it must be extrinsic to the constitutional text and to any original understandings as to the meaning of that text.[70]

Another ground of distinction in the Supreme Court's constitutional custom cases is that at least some of those precedents deal with an analytically distinct question: statutory desuetude. This has been a long-standing puzzle, one that was recognized in both Roman law and in doctrinal literature.[71] In U.S. constitutional law, only one significant precedent even notionally recognizes the possibility that an act of Congress may be superseded, not by a later repealer statute, but by the contrary practice of the executive branch in deviating from the law's enforcement, provided that Congress actually acquiesces in that deviance. In the 1915 decision in *United States v. Midwest Oil Company*, the question was whether the president could unilaterally withdraw oil tracts from the public lands without express congressional approval. In answering in the affirmative, the Court acknowledged a long string of executive branch action,[72] and went on to note:

> It may be argued that while these facts and rulings prove a usage, they do not establish its validity. But government is a practical affair, intended for practical men. Both officers, lawmakers, and citizens naturally adjust themselves to any long-continued action of the Executive Department, on the

presumption that unauthorized acts would not have been allowed to be so often repeated as to crystallize into a regular practice. That presumption is not reasoning in a circle, but the basis of a wise and quieting rule that, in determining the meaning of a statute or the existence of a power, weight shall be given to the usage itself, – even when the validity of the practice is the subject of investigation.[73]

In upholding the president's power, it is apparent that the Court was not only ruling that statutes can enter desuetude by contrary practice, but also that the balance of powers between the presidency and Congress can be altered in that same manner.

There are thus a number of canonical decisions where the Court has ruled that Congress has progressively acquiesced in the president's acquisition of power. These are especially evident in the foreign relations field,[74] but have also been significant in the realm of the president's authority to remove officials he has appointed, a question finally settled in the Supreme Court's 1926 *Myers v. United States* decision.[75] But, quite curiously, the customary crank for separation-of-powers may ratchet in only one direction. The Supreme Court has, on no fewer than two occasions, struck down well-documented "practical constructions" of constitutional provisions running in *favor* of congressional power as being contrary to express textual commands.

In *Fairbank v. United States*, the Court ruled unconstitutional a statute authorizing a stamp tax on exports as violative of the textual prohibition on such duties, even though there was evidence (dating from the First Congress) that such imposts were permissible.[76] In response, the Court held that the practical construction of a constitutional provision by legislative action is entitled to no force, except in cases of doubt,[77] and in that case there was none.[78] This was exactly the tack taken by the Court in 1983, in *Immigration and Naturalization Service v. Chadha*,[79] of striking down the practice of "legislative vetoes." These were statutory provisions that granted power to the executive branch to carry out certain actions, but with the proviso that both congressional houses (or even just one) could cancel that action. This ostensibly violated the Constitution's Presentment Clause, which requires that every congressional action having the force of law be presented to the president for his approval or veto. Despite a long history of legislative vetoes as part of the accommodation by Congress with the regulatory state created by the New Deal,[80] the Court adhered to a formalistic notion of separation-of-powers and struck down such provisions.

As has been seen with the other doctrinal fields considered in this volume, proof of a binding constitutional custom is premised on two broad components. The first element is the objective extent, duration, and consistency of the practice.[81] Tracing the historical pedigree of a usage back to the founding of the Republic seems to be irrelevant, unless the constitutional custom is being used as a surrogate for a showing of the framers' original intent. That a practice can be dated to the early Republic is obviously helpful, as in *Dames & Moore*, where at issue was the president's power to conclude settlement agreements with other nations, and a prime exhibit was President Washington doing just that in 1799.[82] But a consistent practice over a shorter duration is also fine.[83] Otherwise, showing "scores and hundreds"[84] of iterations of the practice will do.[85] Conversely, failing to prove even a threshold level of occurrence for a practice will usually be fatal to a constitutional custom claim,[86] as will a finding that the practice was isolated.[87]

Even if the objective element of constitutional custom can be overcome, something more is required. Although it would be a mistake to think that this extra ingredient is *opinio juris* – in the sense of requiring a governmental entity to accept a practice as law[88] – the subjective element in U.S. constitutional law boils down to whether the opposing branch in the separation-of-powers struggle has actually accepted or "acquiesced" in the practice.[89] Or, as Justice Frankfurter put the matter in his *Youngstown Steel* concurrence: The executive practice must be "long pursued to the knowledge of the Congress and never before questioned."[90] The problem, though, is how to interpret what may be a branch's silence, for in situations where it is Congress extending its power by statute, an executive branch response may be indeterminate (as with signing a bill but still asserting its unconstitutionality). Likewise, when it is the presidency that seeks to expand its power, short of a statute resisting such an assertion (overriding a veto[91]), Congress may have little scope for positive action, and its objection to the practice may be ambiguous.[92]

For these reasons, the Supreme Court has appeared to require that the branch making the assertion of authority do so in the form of an act that places the coordinate branch on notice of its position and requires a response.[93] Effective notice of the practice is thus essential.[94] When an objection is forthcoming from the opposing branch, its effect may still be uncertain. In *Chadha*, the fact that eleven of thirteen presidents, from Woodrow Wilson to Ronald Reagan, objected to the legislative veto seemed to be decisive for the Court.[95] In *Haig v. Agee*, that Congress had declined the executive branch's request to authorize it to revoke passports on national security grounds[96] did not apparently register. The president's authority in that respect was upheld by the Court, although perhaps premised on the president's independent foreign relations powers.[97]

Whether the acquiescence requirement for a binding constitutional custom unduly favors the presidency in its separation-of-powers struggles with

Congress remains hotly contested.[98] It is evident that Congress can impliedly ratify presidential assertions and such will be "[c]rucial" in any separation-of-powers calculus.[99] This will especially be so in the realm of the president's war powers[100] and treaty authority.[101] Yet, despite the pervasive role of constitutional custom in separation-of-powers controversies, potent critiques remain. Aside from concerns about the acquiescence requirement's modalities for congressional responses to executive power,[102] there is a philosophical concern that this doctrine embeds some form of "Burkean minimalism" into separation-of-powers discourse,[103] a path dependence leading us down a road to constitutional infidelity and perdition. Yet, we need not fear to trod this path. If anything, courts have been more likely – as seen in *Chadha* – to heed Justice Frankfurter's warnings that practice cannot "supplant" a clear constitutional requirement[104] and that "[i]llegality cannot attain legitimacy through practice."[105] Or, as the patristic writers of the canon law tradition (introduced in Chapter 2) observed: "Custom without truth is only error grown old."[106] Henry I, in his denunciation of "bad customs," would have approved.

* * *

From the foregoing, it seems evident that custom remains a significant – if sometimes subliminal – source of law in contemporary legal systems. Far from being some antithesis of legal order, custom has managed to buttress doctrines within many legal fields that span the continuum of private and public law. Customary norms are thus often found as the essential elements of modern law.

Custom permeates law through two primary vectors. The first, and most palpable, is through the common law or the decisional processes imposed by codes in civil law jurisdictions.[107] Custom has engrained itself into the most basic of common-law doctrines, whether it is the notion of the "reasonable person" in the law of negligence, or in the use of commonages in property, or in the recognition of merchant usages. Far more subtly, custom can also act on the level of a jurisdiction's fundamental law, generally effectuating community expectations: whether the family relationships common to a region or people, or the power grabs of competing branches of a polity's administration. Where there is a confluence of these constitutional and common-law vectors (say, in Hawai`i or South Africa), the results can be particularly dramatic.

Custom's chameleonlike character in contemporary jurisprudence has been partially achieved by breaking from common-law formalisms. Blackstone's elements for the proof and application of custom have rightly been confined to the context in which he originally intended them: limiting inchoate local servitudes over land. Otherwise, streamlined metrics for the determinations of custom and usage prevail, whether Karl Llewellyn's UCC provisions or the precedents for a showing of doctors' standards of care as a defense to medical malpractice actions. Likewise, the extra ingredient that converts a mere "practice" into a legally binding "custom" has undergone its own transmutation. The old Roman law requisite of *opinio juris* has given way to pragmatic (but equally standardless) judicial determinations of a custom's compatibility with modern living conditions (in family law), its reasonableness or efficiency (in commercial cases), or acquiescence (in separation-of-powers disputes).

There remain, however, many puzzles as to the application of custom in domestic legal systems. Despite our sense that there should be a strict hierarchy of legal sources – a pyramid in which fundamental law is at the top, legislation and judicial precedents next, and with custom forming a solid (if unformed) mass at the base – the reality is more nuanced. Custom's competition with statutes is as old a problem as Roman *lex*, but even today there may be situations where the conditions of statutory desuetude may be occasionally accepted by courts. Even more tellingly, custom constantly vies with text – whether the terms of a contract, the caveats of a will, or the separation-of-powers provisions of a constitution. Where text is neither vague nor ambiguous, customary variations with such commands are unlikely to receive acceptance. But introduce any element of uncertainty into the textual language, any room for variant community expectations (however that community is defined), and custom will rise again.

Lastly, custom still suffers from its own observer effect,[108] its own priority paradox. Ethnographers like Malinowski, Gluckman, and Hoebel understood that the legal cultures they were examining would be changed by their own acts of observation. So, too, it is sometimes indeterminate which must come first: the community practice, or the judicial or legislative recognition of the custom – the practice "chicken," or the recognition "egg." Whether one views custom as autonomous of precedent and statute (and independent of their endorsement), or as solely an adjunct to those positive sources, remains a central conundrum for custom's role in domestic law. These considerations for custom are even more compelling – and convoluted – in the realm of international law.

PART THREE

Custom in International Law

10

Private International Law
International Commercial Usage

Custom and commerce in transnational trade have been inextricably linked for millennia.[1] The customary norms of international commerce have been a traditional part of what has been called the *lex mercatoria* and *lex maritima*, that body of law respected and followed by merchants and ocean-traders. But international commercial norms present a number of doctrinal puzzles, and these will be considered in this chapter.

The first is the extent to which they can ever be truly independent of domestic legal systems. The traditional historical account[2] is that from antiquity and the Middle Ages, the customary regimes of the law merchant and maritime law were created and enforced in a manner that was utterly free from interference by law-making mechanisms in any one polity. While these customs were often compiled and codified, they still reflected the actual usages of trade by the merchants and mariners involved. Indeed, the way in which disputes under these norms were typically resolved was by expedited recourse to panels of arbitrators selected from the relevant commercial community. Over time, merchant tribunals were co-opted as merchant juries by regularly constituted local courts. With the positivist legal revolution of the mid-nineteenth century, even this last vestige of autonomy for the *lex mercatoria* disappeared, and international commercial law became the creature of domestic courts and legislatures. But is this standard legal history narrative accurate? Did transnational commercial customs really disappear? And has there today been a renaissance for the international law merchant, reinvigorated and reconceptualized, and now truly globalized and autonomous?

The second conundrum is even more palpable: Do cross-border norms really matter in contemporary commerce? Do trade usages, actually made by the participants in commercial communities, receive recognition and enforcement by either national courts or international arbitrators? Do merchant usages matter less now than the informal harmonization that is under way by transnational networks of government regulators and bureaucrats? The answers to these questions implicate what may be a new pluralism in economic globalization, and it is precisely in these contexts that customary regimes are most likely to flourish.

That leaves the biggest jurisprudential enigma of all for customary law – one especially resonant with transnational commercial norms – and that is whether, or why, any party would obey them. The basis of obligation for trade usages is particularly tricky in domestic law (as was discussed in Chapter 7), and the problems are only amplified with multinational parties and cross-border transactions. There is thus a lively debate as to whether international commercial customs should manifest a normative element of compulsion in their observance, or whether it is enough that they reflect repeated, reasonable, and efficient conduct. This duality with custom can almost be schizophrenic. When is a "behavioral" norm elevated to the plane of "normative" recognition? And why should the transnational character of the commercial exchange matter in our expectations as to what kinds of custom count?

HISTORICAL ROOTS OF THE *LEX MERCATORIA* AND *LEX MARITIMA*

Two great traditions have enriched our contemporary understanding of transnational commercial norms: one intellectual, the other technical. The first is the concept of *ius gentium* under Roman law (mentioned in Chapter 2). The modern historiographic jurisprudence of the *ius gentium* is extensive, beginning with Sir Henry Maine's thesis that it represented the totality of customs and usages practiced by Rome and her Latin neighbors in the conduct of their international and commercial relations.[3] This view was, of course, a restatement of Savigny's assertion[4] that the *ius gentium* was strictly a private law phenomenon in Rome, a view that has prevailed to this day.[5] Indeed, a careful reading of the Roman law sources[6] makes clear that the *ius gentium* was viewed as a rational collection of unwritten laws or customs.[7]

Of relevance to the modern *lex mercatoria*, the Roman *ius gentium* was the body of law administered by the *praetor peregrinus* in Rome in disputes between two non-Roman aliens, or between a citizen and an alien. This is the "private law" conception of a law of nations later recognized by Savigny and Maine, a body of law that governed the commercial, financial, and personal relations of all individuals. But, make no mistake, the *ius gentium* as understood by anyone living in the time of the Roman Republic, or later the Roman Empire, was a hegemonic construct. The regularization of relations with foreign nationals residing in Rome (engaged in commerce) may have had the effect of benefitting all sides, but ultimately, this was a cohesive body of law linked to a robust, dominant legal order. There should be no doubt that the Roman *ius gentium*'s thrust towards world law was the authentic product of a hegemonic system.

Harold Berman persuasively wrote of the emergence of a common commercial law in medieval Europe that traces its intellectual lineage back to the ancient models of *ius gentium*.[8] The maritime elements of such commercial law, a *lex maritima* that was premised on such codes as the Rolls of Oléron (1160 CE), the Consolato del Mare (1340), and the Amalfi (954 CE) and Visby (c. 1350) Tables, were all in pedigree with the Rhodian Sea Law (developed around 200 BCE), which the Romans adopted wholesale into their *ius gentium*.[9] Admiralty practices in the Middle Ages were obviously driven by the needs of a community of sea merchants that depended on a body of consistent rules, universally recognized and enforced. Likewise, land-based commerce – especially in regularly held trade fairs[10] – depended on these principles of universal rules, predictable results, consistent enforcement, and transparent procedures.

It was thus no accident that, as noted in the last chapter, the Magna Carta of 1215 provided that "All merchants shall have safe conduct to go and come out of and into England ... by land and water for purposes of buying and selling, free of legal tolls, in accordance with ancient and just customs."[11] Centuries later, English chancery courts (which, along with courts of admiralty, were the most likely to apply the *ius commune*) would recognize a universal *lex mercatoria*.[12] Italian cities – especially Genoa, Pisa, and Milan – came to adopt commercial codes in the early Middle Ages.[13] Unlike the Roman *ius gentium*, the medieval *lex mercatoria* was pluralistic. In medieval England, for example, even royal courts (as distinct from merchant tribunals) resolved disputes between local and foreign merchants on the basis of law merchant and not ordinary principles of common law.[14] As Gerard Malynes, an English writer in the late seventeenth century, observed: The law merchant "is a customary law approved by the authority of all kingdoms, and not a law established by the sovereignty of any prince."[15]

The universality of the law merchant was not only a benefit to individual traders or financiers, but also to national economies. Just as the *ius gentium* had a public international law aspect, so did the *lex mercatoria*, to the extent that medieval polities concluded most-favored-nation agreements.[16] In addition, the development of a European common law of commerce revolutionized the process of reducing transaction costs for exchanges across borders, extending large amounts of credit and finance, and developing the instruments and structures for business enterprises.[17] All in all, these initiatives made possible the rise of a commercial middle class in late medieval Europe, the economic revolutions of the Renaissance and early modern period, and, indeed, laid the groundwork for the Industrial Revolution and today's global economy.

Medieval Europe's *ius commune* (discussed also in Chapter 2), especially in its manifestation as a transnational system of commercial law through the law merchant and *lex maritima*, illustrates the possibilities of a nonhierarchal, but still coherent and universal, system of international law. Unlike the hegemony of Rome's *ius gentium*, there was no dominant domestic legal system at work with the customary regimes of commerce in the Europe of the Middle Ages and Renaissance. Through an extraordinary process of legal transplantation (to use Alan Watson's concept[18]), or, at a minimum, a parallel evolution in disparate legal systems,[19] Roman law concepts managed to merge with a functional necessity of universality in many material realms of medieval and early modern commercial life, marking a watershed event in historical jurisprudence.[20]

In contrast with the intellectual tradition of the *ius gentium* and *ius commune*, the technical content of transnational customary norms arose from common practices and institutions necessary for cross-border trade. One of these was documentary transactions, where a written medium (whether a cuneiform object from ancient Sumeria[21] or a vellum from medieval Lombardy[22]) served as a proxy for a consignment of goods (a bill of lading) or financing instrument (a bill of exchange or bearer note). Possession of these documents became the *sine qua non* for commercial transactions, establishing an unconditional right of payment. Because of the long-distance character of commerce, sellers had the right to stop goods in transit on default by the buyer.[23]

A second technical tradition lay in the domain of commercial dispute resolution. Specialized merchant courts were inaugurated as spontaneous and *ad hoc* institutions at trade fairs, or more permanently, by medieval monarchs and princes (called *piepowder* or staple courts in England). They were deliberately structured to be insulated from the provincialism or biases of local tribunals applying local law by allowing appointed panels of merchants to decide cases among themselves. These courts were also intended to offer speedy and efficient justice, an innovation that some scholars suggest was derived from the summary procedures of canon law tribunals.[24] An additional feature of these commercial courts was the mixed jury (known later as the jury *de medietate linguae*, "jury of the half-tongue"), on which foreign merchants sat in approximately equal numbers with local traders.[25] This right was codified into English law in 1303, in Edward I's Carta Mercatoria.[26] As an adjunct to these specialized dispute-settlement institutions, English law (dating from the 1283 statute of Acton Burnell[27]) also provided a streamlined mechanism for the enforcement and payment of judgments.[28]

The "romantic"[29] notion that the medieval *lex mercatoria* was a system of law autonomous from domestic forces – and, by implication, will rise again in that form[30] – has been deeply contested in recent scholarship.[31] Indeed, there seems to be persuasive evidence that for England's leading fair of the Middle Ages – at St. Ives – the norms for resolution of trade disputes were not wholly dependent on a "voluntarily produced" set of customary commercial norms by participating merchants.[32] There were a number of documented cases in which trade customs were disclaimed by the Abbott of Ramsey, under whose official authority the fair operated.[33] As Stephen Sachs has noted, even when trade usages were applied at the St. Ives Fair Court,

> these customs were not necessarily constitutive of a coherent legal order, nor were they necessarily shared across any great distance. Within St. Ives, the use of the phrase "secundum legem mercatoriam" did not invoke a specific body of substantive principles ("according to the law merchant"), but rather referred indefinitely to whatever principles might be appropriate to the case, according to a mixture of local custom and contemporary notions of fair dealing.... Claims that these principles were universal foundered on the clear differences among the various customs of English fairs and towns.[34]

Or, as Emily Kadens has trenchantly written, "The historical *lex mercatoria* was not a single, uniform, essentially private legal system, but rather *iura mercatorum*, the laws of merchants: bundles of public privileges and private practices, public statutes and private customs."[35]

These critiques really implicate only the coherence of an intellectual pedigree for a transnational *lex mercatoria* that was truly autonomous from exogenous sources of substantive norms, particularly domestic legal strictures. Autonomy is not an essential fertilizer for the growth of transnational commercial norms. Nor, for that matter, is a slavish adherence to universal regularity. The medieval law merchant may well have been promoted by public institutions and forces, and its customs may have varied slightly from fair to fair, town to town.[36] Even critics of an overweening role for a medieval *lex mercatoria* still concede that adherence by market participants to the "technical tradition" of customary commercial law – the basic modalities of documentary transactions, resort to dispute-settlement mechanisms, and some specific rules of exchange in various trades – was quite robust and uniform.[37]

THE POSITIVIST REVOLUTION AND CROSS-BORDER TRADE USAGES

It appears that the romantic saga of the customary *lex mercatoria* is not as consistent a narrative as traditionally believed. The Middle Ages were not necessarily a halcyon time for a completely autonomous and uniform system of transnational commercial norms. But, is the story's sequel – the vicious positivist backlash against inchoate merchant customs – any more reliable? Not really. So, if the *lex mercatoria*'s medieval golden age was not so bright, nor was its nineteenth-century nadir so dark. A careful review of both legislative enactments (especially on the Continent) and judicial precedents (especially in England and the United States) reveals that merchant custom continued to exert a powerful pull in transnational commercial disputes.[38]

One jurisprudential distraction can be readily resolved: common-law courts assuredly did supplant merchant tribunals and juries from the seventeenth century on. In England, this was part of a larger phenomenon of the common-law courts (led by such figures as Sir Edward Coke and Lord Mansfield) challenging the prerogatives and jurisdiction of admiralty tribunals, which had come to assume the mantle of *ius gentium* authority, especially in commercial disputes.[39] Commercial customs – both domestic and international – were submitted to lay juries and proven as fact.[40] In Lord Mansfield's famous 1765 formulation in *Pillans v. Mierop*, merchant customs were also subject to integration with, and being overridden by, the common law.[41] To some, this reflected a wholesale incorporation of the law merchant into English common law.[42] This was nothing more than a restatement of the principle, discussed in Chapters 3 and 7, that a custom (whether local or trade) could not be contrary to right reason and thus subject to being nullified by judicial decree. That is not the same thing as a positivist abrogation of all international trade usages.

Likewise, it has been suggested that the codification of commercial norms in the late nineteenth and early twentieth centuries utterly obliterated an autonomous role for custom.[43] As was earlier considered in relation to the 1897 German Commercial Code and the U.S. Uniform Commercial Code, that was not the case at all. Indeed, the intellectual progenitors for these projects – Levin Goldschmidt in Germany[44] and Karl Llewellyn in America – embraced the notion that a dynamic merchant custom should be recognized in their codifications, not frozen in place by legislative fiat.

Even with these shadowy nuances, there remains the harsh glare cast by John Austin's mid-nineteenth-century high-positivist critique of custom.[45] His attack was particularly focused on recognition of merchant practices:

> By many of the admirers of customary laws … they are thought to oblige legally (independently of the sovereign or state), because the citizens or subjects have observed or kept them. Agreeably to this opinion, they are not the creatures of the sovereign or state, although the sovereign or state may abolish them at pleasure. Agreeably to this opinion, they are positive law … inasmuch as they are enforced by the courts of justice: But, not withstanding, they

exist as positive law by the spontaneous adoption of the governed, and not by position or establishment on the part of political superiors. Consequently, customary laws, considered as positive law, are not commands. And, consequently, customary laws, considered as positive law, are not laws or rules properly so called....

At its origin, a custom is a rule of conduct which the governed observe spontaneously, or not in pursuance of a law set by a political superior. The custom is transmuted into positive law, when it is adopted as such by the courts of justice, and when the judicial decisions fashioned upon it are enforced by the power of the state. But before it is adopted by the courts, and clothed with the legal sanction, it is merely a rule of positive morality: a rule generally observed by the citizens or subjects; but deriving the only force, which it can be said to possess, from the general disapprobation falling on those who transgress it.[46]

As H. L. A. Hart observed in his famous critique of Austinian positivism, not every norm needs the sovereign's express imprimatur to be law. Rather, many laws "confer powers on private individuals to make" their own rules, with the advance expectation of official enforcement.[47]

Judicial recognition and treaty codification of transnational commercial norms are two mechanisms by which the Austinian paradox of custom can be reconciled. Moreover, this is consistent with Harold Berman's observation that

Nobody denies that there is a body of international rules, founded on the commercial understandings and contract practices of an international community principally composed of mercantile, shipping, insurance, and banking enterprises of all countries. That body of rules antedates the emergence of strictly separated national legal systems; it has never ceased to exist; moreover, it is continually being developed. It should be recognized by national legal systems as customary law....[48]

When one examines the full breadth of doctrinal rules covered by transnational commercial norms,[49] trade usages have certainly been confirmed in the case law. That has been so since the mid-nineteenth century (and the supposed era of high positivism's active suppression of custom), as well as throughout the twentieth century.

Even contemporaneous with John Austin's high positivism, judicial doubts were expressed. Justice Joseph Story famously observed in the U.S. Supreme Court's 1842 decision in *Swift v. Tyson* that the true interpretation of commercial law was "to be sought, not in the decisions of the local tribunals, but in the general principles and doctrines of commercial jurisprudence,"[50] and that the law of negotiable instruments "was not the law of a single country only, but of the commercial world."[51] In other Supreme Court cases of this period, the general maritime law (or *lex maritima*) was characterized as "not [being] derived from the civil law... nor from the common law. It had its source in the commercial usages and jurisprudence of the middle ages."[52] There was, however, a catch here, owing to the unique character and jurisdiction of federal courts in the United States. Just as *Swift's* holding of a federal general common law of commerce was famously repudiated in *Erie Railroad Co. v. Tompkins* in 1938 (as discussed in Chapter 3),[53] so, too, was the idea that inchoate commercial or maritime customs could prevail over contrary federal law.[54] Nothing in these rulings was, however, a direct renunciation that commercial or maritime usages could form and become the rule of decision in appropriate cases.

INTERNATIONAL TRADE USAGES IN ANGLO-AMERICAN CASE-LAW

Several types of contemporary transnational business dealings will serve as concrete examples of customary norms at work. The first of these already has been mentioned in historical context: documentary transactions for the export or import of goods. Bills of lading are commonly used to express no fewer than three transactional modalities. They can be a receipt for the goods in transit, a contract for carriage of the goods, and a document of title. In international trade, "c.i.f." contracts ("cost, insurance, and freight") are agreements for the sale and shipment of goods to an agreed destination, with the seller bearing the responsibility of seeing that the items safely get to that delivery point. The buyer makes payment against the production of the appropriate documents according to the contract. Metaphorically, a c.i.f. contract is a sale of goods performed by the delivery of documents. Of course, the buyer wants receipt of conforming goods, not a set of documents symbolically representing those items. On this significant disparity in party interests for this form of transaction, much trade usage turns.

One of the best explications of transnational customary norms in this context remains the *Biddell Brothers v. E. Clemens Horst Company* case decided by English courts in 1912.[55] In 1904, Horst (a firm in San Francisco) agreed to sell consignments of hops "c.i.f. to London, Liverpool, or Hull.... Terms net cash," with no express provision allowing the buyer to challenge the quality of the goods after delivery.[56] In 1910, Biddell demanded that advance samples of consignments be submitted for its approval, "in accordance with the universal practice of the trade and the custom adopted by" Horst.[57] Horst insisted that a certificate of quality issued by the San Francisco exchange sufficed, but Biddell refused, whereupon Horst declared the contract in breach and would not ship the next consignment. Biddell sued in the English King's Bench Commercial Court. The trial court found in favor of Horst, ruling that Biddell was obliged to pay against conforming documents and could not insist on an independent inspection.

The English Court of Appeal, Lord Justice Vaughn Williams writing, reversed, holding that because the contract did not expressly say "payment against documents," Biddell could decline payment until satisfied by its own inspection of each shipment. The majority was particularly harsh in its conclusion that the trial court erred in taking judicial notice of a merchant trade usage that the mere inclusion of a "c.i.f." term was alone sufficient to indicate a payment against documents.[58] The Court of Appeal insisted that proof of such a usage must be made, and since there was no evidence in the record as to the conclusive meaning of a bare "c.i.f." term, the defendant's position was unsustainable. In his dissent, Lord Justice Kennedy took the majority to task for, among other things, its too-ready dismissal of the relevance of custom and its ignorance of commercial realities in not giving a "c.i.f." term its plain meaning as a documentary transaction.[59] On further appeal, the House of Lords reversed and found in favor of Horst, mainly along the lines expressed by Justice Kennedy. Although the House of Lords did not offer any further analysis of the underlying trade usages at issue, its opinions later drew praise from no less an authority than Karl Llewellyn.[60]

If English courts were ultimately solicitous of trade usages for bills of lading and documentary transactions in the *Biddell Brothers* case, there were other instances where rulings did not lead to such salubrious results. In a 1949 decision, in *The JULIA*,[61] the House of Lords essentially rejected evidence of a local trade usage construing the use of delivery orders as an adjunct to bills of lading, by which portions of fungible goods shipped could be separated and sold to different buyers in separate consignments subsequent to the issuance of the bill of lading. In essence, delivery orders were – at least at the port of Antwerp on the eve of World War II – a customarily sanctioned way to amend a bill of lading and represented a title document to a subsequent buyer. Nevertheless, the House of Lords rejected their use in that fashion, a decision that marked a fundamental departure from openness to overseas trade usages that might be at variance with British practices.[62]

In a 1957 decision, *Brown, Jenkinson & Company v. Percy Dalton*,[63] the English Court of Appeal went even further and struck as unreasonable a fairly common trade practice by carriers to issue a "clean" bill of lading indicating that the goods were properly shipped, even when (in that case) the shipper's containers were decrepit. The court held, irrespective of the custom,[64] that it was contrary to public policy to allow the carrier to recover from the shipper under an indemnity agreement, even though the consignee injured by the fraudulent clean bill was fully compensated by the carrier's insurer. As Lord Justice Pearse wrote, "[i]t is not enough that the banks or purchaser who have been misled by clean bills of lading may have recourse at law against the ship-owner. They are intending to buy goods not law suits...."[65]

In the field of marine insurance for cargo, we see this same mixed record for judicial recognition of trade usages. Until the twentieth century, the law of marine insurance was based entirely on commercial usage and judicial decisions interpreting such customary norms. This was as much as acknowledged in the first attempts at codification.[66] As has become evident in many other contexts in this volume, the act of codification does not interrupt the lifecycle of customary law formation, although it may channel it into disputes about the possible interpretations of statutory passages or their desuetude in the face of completely novel, and contrary, usages.

This is nicely illustrated from two cases drawn from the law of marine insurance: one decided by a British court, the other by an American tribunal. In *Diamond Alkali Export Corporation v. FL. Bourgeois*,[67] the Court of King's Bench in 1921 was faced with a c.i.f. transaction in which the buyer (a British firm) refused payment to a seller (an American company) on documents that, it alleged, were nonconforming with the underlying contract. Specifically, the buyer rejected the use of a "certificate of insurance" tendered by the seller as a substitute for a complete "policy of insurance" required by the contract. The seller, relying on other decisions regarding analogous bill-of-lading practices,[68] alleged that its use of a certificate conformed with trade usages for c.i.f. terms. But this was rejected by Judge McCardie. And even though he acknowledged that his decision "may well be ... disturbing to business men,"[69] he noted that "there is no finding or evidence before me of any custom or general usage which modifies the long and clearly established legal rights of a buyer under a c.i.f. contract...."[70] He left open the possibility that such a usage could later be proven to have arisen, but he was skeptical that such could be shown.[71]

Three years later, in 1924, exactly the same issue was decided by a U.S. district court in New York City. The deciding judge was none other than Learned Hand, introduced in Chapter 8 as the author of the landmark torts decision in *The T. J. HOOPER*. In *Kunglig Jarnvagsstyrelsen v. Dexter & Carpenter*,[72] the Swedish plaintiff bought a cargo of coal from the U.S. defendant and paid on the presentation of documents that included an insurance certificate, and not a full policy. As luck would have it, the consignment was lost at sea, and the certificate did not have a real insurance policy backing it up, although such could be demanded by the buyer from a broker.[73] The buyer sought a refund of the amounts paid, relying on the English decision in *Diamond Alkali* for the proposition that the tendering of an insurance certificate was unacceptable for a c.i.f. contract.[74]

Nevertheless, Judge Hand decided to reject the English precedents and embrace the commercial usage of accepting certificates of marine insurance under these circumstances. "Much as I should hesitate to diverge from the settled law of so great a commercial country, it seems to me," Judge Hand wrote, that

> [w]hen a usage of this kind has become uniform in an actively commercial community, that should be warrant enough for supposing that it answers the needs of those who are dealing upon the faith of it. I cannot see why judges should not hold men to understandings which are the tacit presupposition on which they deal. From Lord Holt's time on they have generally in one way or the other been forced in the end to yield to the more flexible practices of commercial usage. So far as I know, the results have been generally acceptable to every one, once they were settled.[75]

Judge Hand then ruled that the custom of proffering insurance certificates was not unreasonable, either by virtue of the fact that a buyer could never really know the terms of the policy he might later depend upon or that there might be a broker's lien upon the policy (and payable by the buyer) for premiums.[76] Judge Hand offered this elegant explication of the underlying transactions, the calculus of risk, and the implications for commercial customs:

> Therefore [plaintiff's] objection comes to this: Though the seller pays the premium to the New York broker, a usage is unreasonable which exposes the buyer to the possibility of a lien for that premium in favor of the London broker, whom the New York broker does not pay. In the first place, is it altogether clear that the London broker could hold his lien, if he knew that the certificate was to pass to a third person and would represent the policy which he retained? Assuming that he could and that the usage leaves the buyer exposed to such a risk, it does not on that account appear to me to be beyond reasonable limits because of that possible injustice. Usages are never of importance, unless they modify rights which would otherwise result. The fact that the usage imposes a risk upon the buyer, which he would not incur if a policy were delivered, is not, I think, so vital to the substance of the contract that it may not be interpolated into the contract by implication.[77]

The rule adopted by Judge Hand in *Dexter & Carpenter* was not only later codified in the Uniform Commercial Code,[78] but also reflects his jurisprudence of custom. While in *The T. J. HOOPER*, Hand was skeptical of inefficient or irrational customs,[79] in *Dexter & Carpenter*, he was more willing to defer to the marketplace of "settled" usages as a means of calibrating contractual understandings and risks. At the same time, there is nary a mention in Judge Hand's analysis in *Dexter & Carpenter* of a compulsive requirement for proving the usage of accepting insurance certificates. This was consistent with a general rejection of an *opinio juris* requirement in transnational commercial custom cases, an approach that has remained in the law of insurance to this day.[80]

These trends are evident in cases construing letters of credit, the last form of international transaction considered here. The 1944 decision of the Second Circuit in *Dixon Irmaos*, mentioned in Chapter 7,[81] was the ultimate repudiation of *opinio juris* for international commercial norms. In that case, the beneficiary of a letter of credit was unable to tender the required "full set" of bills of lading. The beneficiary offered an indemnification by a prime bank in the event of any loss if the full set could not later be produced. The confirming bank refused. The beneficiary sued the confirming bank, alleging a commercial custom to honor indemnities in such situations. The trial court found that such a practice existed, but that banks regarded it as completely discretionary.[82] The court of appeals reversed. Judge Swan, who had earlier sat with Learned Hand in *The T. J. HOOPER* appeal, wrote for the court. He held that since expert witnesses for the confirming banks could not testify to any previous occasion in which discretion had been exercised to *refuse* an offer of indemnity, a uniform usage had been established, which was a tacit presupposition of all letter of credit transactions.[83] As one commentator later observed, "[t]he fact that the banks did not feel bound by the usage was held to be immaterial."[84]

Over a half-century later, letter of credit disputes are still being resolved in reference to usages, although they have now been compiled in documents such as "Uniform Customs and Practice for Documentary Credits (UCP)," issued by private organizations like the International Chamber of Commerce (ICC).[85] Recent U.S. court decisions have accepted the UCP as a relevant trade usage. In the 2002 *Voest-Alpine Trading v. Bank of China* decision, the issue was whether the defendant's refusal of payment under a letter of credit complied with UCP 500 article 14(d), which established a deadline for a bank's notice of dishonor.[86] The Fifth Circuit held that even though "the UCP 500 has acquired the function and status of law with respect to letters of credit which incorporate its terms," the district court's finding that the bank's conduct did not comply with such usages of trade was "a factual conclusion subject to review for clear error."[87] The court of appeals found there was ample evidence supporting a finding that the bank had breached "standard international banking practices" in handling a discrepant letter of credit.[88]

Essentially, the appeals court gave deference to the UCP, not as "law," but as a "usage" incorporated by implication into the terms of a transaction.

USAGE IN INTERNATIONAL CODIFICATIONS

If substantive transnational commercial norms are being notionally codified in instruments like the ICC's UCP 500, what remains of inchoate usages? Must a norm be vetted, or at least recognized, in a compilation of customs (modern equivalents of the medieval Consolato del Mare or Rolls of Oléron) in order to receive judicial sanction? That would vastly limit the horizon for transnational commercial norms. And recognizing that there have been attempts to codify the law of international transactions, none of these have gone so far as to limit the ambit of trade usages in this fashion. In the same way that Karl Llewellyn in the UCC sought to refashion commercial custom into an integrative jurisprudence of trade usages, so, too, with these international codification efforts.

The first of these was the 1964 Hague Conventions for a Uniform Law on the International Sale of Goods ("ULISG")[89] and for a Uniform Law on the Formation of Contracts for the International Sale of Goods ("ULFC").[90] ULISG Article 9 contained these provisions:

2. [Parties] shall also be bound by usages which reasonable persons in the same situation as the parties usually consider to be applicable to their contract. In the event of conflict with the present Law, the usages shall prevail unless otherwise agreed by the parties.

3. Where expressions, provisions or forms of contract commonly used in commercial practice are employed, they shall be interpreted according to the meaning usually given to them in the trade concerned.[91]

This was fairly boilerplate, and perhaps no more than an international riff on Karl Llewellyn's UCC article 1–205.[92] But, somewhat curiously, it is in the ULFC that greater attention was given to the role of usages in the various aspects of contract formation for cross-border transactions.[93] Usages, according to the ULFC, can be weighed in the interpretation of communications between the parties, firm or irrevocable offers, and acceptances, as well as determinations of the contracting capacity of the parties.[94]

The Hague Uniform Law projects failed for a variety of reasons, most of which had nothing to do with their handling of trade usages as a source of substantive obligation in international contracting. Nevertheless, there are marked differences between the ULISG/ULFC provisions on usage and those that appeared in the 1980 Vienna Convention on the International Sale of

Goods ("CISG").[95] After much heated debate,[96] article 9(2) of CISG provided that

> [t]he parties are considered, unless otherwise agreed, to have impliedly made applicable to their contract or its formation a usage of which the parties knew or ought to have known and which in international trade is widely known to, and regularly observed by, parties to contracts of the type involved in the particular trade concerned.[97]

Usages are also mentioned in CISG as a means of determining the intent of the parties[98] and as a modality for acceptance.[99]

The CISG's formulation on usage is significant in several respects. By speaking of "usage" and not "custom," it seems to follow Llewellyn's rejection of an *opinio juris* requirement for a commercial norm, and so a "normative custom is assimilated to what may be called behavioral custom, and the presumed expectations of the participants in the usage are sufficient to give rise to the obligation to observe it."[100] The ULISG provision, with its emphasis on "usages [which parties] … usually consider applicable to their contracts,"[101] arguably embraces an *opinio necessitatis* position.[102] The CISG's linkage between a usage and the intention of the parties is somewhat "ethereal"[103] and article 9(2) seems to create a "legal fiction"[104] that a usage in all circumstances is the basis of an implied agreement between the contracting parties.

In light of the objections of socialist and developing nations (who opposed the wholesale adoption of usages they might not even be aware of, and could well disfavor in their transactions),[105] the CISG takes no position on whether a usage can serve as a source of legal obligation other than with respect to construing a contract in accordance with the actual intentions of the parties.[106] Nor does the CISG appear to distinguish between general and local usages, the problem that arose in *The JULIA*.[107] In contrast with UCC section 1–205, trade usages under the CISG are not placed in a strict normative hierarchy and may thus prevail over conflicting contract terms or courses of dealing among the parties.[108] Yet, the CISG rejected the ULISG's requirement that any usage to be applied must necessarily be "reasonable,"[109] an astonishing position in light of the case law rejecting such usages as indemnifications for "foul" bills of lading and repugnant c.i.f. clauses.[110]

The CISG's provisions on usage have thus been rightly critiqued as the unworkable and incoherent product of diplomatic compromise.[111] These defects have been partially addressed[112] in the International Institute for the Unification of Private Law's 1994 Principles of International Commercial Contracts ("UNIDROIT Principles").[113] The UNIDROIT Principles define usages (as distinct from courses of dealing, or "practices") in this way:

(1) The parties are bound by any usage to which they have agreed and by any practices which they have established between themselves.
(2) The parties are bound by a usage that is widely known to and regularly observed in international trade by parties in the particular trade concerned except where the application of such a usage would be unreasonable.[114]

As with the ULISG, the UNIDROIT Principles also incorporate usages into provisions on modes of contractual acceptance,[115] contract construction,[116] and implied obligations.[117] The UNIDROIT Principles thus allow that trade usages can be binding, even without the express intention of the parties, provided they meet certain objective criterion that the norms are: (1) "widely known … and regularly observed," (2) "in the particular trade concerned," and (3) not "unreasonable" in application.[118] Although the UNIDROIT Principles have no official standing as a codification, they may better express contemporary understandings of the role of commercial norms in international transactions, and thus have a greater influence in restating the relevant *lex mercatoria*.

However construed, the ULISG/ULFC, CISG, and UNIDROIT projects are all in agreement on one point. They each serve to enable the recognition of usages in particular circumstances. What those conditions or requirements may be, does vary between these instruments. So, we have here a clear example of official law-making, in H. L. A. Hart's vocabulary, "confer[ring] powers on private individuals to make" their own rules. But is such a general grant of private legislative authority to transnational commercial actors enough?

COMMERCIAL CUSTOM AND THE "NEW" LEX MERCATORIA

Two new frontiers have thus been opened for the contemporary law merchant and the application of commercial norms to transnational business disputes. The first is in the realm of international commercial arbitration as a means of dispute settlement. The other is in relation to new regimes of norm harmonization, through such institutions as the International Chamber of Commerce (ICC) or other private standard-setting bodies. Both of these sets of initiatives have sought to distinguish the two faces of the modern *lex mercatoria*: inchoate universal principles of international commerce and specific regimes of usages for particular sectors, trades, and transactions.

While the results of much contemporary international commercial arbitration (or, at least, those involving private business parties on both sides) remain hidden from view because of secrecy and confidentiality, some broad patterns have been discerned.[119] One phenomenon that has emerged is that arbitrators in some situations will seek to base their decisions not on the law selected by the parties in their contracts, or not even a domestic law applicable to them, but, rather, based on "general principles" of commercial law applicable in some universal sense.[120] Such a technique has the advantage of avoiding the use of what may be regarded as eccentric provisions of substantive domestic law. It is also subject to criticism for being vague and unprincipled, as well as violative of the party autonomy that manifested itself in the selection of an applicable law for the contract.

More defensible are situations where arbitrators apply specific usages of trade to a commercial dispute. On occasion, such recourse has been sanctioned by the relevant procedural rules of the arbitration. For example, Article V of the Claims Settlement Declaration, which constituted the Iran-U.S. Claims Tribunal in 1981, authorized the "[t]he Tribunal [to] decide all cases on the basis of respect for law, applying such choice of law rules and principles of commercial and international law as the Tribunal determines to be applicable, taking into account relevant usages of the trade, contract provisions and changed circumstances."[121] The UNCITRAL Arbitration Rules also provide that "[i]n all cases, the arbitral tribunal shall decide in accordance with the terms of the contract and shall take into account the usages of the trade applicable to the transaction."[122] In reviewing arbitral awards issued under these institutions and rules, domestic courts have upheld arbitrator action in applying trade usages, even those not expressly incorporated by the law of the contract.[123]

None of this is to suggest, however, that parties to transnational deals have adopted wholesale the *lex mercatoria* as the law of their contracts in preference to a designated domestic legal system. That particular mythology of the new law merchant has been effectively debunked.[124] In this respect, we are not really today witnessing a Hayekian "spontaneous evolution of commercial law."[125] The current role of custom in transnational commerce is thus less overreaching and systemic, but, perhaps, more profound and subtle. Courts and arbitrations are more commonly using commercial norms and trade usages as interstitial devices to fill gaps in contract terms or the parties' manifest intent.[126] In many of these decisions and awards, the judges and arbitrators are not invoking "general principles" of international commercial law, an immanent *lex mercatoria*, at all.[127] They are far more likely to be applying very specific merchant or trade usages.

The second frontier for the "new" *lex mercatoria* is the sure and certain knowledge of its resurrection from earlier models. The "technical" tradition of transnational commercial norms has been quite durable. Indeed, it has been far more lively than any rhetoric of continuity for an "intellectual" tradition that can trace its pedigree from the Roman *ius gentium*, the medieval *ius commune*, the early modern *lex mercatoria*, and reincarnated as today's new law merchant. The hagiography for a *lex mercatoria* is simply unjustified, whether viewed historically or empirically. The realities of commercial custom are palpable, provided one knows through which prisms to look.

The first optic is that contemporary transnational business norms operate in a pluralistic legal environment, not a hegemonic one. There is no truly decentralized and autonomous, and yet integrated and complete, body of customary international commercial law operating today. Indeed, such a system may never have existed. Merchant custom subsists side by side with norms generated by particular contracts and background rules enacted within domestic polities. For every niche of contemporary international commerce – whether global currency trading,[128] export credit insurance,[129] the governance of cyberspace,[130] or letters of credit[131] – sets of customary trade practices exert a strong pull on the behavioral expectations of the communities that created and follow them. Custom's integration in pluralistic legal systems is well documented.[132] It had already been discussed in this volume in contexts as varied as family law in South Africa or property regimes in Hawaii.[133]

Understanding how contemporary transnational commercial norms are pluralistic means an appreciation of the multiple sources for their generation. These can include localized trade usages, generalized practices for certain sectors, treaty codifications, decisions by arbitrators and judges, and domestic legislation. As has already been mentioned, "bottom-up" usages have been enabled in transnational commerce to a degree that is virtually unprecedented in other doctrinal areas.[134] This has spawned its own set of criticisms, inasmuch as these forms of private law-making are hidden from view, and thus lack transparency and democracy in development and accountability in execution.[135]

This is hardly a novel critique, and one that seems particularly inapt in the field of transnational commerce. Despite calls today for more robust forms of regulation to counteract "irrationally exuberant" markets, most law merchant norms have been subject to a substantial degree of oversight, most notably (and traditionally) in the form of domestic courts' refusal to accept unreasonable usages. If there is a criticism to be leveled against the transparency, accountability, and democracy of transnational commercial norm-setting, it is not in the domain of such purely "private legislatures" as the ICC or the International Union of Credit and Investment Insurers.[136]

Rather, the worry may be that in a rush to control markets, there will be a concomitant push to constrain commercial customs. This is the second optic through which globalizing moves for business norms have to be observed.

"Private" transnational standard-setting bodies are under increasing pressure from public international institutions, which desire to enter the market for regulation. Bodies such as the International Monetary Fund, Bank for International Settlements, World Trade Organization, or Multilateral Investment Guarantee Agency have all sought to open regulatory initiatives that have hitherto been the prerogative of merchant or trade organizations. Just as the dividing line between public and private international law has been dissolved along its most general boundaries,[137] so, too, in this area of transnational commercial norm-creation.[138]

This development, more than any other, puts into sharp relief the main themes of this chapter. Whether, as a historical matter, nation-states exercised authority over the *lex mercatoria* in the Middle Ages and early modern period will always be disputed. Surely, a truly novel feature of the "new" law merchant is the role of public international institutions to engage in norm-formation and regulation in competition with the constituent actors and participants of transnational commerce. Nevertheless, purely "bottom-up" law-making remains a potent force in transnational commercial law.

That leaves the fundamental jurisprudential question of what converts the fact that a norm is followed by a relevant commercial community into a binding custom. All of the relevant international codifications on the scope and application of trade usages (ULISG/ULFC, CISG, and UNIDROIT Principles) all seem to accept that a sense of compulsory obligation among the market participants (*opinio juris*) is *not* required. Little else remains settled on this score. The extra ingredient that makes a usage legally cognizable as a custom may well be the test of its reasonableness or utility. As we shift from the domain of private international law (cross-border business usages) to public international law (customary norms among nations), this problem will continue to follow us.

11

Public International Law
Custom Among Nations

Customary international law presents the greatest concentration of theoretical and doctrinal problems reviewed in this book. This is, in and of itself, a bit of a puzzle. Why has the role of custom in public international law been so hotly disputed for so long? Why, especially in comparison with discussions about the place of custom in domestic legal doctrines (see Chapters 5–9), has customary international law (CIL) been overemphasized and overtheorized? Why are the doctrinal features and contours of CIL so distinct, even in relation to other, purely public law subjects (such as constitutional law, discussed in Chapter 9)? And, why, after nearly half a millennia of debate, are we no closer to conclusive answers as to what makes a binding custom among nations, the relation between CIL and other international law sources of obligation (particularly treaties), and the process by which customary international law changes or dies?

There are, perhaps, a number of reasons for what may be called exceptionalism for CIL. The first of these is that, alone among legal fields, public international law acknowledges custom as being a leading source of obligation. There is currently enshrined a definitive statement of the sources of international law. It can be found in Article 38 of the Statute of the International Court of Justice (ICJ), or World Court, which indicates that, in disputes submitted to it, the Court shall apply:

a. international conventions, whether general or particular, establishing rules expressly recognized by contesting states;
b. international custom, as evidence of a general practice accepted as law;
c. the general principles of law recognized by civilized nations;
d. ... judicial decisions and the teachings of the most highly qualified publicists of the various nations, as a subsidiary means for the determination of rules of law.[1]

Article 38(1)(b)'s laconic definition of customary international law as "evidence of a general practice accepted as law" will be intensely considered here. But it is worth remembering that Article 38 makes a clear sentiment that it is enunciating *legal* sources of norms in resolving disputes between states (the only parties that can appear before the World Court). The Court is thus a judicial institution and is thus bound to decide controversies on the basis of respect for a rule of law. By implication, this is supposed to confer also on the sources mentioned in Article 38 the unalloyed status of international law. Contributing to CIL exceptionism is that substantial methodological confusion continues to surround even the basic structure of international law sources. A literal reading of Article 38 suggests there is no hierarchy established among the sources, and, indeed, one might believe that the ones mentioned may not even have an obvious interrelationship; they are separate and distinct, hermetically sealed in practical application.

But the mere recognition of custom as a source for obligation in a particular legal domain cannot be regarded as exceptional. As discussed in Chapter 7, Uniform Commercial Code section 1–205 provides clear grounds for the incorporation of usages of trade into the construction of contracts.[2] Likewise, as mentioned in Chapter 5, various African and Pacific polities have constitutionally or statutorily enabled the application of customary family law norms into their legal systems.[3] So what distinguishes custom among nations in public international law? An answer may lie in the sheer volume, breadth, and density of CIL norms. Custom – as distinct from treaty obligations or the application of inchoate "general principles of law" – continues to dictate broad swathes of international legal obligation. Certain, "classic" realms of international law are governed by custom. These include diplomatic privileges and immunities, and the rules by which one nation may protect the interests of its nationals against injury by another state.[4] Many sets of norms on the use of force in international relations and the peaceful resolution of disputes are governed by CIL.[5] International rules concerning the use of "common spaces" – including the oceans and international environment – are dictated by custom.[6] Much of the post–World War II project of ensuring that states protect the human rights and dignities of their citizens, and that countries observe restraint in the treatment of noncombatants in wartime, has been elucidated through customary international law.[7]

Finally, and (perhaps) most influentially, CIL norms dictate the construction and application of "meta-norms" of public international law. These include what H. L. A. Hart would call secondary rules of recognition for other international law sources, as with principles of treaty formation, interpretation, and termination.[8] Likewise, the substance of the international law of state responsibility and the procedures under which states make claims for redress of international wrongs are dictated by custom.[9] So, it would appear that CIL has permeated many domains of public international law – not only particular doctrinal niches, but also the very architecture of the system.

Appearances may, however, be deceiving. It might be suggested, as in Chapter 1, that the presence of customary norms is a tell-tale sign of a primitive legal order, and, as Hart argued,[10] that legal cultures that extensively and pervasively employ custom will either modernize or perish. Some jurisprudes – most famously, Hans Kelsen – have maintained that, over time, treaty-based sources of international norms will dominate over customary principles.[11] There is a natural tendency, as in any "mature" legal system, for legislation to crowd out custom. One might, therefore, believe that custom is actually waning as an influential or legitimate source for international legal obligation. This will be considered in the final pages of this chapter, but, for the time being, it would be more prudent to assume that custom remains a potent and robust form of law-making in international relations.

Such an assumption, however, does not resolve the problem of exceptionalism for customary international law. Indeed, some writers have forcefully reasoned that CIL actually *lacks* many of the attributes that make customary norms binding in private law-making contexts (as in contracts, torts, and property).[12] But, as previously noted, custom exists in such purely public-law domains as domestic constitutional law (albeit with different requirements for its formation and recognition), so the clichéd distinction between private and public law cannot be the ground for believing that CIL must be intrinsically different and distinct from all other forms of customary law.

The balance of this chapter grapples with these conundrums. After a brief review of the historical trends and moments that have brought us to our current jurisprudential juncture for CIL, the key problem of customary international law's actual formation will be addressed. This involves a searching analysis of what has been taken as a canonical set of elements for the proof of any customary international law norm: ICJ Statute Article 38's requirements of a "general practice" of states, which is "accepted as law." This mix of ingredients between usage and *opinio juris* is at the heart of the problem for CIL's formation.

But there are other perplexities as well. These include distinctions between universal norms, and those that may be confined to particular geographic regions or as between contesting states in a dispute. Likewise, the relationship between customary norms and treaty regimes remains intensely intractable, especially as the equilibrium between these two sources of international legal obligations shifts in favor of written international agreements. And, yet, public international law has privileged a select group of CIL norms as "*jus cogens*" or "*erga omnes*" in character, which makes them either immune from alteration by treaty or assertable by any nation. There is also the understudied issue of how international customs are modified or outright terminated over time. All of this should lead to a new synthesis (or, at a minimum, a new appreciation) of whether CIL is a real, efficient, legitimate, and enduring source of international legal obligation.

TRENDS AND MOMENTS FOR CUSTOMARY INTERNATIONAL LAW

A historical disquisition on the evolution of CIL need not long detain us because most of the broad contours have already been explored here (especially in Chapters 2 and 10). Customary international law's evolution is the product both of a historical lineage dating back to Roman law's *ius gentium* and its formulation of the elements of custom, as well as a dramatic reimagining of custom's positivist character in the late Middle Ages and, again, between 1880 and 1920. What is most pronounced about this timeline is the extent to which the form of CIL has been dictated by what has been perceived (sometimes incorrectly) as the dictates of a civil law tradition that began with Rome and was transmitted to medieval Europe through the Roman Catholic Church's canon law and the secular *ius commune*. This is especially evident in the supposition that the crucial ingredient of custom – the magic elixir that drives the alchemy of transmuting a "mere" usage, or pattern of conduct, into a binding norm – is that the participants are following that practice out of a sense of legal obligation, and not as a moral prescription or courteous behavior.[13] The doctrine of *opinio juris sive necessitatis* is thus at the center of all doctrinal debate about the formation of customary international law.

As has been previously noted,[14] the notion of *opinio juris* had only a tenuous foundation in Roman law, and may have been the product of later, medieval jurisprudence. But for customary international law, a significant transformative moment occurred in the late Middle Ages. This can largely be seen in the writings of the Spanish legal philosopher and theologian, Francisco Suárez (1548–1617). His seminal work, *Tractatus de legibus ac deo legislatore* (1612), revolutionized an understanding of CIL, just as the entire body of international law was being remade with the advent of the modern, nation-state after the bloody Thirty Years War (1618–1648) in Europe, concluded by the Peace of Westphalia.[15]

Before Suárez, the basis of obligation in the law of nations was strongly rooted in natural law principles. Indeed, the works of writers we normally associate as the progenitors of "modern" international law – most notably, Hugo de Groot (Grotius) (1583–1645) – were vigorously naturalist in their orientation. But Suárez took issue with the notion that his contemporary *ius gentium* was based on natural law or generally derivative international morality.[16] This was not a semantic distinction for Suárez, but a real one.[17] The *"ius gentium,"* Suárez wrote, "differs from natural law because it is based on custom rather than nature."[18] This was one of the very first positivist enunciations for custom and the law of nations.

Borrowing from canon law, Suárez indicated that "[c]ustom is a kind of law [*ius*] introduced by usages and accepted as law...."[19] At great length, he enunciated an *opinio juris* requirement for custom,[20] but only when distinguishing, in municipal law, a "custom as fact" (usages that people engage in without legal compulsion) from "custom as law" (acts performed under penalty of law).[21] Relying on Julian's comment that custom is what "the populace has approved without any writing [and] shall be binding upon everyone, [irrespective of] whether the people declares its will by voting or by the very substance of its actions,"[22] Suárez believed that custom was established as both a fact (proof of the practice) and a "will and intention"[23] to be bound. In short, custom could create legally binding norms because "in a legitimate custom all the elements necessary for the establishment of a precept or law can exist together[:] fitness of subject matter, power, and will[,] sufficiently manifested externally."[24]

In connecting the *ius commune*'s customary law with the *ius gentium*, Suárez observed "[j]ust as in city or province custom introduces law, so too in the whole human race[,] laws could be introduced by the usages of peoples."[25] Then he made this positively crucial distinction:

> A matter can be said to pertain to the *ius gentium* in two ways: in one way because it is a law that all the various nations and peoples should observe toward one another (*inter se*); in another way because it is a body of law that particular cities and kingdoms observe within their own borders (*intra se*), which is called the law of nations because of the similarity and agreement of these laws.[26]

Suárez's first version of the *ius gentium* is what we could properly call the law of nations or public international law; his second version was the old *ius commune*, which has lived on as private international law. And, unlike domestic versions of customary law, Suárez believed that, for the *ius gentium inter se*, custom was introduced little by little by usage, but without any special consent of all the nations concerned at a particular time.[27]

Suárez acknowledged that his construct of CIL was not free of difficulties. He recognized that once a norm was established, it would be exceedingly difficult in practice for a contrary consensus of nations to arise to change it.[28]

More significantly, nations could opt out of particular norms. This was not just a matter of objecting to a custom (Suárez did not really recognize the phenomenon of a persistent objector). Rather, he wrote that "what is contrary only to the law of nations is not intrinsically evil"; whereas what is contrary to the law of nature definitionally is.[29] So long as a contrary local custom did not seriously injure another people or country, it was tolerable.[30] So, even though Suárez maintained that "the *ius gentium* is truly law and binds as true law,"[31] it is not immutable and unchangeable, although the mechanism for its transformation is uncertain.

Suárez's theory of CIL was revolutionary on three grounds. He firmly placed customary international law on a positivist basis: It is made by nations and peoples through a process of practice and consent. Next, Suárez seemingly relaxed a strict *opinio juris* requirement by allowing that the consent ("will and intention") of a nation to be bound to a custom could often be manifested through acquiescence.[32] And, last, because of its positivist footing, CIL can be changed or opted out from, albeit with conditions and caveats. These CIL postulates would prove to be quite influential,[33] at least until the period of "high positivism" beginning in the mid-nineteenth century.

High positivism's primary intellectual project was to establish a linkage between sovereignty and a positivist basis for the sources of international law. One of the leading conjectures for a positivist basis for international legal obligation is consent. Under this theory, the rules of international law become positive law when the will of the state consents to being bound by them either expressly or impliedly. The doctrine of consent generally teaches that the common consent of states voluntarily entering the international community gives international law its validity. States, and presumably other international actors, are said to be bound by international law because they have given their consent. The notion of consent is supposed to be applicable, irrespective of the particular source of an international legal obligation. Consent positivists have sharply disagreed on this point. Alf Ross, for example, observed that "[t]he positivist theory takes it for granted that all International Law is conventional [treaty] law … and that all validity of International Law is in the last instance derived from a union of the wills of sovereign states."[34] But the majority view, dating as far back as Emmerich de Vattel and Cornelius van Bynkershoek,[35] is that state consent to international law norms need not be made only in reference to written treaties, but may be also tacitly manifested in regard to customary obligations. According to the proponents of this approach, because consent can be either express or tacit, that allows a broader range of obligations to be made binding on states.

Consent certainly has been regarded as the most intelligible of positivist theories of obligation in international law. Nevertheless, it suffers from many of the same analytic failings as its competitors. Charles Fenwick raised the same kind of chicken-and-egg paradox as previously described: Do states, at the beginning of their international life or at the commencement of an authentic international community, really consent to certain basic principles of international law? The consent theory, according to Fenwick, is "inadequate to explain the assumption upon which governments appear to have acted from the beginning of international law."[36] Likewise, James Brierly suggested that to believe that international law consists only of rules that states have consented to does not account for the reality and complexity of the international system. At a bare minimum, he said, consent has difficulties explaining the integrity of norms drawn from nonexpress sources, such as custom.[37] Another difficulty, also noted by Brierly, is that if consent becomes the benchmark for international obligation, what happens when an international actor withdraws its approval of a particular legal norm (whether reflected in a treaty, custom, or another manifestation of consent)?

All of these theoretical considerations and jurisprudential wrangles came to a head when, in the summer of 1920, an Advisory Committee of Jurists assembled in Brussels to draft a statute for the Permanent Court of International Justice (PCIJ), the first global, standing tribunal. Part of the charge for the Advisory Committee was to draft a provision on the sources of international law to be applied by the Court in disputes before it.[38] Thus was born the provision that later became Article 38 of the ICJ Statute and its definition of customary international law as "a general practice accepted as law." Ironically, many of the preparatory documents for the PCIJ Statute virtually ignored the role of CIL as a source of international law, preferring instead to concentrate on "any Treaty in operation between the contesting parties, such Treaty [directly or indirectly] to form the basis of the judgment."[39]

At the Advisory Committee's deliberations, the role of custom as a source of public international law – as distinct from international agreements – was hotly debated.[40] It was Baron Descamps, the chair of the Advisory Committee and the Belgian Minister of State, who offered the formula of "international custom, being practice between nations accepted by them as law."[41] Descamps also observed that "when a clearly defined custom exists or a rule established by the continual and general usage of nations, which has consequently obtained the force of law, it is also the duty of the judge to apply it."[42] But former U.S. Secretary of State Elihu Root was skeptical that countries would "accept the clause relative to international custom" and argued that nations "will not submit to such principles as have not been developed into positive rules supported by an accord between all States."[43]

Members of the Advisory Committee disagreed about some aspects of the formulation of sources for international law, and those from common-law jurisdictions (most notably Root and Lord Phillimore from Britain) were at sharp variance with those from civil law nations (particularly Descamps and Raoul Fernandes from Brazil).[44] But there seemed to be unspoken unanimity in requiring, as an element of CIL, that a norm be "accepted as law." The League of Nations, in considering the Advisory Committee draft, made no changes to what later became Article 38(1)(b)'s formulation of customary international law.[45]

What explains this apparent consensus in 1920 that *opinio juris* is a necessary ingredient for CIL? In large measure, this ostensibly authoritative definition of customary international law is nothing more than an artifact of a peculiar jurisprudential debate from the late nineteenth and early twentieth centuries.[46] As mentioned in Chapter 2,[47] the Historical School sought to integrate a theory of custom as the ultimate source of domestic law, based on the will of the people accepting it as law (*volkgeist*).[48] It was François Gény, in his *Méthode d'interprétation et sources en droit privé positif* (1899), who was the first to articulate an "immaterial or psychological" component to the formation of custom and call it *"opinio juris seu necessitatis."*[49] But Gény was writing exclusively about domestic law, and he was seeking to distinguish legal usages (custom) from social usages (morals or courtesy).

Some writers have thus suggested[50] that the Advisory Committee's formulation of CIL was a vestige of the Historical School's notion that custom was both positive and immanent – something that was spontaneously divined from the will of the participants in a legal system but not made or legislated in any traditional sense.[51] As strange as it may sound to contemporary ears, this notion of CIL should not be conflated with a natural law construct that international custom reflected some underlying set of moral values embraced by the community of "civilized" nations. Although this was a popular idea in the late nineteenth century – especially among British publicists[52] – the formulation of customary international law arrived at by the Advisory Committee in 1920, and since enshrined (despite its manifest faults), was expressly regarded as a positivist view of custom.

The academic criticism of Article 38(1)(b) has been legion.[53] The primary critique is that the provision is semantically backwards: It is not the "custom" that is the evidence of the practice, but, rather, the "general practice" that is proof of a custom.[54] Nevertheless, whenever international bodies (including the U.N.'s International Law Commission (ILC) or the World Court) have had the opportunity to revisit the Advisory Committee's formulation of CIL, they have steadfastly declined.[55] A 1950 report prepared by the American jurist Manley O. Hudson approvingly cited James Brierly's summary of the "necessary elements" of proof for CIL, even though Hudson recognized they were "somewhat lacking in precision"[56]:

    (a) concordant practice by a number of States with reference to a type of situation falling within the domain of international relations;

    (b) continuation or repetition of the practice over a considerable period of time;

    (c) conception that the practice is required by, or consistent with, prevailing international law; and

    (d) general acquiescence in the practice by other States.

[T]he presence of each of these elements is to be established as a fact by a competent international authority.[57]

If Hudson was expecting quick approval of his gloss on Article 38(1)(b), he was sadly disappointed. Members of the ILC voiced strong objection to element (c)'s assumption that CIL, once created, could not be altered, or that a new custom could not form in the face of previous practice. Even more significantly, the Commission outright rejected Hudson's requirement in element (b) that a practice had to be iterated "over a considerable period of time." In addition, Hudson's process requirement that a custom be first validated by a "competent international authority" was likewise rejected as precluding the normal process of CIL formation: the give and take of international negotiations and the claims and defenses made by contesting states to a dispute.[58]

But, rather curiously, ILC members generally endorsed Hudson's most radical move: that elements (c) and (d), when read together, adequately described the *opinio juris* requirement, inasmuch as "acquiescence" or lack of protest could be material in determining whether states viewed a practice as being "accepted as law." Hudson's assertion was consistent with a large body of scholarship, especially from the interwar period,[59] that CIL was supported by the tacit consent of states as members of the international community. And although Kelsen criticized such a position as relying on a "fiction,"[60] it nevertheless captured the dynamic of CIL creation by which groups of states may "bid" new norms, while others may object, and yet other countries may simply remain silent and so acquiesce.[61]

FORMATION OF CUSTOMARY INTERNATIONAL LAW

To show a rule of customary international law, one must prove to the satisfaction of the relevant decision-maker (whether it be an international tribunal, domestic court, or government or intergovernmental actor) that the rule has (1) been followed as a "general practice," *and* (2) has been "accepted as law." The first part of the equation (the general practice element) is an objective inquiry: Have international actors really followed the rule? Has the practice been consistent? Has the practice been followed for a sufficient period? The second part of the equation (the "accepted as law" element) has often been called a subjective, or even (as Gény wrote) a psychological, inquiry. It asks *why* an international actor has observed a particular practice. The *opinio juris* inquiry attempts to ascertain whether a practice is observed out of a sense of legal obligation or necessity, or, rather, merely out of courtesy, neighborliness, or expediency.

There is an inherent tension between these two elements, and practicing international lawyers (as distinct from legal academics) suspect that they are deliberately redundant. The tendency has been, in proving whether something is a rule of customary international law, to simply satisfy oneself that a particular practice is really followed by states and other international actors and to forget about the motives for the norm's observance.[62] But there really is a need to have an extra element, an additional "ingredient" for the recipe that makes customary international law. Otherwise, international actors will be bound to follow practices that may not really reflect their own expectations of lawful international conduct, or, worse yet, may be unreasonable or anachronistic. Whether one thinks of an *opinio juris* requirement or instead focuses on the reasonableness or utility of a rule of custom, something in addition to the fact that states and other actors follow the practice is necessary.

Some writers have suggested, based on this dichotomy of general practice and *opinio juris*, that there is a distinction to be made between the "traditional" formulation of custom (as reflected in Article 38) and "modern" custom that has arisen particularly with the human rights revolution following World War II. Traditional custom, Anthea Roberts has written, is "evolutionary and is identified through an *inductive* process in which general custom is derived from specific instances of state practice.... *Opinio juris* is a secondary consideration invoked to distinguish between legal and nonlegal obligations."[63] "By contrast, modern custom is derived by a *deductive* process that begins with general statements of rules rather than particular instances of practice. This approach emphasizes *opinio juris* rather than state practice because it relies primarily on statements rather than actions."[64] Some scholars[65] have suggested that traditional CIL is outmoded and anachronistic, and have lauded the dynamic and progressive character of modern custom. Others have warned that modern CIL lacks the legitimacy of state consent and could either be enlisted in the service of great power interests[66] or advance norms that are not really founded in state practice at all.[67]

Putting aside the relative weight of words versus deeds in the proof of state practice (which will be taken up presently), the relative strengths and weaknesses of both the "traditional" and "modern" approaches to CIL are notorious.[68] Traditional custom labors under some procedural dysfunctions and the plain difficulty of discerning patterns of authoritative state practice from the actions of nearly 190 states as part of the international community. The key defect of modern custom is that in lauding ideal standards of state conduct, it has become detached from actual state practice. If legitimacy and transparency matter as metrics for customary international law (more on that at the end of this chapter), then the traditional view of CIL – even as imperfectly captured in Article 38(1)(b)'s formulation – should continue to be embraced.

As argued by a number of publicists, one way to reconcile traditional and modern approaches is to view the entire process of CIL formation as a series of stages of growth,[69] or a kind of sliding scale of normativity.[70] Whether one uses an idiom of growth (a norm "hardens" over time with increasing state practice and then, later, the necessary acceptance as law)[71] or the metaphor of a continuum (custom can be supported by high degrees of state practice but relatively little evidence of *opinio juris*, and vice versa), a reconciliation between traditional and modern views of CIL can be achieved without sacrificing essential process safeguards or substantive values of integrity for CIL formation.

How, then, can one prove that a norm of international conduct is really a "general practice" that qualifies it as a binding rule of customary international law? States rarely oblige by disclosing and handily collecting all of their relevant international practices in one location. (The exceptions include such legally sophisticated nations as the United States, United Kingdom, Japan, and others, which periodically publish compendiums of their practices of, and positions on, international law.[72]) Remember, customary practices are often not formally recorded at all. More than that, what states *do* should matter a lot more than what they *say*. But, necessarily, international lawyers rely on written evidence of state practice (even if it is diplomatic correspondence, military manuals, or newspaper accounts of contemporary events).[73] And while customary international law is very much a "struggle" between competing positions, no international lawyer would desire that in their exuberance to show what their positions are, states would more readily resort to muscular and violent means of asserting their rights.

But this leads to a problem of what sorts of state practice should really count in the formation of CIL. Are government pronouncements as to the content of a customary norm more reliable than an actual assertion of a right under such a rule?[74] Some publicists (such as Anthony D'Amato) would limit evidence of state practice to situations where a state has made an affirmative claim of right under a rule of CIL, and consigning less assertive government actions or statements to the proof of some ostensible *opinio juris*.[75] But that can leave out of the equation unilateral acts of adherence to CIL norms, conduct performed by a state without relation to a pending claim or incident.[76] In this category would also be municipal legislation and the decisions of domestic courts, which might recognize CIL principles, even if not in the context of interstate disputes.[77] And, as already alluded to above, to what extent should a state's passivity or acquiescence be considered consent to the formation of new CIL norms?[78]

There is also authority in some international decisions that the practices that should count the most are those of "specially affected" states, those nations that have the greatest stake in a dispute as to the content of a CIL norm.[79] This is not, however, a thinly disguised bid for great power mastery over the levers of CIL formation.[80] Rather, it is a recognition that, in measuring compliance with a supposed custom, what matters are the usages of states that had the opportunity to engage in such a practice.[81]

An excellent illustration of the "traditional," inductive method of finding evidence of state practice is shown in *The PAQUETE HABANA*, a case decided by the U.S. Supreme Court in 1900.[82] The facts and issues presented in the case were deceptively simple. Two Cuban fishing boats had been captured by U.S. naval forces in the Spanish-American War and condemned as "prizes" of war. The question was whether small coastal fishing boats were immune from capture under customary international law. The U.S. government confidently asserted they were not so protected. The attorney for the Cuban boat owners, J. Parker Kirlin, was obliged to show the content of customary international law. Drawing from sources as varied as medieval English royal ordinances, agreements between European nations, orders issued to the U.S. Navy in earlier conflicts, and the opinions of treatise writers,[83] Kirlin staged one of the most stunning upsets in U.S. Supreme Court history. He persuaded the Court that his clients, and not the U.S. government, knew better what customary international law was. The Court held that CIL barred the capture of small fishing boats.

Kirlin's victory was not only a demonstration of an eclectic and scholarly collection of evidence of state practice. It was a *tour de force* of powerful argument insofar as Kirlin persuaded a majority of the justices that the immunity granted to coastal fishing boats was grounded in humanitarian concerns, as well as supported by legal obligation. The United States had particularly relied on one earlier case, *The YOUNG JACOB*, decided by the English High Court of Admiralty in 1798.[84] That case had held that the practice of immunizing fishing craft was not a rule at all, but instead was only "comity" or courtesy.[85] The English court had ruled that the practice was not supported by *opinio juris*, and the United States government (some 100 years later) seized on this as a basis for arguing that protecting enemy fishing boats was a matter of "grace" only. Kirlin persuaded the Court, however, that within the intervening century the practice *had* become obligatory; it was no longer optional and was, indeed, binding on the United States.

Kirlin had the advantage, of course, of proving a customary usage that was supported by an impeccable evidentiary pedigree: nearly two centuries of consistent and well-documented state practice.[86] But must all evidence of a general practice be confirmed by this high threshold of uniformity, consistency, and longevity of the usage? The International Court of Justice has indicated that uniformity need not be perfect and that minor inconsistencies in the observance of the practice are acceptable. Likewise, the ICJ has held that for a rule to be established as customary, the corresponding practice need not be in absolutely rigorous conformity with the rule. Instead, the conduct of States in such situations should be consistent with such rules, and to the extent they are not, such inconsistencies should be treated as breaches of the rule and not as an indication of the emergence of a new rule.[87]

There also is no requirement that a practice necessarily be observed for a long period before it will be confirmed as a binding custom.[88] The history of international law is replete with instances of state practice that enjoyed such immediate popularity, and around which formed such a complete consensus of the international community, that they were recognized almost as "instant custom."[89] One well-known example was the development of state claims to offshore oil and gas deposits under a theory of continental shelves that took barely 15 years to form into binding law.[90] It is not the age of a practice that makes a custom. Rather, it is the high degree of consistency and uniformity of observance by most (if not all) of the international community that satisfies the objective element of confirming it as a "general practice."[91]

If one thinks it is easy to prove a rule as a general practice, one might do well to consult the French counsel in *The S.S. LOTUS* case decided by the Permanent Court of International Justice (PCIJ) in 1927.[92] Another nautical case, the facts are again wonderfully simple. A French vessel, *The LOTUS*, negligently collided with a Turkish vessel on the high seas (beyond any nation's control), killing eight Turkish nationals. *The LOTUS* foolishly

sailed into Istanbul, whereupon Turkish authorities arrested the French officer on whose watch the accident occurred and charged him with negligent
homicide. France protested Turkey's assertion of criminal jurisdiction over a
French national for an act that occurred on a French vessel outside of Turkey's
territory.

The question here is how the PCIJ determined the relevant customary
international law principles to apply.[93] To France's dismay, the Court ruled
at the outset that since France was challenging Turkey's exercise of jurisdiction, it was incumbent on France to show that Turkey violated customary
international law.[94] That pretty much sunk France's chances of winning
the case, because it meant that French counsel were obliged to collect sufficient evidence of state practice indicating that Turkey's prosecution was
improper.[95] Unfortunately for France, its advocates were given the task of
showing evidence of state practice indicating that exercise of criminal jurisdiction over a foreign national on a foreign-flagged vessel on the high seas
was improper.

That proved impossible. The PCIJ was able to distinguish every earlier case
or incident relied upon by France for the proposition that the state of nationality or the "flag-State" had exclusive jurisdiction in circumstances such as this.
Not only was there a lack of objective evidence supporting France's supposed
general practice, but even if there had been (the Court intimated) it would
merely show that states had often abstained from instituting criminal proceedings, but had not necessarily felt obligated to do so.[96] In short, even if France
had proven a usage, there was no *opinio juris*.[97] So, even if the French lawyers
had shown (which they could not) a "smoking gun" of an earlier incident
where Turkey had declined to prosecute a foreign national, that would not
have been conclusive. The only possible way that France could have carried
its burden was to have documented a case where a *Turkish* vessel had collided
with a foreign ship, that foreign country had prosecuted a Turkish mariner,
and then Turkey had protested and prevailed. Only in this classic "shoe-on-
the-other-foot" scenario could France have proven a contrary general practice
accepted as law by Turkey.

The LOTUS has proven to be a most problematic case for international lawyers. Its core holding is that international law is a permissive system: Everything
is allowed, except that which is expressly prohibited. The burden was thus
placed on the country challenging another's conduct. Aside from this presumption (which has certainly been questioned and attacked in the context of
exercises of jurisdiction), *The LOTUS* remains a powerful cautionary tale for
international lawyers attempting to prove the existence of a general practice
accepted as binding customary international law.

An excellent example of a "modern," deductive approach to CIL formation is in *Filártiga v. Peña-Irala,* where a U.S. court decided that torture constituted a violation of the "law of nations" for purposes of invoking the court's jurisdiction under the Alien Tort Claims Act.[98] In reaching that conclusion, the Second Circuit of the U.S. Court of Appeals relied on U.N. General Assembly resolutions, while properly noting that they constituted evidence only (but persuasive evidence) of state practice and *opinio juris.* The votes themselves, the court was careful to say, were not dispositive as a source of international legal obligation. One point that has often been made by commentators is that General Assembly resolutions, precisely because they are recommendations, lack the necessary *opinio juris* for custom.[99] This is so even though states may repeatedly vote for a resolution and profess their support for the legal rule it stands for. States, for example, overwhelmingly voted in the General Assembly for resolutions condemning state-sponsored torture, yet (as such groups as Amnesty International have reported) some of these same states actually engage in the torture of their own citizens.[100] Which do we prefer to believe: the professed position of the state or the empirical evidence of its actual conduct? In some instances, international lawyers and judges will take states' words at face value.

It is by no means an easy task even to establish the "objective" prong of a custom as a general practice. But it is the "subjective" element of *opinio juris* that remains the most problematic for international lawyers. The most obvious difficulty with this vision of the binding nature of custom – that nations obey a practice out of a sense of legal obligation – is one that even the Romans recognized (see Chapter 2). It cannot explain the motivation of "first movers": the handful of international actors that follow a new practice, or the attitudes of states in opposing a currently accepted usage.[101] International tribunals have not been helpful in resolving this *circulus inextricabilis.*[102] In some cases, they have adopted lax standards of *opinio juris* in some cases (making it almost self-proving),[103] while in others imposed a demanding test that was all but impossible to satisfy.[104] Nothing necessarily distinguishes the disputes, save the cynical view that the World Court was desirous in some instances of validating a rule as a custom and not so obliging in the other matters.[105]

Ascertaining *opinio juris* has always been difficult. Indeed, in many World Court judgments, the balance of equities has usually swung against a finding that a state practice is supported by *opinio juris.*[106] Whether the ostensible custom was fishing rights in offshore waters,[107] particular methods of treaty construction,[108] the nationality of corporations,[109] or a prohibition on the use of nuclear weapons,[110] the ICJ has declined enforcement of the rule based on a lack of proof that it has been truly consented to as binding law.[111] And, yet, in other instances, international tribunals have found persuasive evidence of *opinio juris* by simply cataloguing evidence of state practice, what one decision described as a "test[] by induction based on the analysis of a sufficiently extensive and convincing practice, and not by deduction from preconceived ideas."[112] Or, put another way, practice can be "illustrative of belief," or "confirm[ing]" of *opinio juris*.[113] Proof of *opinio juris* is often drawn by inference from strictly domestic enactments or rulings (including judicial decisions)[114] and can further attenuate or dilute this state scienter inquiry, although a countervailing trend is to use the resolutions of international institutions and adherence to multilateral treaties as persuasive evidence of *opinio juris*.[115]

It has been suggested that the real binding force behind a custom is not the tautological "sense of legal obligation" that international actors may or may not espouse (and which we will never know, of course). Rather, it must be that actors follow a custom out of a sense that it is reasonable or functional for the international community.[116] This approach tends to substitute a naturalist test of reasonableness, utility, fairness, or justice for every emerging or conflicting custom,[117] at least in the absence of the express evidence of state consent to be bound to a legal custom, which is so often lacking. But just because a norm is reasonable, does not necessarily explain why it has acquired binding force.[118] Indeed, in at least one case, the ICJ has ruled that a norm having the character of "practical convenience and certainty of application"[119] was, nevertheless, not supported by *opinio juris*.

The ultimate riddle of *opinio juris* is whether "accept[ance]" of a norm "as law" must be specific as to a particular nation concerned, or may be inferred from the international community at large.[120] This is nothing more, of course, than a restatement of the quandary for the "objective" element of state practice of whether acquiescence or silence can suffice to confirm a usage.[121] If specific intent is required for a nation's *opinio juris*, then it well and truly becomes a psychological inquiry of whether a nation "belie[ves] that th[e] practice is rendered obligatory by the existence of a rule of law requiring it."[122] But if inferred consent is embraced in the proof of a particular state's *opinio juris* for a specific norm, the legitimacy of CIL formation can still be retained.[123]

All of this may beg, however, the larger question of how exactly customary international law is made. This problem is particularly acute when one realizes that for most evolving rules of international behavior or conduct there is *no* consensus. Instead, there is a dynamic "struggle for law," in which countries are actively competing in a marketplace of rules.[124] A country might, by both its words and deeds, attempt to build support for a new custom. Other nations might join this bid. Another group of countries might actively resist the creation of a new norm. They might lodge diplomatic protests and – in extreme circumstances – actually undertake affirmative steps to block the formation of a new practice or, at a minimum, to deny that new usage the legitimacy of *opinio juris*.

REGIONAL AND SPECIAL CUSTOM; ACQUIESCENCE AND OBJECTION

International tribunals have developed some definitive methods for identifying an emerging custom under these conditions of conflict and competition. It is important to appreciate these approaches because they illustrate not only the practical reality of custom as a source of international law, but also show how the ICJ and international advocates can use custom to achieve different sorts of client objectives and decisional outcomes. The best way to understand these approaches to custom is by comparing two cases decided by the World Court.

The first of these, The *Asylum* Case,[125] implicated a most peculiar custom. The case arose when a Peruvian military leader, Victor Raul Haya de la Torre, took refuge in the Colombian embassy in Lima after leading an unsuccessful coup attempt. Elsewhere in the world, this would have resulted in a very long stay for Haya de la Torre, for while all nations respect the inviolability of foreign embassy premises, there is certainly no rule requiring a host state to allow a political refugee safe passage out of the embassy, out of the country, and to the asylum state. Nowhere, that is, except Latin America, where a regional custom of diplomatic asylum evolved.

Imagine, then, the surprise of the Colombian authorities, who, after waiting a decent interval, made what they assumed was a *pro forma* request to Peru to grant Haya de la Torre safe passage to Colombia. The Peruvians turned them down flat, asserting that they were not bound by the regional custom of diplomatic asylum. And the Court ultimately took Peru's side in the dispute, ruling that the regional custom was not binding.[126] As in *The LOTUS* Case, once it became clear that Colombia bore the burden of showing that Peru's conduct violated international law (as opposed to Peru being required to explain its actions), the result was inevitable.

The most significant aspects of this case were the ICJ's treatment of a state's reaction as proof of its opposition to the formation of a custom and its discounting of regional custom as a source of international law. What the Court ruled was that where a regional (as distinct from a global) custom was concerned, silence on the part of the state in the face of an emerging practice meant that the state objected or protested to the rule. In short, a silent or ambiguous response meant rejection. This was contrary to the general presumption that states were obliged to protest loud and often if they wished to avoid being bound by a rule of emerging global custom.

Why, then, did the World Court change the calculus of consent for regional custom in The *Asylum* Case? One can only conclude that the Court wished to suppress regional custom, and there is no more effective way to do so than to declare a presumption that fundamentally disrupts the formation of such regional practices. While the ICJ has no qualms about applying rules derived from regional (or at least nonglobal) treaties, it was concerned that development of distinctive bodies of regional rules – not just for Latin America, but perhaps also for Europe, Africa, and Asia – might unduly interfere with the universal aspirations of international law. More pertinently, the allowance of easy-to-make regional customs might also challenge the institutional role of the World Court as a place for authoritative pronouncements on international legal rules. I speculate this because in an analytically similar case, *Right of Passage Over Indian Territory*, decided by the Court in 1960,[127] the ICJ reached a very different conclusion.

The problem raised in that dispute was Portugal's asserted right to be able to transit both civil administrators as well as troops and munitions from the Portuguese colony of Goa (on the coast of India) to little Portuguese-controlled enclaves in the interior of India. It was the late 1950s – a critical time for the process of decolonization around the world – and India made no pretense of its desire to drive the last vestiges of colonialism from the Indian subcontinent. So the Indian authorities denied Portugal's right of passage, assuming (correctly) that if the enclaves could not be resupplied they would be ripe for the picking.

The ICJ could have decided the dispute as a matter of global custom: whether there was some inherent right of passage by one nation over the territory of another, especially in situations where part of one nation's territory was completely surrounded by another. The judges on the Court declined to undertake this analysis, and one can hardly blame them. It would have been a daunting and difficult task of collecting many centuries of state practice over many continents in order to derive a set of global customary rules for these situations.

Instead, the World Court chose to limit the Lens of the analysis to an exceedingly narrow shutter. The question became whether Portugal and India (and its predecessors, the British and Maratha rulers) had developed a special, or local, custom allowing Portuguese right of passage. The Court sifted through evidence of the course of dealing between the two sides, developed over many centuries. The ICJ ultimately concluded that Portugal's right of passage for civil administrators was binding custom on India, although India retained the right to exceptionally suspend such passage. But as for a right to move troops and weapons over Indian territory, previous permissions to do so had been "mere" comity or courtesy, and in so lacking *opinio juris*, it failed as a custom.[128]

The Court essentially decided in *Right of Passage* and its 1952 *Nationals in Morocco* opinion[129] that it was futile to declare a global custom in a case where it was easier to simply describe and characterize a "course of dealing" between the two parties to the dispute. And in using a special custom – which can be analogized to commercial courses of dealing discussed in Chapters 7 and 10, or local property customs explained in Chapter 6[130] – the Court resorted to the typical presumption that silence in the face of an emerging practice means acquiescence or acceptance. In these bilateral situations, it appears especially incumbent on states to protest if they are unhappy with the legal positions taken by their neighbors.

For example, in the 1951 *Anglo-Norwegian Fisheries* Case,[131] the United Kingdom and Norway contested access to fisheries off the Norwegian coast. Norway had attempted to claim ocean areas through some creative cartography: by drawing "straight baselines" from points along its rugged coastline and asserting that the enclosed areas were exclusive Norwegian fisheries. Norway's zealous "bidding" of a straight-baseline rule, combined with Britain's lack of effective (and well-documented) protests in the early 1900s, meant that Britain had waived its subsequent objection.[132] The Court indicated that Norway's straight-baseline rule was thus not "opposable" by the United Kingdom.

In the Court's divergent treatment of regional custom and local (or special) custom, one also has two very different models of the role of CIL in the settlement of international disputes. In The *Asylum* Case, the ICJ was emphatic in asserting that it was its prerogative to declare the content of customary international law, not only for the benefit of the parties to the case, but, more importantly, to the global community at large. And whenever the ICJ takes on the difficult task of defining principles of global custom, it is as much to declare what the law is as to settle a dispute. But in *Right of Passage*, one observes a far more modest (and typical) role for the Court: simply settling a dispute, without making great pronouncements. That is why, in such situations, recourse to special custom and to the very particular course of dealing between two nations is so very attractive for the ICJ.[133] Essential to either approach is the Court's understanding of the role of consent in making customary rules.

If one regards this pattern of assumptions and presumptions about the formation of customary international law as troublesome, one would be correct to be concerned. It would seem that, with the exception of regional custom, fortune favors those states that aggressively stake out new rules and hope that other nations simply do not notice or fail to act in a timely or compelling manner. Aside from the basic question of what constitutes an effective protest of an emerging custom, how can one know whether a new practice is successfully supplanting an old usage? One could, I suppose, look at the extent, frequency, and consistency of departures from old customs and tally the numbers of states that adhere to one rule or the other, or try to trace a linear progression as states shift from one practice to another.

That leaves the question of how states can effectively "opt out," or block the application of a customary rule. While the formation of customary obligations can be foiled by a lack of duration or consensus in the practice, or the occasional denial of *opinio juris*, once a usage has gained momentum, it is hard to stop. The general presumption is that unless a state has persistently objected during the process of crystalizing a customary norm, it will be held to that rule, even if it later regrets or denounces the norm in question.[134]

This is perhaps the decisive feature of the customary regime in international law. It means that states are obliged to protest loud and often if they wish to avoid being bound by a norm of emerging global custom. Subsequent objections to an already formed custom are likely to be ineffective, and the only way for a state to liberate itself from a CIL obligation is to demonstrate that the norm has been superseded or entered desuetude.[135] But it is worth observing that, with the exception of the acquiescence of coordinate branches of government in constitutional separation-of-powers disputes,[136] in no other domain of customary law is persistent objection by a particular actor in a legal community entertained as a ground for refusing to enforce a custom.[137] Public international law thus has two peculiar features for customary norms: They may be objected to by a vociferous minority, but, once acceded to, they may not (apparently) be breached, except in the absence of a new rule.

Moreover, these general presumptions for global custom seem unfair. They expect that all countries in the world have minions of international lawyers in their employ who have nothing better to do than closely monitor what other nations are "bidding" and "claiming" as new rules of custom, and then effectively protest them.[138] The reality of legal staffing for foreign ministries around the world is quite different. Nevertheless, it has always been understood that customary international law could never really develop if it required the affirmative and express consent of nations to produce a binding state practice.[139] Hence, the general assumption is that, for global custom, silence means acceptance of a new rule.

The structure of customary law is thus skewed in favor of rule formation, at least once a magic threshold has been crossed. Persistent objection can thus be difficult to sustain.[140] As the International Law Association has reported, the persistent objector rule

> respects States' sovereignty and protects them from having new law imposed on them against their will by a majority; but at the same time, if the support for the new rule is sufficiently widespread, the convoy of the law's progressive development can move forward without having to wait for the slowest vessel.[141]

Tribunals will occasionally allow states to silently abstain from a usage (or to substitute another rule), and if other interested nations themselves fail to object, that lack of "opposability" might have the same effect as a successful persistent objection.[142] But this is a strategy fraught wish risk, and the dynamic of tacit acceptance and persistent objection best describes the formation of CIL.

CUSTOMARY INTERNATIONAL LAW AND TREATIES

Profound tensions can arise between rules based on treaties and those based on CIL. As has already been observed, in ICJ Statute Article 38's canonical (and delphic) statement of the sources of international law, no hierarchy is imposed.[143] Custom and treaty are co-equal sources of international obligation. The relationship between CIL and treaties is thus every bit as complex as the interplay of custom and statutes in domestic law.

One such problem is presented where a state deliberately does not become party to a treaty, but it is nevertheless asserted that it has become bound to a custom codified or progressively developed in that agreement.[144] This was the situation in the *North Sea Continental Shelf* Cases,[145] where Denmark and The Netherlands asserted that the Federal Republic of Germany was bound to a rule of equidistance in delimiting their respective continental shelves, even though Germany had purposefully not signed the 1958 Convention on the Continental Shelf. Needless to say, Germany had declined to sign that instrument precisely because adoption of the equidistance rule would have had disastrous consequences for its legal claim to offshore oil and gas in the North Sea.[146]

The ICJ ruled that the equidistance rule – unlike the basic concept of a nation's claim to a continental shelf – was a progressive development, and not a codification of existing custom. Holland and Denmark could not, thereby, assert that the equidistance rule contained in the 1958 Convention had quickly matured into a custom (the dispute arose in the mid-1960s, and was decided in 1969). This saved Germany from proving that it had persistently objected to the new custom, as distinct from merely rejecting the treaty.[147]

The important thing to remember here is that a rule can develop through a parallel evolution in both treaties and custom.[148] Even though a country rejects a treaty provision containing a rule, if it fails to object as that same norm is renewed in state practice, it will later become bound to it.[149] For example, in the *A/18 Decision* rendered by the Iran-United States Claims Tribunal in 1984,[150] the issue was whether dual nations of both the United States and Iran could bring claims. Iran stoutly resisted such a move and argued that as a matter of construing the Tribunal's constituent document, the 1981 Claims Settlement Declaration (CSD),[151] such claims were precluded. But the Tribunal held, in construing the ambiguous provisions of the CSD, that a rule of allowing dual national claims (provided they were brought by individuals having a "dominant and effective" nationality of the opposing state) *was* allowed by CIL. And, as evidence of that customary norm, the Tribunal relied on treaties to which Iran was not a party, suggesting that the rule was nonetheless incorporated into custom. This analytical approach was identical to the ICJ's earlier ruling in the 1955 *Nottebohm* Case.[152] Moreover, in the Court's 1986 *Nicaragua (Merits)* Judgment, it was expressly held that the incorporation of a norm into a treaty does not exclude its parallel existence and application in CIL.[153]

And if treaty rules and custom can converge, they can also clash. Despite the fact that more and more areas of international law are being governed by rules contained in international agreements, it would be profoundly mistaken to believe that in case of conflict, custom will be trumped by treaty. Indeed, a number of diplomatic incidents and tribunal decisions have given customary international law norms precedence over treaty rules.[154] In diplomatic correspondence between the United States and United Kingdom, just before America's entry into World War I,[155] the United States successfully protested the British practice of stopping U.S. vessels and arresting German nationals. Britain justified this practice based on an extensive network of treaties, but the United States relied on a customary rule granting immunity to neutral vessels. Absent an explicit agreement between Britain and the United States sanctioning such arrests, the United States was correct to rely on custom. By contrast, in the *S.S. WIMBLEDON* Case, the World Court (in its first case)[156] was faced with a collision between customary principles of neutrality and treaty-based rules of access to an international canal. The PCIJ opted for the treaty and compelled Germany to grant passage through the Kiel Canal to a vessel carrying munitions to Poland, then engaged in a war with the Soviet Union. Germany was thus caught in a classic "whipsaw." By satisfying its obligations under the Treaty of Versailles, it was violating its customary international law obligation of neutrality to the Soviets, which was *not* a party to Versailles.[157]

But there is a fundamental evidentiary problem when a CIL norm is sought to be proven from contrary treaty provisions. Ironically enough, it has been domestic courts that have observed this paradox, often using an idiom of general principles of customary law. For example, the Irish Supreme Court observed in a 1951 case that it did "not accept the view that a principle of [customary] international law can be established [by citing treaties] – at least where the principle sought to be established is contrary to, or qualifies, an existing rule."[158] Even more pointed was the English Court of King's Bench ruling in *West Rand Central Gold Mining*:

> the reference ... to stipulations in particular treaties as evidence of international law is as little convincing as the attempt... to establish a trade custom... by adducing evidence... of particular contracts..... We have already pointed out how little value particular stipulations in treaties possess as evidence of that which may be called international common law.[159]

In the synergistic relationship between treaties and CIL, it is sometimes quite difficult to discern when international agreements (especially bilateral instruments or multilateral treaties with relatively few adherents) are simply "bidding" a new norm or when they truly are codifying already existing custom.

But the dynamic does not even end with a successful codification effort. Just because a norm is enshrined in a treaty does not necessarily mean that the parallel custom withers away and dies. State practice presumably continues and holds the potential for supervening even the codificatory treaty.[160] And, as already discussed, it is clear that treaty provisions can be construed in accordance with "any relevant rules of international law applicable in the relations between the parties,"[161] which would (of course) include CIL. Far more controversial is the notion that an earlier treaty's provisions may be expressly modified by customary developments. The U.N.'s International Law Commission actually proposed a clause on this issue,[162] but it was ultimately not included in the 1969 Vienna Convention on the Law of Treaties (VCLT).

Nevertheless, state practice is replete with examples of countries recognizing that their previous treaty obligations have been altered by supervening norms of customary international law.[163] And, in at least a few decisions by international tribunals, the role of newly formed CIL has been recognized.[164] Indeed, this has been controversial in the work of the Iran-U.S. Claims Tribunal in the context of its expropriation jurisprudence. In a number of cases, U.S. companies seeking relief for the taking of their properties in Iran during the Islamic Revolution relied on the relevant provisions of a 1955 Treaty of Amity between the two nations,[165] articulating the standards of compensation in such circumstances. Iran argued that the 1955 Treaty provisions had been supervened by a more forgiving standard of compensation embodied in customary international law. At least one Tribunal decision appeared to examine supervening developments in the CIL of expropriation and compensation, if only to conclude that the 1955 Treaty standard and the CIL norm were identical.[166]

In a similar vein, a series of World Court cases construing the United Nations Charter eerily parallel the U.S. Supreme Court's separation-of-powers jurisprudence.[167] For example, in the 1971 *Namibia* Advisory Opinion, the ICJ essentially ruled that Charter Article 27(3)'s formulation on the effect of abstentions in the Security Council had been conclusively modified by the practice of that body.[168] Even more extraordinarily, in the 1962 *Certain Expenses* Opinion – which featured a true separation-of-powers dispute, pitting the U.N. Security Council against the General Assembly – the Court ruled that the practice of the General Assembly in authorizing peacekeeping missions was an authoritative interpretation of Charter Article 17(2), and the Council had essentially acquiesced in the Assembly's assertion of power.[169] So, here we have instances of the customary practices of the organs of an international institution amending (or authoritatively construing) that organization's constituent instrument.

The last ground for potential conflict between treaties and custom is presented with *jus cogens* obligations. These are definitionally "peremptory norms" – rules of custom that may not be abrogated by treaty.[170] More specifically, the 1969 VCLT defines *jus cogens* rules as those "accepted and recognized by the international community of States as a whole as a norm from which no derogation is permitted and which can be modified only by a subsequent norm of general international law having the same character."[171] Like provisions of domestic contracts that are "void for public policy," treaties that violate *jus cogens* (such as an agreement sanctioning genocide or to enslave individuals or to engage in aggressive war[172]) are void when made, or, if a peremptory norm later develops in conflict, such an agreement is subsequently voidable.[173]

There are thus some rules of custom that are so significant that the international community will not suffer states to "contract" out of them by treaty. *Jus cogens* norms can thus bind states that have expressly withheld their consent to that custom.[174] The only domestic-law analogy to CIL's *jus cogens* doctrine would be the notion that a statute could enter desuetude by virtue of a supervening custom. This tantalizing scenario has been previously considered in this volume, but, aside from the recognition of the possibility in Roman canon law sources and scholarly writings,[175] and very occasional modern judicial decisions,[176] it has hardly registered as a serious jurisprudential possibility. Until now, that is.

Likewise, some customary international law obligations are so significant that the international community will permit *any* state to claim for their violation, not just the countries immediately affected. These are *erga omnes* norms.[177] *Erga omnes* norms are analytically distinguished from *jus cogens* rules, inasmuch as the former is a rule of "standing" and thus the underlying custom can be subject to persistent objection and to more easily executed modification (through the creation of supervening regional or special custom).[178] Moreover, the set of norms encompassed within the set of obligations *erga omnes* may be different, and wider, than *jus cogens* rules.[179] Or, put another way, all *jus cogens* norms are *erga omnes* obligations, but not vice versa.

Accordingly, we have some principles of customary international law that seem to transcend state consent and are seemingly immune from the "bidding" and "blocking" process of objection. Indeed, the *jus cogens* doctrine appears to have been developed as the ultimate antidote to the persistent objector,[180] and especially the white-minority government of South Africa's legalistic defense of its apartheid policies from 1945 to 1994. How these particular rules of "super-custom" are designated and achieve the exceptionally high level of international consensus they require is, however, a bit of a mystery.[181] And, not surprisingly, the whole intellectual project of *jus cogens* norms as some form of natural law "super-custom" has been viciously attacked in the academic literature[182] and by some governments.[183] But it also has been surprisingly robust, with an intellectual pedigree that ties the human rights revolution of the post–World War II era to the natural law traditions of the discipline.[184]

CHANGE AND DEATH FOR CUSTOMARY INTERNATIONAL LAW

The paradox of *jus cogens* thus places in sharp relief the positivist basis of CIL, at least as conceptualized from the time of Francisco Suárez. *Jus cogens* is simply entrenched CIL, a customary rule of a "higher normativity"[185] that enshrines "fundamental or cardinal principle[s]"[186] of international order. *Jus cogens* norms are, in a sense, "constitutionalized." But they are not immutable, as the 1969 VCLT acknowledged.[187] And, yet, that leads to broader – and even more intractable – problems of how a norm of CIL, once formed, later is modified or terminated in application or effect. Put simply, how can there be *desuetudo* for custom (*consuetudo*)?[188]

One myth, derived from the Roman law conception of custom,[189] is that, once born, a norm of customary international law can never die.[190] But this is "a wholly erroneous belief,"[191] and is refuted in state practice – custom can evolve over time. The opposite line of argument is that every act contrary to an existing custom "contains the seeds of a new legality," and that "each deviation contains the seeds of a new rule."[192] Indeed, the ICJ in the 1986 *Nicaragua* judgment seemed to sanction this approach when it observed that instances of state conduct inconsistent with a particular customary norm could be treated not only as "breaches" of the rule, but also as "indications of the recognition of a new rule."[193] In this Freudian construct, every aberrant usage really is a "bid" for a new custom. As in psychoanalysis, however, sometimes a cigar really is just a cigar, and a violation of a CIL norm is just that – an unlawful act that does not really purport to establish a new rule.[194] Similarly, it surely cannot be enough for states to unilaterally declare that a custom is no longer real or binding.[195]

To unwind an existing custom, it must no longer be constituted by its essential ingredients – there must be a contrary state practice, and the old norm is no longer supported by *opinio juris*.[196] This more nuanced stance also has support in the *Nicaragua* judgment, when the Court noted that "[r]eliance by a state on a novel right or an unprecedented exception to the principle might, if shared in principle by other states, tend towards a modification of customary international law."[197] This may, however, beg the question of whether "a *lack* of state practice consistent with [a norm,] rather than directly contrary practice"[198] is what triggers desuetude for a custom. There is, however, a split among publicists as to whether, in order to complete the process of desuetude, the old custom must be entirely supplanted by a new one. Some authorities insist this must be so, if for no other reason than to avoid lacunae in CIL.[199] But others argue that "the evidence of the absence of general consensus in respect of a customary rule causes its disappearance even before the replacing customary rule has matured."[200]

Despite these disagreements, we can accept the notion that existing customs should not be lightly discarded. Indeed, there should be a higher threshold of uniformity, consistency, and volume of state practice in order to terminate "an old, well-settled customary rule,"[201] as opposed to creating a new one in a hitherto unregulated realm of international relations.

One can be agnostic on these questions but still believe, as Judge Jiménez de Aréchega noted in his separate opinion in the 1982 *Tunisia-Libya Continental Shelf* Case, that it cannot be enough to subvert an existing custom by vague or inchoate statements[202] – "in order to have this abrogating effect the new rule must necessarily partake of the nature of a rule of customary law. Only a legal rule may abrogate a preexisting one."[203] This statement was clearly intended as a complement to Kelsen's assertion that "[i]f a substantial number of states repeatedly and effectively violate a rule of custom, and particularly do so with the conviction that they are creating new law, it is difficult to maintain that the old law remains unimpaired."[204]

For an existing custom to enter desuetude, patterns of state practice really must change *or* there must be very clear evidence that the usage is no longer "accepted as law." Or, put another way, there are two ways to kill a norm of customary international law: divert the course of state practice or deprive the rule of its legitimacy via *opinio juris*.[205]

A NEW SYNTHESIS FOR CUSTOMARY INTERNATIONAL LAW

Of all the contemporary challenges to customary international law, the line of inquiry that suggests that CIL can never be a "real" source of international legal obligation can be most readily dispensed with. Although most recently popularized in the work of Jack Goldsmith and Eric Posner,[206] this critique of CIL obviously has, as its intellectual roots,[207] Hans Kelsen and H. L. A. Hart's two-edged attack on international law. Kelsen and Hart famously argued that, to the extent that custom plays any role in international legal obligation, it is a sign of a "primitive" legal order[208] and, even worse, a thinly disguised natural-ist one based on inchoate notions of "international morality."[209] Of course, as I have contended here, CIL really is an intensely positivist construct, and, far from being a "subordinate"[210] source of international legal obligation, is actu-ally quite central to current doctrinal debates.

Goldsmith and Posner take a different methodological tack, but their provi-sional[211] conclusion is still the same as Kelsen and Hart's: There can be no real legal obligations for states in following CIL rules. Using rational choice and game theory approaches,[212] Goldsmith and Posner posit four models of behav-ioral compliance with customary international law norms: coincidence of interest, coercion, cooperation, and coordination. Coincidence occurs when states follow a norm irrespective of the behavior of other nations.[213] Coercion occurs where strong states force weak nations to comply.[214] Cooperation and coordination occurs where states, out of pure self-interest and the expectation of reciprocity, observe a rule.[215] In none of these situations, Goldsmith and Posner assert, are norms being followed out of a sense of legal obligation.[216]

The flaw in this contention is not so much the game-theoretic perspec-tive (which may, as far as it goes, describe the dynamic of some state behav-iors[217]), but its fundamental assumption as to *why* states obey international law.[218] Using a hyperactively realist perspective on international relations,[219]

Goldsmith and Posner conclude that "[m]ainstream international law scholars would not view a behavioral regularity that arises from" their four models "as an example of customary international law."[220] For Goldsmith and Posner, to follow a CIL norm because of its inherent value (coincidence), or out of self-interest (cooperation and coordination), or even because of fear of negative consequences (coercion) is inimical with it being a *legal* rule.

That conclusion ignores the rich experience of functional cooperation in the international community. Whether one views function in Malinowski's sense of expected reciprocities for behavior[221] or through a wider lens, we realize that a state's compliance with a norm may begin with expectation, apathy, or (even) fear, but end with the certainty of legal duty. Functional cooperation between states and international actors is conditioned largely by forces that may have nothing to do with law. These might include developments in the international economy; movements of people, goods, and services; and the globalization of culture and intellectual life.[222] The phenomenon of functional legal cooperation between states has been overwhelmingly responsive or reactionary. International law has acknowledged the demands of international life, rather than anticipating or directing them. That is not entirely a bad circumstance; some of the signal failings of international law have arisen when lawyers and diplomats have moved ahead of the needs of the international community. International law is doctrinally most vulnerable – and most illegitimate – when it loses touch with its constituencies and function. So, Goldsmith and Posner's belief that there should be a schism between the "true" motivations of states in obeying CIL and their sense of legal obligation is no criticism at all. Or, put another way, one can be instrumental about the role of CIL in international relations[223] without falling into a realist trap that disclaims any proof of norm-compliance as evidence of an international legal obligation.

But just because customary international law easily escapes the clutches of the realist critique does not make it immune from other charges. Standard accounts of customary law – including CIL – laud its efficiency and nimbleness in incorporating into a legal system the actual behaviors and expectations of that system's constituents. As has been observed throughout this book, custom remains a powerful, if subliminal, source of law, even in "mature" legal systems. But public international law is not a fully mature legal system at all – aspects of it remain strikingly primitive, in the sense of being highly decentralized and institutionally undeveloped, not ineffective or unsophisticated.[224] And customary international law is supposedly a source of signal strength and flexibility for international law.[225] It allows international legal actors to informally develop rules of behavior without the necessity of resorting to more formal and difficult means of law-making (like treaties). Custom "tracks," or follows, the conduct of such actors as states, international institutions, transnational business organizations, religious and civic groups, and individuals involved in international matters.[226]

Indeed, CIL's ostensible efficiency appears to have been a primary motivation for its incorporation into Statute Article 38's formulation of the sources of international law. As Baron Descamps, president of the Advisory Committee of Jurists, noted in 1920: CIL is "a very natural and extremely reliable method of development [of international law] since it results entirely from the constant expression of the legal convictions and of the needs of the nations in their mutual intercourse."[227] But efficiency and "reliab[ility]" may have two very different meanings here. The extent to which CIL effectively tracks State behavior (the sense that Descamps employed) is a very different inquiry than whether a particular customary norm is rational or reasonable.[228]

As has already been observed,[229] a norm's reasonableness does not necessarily grant it the imprimatur of *opinio juris*. From this, some scholars have inferred that CIL is more forgiving in embracing unreasonable norms than any realm of domestic law, public or private,[230] where irrational customs are routinely struck by judges.[231] Among the factors that (in any legal community) would tend towards the promotion of efficient customs,[232] some are notably absent in international relations.[233] These are, most particularly, the lack of homogeneity among states in the international community and the unlikelihood that states will play reciprocal roles on most contentious issues (that is, find themselves routinely on both sides of the problem, such as being *both* buyers and sellers in a commercial transaction).[234] Nevertheless, CIL norms are most likely to flourish precisely in the interstices of international relations, where states have homogenous objectives and are likely to appreciate both sides of an issue in relatively *non*contentious circumstances.[235] While it may well be true that there is no prohibition on CIL's incorporation of irrational norms, such is a highly unlikely occurrence.

All of this may beg the larger implications of the efficiency paradox for CIL. Here, Goldsmith and Posner's critique hits closer to the mark. "Multilateral coordination problems," they argue, cannot "easily be solved in the informal, unstructured, and decentralized manner typically associated with customary international law."[236] This, of course, converts CIL's supposed signal strengths – its informal, unstructured, and decentralized character – into fatal flaws. But in an international legal system that already features many highly structured mechanisms for law-creation (such as functional international institutions, the International Law Commission, and treaty-drafting or -review diplomatic conferences), it certainly makes sense that there should also be an alternative set of processes. The dynamic of state practice and CIL offers the best hope for such an alternative to the glacial pace of treaty-making and sclerotic attempts at treaty enforcement,[237] application, and compliance.

At a time when customary international law is coming under simultaneous attack from both extreme positivists (who suggest that its processes are illegitimate and nontransparent[238]) and by those of a naturalist bent (who regard it as merely pandering to state interests[239]), it might be useful to recall that in some ways custom is the *most* positive and progressive of international law sources. It is certainly the most likely to track (although, as I just concede, a bit inelastically[240]) the actual behavior of international actors. The market aspect of customary norm-creation largely ensures that. Moreover, as Anthony D'Amato has observed, "[c]ustom is a dynamic process of law-creation, yet it is also a restraint on illegal dynamism."[241] So, any view of CIL "must provide for change and adaptation in customary law, yet it must also ensure enough stability...."[242]

That leads, inevitably, to an inquiry of whether customary international law is sufficiently transparent and legitimate. Transparency, of course, turns on whether the processes of CIL formation, modification, and termination are sufficiently visible to the participants in the international legal system. As has already been discussed, one of the ostensible virtues of CIL is that it depends on a robust and thick flow of signaling data of "bids" and "blocks" to customary norms. Whether all actors in the international community (both states and nonstate actors) can equally and effectively monitor this signal traffic – and intervene (when they deem necessary) with their own communications, claims, and conduct – is an open question. It does bear remembering that states definitionally control the levers of CIL creation and, in this process, occasionally engage in subterfuge and recourses to "constructive ambiguity" to obfuscate their intentions. But that is a natural part of diplomacy, and, make no mistake, the dynamic of customary international law is an adjunct to the essential processes of international relations.

Legitimacy captures broader substantive and process issues than the communication concerns embedded in transparency. As Thomas Franck famously observed: "[i]n any community organized around rules, compliance is secured – to whatever degree it is – at least in part by the perception of a rule as legitimate by those to whom it is addressed."[243] CIL's inchoate and indeterminate character has often been cited as a ground for denying it legitimacy.[244] Insofar as CIL norms do not (unless codified or embedded in authoritative decisions) ever have textual determinacy, nor necessarily a coherent and consistent content,[245] that also undermines customary international law's normative authority. These are fair criticisms, but, of course, apply to *all* customary law. They seem more relevant, and can be better employed, as challenges to whether particular norms qualify as custom in the first place.

Less serious is the critique that CIL processes lack "symbolic validation," in the sense that Franck used,[246] and would have been intuitively understood by writers as diverse as Blackstone, Malinowski, Llewellyn, and Hayek. While it may be quaint to refer to CIL processes in the argot of "rituals" and "symbols," the metaphor of custom as a "struggle for law" does nicely capture the inherent basis of CIL as exchanges of "signals," "cues," "bids," and "responses."[247] And although there is nothing of Hayekian "spontaneity" in today's fashioning of CIL norms, neither is there Blackstonian formalism. Rather, customary international law manages to validate the norms it endorses through a stable process of vetting, iterated by the constant interactions of players in the international system.

Customary international law may, however, suffer from a "democracy deficit," in the sense that powerful nations (larger "market players") are more likely to exercise substantial influence over the processes of its formation and revision than smaller or weaker nations.[248] This is nothing more than a restatement of the concern as which nations' practices matter most in the objective proof of usage for a custom.[249] Such a power differential applies also for adherence to various treaty regimes, and so might be a systemic concern with all international law-making.

There is another form of democracy deficit for customary international law. That is the positivist criticism that, to the extent that individuals, nongovernmental organizations, and international "civil society" are influencing the formation of CIL norms, and thus supplanting traditional state practice as the primary engine for CIL growth, customary international law has been hijacked by "cosmopolite" elites, which are not accountable to national populaces.[250] But this also rings false. As already indicated, the apparatuses of states are firmly in control of the levers of customary international law. Maybe the complaint really is that traditional state organs that participate in CIL formation (ministries of foreign affairs, diplomatic corps, and national parliaments) have been captured by "cosmopolite" elites and are not really democratically accountable. If so, then that charge tends to a condemnation that CIL caters too much to the interests of states, irrespective of how the "national interest" of each state is legitimately derived. In any event, that view condemns customary international law for doing its job *too* well: tracking the behavior of states and ordering that conduct in ways that are consistent with the interests of the international community.

Reports of the imminent demise of customary international law – which have been circulating for decades[251] – thus seem premature. It is highly unlikely that the treaty-making process in international law will ever completely supplant CIL,[252] even though (admittedly) more and more areas subject to exclusively customary regulation will be codified over time. And, as already observed here, codification is not an "end of history" for customary international law. It merely shifts it to a new ground of treaty construction and application, as well as the potential for new customary norms to emerge.

The crucial challenge for customary international law is to at once retain its dynamism and its legitimacy.[253] As I have tried to argue here, the traditional formula for CIL enshrined in Statute Article 38 is not a musty formalism or some artifact from the deep recesses of international law's intellectual history. Rather, the combined objective and subjective inquiries for CIL formation (state practice and *opinio juris*) remain the crucial algorithm for establishing whether a norm really rises to the level of international custom, and is thus deserving of recognition and enforcement. To dispense with, or relax, either of these requirements in a misguided attempt to increase CIL's dynamism and relevance (especially to pursue favored objectives, such as the promotion of human rights) would fatally undermine its legitimacy. Likewise, to abandon customary international law's strong positivist intellectual roots in favor of a new naturalism (whether expressed in the idiom of the "rationality" or "humanity" of favored norms) would also be folly. For that reason, and despite the manifest temptations, any attempts to expand the scope of the *jus cogens* and *erga omnes* doctrines must be restrained.

Within these theoretical limitations, I favor an approach to customary international law that emphasizes its diverse and robust (even combative) character. The processes of customary international law work best when all international actors realize that there is much at stake. That is why I have argued here for the continued embrace of the tacit acceptance (through acquiescence) of emerging CIL norms, so long as the privileged place of the persistent objector is recognized. This should apply to manifestations of global custom, as well as special or local custom, but not for regional custom. Just as we should remove structural impediments to the formation of CIL (even while rigorously observing the requirements of state practice and *opinio juris*), symmetry and legitimacy demand that the same process should be able to ratchet in reverse. Those norms that have outlived their usefulness and are no longer supported by either constituent ingredient for CIL should be accorded a decent burial.

There may well be reason to regard as exceptional customary international law's processes and dynamics. The international community of states (as distinct from the global community of private actors, considered in the last chapter) is surely unique as to the make-up of its constituents, the character of various CIL norms, and what is at issue for global order. Nevertheless, CIL remains a form of customary law, with all the strengths and weaknesses that we have observed in other domestic and international contexts. Whether one regards the international legal system as "primitive" or "mature" – or simply one in transition and facing great challenges – custom will remain a potent and influential source of obligation.

Conclusion

How and Why Custom Endures

Custom lives! It may not be the jurisprudential "king of all," as Pindar wrote, but customary law remains a key source of obligation, even in "modern" and "mature" legal systems. One has to know, however, where to find the subtle evidences of unofficial and unenacted norms, and a large part of this book has been an exposition of the role of customary law in contemporary doctrinal debates in various domestic polities, as well as in international law. There remain, however, some lingering questions and nagging concerns as to how custom lives today, its constituent elements, the limits of its applicability, and its ultimate status as a source of law.

FALSE CONSTRAINTS ON CUSTOM

Throughout this volume, some ideas have recurred that, acting singularly or together, purport to place strong limits on the role of custom in law. Most of these are, however, false or misleading, and it is worth summarizing why that is so.

The first of these – the purported distinctions in the application of custom in public- and private-law settings, and in domestic (as opposed to international) jurisdictions – is just unhelpful. Aside from the obvious point that the public/private divide has become as indistinct as the boundary between domestic and international law subjects,[1] it seems that customary law has thrived in the interstices of these divisions. Whether it is commercial law (which has strong domestic and transnational components) or family or property law (which each combines features of public and private law), customary norms have continued to flourish. As for the old canard that custom can only change private-law obligations (especially those sounding in property, contract, and torts) and never have any influence in the public-law realm, that has been demonstrably disproven here. Even if one were to discount the role of custom in public international law as "exceptional," that does not explain the role of customary norms in adjusting separation-of-powers disputes in U.S. constitutional law,[2] family law and gender equality cases in South Africa,[3] or property takings in Hawai'i or Oregon.[4]

A second source of confusion is the notion, derived from the Roman law *mos iudiciorum*,[5] that custom is just the practice of courts. Under this theory, the only relevant "community" for purposes of norm-formation are judges. Putting aside the implications of this as an expression of high positivism (which will be considered next), this is really a historic artifact of the debate as to the place of judges in the English common-law system.[6] It also reflects two very different definitions of custom. In England, the *consuetudo regni* ("custom of the realm") formed the basis of English common law.[7] It was analytically distinct as a source of law from the practices of discrete communities – whether of property holders in a specific locality or of merchants in a particular trade. This distinction should be obvious, but it isn't necessarily. Where common-law judges (as in Oregon[8]) have sought to conflate "local" customs with the "general" common law, jurisprudential problems have ensued.

In a related way, a problematic legacy for contemporary customary law is William Blackstone's authoritative statement of its scope in his 1765 *Commentaries on the Laws of England*. His elements of proof for a custom have exercised a strong influence on the Anglo-American law of property, contracts, and torts, even though they were surely intended to cover only local servitudes on land. Over the course of the last quarter-millennia, the Blackstonian conception of custom has been definitively transformed. Gone is the musty formalism, but, by the same token, absent also today is the inherent restraint and judicial caution that Blackstone expressed about judicial recognition (or refusal) of customary norms at variance with the general common law. While this transformation has certainly been seen in recent property-rights litigation in the United States, its real impact is likely to be felt in the realm of tort standards-of-care, especially in cases involving safety standards for sectors as diverse as shipping (as in *The T.J. HOOPER*) or medicine (as in *Helling v. Carey*).[9]

Blackstone, of course, is not the figure to blame for customary law's low jurisprudential standing at present. He merely codified and conflated the English common-law view of the subject. No, if there is intellectual villainy here, that can be laid at the doorstep of the likes of Alexander Hamilton,[10] John Austin,[11] Hans Kelsen,[12] and H. L. A. Hart.[13] While Hart famously disagreed with Austin's account of legal positivism,[14] they all seem in one accord on the issue of custom as a source of law. For Austin, custom definitionally lacks sovereign compulsion – he fervently believed that customary norms, as "bottom-up" law, were an oxymoron. Hamiltonian and Austinian "high positivism" has insinuated itself as the "modern view" of custom, and has led to it being dismissed as epiphenomenal, or worse, by various modern scholars.[15]

Kelsen and Hart's take on custom is more nuanced, but no less invidious. To describe (as Hart does) all customary law systems as "primitive" because they lack the mechanisms of secondary rules of recognition is a gross caricature. It was equally heedless of the subtleties and complexities of indigenous legal systems (say, in Nigeria or South Africa) and that of the community of nations. Hart's saving move of characterizing customary norms as "subordinate," insofar as they are informal private law-making, dependent on the whim of formal legal institutions,[16] is to damn custom with faint praise.

The fundamental error of Austinian high positivism or Hart's "custom as primitive law" thesis is the notion that community-based norms can never be successfully elaborated or enforced. As has been maintained throughout this book, custom is, indeed, a species of positive law-making and should not be confused with some naturalist expression of an exogenous moral or ethical value system. I acknowledge, however, that this book, inasmuch as it has sought to define the relationship of custom to law, has relied on the evidences of formal legal institutions (statutes, treaties, court and tribunal decisions) for its proof that custom remains a vibrant source of legal obligation. This methodology exposes me to the risk of blithely falling into the trap of conceding that a customary norm only matters when it is codified by a law-maker or recognized by a judge. According to this blend of Austin's and Hart's idioms, custom can never be self-executing; it always depends on sovereign actuation.

My response to this "modern" view of custom has proceeded on a few different tacks. First, and most obviously, there is nothing modern about this critique of custom at all. It is as old as the foundations of the Western legal tradition.[17] There has always been a definitive tendency by legal cultures that regard themselves as both "sophisticated" and "autonomous" (whether Roman or canon law at their apogees, or the Anglo-American common law of the nineteenth century) to regard customary norms with disdain. Precisely because of its inchoate and informal character, custom has often been viewed with hostility because it is seen to pose a threat to order and stability, especially to established legal institutions endowed with sovereign authority (legislatures and courts). "Law from the bottom" was certainly perceived by Austin as something profoundly threatening. Ironically enough, those that have espoused customary norms are rarely legal revolutionaries. Quite the opposite, in fact, as Edmund Burke and the adherents of the Historical School so vigorously maintained.[18]

Next, this volume's emphasis on "formal" recognitions of customary norms – whether through treaty or statutory enablements and codifications, or through judicial discussions and applications – has never meant to imply that custom cannot be robustly enforced without such official interventions. To the extent that there is empirical literature on informal enforcement of customary norms, I acknowledge that the results are mixed. Where one would expect effective enforcement to be highest – say, through trade associations policing their members' commercial practices[19] – it may not be. But in many other contexts reviewed in this book (including family law, torts, separation-of-powers, and public international law disputes), the degree of informal compliance with customary norms may be quite high. Further research is needed on this empirical angle of custom's informal enforcement, and such project designs (in order to produce coherent and correlatable results) may have to be limited to very particular norms in very specific legal domains.

This lack of data should not, however, detract from the main point here that irrespective of whether custom is enforced "formally" (through the traditional legal institutions of sovereign power) or "informally" (through unofficial, community-based agents), it *is* being recognized and applied. Indeed, Hart's point that sophisticated legal systems often co-opt private law-making and enforcement[20] is especially relevant because it acknowledges that the bright-line boundary between the sovereign's legal institutions and those of private legal actors is starting to become quite blurry. The institution of arbitration in transnational commercial disputes is certainly reflective of this.[21]

It needs also to be recognized that customary norms are "internalized" in many communities. The expectation that the only way they can be truly reflected is through external application is thus manifestly false. Whether it is communities of care-practitioners (introduced in Chapter 8) or the community of nations (see Chapter 11), norms have a tendency to find their own proper level of execution within any relevant community, irrespective of the character of the enforcement mechanisms available. All of this tend to belie the "modern" view of custom, which is dismissive of its role in law.

THE ELEMENTS OF CUSTOM

Much has been written here about the ingredients that create a binding customary norm. Throughout this volume, I have adhered to a fairly traditional account that what makes an enforceable custom is strong objective evidence of a community practice or usage, combined with a more subjective calculus of the norm's value as a legal obligation. I am mindful that this traditional formulation has been criticized in many different contexts. The dual "objective-subjective" inquiry may have rather less relevance for doctrinal domains such as family law and torts, where the nature of the relationships at issue is such that the motivations of community actors to follow particular standards of conduct are less decisive as to the value of the norm. It should be enough that constituents follow a rule, but for commercial and constitutional norms (both domestic and international), such motivations appear to matter a great deal. Suffice it to say, for the moment, that two ingredients are needed for customary law: objective usage and subjective value.

Before addressing the central paradox of custom's formation – whether the subjective "value" ingredient is best expressed in the idioms of compulsion, *opinio juris*, consent, reason, or utility – there are some incidental issues as to the objective proof of usage. One of these can easily be dispensed with. Despite custom's popular association with the antiquity of the norms it embraces, there is no contemporary justification for asserting that proof of a norm's usage depends on the age of the practice. Showing the great age of a usage was, ironically enough, never required in either Roman law or in the Roman Catholic Church's canon law.[22] It was only in the English common law's strident reaction to customary law, as reflected in the jurisprudence beginning in the early sixteenth century, that a hard requirement for the antiquity of a custom came to be embraced.[23] Combining the English common-law concept of "legal memory" and strong notions of the continuity of a practice over a long period, Blackstone's temporal restrictions on custom[24] came to be viewed as the single greatest impediment to a customary norm's judicial recognition.

As I have already suggested, these antiquity bars on the formation of custom – as with the other elements of Blackstonian formalism – have long been hurdled. With the exception of the original context that Blackstone proposed (local servitudes on land), no other area of law has sought to limit the application of customary norms to those than can be proven to be of great age. That is not to say, of course, that proof of a long and continuous duration of a usage will not greatly aid in the objective showing of the necessary community practice. But it is by no means decisive, as has been shown for various commercial norms,[25] separation-of-powers disputes,[26] and particular examples of "instant" customary international law.[27]

So, the objective proof of a practice has really boiled down to generalized evidence of a certain norm's consistent observance by a critical mass of community participants over a statistically significant period. Certainty, duration, consistency, and widespread conformity appear to be the key elements for a usage. That leads to an issue of how individual community members can block the formation of an emerging customary norm, and thus exempt themselves from its subsequent application. As has already been noted,[28] with the exception of two purely public-law domains – separation-of-powers disputes in U.S. constitutional law and customary international law (CIL) – it is simply irrelevant whether a particular community member persistently objects to the formation of a new customary norm. Indeed, this may be the only issue for which there is any relevance of a public-law/private-law divide. It may well turn on the notion that when sovereign actors (states or their internal branches) are the relevant community-participant, we *do* care as to whether they might individually object to a new norm. Otherwise, an actor's refusal to follow a custom may be relevant for other purposes – say, as a particularized course of dealing in commercial transactions[29] – but does not otherwise block the formation of a community norm.

That leaves, of course, the question consistently mooted in this book: What defines that extra, subjective ingredient for custom? I have tried to narrate here an intellectual history on that question, and I must confess the results are somewhat indeterminate. Roman law tended to emphasize the consent of the relevant community embracing the practice.[30] Canon law introduced a naturalist vision of the reasonability and necessity of the usage.[31] English common law, as enshrined in Blackstone, espoused the "artificial reason" of judges in assessing the value of customs, while also, at the same time, speaking in an almost Austinian idiom of the "compulsion" of those who follow them.[32]

In addition to these historical traditions, there have been more recent innovations. The almost psychological inquiry of whether an actor follows a norm out of a sense of legal obligation resonates with Blackstonian compulsion and Roman law's *consensus omnium*. Yet, contemporary public international law's doctrine of *opinio juris* bears no real resemblance to antecedents in Roman law, canon law, the *ius commune*, or English common law. This is the strictest form of a subjective ingredient for custom, and it is entirely a modern invention. It sits as an oddity in the law of nations, and, perhaps, is the only thing that distinguishes the exceptional character of CIL. Also added to today's panoply of potential extra ingredients for customary practices are well-defined economic analyses of a norm's efficiency, as well as vague references to the social utility of a usage.

One would thus look in vain for a single answer to what makes a practice truly binding as a custom. As tempting as it would be to propose here a unified theory for custom's formation, such, alas, is impossible. It may well depend on the kind of norm at issue. For family and tort law, the social utility of the practice seems decisive. For commerce (both domestic and international), the economic efficiency of the trade usage matters in marginal cases of enforcement. For property law and truly local customs, the compulsory character of the norm is what counts. For both constitutional separation-of-powers and customary international law disputes, it appears that, at a minimum, the relevant actor's tacit consent or acquiescence is required.

This problem in isolating a key extra ingredient for a customary norm has broad jurisprudential implications. Where regimes of customary norms are truly autonomous of formal enforcement mechanisms, none of this matters, of course. It is only where the sovereign intervenes to statutorily enable or codify a custom, or (more likely) where a court is called upon to recognize and enforce it, that this becomes an issue. In this one way, then, all customary regimes remain captive to Austinian high positivism. Moreover, a wide degree of discretion is afforded to decision-makers wielding sovereign power in passing on the validity of customs. This analysis turns on a general calculus of economic efficiency or social utility, or a more particularized review of an actor's motivation or conduct in the face of a norm. In any event, legislators and judges generally feel themselves able to substitute their collective or individual judgment for that of the relevant community of norm-practitioners.

What is quite remarkable is how this discretion has been cabined – and how legislatures and judges have often avoided the temptation to subvert established customary law systems. As already noted, if contemporary courts and legislatures truly believed that custom was a threat to the rule of law, they would ruthlessly suppress it in all its manifestations. That they have not says much about custom's continued vitality. More importantly, it is by no means clear that sovereign legal institutions have the capacity to eradicate customary regimes, even if they really desired to do so. If anything, the search for the extra ingredient that makes a custom binding has its own set of social and historical constraints, and these are now firmly ingrained in the fabric of the law.

CUSTOM'S TRUE LIMITS

Despite my thesis that customary norms live as an authentic source of legal obligation, this volume has been no paean to custom. Customary regimes operate within definite restraints. These must be recognized and accepted before reaching any final conclusions on the proper role of custom in law. Some of these constraints have only mild repercussions for the coherence of customary law; others pose more fundamental jurisprudential challenges.

For starters, it is clear that customary norms cannot today safely intrude into certain doctrinal domains. Despite the use of custom as a source of criminal sanction in preliterate societies,[33] no one seriously advocates the notion that unofficial and unenacted norms should be the basis of substantive criminal liability in any society. Ironically, the only exception to this rule – the continued influence of CIL norms in international criminal law – has been immensely controversial. At the Nuremberg and Tokyo trials of the top German and Japanese military and political leadership after World War II, one of the crucial counts against some of the defendants was the "planning, preparation, initiation or waging of a war of aggression."[34] But it was by no means clear that at the outbreak of hostilities that a firm international consensus, as evidenced through CIL, had developed against aggressive war. When these counts were challenged by the defendants as impermissible *ex post facto* criminal liability, such objections were brushed aside. What is most surprising is that the Nuremberg Tribunals held that there was no positivist limit on using custom as a source of criminal liability in such circumstances.[35] This approach has been extended by more recent international humanitarian law tribunals, such as those for the genocides in Rwanda and the former Yugoslavia.[36]

Even though custom's role in deterring and punishing wrongdoers has diminished over time, one criticism of customary norms does not appear to want to fade away. That is the issue of atavistic, irrational, or just strange customs. A perennial worry for any legal system that seriously entertains customary norms is that "bad" customs will be encouraged to thrive. Judges and economists (sometimes, as with Richard Posner,[37] one and the same) wring their hands about this.

They need not fret. If there is any positive legacy of Blackstonian formalism it is that common-law judges have learned – like pigs in Provence – to sniff out and devour unpalatable customs. Whether it is an analysis of social utility that drives modern-day repugnancy determinations for customary family law norms in Africa,[38] or a calculus of economic efficiency and unconscionability for commercial usages,[39] or cost-benefit determinations of accident prevention standards-of-care in tort,[40] it seems unlikely that truly "bad" customs will long persist. Indeed, when customs have been struck (whether on constitutional, statutory, or common-law reason grounds), there has usually been nary a protest by the community concerned. Furthermore, where there is even a hint that a customary norm is being purportedly applied to the detriment of an individual who is not really a member of the relevant community that accepted it – the proverbial "stranger to the custom" – the custom will be ignored. That is as it should be.

It just seems extravagant to suppose that customary legal systems readily countenance dysfunctional norms. If anything, such systems may err too much in favor of a golden mean of rationality and not be as forgiving as they might with the outlying conduct of certain actors. This was certainly a phenomenon with African customary law[41] and has been seen in other contexts in this study.[42]

There is a definitive tension in customary law systems between freedom and conformance. One of the posited virtues of custom is that norms are made by community participants and not by some sovereign overlord. In the constitutional mythology of English common law, custom was always equated with the essential liberties of the people.[43] This has been perpetuated in the writings of Friedrich Hayek, who emphasized the "spontaneous order" and "law of liberty" created by customary (or, at least, nonstatutory) legal regimes.[44]

This is all a needlessly romantic gloss on custom, and may well ignore its "dark side." As Richard Posner has explained,[45] enforcement of informal customary norms definitionally reduces human freedom, inasmuch as freedom of choice is deflected from individual discretion to that of a group. That, of course, is the price of all norms of human conduct. It really should make no difference whether a rule is being imposed by a formal, sovereign institution or an informal, customary one. In some contexts reviewed in this study,[46] custom has manifested itself as a very purposeful expression of communitarian values at the expense of civil rights and individual liberties, especially rights in property and freedoms of association. Just because custom is made by communities, that should not make all customary norms communitarian or majoritarian in character.

That leads to a related concern of whether custom is a truly democratic and legitimate source of legal obligation. At least in preliterate and early modern societies, there was a substantial concern that customary regimes were actually the product of institutional elites, and were often wielded at the expense of the masses.[47] We have even seen instances of custom being confected into an "invented tradition" and abused by colonial governments, minority regimes, or just tyrannical rulers.[48] The overwhelming evidence of this study is, however, that custom was – and remains – a popular mechanism for law-making. As transmitted to us within the Western legal tradition – through Roman law, the *ius commune*, civilian systems, and English common law – customary regimes still retain their inchoate and amorphous character as "bottom-up" law-making. And while the levers of this law-formation process are certainly susceptible to being hijacked by elite forces or particularly powerful actors (as was seen in certain commercial law and tort contexts[49]) or by states where they are the constituents of the relevant community (as in the law of nations[50]), these are the exceptions that prove the rule of custom's popular character.

Is custom a legitimate form of law-making in contemporary democratic societies? Putting aside CIL's legitimacy in the unique discourse of public international law (just discussed in the last chapter[51]), custom's consistency with the ideals of democracy under the rule of law does not appear to be seriously questioned today. In a clichéd sense, custom is pure democracy at work: the "people" making their own "laws" without recourse to "formal" institutions or impediments. That goes too far, of course. Custom is typically made by discrete and insular communities, and can sometimes reflect norms at sharp variance with society at large.

Customary regimes flourish, however, in pluralistic legal environments, or at least those open to tolerable variances in legal obligations. Legal cultures derived from English common law (which have been central for this book's case studies[52]) have been generously pluralistic in this sense. Contemporary jurisdictions from the civilian tradition, especially those that have embraced a highly centralizing (and commanding) role for law, have been somewhat less tolerant in this regard,[53] although that is matter for further research and empirical study.

To use another idiom, custom is certainly consistent with democratic institutions, at least those that have come to appreciate and address the majoritarian dilemma. Pluralism offers one antidote to that, and the presence of customary legal regimes offers a useful escape valve from what may become insuperable problems of minority rights, or even separatism. What degree of variance from majority norms can a customary regime sustainably support, and which will be tolerated? In a world of Austinian high positivism – or pure republicanism (as distinct from democracy) – the answer would turn on the whim of the sovereign's own legal institutions: Custom can survive only to the extent that legislators or judges allow it. As has been seen repeatedly in this volume, however, customary regimes have been perpetuated without any real statutory enablement (as with commercial custom[54]) and only occasional judicial recognition. So, consistent with the pluralistic character of custom, relatively high degrees of variance with majority norms are possible – and permissible.

Then there is the ultimate constraint for custom: its capacity to change with the times. This problem was mooted in Roman law, expounded upon by canon law scholars, debated by such English common-law figures as Coke and Blackstone, and today features prominently in the writings of scholars as diverse as Bronislaw Malinowski, Friedrich Hayek, and Richard Posner. The oft-suggested criticism of customary regimes – that they are glacial in their response to social and economic imperatives – has not been borne out in the sources reviewed or case studies presented in this book. Even in the realm of customary family law norms – where one might expect the greatest resistance to change because at issue are "fundamental" values of gender roles, wealth transfers, and family functions – that has not necessarily been the case. This has been witnessed through legal evolutions in South Africa.[55] If anything, what has been demonstrated here is that norms can fluidly change within customary legal systems. This is particularly so in response to economic or business conditions (as with commercial customs) or emerging standards of care to avoid accidents (as in tort law). What takes time, it seems, are the *external* recognitions of such altered practices, usually through judicial decisions that acknowledge that a customary norm has changed in the face of new circumstances.

That brings us to the problem of codification. At the outset, a crucial distinction needs to be made between a statute that enables the development or recognition of a customary law regime as distinct from a law that actually codifies a specific and substantive customary norm. Uniform Commercial Code section 1–205[56] and its treaty analogues in the sphere of transnational commercial usages[57] are examples of enabling instruments. England's 1832 Prescription Act and South Africa's Recognition of Customary Marriages Act are obvious examples of "pure" codification statutes.[58]

As has been made clear throughout this book, not even a purely codificatory instrument – one that purports to transcribe and enact a previously unwritten and unofficial customary norm – really ends a custom. It does shift enforcement of the norm to a statutory basis and the application of the norm to the realm of statutory construction.[59] As is seen most prominently in the realm of public international law,[60] it is entirely possible to imagine a norm being recognized and enforced on two tracks. The first is through its statutory or treaty form. The second is through its continuing character as a custom. There are strong synergies between these two paths, with the continuing custom being used as the yardstick by which the codification is measured. As the Roman jurist, Paul, observed: "custom is the best interpreter of statutes."[61]

Can custom supervene a formal legislative enactment, whether a statute or treaty? This tantalizing question of statutory or treaty desuetude in the face of contrary custom has preoccupied the speculations of scholars for millennia. Finding true examples of such desuetude in actual practice is extremely difficult. Aside from Pliny's narration of the Emperor Trajan's dilemma,[62] Lord Justice Bowen's ruling in the 1885 case of *Perry v. Barnett*,[63] and the U.S. Supreme Court's 1915 opinion in *Midwest Oil*,[64] the historical record is bereft of desuetude in domestic law systems. It is only in the realm of public international law that modification of treaties by supervening custom, along with the doctrine of *jus cogens*, makes custom a truly coequal source of legal obligation.[65] In all other contexts, custom must be viewed – as H. L. A. Hart surmised[66] – as a "subordinate" source of law.

CUSTOM'S DEEP JURISPRUDENTIAL FOUNDATIONS

All of the foregoing may account for *how* custom endures, but does not necessarily explain *why*. The whole notion of "bottom-up" law-making is, at once, intuitive and appealing for anyone who lives and works within communities of legal actors, and yet deeply unsettling for those who cleave deeply to strongly positivist positions as to the legitimacy and authority of legal rules. The reason why customary norms and customary law remain durable features of many contemporary legal systems lies at the intersection of two sets of insights – one jurisprudential, the other practical.

As Part One of this book narrated, there is no single jurisprudential explanation for custom. There are many, and together they combine to give customary norms the symbolic validation and legitimacy they require to endure. One strand of thought that justifies custom is functionalism. Whether in the argot of Jeremy Bentham or Bronislaw Malinowski,[67] this is the idea that people respect customary norms because of reciprocity and the expectation of social gain. Another line of thought, generated by both anthropologists (such as Max Gluckman[68]) and socioeconomists (like Ronald Coase, Richard Posner, Richard Epstein, and Richard Craswell[69]), is that the human impulse towards following customary norms is generated in direct relation to their utility, rationality, and efficiency. Lastly, there is the whole bundle of positivist positions – fashioned through the Western legal tradition and the English common law – that have sustained custom as a source of legal obligation for millennia.

The confluence of these intellectual streams – functionalism, rationalism, and positivism – is what has given custom its enduring character. Positivist attacks on custom gain little traction in the face of strong functional-reciprocal and rational-utility justifications for a norm. Likewise, even when a norm lacks either a reciprocal basis of obligation or a very compelling efficiency ground, it can still be legitimized by a countervailing justification. All of this helps to explain why the search for the "extra ingredient" that transmutes mere practices into binding customs can sometimes be so elusive. As already noted here, the jurisprudential basis for that extra element really reduces either to the expectation that others will also follow a norm (reciprocity) or that the norm is inherently useful or efficient (reasonableness). There can be no single basis for what makes a general practice into a legal custom, for the same reason that there is no unitary jurisprudential ground for custom.

This book has likewise offered three sets of practical insights for custom's endurance. One of these has just been mentioned: Custom thrives in legal cultures that are accepting of multiple sources of legal obligation and the possibility that different rules could be applied on the same facts to the same actors. Pluralism allows customary law regimes to "nest" in larger, more diverse legal systems. As acknowledged, this nesting is not always comfortable and natural tensions arise. As has been seen throughout this volume, these conflicts – whether as between different sets of customary norms or with a system's fundamental or constitutional values – are usually resolved in a way that at least allows the customary legal system to continue intact, even though particular norms may need to give way.

Another practical discernment raised in this book is that customary norms depend for their formation and propagation on communication between the members of the relevant law-making community. In the paradigmatic fields of private law – property, contracts, and torts – this communication feature is manifested in a process by which norms are "bid," "countered," "accepted," or "rejected."[70] Particularly in the realm of commercial law (both domestic and international) there should be a thick flow of signaling cues for the emergence of new customs, the modification of old rules, and the termination of outmoded norms. The doctrinal puzzle that is the application of customary norms to standards of care in tort law is precisely attributable to the fact that such information flows are often constricted and asymmetrically convey to the injured party the data needed to efficiently avoid accidents.[71] We also see this phenomenon in public law, whether manifested in strong principles of notice and acquiescence in U.S. constitutional separation-of-powers disputes[72] or in the persistent objector rule from the law of nations.[73]

The last practical sensibility advanced in this book is that customary law processes are just the most visible and palpable form of a wider "struggle for law" in many legal cultures. While this is certainly evident in the international community's formulation of CIL norms,[74] it has been seen and heard here in many other contexts as well. The content of customary norms *matter* for the community constituents concerned. Customary rules are often central to the lives of the participants. They can govern a person's most intimate relationships, the disposition of their property, their commercial livelihood, their safety and security, or the governance of their essential institutions. It is natural, therefore, that when the stakes are so high community members will struggle mightily to ensure that their individual, group, or collective interests are properly reflected in and protected through these customary norms. Whether it is the institution of polygynous marriages in South Africa, the breadth of native Hawai`ian property rights, the appropriate standards of care in medical malpractice cases, the recognition of what may be overreaching or unconscionable commercial usages, or the resolution of war powers disputes between the president and Congress, customary law can be contentious. The struggle for custom can define a legal culture.

Custom's pluralistic character, its actuation through signaling processes, and its sometimes confrontational stances, all contribute to its endurance. These peculiar qualities might be assumed as ways to distinguish custom from law or, to go even further, to argue that law and custom are inimical. This position has been espoused by a variety of scholars from a diversity of perspectives – including James Coolidge Carter, Karl Llewellyn and Adamson Hoebel, Richard Posner, and Robert Ellickson.[75] But I do not believe that custom is really "antilaw," some form of jurisprudential dark matter that will annihilate law upon contact. If battlelines are to be drawn, it has been to the advantage of both extremist camps – high positivists on the one side; communitarians on the other – to accentuate the differences between law and custom. But this is a false schism. If this study has shown anything, it is that customary norms can be successfully integrated into most legal systems.

Custom lives because it reflects the most essential impulses of social order under the rule of law. It serves as a vital counterweight to what are seen today as traditional, "top-down" legal sources, institutions, and doctrines. Customary regimes have often been perceived as a bulwark of liberty, or as the English poet and playwright, Charles Davenant, penned in 1677, "Custom, that unwritten law / By which the people keep even their kings in awe."[76] Custom is not only, as David Hume wrote, "the great guide of human life";[77] it is the ultimate repository of values for a legal culture. All of this is not to dispute, of course, that some customs – as with laws of any sort – are "[m]ore honored in the breach than the observance."[78] Even so, the real value of custom as a source of law, and its true role in contemporary legal systems, is the extent to which it successfully mirrors changing social expectations for norms of behavior and then channels those beliefs into legally cognizable rules of conduct. Customary law is all around us, and always will be. This book has offered a glimpse of where to look for it today and where it might be found tomorrow.

Notes

PREFACE

1. Herodotus, The Histories 186 (Robin Waterfield transl.; Oxford: Oxford Univ. Press, 1998) (passage iii.38) (quoting Pindar). For more on this passage, see Sally Humphreys, Law, Custom and Culture in Herodotus, 20 (1, 2) Arethusa 211 (1987).
2. See U.C.C. §§1–103, 1–205 (2004) (recognizing industry customs and trade usages).
3. See The T.J. HOOPER, 53 F.2d 107 (S.D.N.Y. 1931), aff'd, 60 F.2d 737 (2d Cir. 1932) (industry practice of using radios as evidence of seaworthiness).
4. See Dames & Moore v. Regan, 453 U.S. 654, 678–83 (1981) (using evidence of long-standing practice and interbranch acquiescence to sustain a presidential exercise of power).
5. This anecdote is drawn from my tribute to the memory of Harold J. Berman (1918–2007). See David J. Bederman, The Customary Law of Hal and Ruth, 57 Emory L.J. 1399 (2008).
6. See Chapter 1, at note 54 (for the view of R. F. Barton questioning "if custom can be presumed to have a theory").
7. See David J. Bederman, The Curious Resurrection of Custom: Beach Access and Judicial Takings, 96 CLR 1375 (1996) (material in Chapters 3 and 6); David J. Bederman, International Law Frameworks (2d ed.; New York: West Publishing, 2006) (material in Chapter 11).

1. ANTHROPOLOGY

1. See, e.g., A. S. Diamond, Primitive Law, Past and Present (London: Methuen, 3d ed. 1971); H. L. A. Hart, The Concept of Law 89–90 (Oxford: Clarendon Press, rev. ed. 1972 (with notes)) (referring to "primitive communities"); E. Adamson Hoebel, The Law of Primitive Man (Cambridge, Mass.: Harvard Univ. Press, 1954); K. N. Llewellyn & E. Adamson Hoebel, The Cheyenne Way: Conflict and Case Law in Primitive Jurisprudence (Norman: Univ. of Oklahoma Press, 1941); Bronislaw Malinowski, A New Instrument for the Interpretation of Law – Especially Primitive, 51 YLJ 1237 (1942).

2. See Bronislaw Malinowski, Crime and Custom in Savage Society (London: Routledge, 1926; rep. 1982).
3. See discussion in the preface, text at note 5.
4. See Sir Henry Sumner Maine, Ancient Law: Its Connection with the Early History of Society and Its Relation to Modern Ideas 16 (1861) (Ashley Montagu ed., Tucson: Univ. of Arizona Press, 1986) ("usage which is reasonable generates usage which is unreasonable. Analogy, the most valuable of instruments in the maturity of jurisprudence, is the most dangerous of snares in its infancy.").
5. See id. at 11–12 ("these aristocracies were usually the depositaries and administers of law"). See also Sir Carleton Kemp Allen, Law in the Making 120, 126–27 (Oxford: Clarendon Press; 7th ed., 1964) (glossing Maine). For the related work of Jeremy Bentham on primitive custom, see Gerald J. Postema, Bentham and the Common Law Tradition 309 (Oxford: Clarendon Press, 1986).
6. Hart, supra note 1, at 89–90.
7. See id. at 89–96.
8. See id. at 89–91.
9. See also id. at 244 (citing work of Diamond, supra note 1, at 260–70; Malinowski, supra note 2; and Llewellyn & Hoebel, supra note 1).
10. See Maine, supra note 4, at 15. ("The usages which a particular community is found to have adopted in its infancy and in its primitive seats are generally those which are on the whole best suited to promote its physical and moral well-being; and, if they are retained in their integrity until new social wants have taught new practices, the upward march of society is almost certain.") See also Sir Henry Maine, Village-Communities of the East and West (1871) (New York: Henry Holt, 1880 rep.); Sir Henry Maine, Dissertations on Early Law and Custom (New York: Henry Holt, 1883); Lon L. Fuller, Anatomy of the Law 82 (New York: Praeger, 1968) (reviewing Maine's account of legal anthropology).
11. See E. Sidney Hartland, Primitive Law 138 (London: Methuen, 1924). ("The savage is far from being the free and unfettered creature of Rousseau's imagination. On the contrary, he is hemmed in by the customs of his people, he is bound in the chains of immemorial tradition … in … every aspect of his life.") See also id. at 5. ("Primitive law is in truth the totality of the customs of the tribe.")
12. For more biographical data on Malinowski's extraordinary life and career, see John M. Conley & William M. O'Barr, Back to the Trobriands: The Enduring Influence of Malinowski's Crime and Custom in Savage Society, 27 LSI 847, 848–55 (2002).
13. See Malinowski, supra note 2, at 9–16 (criticizing notion that primitive people automatically submit themselves to customary norms).
14. See id. at 63. ("In modern anthropological jurisprudence, it is assumed that all law is custom to the savage and that he has no law but his custom. All custom is again obeyed automatically and rigidly by sheer inertia.… Modern anthropology … ignores and sometimes even explicitly denies the existence of any social arrangements or psychological motives which make primitive man obey a certain class of custom for purely social reasons.")
15. Id. at 23.
16. Id. at 31. See also id. at 46–59.
17. See id. at 39–41 ("The real reason why all these economic obligations are normally kept, and kept very scrupulously, is that failure to comply places a man in an

intolerable position, while slackness in fulfillment covers him with opprobrium. The man who would persistently disobey the rulings of law in his economic dealings would soon find himself outside the social and economic order...."). See also Robert D. Cooter, Inventing Market Property: The Land Courts of Papua New Guinea, 25 & L.. & Soc'y Rev. 759 (1991); Janet T. Landa, The Enigma of the Kula Ring: Gift Exchanges and Primitive Law and Order, 3 Int'l Rev. L. Econ. 137 (1983).

18. Malinowski, supra note 2, at 52.

19. Id. at 68.

20. Id. at 100; see also id. at 107.

21. See Conley & O'Barr, supra note 12, at 856.

22. Id.

23. In his 129-page volume, Crime and Custom in Savage Society, Malinowski presents only three case studies of actual events – including the case of Kima'i (involving incest, exogamy, suicide, and social ostracism; see Malinoswki, supra note 2, at 77–84), the case of Guya'u and Mitakata (implicating mother-right and father-love, favored social relations, and social ostracism; see id. at 101–05), and the case of Si'ulobubu (insults and challenges to authority; see id. at 92). All of these case studies will be considered further below. For a discussion of Malinowski's protean use of case studies, see Conley & O'Barr, supra note 12, at 869–70. See also Bronislaw Malinowski, Magic, Science and Religion and Other Essays (New York: Free Press, 1948).

24. Conley & O'Barr, supra note 12, at 858. Cf. Malinowski, supra note 2, at 58 (Trobriand civil law consisted of a "body of binding obligations, regarded as a right by one party and acknowledged as a duty by the other, kept in force by a specific mechanism of reciprocity and publicity inherent in the structure of their society."). See also Hoebel, supra note 1, at 36–39, 190. For more on the debate about structural-functionalism, see Chapter 4, text at notes 1–16.

25. See also Malinowski, supra note 1, 51 YLJ at 1243–44 (explaining four different conditions for law, all of which could subsume custom). See also Conley & O'Barr, supra note 12, at 864–65 (detailing significance of Malinowski's final article in the *Yale Law Journal*).

26. See Conley & O'Barr, supra note 12, at 864. See also Isaac Schapera, Malinowski's Theories of Law, in Man and Culture: An Evaluation of the Work of Bronislaw Malinowski, at 139–44 (Raymond Firth, ed.; London: Methuen, 1957).

27. Malinowski, supra note 1, 51 YLJ at 1242.

28. Malinowski, supra note 2, at 52.

29. See N. E. H. Hull, Roscoe Pound and Karl Llewellyn: Searching for an American Jurisprudence (Chicago: Univ. of Chicago Press, 1997); William L. Twining, Karl Llewellyn and the Realist Movement (London: Weidenfeld & Nicolson, 1973).

30. See Obituary, Adamson Hoebel 86, Studied Pre-Literate Groups, N.Y. Times, July 26, 1993, at B11. See also E. Adamson Hoebel, Man in the Primitive World: An Introduction to Anthropology (New York: McGraw-Hill, 2d ed., 1958).

31. See Ajay K. Mehrotra, Law and the "Other": Karl N. Llewellyn, Cultural Anthropology, and the Legacy of the Cheyenne Way, 26 LSI 741 (2001); John M. Conley & William M. O'Barr, A Classic in Spite of Itself: The Cheyenne Way and the Case Method in Legal Anthropology, 29 LSI 179 (2004).

32. Llewellyn & Hoebel, supra note 1, at viii.

33. See Mehrotra, supra note 31, at 755–61 (discussing origin of funding and project design for "Indian Law Project #81" as developed by Llewellyn).
34. Llewellyn & Hoebel, supra note 1, at viii.
35. See id. at 341–46 (drawing from the authors' own oral histories, as well as those presented in George Bird Grinnell, The Fighting Cheyennes (New York: C. Scribner's Sons, 1915)).
36. See Mehrotra, supra note 31, at 742.
37. See Franz Boas, The Shaping of American Anthropology, 1883–1911; a Franz Boas Reader (George W. Stocking, Jr., ed.; New York: Basic Books, 1974); Douglas Cole, Franz Boas: The Early Years, 1858–1906 (Seattle: Univ. of Washington Press, 1999); Vernon J. Williams, Rethinking Race: Franz Boas and His Contemporaries (Lexington: Univ. Press of Kentucky, 1996). See also Mehrotra, supra note 31, at 752–54.
38. Conley & O'Barr, supra note 31, at 207–08 (comparing Cheyenne Way, with later work by Max Gluckman and Paul Buhannan).
39. See Mehrotra, supra note 31, at 755–56; Conley & O'Barr, supra note 31, at 188.
40. See Mehrotra, supra note 31, at 752–53.
41. See id. at 751 ("Applauding anthropology's focus on the particular rather than the universal, [Llewellyn] was impressed by the discipline's recent attempt to uncouple law from custom.").
42. Llewellyn & Hoebel, supra note 1, at 25.
43. See id. at 26.
44. Id. at 275. Hoebel, in his individual writings, substantially repeated this thesis. See Hoebel, supra note 1, at 20–23.
45. Llewellyn & Hoebel, supra note 1, at 275 (original emphasis).
46. Id. (original emphasis).
47. Id. at 275–76 (original emphasis).
48. Id. at 276.
49. See Conley & O'Barr, supra note 31, at 180.
50. See Mehrotra, supra note 31, at 765–66 (discussing "malleable and dynamic nature of Cheyenne legal customs").
51. See Conley & O'Barr, supra note 31, at 180–81.
52. See id., at 180–81; Mehrotra, supra note 31, at 742–44, 756.
53. See, e.g., R. F. Barton, The Kalingas: Their Institutions and Custom Law, at v-vii, 6–31 (Chicago: Univ. of Chicago Press, 1949); Max Gluckman, The Judicial Process Among the Barotse of Northern Rhodesia xix-xxv, 1–34 (Manchester: Manchester Univ. Press, 1955); Isaac Schapera, A Handbook of Tswana Law and Custom (London: Oxford Univ. Press, 2d ed., 1955).
54. See Barton, supra note 53, at 198 ("In the theory of custom – if custom can be presumed to have a theory – … circumstances have led to a variance in practice.").
55. See John Philip Reid, A Law of Blood: The Primitive Law of the Cherokee Nation 70 (New York: New York Univ. Press, 1970) (discussing Hartland and Malinowski).
56. Diamond, supra note 1, at 195.
57. Benjamin J. Cardozo, Nature of the Judicial Process 59, 62 (New Haven: Yale Univ. Press, 1928), as quoted in Gluckman, supra note 53, at 289–90.

58. Gluckman, supra note 53, at 261. See also id. at 405 (from Gluckman's 1966 reappraisal).

59. Max Gluckman, Politics, Law and Ritual in Tribal Society 201 (Chicago: Aldine Publishing Co., 1965). See also T. Olawale Elias, Nature of African Customary Law 27–34, 38–52, 66–75 (Manchester: Manchester Univ. Press, 1956); Paul Bohannan, Justice and Judgment Among the Tiv (London: Oxford Univ. Press, 1957).

60. Id. at 201–02. See also id. at 199 (noting that Barotse have distinct terms for custom (*mokgwa*) and law (*molao*)). See also S. F. Nadel, The Nuba: An Anthropological Study of the Hill Tribes in Kordofan 499–502 (London: Oxford Univ. Press, 1947).

61. Harold J. Berman, Law and Revolution: The Formation of the Western Legal Tradition 77 (Cambridge, Mass.: Harvard Univ. Press, 1983).

62. See id. at 79–80, 572–74 nn.65–69 (critiquing views of Maine and Diamond).

63. See Hoebel, supra note 1, at 191–92; Malinowski, supra note 2, at 17–21.

64. See Gluckman, Ritual, supra note 59, at 36–215; Gluckman, Barotse, supra note 53, at 1–34, 357–67. See also Hoebel, supra note 1, at 198–213.

65. Malinowski, supra note 2, at 77–78.

66. Id. at 78.

67. See id. at 77–80.

68. Id. at 79, 80. See also Conley & O'Barr, supra note 12, at 860–62. For a contemporary view of custom and criminal law in Micronesia, see Brian Z. Tamanaha, Looking at Micronesia for Insights about the Nature of Law and Legal Thinking, 41 AJCL 9, 42–47 (1993).

69. See Malinowski, supra note 2, at 101–05. See also Hoebel, supra note 1, at 188–90, 192–93.

70. See id. at 92; see also Hoebel, supra note 1, at 195–96 (while sitting in a tree Si'ulobubu publicly told To'uluwa to "eat shit").

71. See Hoebel, supra note 1, at 196.

72. See id. at 198–202.

73. See Gluckman, Ritual, supra note 59, at 198–201. See also id. at 210–13 (among Tiv people, "debt" obligation could be both in character of a tort or contractual duty).

74. Gluckman, Barotse, supra note 53, at 244. See id. at 241–42 (the Lozi "can treat fairly recent innovations as ancient customs").

75. Compare Gluckman, Barotse, supra note 53, at 238; with Allen, supra note 5, at 157 (for English courts, foreign custom proven as a matter of fact by competent evidence).

76. The most famous critique of Gluckman's thesis was offered in Claude Lévi-Strauss, The Savage Mind 82–163, 387–98 (1962; Chicago: Univ. of Chicago Press, English transl. 1966). See also Lon L. Fuller, Human Interaction and the Law, 14 AJJ 1, 11–12 (1969); Ian Hamnett, Chieftainship and Legitimacy: An Anthropological Study of Executive Law in Lesotho 11–15 (London: Routledge, 1975).

77. Compare Hoebel, supra note 1, at 20–28 ("law may be defined in these terms: A social norm is legal if its neglect or infraction is regularly met, in threat or in

fact, by the application of physical force by an individual or group possessing the socially recognized privilege of so acting"); and Llewellyn & Hoebel, supra note 1, at 229–34, 275; with Gluckman, Barotse, supra note 53, at 405.

78. See Malinowski, supra note 2, at 23. See also Hoebel, supra note 1, at 178–80; Conley & O'Barr, supra note 12, at 856, 864.

79. See Gluckman, Ritual, supra note 59, at 198–201, 208; Gluckman, Barotse, supra note 53, at 124.

80. Gluckman, Barotse, supra note 53, at 138 ("a Barotse [judge] … assesses evidence by the standard of how a reasonable man or woman would have behaved, meticulously according to custom.…"). See id. at 389 (quoting Yevenchi v. Akuffu, [1905] Renner's Rep. 362, 367 (Gold Coast) (Griffith, C. J.) ("Native custom generally consists of the performance of the reasonable in the special circumstances of the case.")).

81. See id. at 241. ("[T]he problem of consistency of established custom as a whole is never raised, because in the absence of writing no-one is at any moment in a position to survey all customs together. Only the customs involved in a particular set of relationships come before the judges at one time.") See also id. at 239.

82. Id. at 243; see also id. at 109–10 (Case 23; provincial Kuta, Lialui, June 1947), 410 (quoting Isaac Schapera, The Sources of Law in Tswana Tribal Courts: Legislation and Precedent, [1957] JAL 150, 161–62).

83. Id. at 241.

84. See Barton, supra note 53, at 196–200.

85. See Reid, supra note 55, at 102.

86. See Llewellyn & Hoebel, supra note 1, at 132–68.

87. See Hoebel, supra note 1, at 297, 306–18 (Andaman islanders, Tshimashian tribe of Pacific Northwest, and Australian aborigines)

88. See Berman, supra note 61, at 55–56; William I. Miller, Bloodtaking and Peacemaking: Feud, Law and Society in Saga Iceland 179–220 (Chicago: Univ. of Chicago Press, 1990).

89. This phrase comes from the idiom of public international law. See Charter of the United Nations, June 26, 1945, 1 U.N.T.S. xvi, 59 Stat. 1031, art. 13, para. 1(a) ("The General Assembly shall initiate studies and make recommendations for the purpose of … encouraging the progressive development of international law and its codification.…").

90. Maine, supra note 4, at 5. See also Adriaan Lanni, Social Norms in the Courts of Ancient Athens, 1 J. Legal Anal. 691, 700–07 (2009) (detailing six categories of general extra-statutory norms enforced in Athenian tribunals).

91. See Allen, supra note 5, at 120, 126–27 ("Customary law [Maine says] becomes crystalized in rules elaborated by interpreters."); Berman, supra note 61, at 79–80.

92. See Gluckman, Barotse, supra note 53, at 236–37. See also id. at 165–66, 378, 402.

93. See Reid, supra note 55, at 36 n.5 (1808 abolition of customary law, but only after years of use alongside codification acts and judicial precedents).

94. See Matthew L. M. Fletcher, Rethinking Customary Law in Tribal Court Jurisprudence, 13 Mich J. Race L. 57, 61–71 (2007); Nell Jessup Newton, Tribal Courts Praxis: One Year in the Life of Twenty Indian Tribal Courts, 22 Am.

Indian L. Rev. 285, 304–09 (1997); Ezra Rosser, Customary Law: The Way Things Were Codified, 8 Tribal L. J. 18 (2008).

95. See Hermann U. Kantorowicz, Savigny and the Historical School of Law, 53 Law Q. Rev. 335 (1937); Robert E. Rodes, Jr., On the Historical School of Jurisprudence, 49 AJJ 165 (2004); 1 Sir Paul Vinogradoff, Introduction to Historical Jurisprudence 103–12 (London: Oxford Univ. Press, 1920). For more on the German Historical School, see Chapter 2, text at notes 95–105.

96. Allen, supra note 5, at 87.

97. See Markus Dirk Dubber, The German Jury and the Metaphysical Volk: From Romantic Idealism to Nazi Ideology, 43 AJCL 227, 242–51 (1995); Munroe Smith, Customary Law, in A General View of European Legal History 269, 290–96 (New York: Columbia Univ. Press, 1927).

98. See Berman, supra note 61, at 51–61, 77–84.

99. Id. at 82.

100. See Miller, supra note 88, at 224–25, 231, 252–56.

101. See Berman, supra note 61, at 78.

102. See Barton, supra note 53, at 5 (introduction by E. Adamson Hoebel) ("International law is primitive law on a world scale."); Conley & O'Barr, supra note 31, at 203–07 (influence of Llewellyn's work on the Cheyenne as reflected in his drafting of the Uniform Commercial Code); Hart, supra note 1, at 3–4; Hoebel, supra note 1, at 331–32; David Ray Papke, How the Cheyenne Indians Wrote Article 2 of the Uniform Commercial Code, 47 Buffalo L. Rev. 1457 (1999).

103. Hart, supra note 1, at 44. See also id. at 240 (where Hart likens custom to "tacit commands," and critiques Austin's theory of positivism). See also George Rutherglen, Custom and Usage as Action Under Color of State Law: An Essay on the Forgotten Terms of Section 1983, 89 VLR 925, 927 (2003). ("In our legal system today, custom does not function as a freestanding source of law capable of generating legal rules, principles, rights, and duties, without first being adopted by a public official.")

2. CULTURE

1. See Berman, supra note 61 (ch. 1), at 1–18.

2. Just. Inst. 1.2.9. See also Sir Paul Vinogradoff, Custom and Right 22 (Oslo: H. Aschehoug & Co. Nygaard, 1925).

3. See A. Arthur Schiller, Custom in Classical Roman Law, 24 VLR 268, 270–71 (1938). But see 5 Dio Chrysostom 253 (H. Lamar Crosby, transl.: Cambridge, Mass.: Harvard Univ. Press, 1985) (On Custom, 76.1) ("Custom is a judgment common to those who use it, an unwritten law of tribe or city, a voluntary principle of justice, acceptable to all alike with reference to the same matters, an invention made, not by [a] human being, but rather by life and time.") (fl. 1st century CE).

4. Cicero, Topica v.28.

5. See Just. Dig. 1.1.6.1 (Ulpian, Institutes 1) ("This law of ours … exists either in written or unwritten form; as the Greeks put it, "of laws some are unwritten, others unwritten"). See also H. F. Jolowicz & Barry Nicholas, Historical Introduction to

the Study of Roman Law 353 & n.2 (3d ed., Cambridge: Cambridge Univ. Press, 1972); Lanni, supra note 90 (ch. 1).

6. Just. Inst. 1.2.9. This notion of "consent" is echoed in a later passage of the *Institutes*, which makes precisely this distinction between positive and natural law: "The laws of nature, which all nations observe alike, being established by a divine providence, remain ever fixed and immutable. But the laws which every state has enacted, undergo frequent changes, *either by the tacit consent of the people* [*tacito consensu populi*], or by a new law being subsequently passed." Just Inst. 1.2.11 (emphasis added).

7. Just. Inst. 1.2.9.

8. Allen, supra note 5 (ch. 1), at 82 (citing Just. Inst. 1.2.9 (for *mores*); Just. Dig. 18.1.34.1; 29.2.8.pr; 50.16.42 (for *mos*)). See also Schiller, supra note 3, at 271 (citing Just. Dig. 4.6.26.2; 48.9.9.pr (for *mos*); 1.7.34; 23.2.8 (for *mores*)); Vinogradoff, supra note 2, at 23.

9. See Allen, supra note 5 (ch. 1), at 82–83; Schiller, supra note 3, at 271–72; J. A. C. Thomas, Custom and Roman Law, 31 *Revue d'Histoire du Droit* 39, 52 (1963).

10. See also Jolowicz & Nicholas, supra note 5, at 354.

11. Id. at 355. See also David Ibbetson, Custom in Medieval Law, in The Nature of Customary Law 151, 151–52 (Amanda Perreau-Saussine & James Bernard Murphy, eds.; Cambridge: Cambridge Univ. Press, 2007); H. F. Jolowicz, Roman Foundations of Modern Law 21 (Oxford: Oxford Univ. Press, 1957).

12. See W. W. Buckland & Arnold D. McNair, Roman Law and Common Law 16–17 (2d ed., rev. F.H. Lawson, ed.; Cambridge: Cambridge Univ. Press, 1965) (citing Just. Dig. 1.2.2.3; 1.2.2.12; 1.3.32.1). See also L. Capogrossi Colognesi, Les *mores gentium* et la formation consuetudinaire du droit romain archaïque (7e – 4e s. avant J.C.), 51 Recueils de la Société Jean Bodin 91 (1990). See also Just. Dig. 27.10.1.pr (Ulpian, Sabinus 1) ("The Law of the Twelve Tables prevents a prodigal's dealing with his property, and this was originally introduced by custom.").

13. See Just Dig. 23.2.39.1 (Paul 6 ad Plaut.); 23.2.8 (Pomponius 5 ad Sab.). See also Rafael Taubenschlag, Customary Law and Custom in the Papyri, 1 J. Juristic Papyrology 41 (1946) (for custom in Ptolemaic and Roman Egypt).

14. See Just. Dig. 1.6.8.pr ("since the right of power over one's family has been established by received custom....").

15. See Just Dig. 24.1.1 (Ulpian 32 ad Sab.) ("As a matter of custom, we hold that gifts between husband and wife are not valid. This rule is upheld to prevent people from impoverishing themselves through mutual affection by means of gifts which are not reasonable, but beyond their means."). See also James B. Thayer, Lex Aquilia – On Gifts Between Husband and Wife 127 (Cambridge: Cambridge Univ. Press, 1929). See also Alan Watson, The Spirit of Roman Law 59 (Athens, Ga.: Univ. of Georgia Press, 1995).

16. See Just Dig. 28.6.2.pr (Ulpian 6 ad Sab.). See also Watson, supra note 15, at 59.

17. See Just. Dig. 29.2.8.pr (Ulpian 7 ad Sab.). See also Watson, supra note 15, at 59.

18. See [Cicero], Rhetorica ad Herennium ii.13.19. See also Watson, supra note 15, at 59.

19. See Gai. Inst. 4.26. See also Jolowicz and Nicholas, supra note 5, at 101.

20. See Alan Watson, The State, Law, and Religion: Pagan Rome (Athens, Ga.: Univ. of Georgia Press, 1992).

21. See Schiller, supra note 3, at 273, 276 (critiquing the eccentric views of Eugen Ehrlich in Beiträge zur Theorie der Rechtsquellen: Grundlegung der Soziologie des Rechts 42–47, 357 (Berlin: Heymann, 1902); reprinted as Eugen Ehrlich, Fundamental Principles of the Sociology of Law 436–42 (Walter L. Moll transl.; Cambridge, Mass.: Harvard Univ. Press, 1936)).

22. Just. Dig. 1.3.32.pr (Julian, Digest 84). See also id. at 1.3.33 (Ulpian, Office of Proconsul 1) ("Everyday usage ought to be observed in place of legal right and statute law in relation to those matters which do not come under the written law."); 1.3.36 (Paul, Sabinus 7) (custom "is held to be of particularly great authority because approval of it has been so great that it has never been necessary to reduce it to writing.").

23. See Werner Flume, Gewohnheitsrecht und römisches Recht (Opladen: Westdeutscher Verlag, 1975); Jill Harries, Law and Empire in Late Antiquity 31 (Cambridge: Cambridge Univ. Press, 1999); Max Kaser, Römische Rechtsquellen und angwandte Juristenmethode 21–33 (Vienna: Hermann Böhlaus, 1986); Wolfgang Kunkel, An Introduction to Roman Legal and Constitutional History 150–52 (2d ed.; Oxford: Oxford Univ. Press, 1973); Enst Levy, West Roman Vulgar Law: The Law of Property (Philadelphia: Am. Philosophical Soc'y, 1951); George Mousourakis, The Historical and Institutional Context of Roman Law 355–56 (Aldershot: Ashgate, 2003).

24. See Allen, supra note 5 (ch. 1), at 81; Buckland & McNair, supra note 12, at 17–18; Schiller, supra note 3, at 277–78; Thomas, supra note 9, at 50–51. See also Jean Gaudemet, La Formation du Droit Séculier et du Droit de L'Église aux IVe et Ve Siècles 114–27 (2d ed.; Paris: Sirey, 1979).

25. Just. Dig. 1.3.34 (Ulpian, Duties of Proconsul 4).

26. See Just. Dig. 26.7.32.6 (Modestinus, Replies 6). See also id. 1.3.37 (Paul, Questions 1) ("If a question should arise about the interpretation of a statute, what ought to be looked into first is the law that the *civitas* had previously applied in cases of the same kind. For custom is the best interpreter of statutes."); 26.7.7.10 (Ulpian, 35 ad Ed.); 50.17.34 (Ulpian, 45 ad Sab.).

27. See Siegfried Brie, Die Lehre vom Gewohnneitsrecht 52–58 (Breslau: Marcus, 1899); Schiller, supra note 3, at 278–79.

28. Just. Dig. 1.3.38 (Callistratus, Questions 1).

29. Just. Dig. 50.13.1.10 (Ulpian, All Seats of Judgment 8) ("As regards the fees for advocates, the judge must proceed in such a way that he sets the level in relation to the nature of the case and the skill of the advocate and the custom of the circuit and the court in which the advocate was to plead, provided the amount does not exceed the legal fee").

30. See Allen, supra note 5 (ch. 1), at 122–23; Ehrlich, supra note 21; Schiller, supra note 3, at 273–75 (discussing work of Schulz); 2 Sir Paul Viongradoff, The Problem of Customary Law, in Collected Papers 410 (London: Wildy, 1963).

31. Just. Dig. 1.3.34 (Ulpian, Duties of Proconsul 4).

32. Just. Dig. 1.3.32.1 (Julian, Digest 84).

33. Just. Dig. 1.3.35 (Hermogenian, Epitome of Law 1).

34. Just. Dig. 1.3.32.1 (Julian, Digest 84).

35. Just. Dig. 1.3.35 (Hermogenian, Epitome of Law 1). See also Epitome Ulpiani 4 ("Custom is the tacit consent of the people, deeply rooted through long usage.").

36. Just. Dig. 1.3.40 (Modestinus, Rules 1).
37. See Allen, supra note 5 (ch. 1), at 83; Brie, supra note 27, at 23.
38. See Alan Watson, An Approach to Customary Law, 1984 U. Ill. L. Rev. 561, 562–63 (discussing Karl Larenz, Methodenlehre der Rechtswissenschaft 338 (2d ed., Berlin: Springer, 1975)). See also La. Civ. C. Art. 3 (1999) ("Custom results from practice repeated for a long time and generally accepted as having acquired the force of law."); id. rev. comm. (b) ("According to civilian theory, the two elements of custom are long practice (*longa consuetudo*) and the conviction that the practice has the force of law (*opinio necessitatis* or *opinio juris*).").
39. Just. Dig. 1.3.32.1 (Julian, Digest 84). See also 1.3.36 (Paul, Sabinus 7) (custom is "of particularly great authority because approval of it has been so great....").
40. See Friedrich Carl von Savigny, System des Heutigen Römischen Rechts 174 (Berlin 1840).
41. Just Dig. 1.3.39 (Celsus, Digest 23).
42. Watson, Approach, supra note 38, at 564.
43. See John Austin, The Province of Jurisprudence Determined 30, 163 (rep. London: Weidenfeld & Nicolson, 1954); 2 John Austin, Lectures on Jurisprudence 222 (London: J. Murray, 1863).
44. For a neo-Austinian view that "custom must be accepted by the sovereign in order to constitute law. To become law, custom ... must be clothed with the requisite form which marks its official acceptance by the sovereign," see Watson, Approach, supra note 38, at 573.
45. See Just. Dig. 1.1.9 (Gaius, Institutes 1). For the problem of Gaius's conflation of natural law with the ius gentium, see John R. Kroger, The Philosophical Foundations of Roman Law: Aristotle, The Stoics, and Roman Theories of Natural Law, 2004 Wis. L. Rev. 905.
46. See Watson, Approach, supra note 38, at 563–64.
47. Just. Code 8.52.2 (Constantine). See also Jolowicz & Nicholas, supra note 5, at 355; Ludwig Mitteis, Reichsrecht und Volksrecht in den östlichen Provinzen des römischen Kaiserreichs 161–65 (Leipzig: B.G. Teubner, 1891). For a related constitution, see Theod. Code 5.20.1 ("Longa consuetudo quae utilitatibus publicis non impedit, pro lege servabitur").
48. See Jolowicz & Nicholas, supra note 5, at 354 and n.9; Schiller, supra note 3, at 273 and n.29, 281; Thomas, supra note 9, at 45 ("There is unanimity that the passage as it stands is not the work of Julian."); Watson, Approach, supra note 38, at 562 n.4.
49. Just. Dig. 1.3.32.1 (Julian, Digest 84).
50. Just. Inst. 1.2.11. See also J. A. C. Thomas, Desuetudo, 11 Revue Internationale des Droits de l'Antiquité (3d ser.) 469 (1964).
51. See Just. Dig. 9.2.27.4 (Ulpian, 18 ad Ed.).
52. See Gai. Inst. 3.17.
53. See Jolowicz & Nicholas, supra note 5, at 354 and n.10 (citing Cicero, Quintillian and Varro).
54. Pliny, Epistulae 10.114–15.
55. See 1 E. C. Clark, History of Roman Private Law 342–76 (Cambridge: Cambridge Univ. Press, 1914); Geoffrey MacCormack, Sources, in A Companion to Justinian's *Institutes* 1, 16 (Ernest Metzger ed.; Ithaca: Cornell Univ. Press, 1998);

A. Arthur Schiller, Roman Law: Mechanisms of Development 253–68, 560–69 (The Hague: Mouton, 1978).

56. See Just. Code 8.52.1 ("nam et consuetudo praecedens et raio quae consuetudinem sausit custodienda est"). See also Quintillian, Institutio Oratorio v.10.13; Cicero, de Inventione ii.65.

57. Just. Dig. 1.3.39 (Celsus, Digest 23). See also Allen, supra note 5 (ch. 1), at 84 and n.1.

58. See Berman, supra note 61 (ch. 1), at 123–27.

59. See id. at 297–303, 310 (compilations of feudal practices), 326 (customs of the manor as promoting cooperation), 328. See also T. F. T. Plucknett, Concise History of the Common Law 308–09, 310–13 (5th ed., London: Butterworth, 1965).

60. See Berman, supra note 61 (ch. 1), at 339–40. See also Plucknett, supra note 59, at 314.

61. See Berman, supra note 61 (ch. 1), at 398–99 ("the writing down of customs by order of public authority did not necessarily deprive them of their quality as customary law").

62. See id. at 406, 517.

63. See R. H. Helmholz, The Ius Commune in England: Four Studies 10 (Oxford: Oxford Univ. Press, 2001); Walter Ullmann, Law and Politics in the Middle Ages (Ithaca: Cornell Univ. Press, 1975).

64. Helmholz, supra note 63, at 13.

65. See id. at 8, 240; see also Berman, supra note 61 (ch. 1), at 427, 456, 480.

66. See John Gilissen, La Coutume 22–24 (Turnhout: Brepols, 1982); Helmholz, supra note 63, at 3–7.

67. See Berman, supra note 61 (ch. 1), at 274, 532.

68. See Helmholz, supra note 63, at 143–45, 158, 170, 244 (customary nature of mortuary or burial payments to the church); id. at 225 (customs concerning allocation of civil and ecclesiastical jurisdiction over clergy).

69. See R. Van Caenegem, Government Law and Society, in The Cambridge History of Medieval Political Thought, c. 350 – c. 1450, at 174, 181–82 (J. H. Burns, ed..; Cambridge: Cambridge Univ. Press, 1988); J. Gaudemet, La Coutume en Droit Canonique, in 2 La Coutume 41 (52 Recueils de la Société Jean Bodin (1990)); Merlin Joseph Guilfoyle, Custom: An Historical Synopsis and Commentary (New York: Paulist Press, 1937) (Catholic Univ. of America Canon Law Studies No. 105).

70. See Gratian, D.1, C.4, as reprinted in Gratian, The Treatise on Laws 4 (James Gordley transl.; Washington, D. C.: Catholic Univ. of America Press, 1993) (Studies in Medieval and Early Modern Canon Law, vol. 2). See also Ibbetson, supra note 11, at 154; Giuseppi Comotti, La consuetudine nel diritto canonico 32–43 (Milan: Giufrè, 1993); Vinogradoff, supra note 2, at 25–26; René Wehrlé, De la Coutume dans le Droit Canonique 87–93 (Paris: Sirey, 1928). For the views of St. Thomas Aquinas on the role of custom, see Summa Theologica 1a2ae 90.3; 97.3 ad 3; 96.4.

71. See Gratian, D.6, p.c.3. Compare with Just. Dig. 1.1.1.3 (Ulpian, Institutes 1) (natural law is "that which nature teaches all animals"). See also Jean Porter, Custom, Ordinance and Natural Right, in Gratian's *Decretum*, in Nature of Customary Law, supra note 11, at 79, 87–88.

72. See Gratian, D.1, C.5.
73. See Gratian, D.8, a.c.2; D.8, C.2; D.8, C.4–9.
74. Gratian, D.1, C.5, reprinted Gratian, supra note 70, at 5–6.
75. Gratian, D.11, a.c.1; D.11, C.4.
76. Gratian, D.8, C.2.
77. Gratian, D.12, C.6–7; D.12, p.c.11.
78. Gratian, D.1, C.5 (gloss by Johannes Teutonicus, c. 1215 CE, to the effect that not every practice has the dignity of a custom because some usages are merely tolerated or actually conflict with other social values). See Porter, supra note 71, at 92 and n.21.
79. See Berman, supra note 61 (ch. 1), at 112–13, 258 (narrating how this maxim was employed in church-state disputes, as with the assassination of Thomas á Becket).
80. Gratian, D.8, C.5. For more on this crucial figure in the papal legal revolution of the Middle Ages, see Berman, supra note 61 (ch. 1), at 85–107.
81. See Berman, supra note 61 (ch. 1), at 144–45 ("The theory that customs must yield to natural law was one of the greatest achievements of the canonists."), 528; Brie, supra note 27, at 67–78; Helmholz, supra note 63, at 153–54; Porter, supra note 71, at 95. See also Decretals of Gregory IX, 1.14.10–11.
82. Gratian, D.12, p.c.11; D.12, C.12. See also Vinogradoff, supra note 2, at 27.
83. See Ibbetson, supra note 11, at 154.
84. In German parlance, this would be the distinction between legal customs (*rechtsgewohnheiten*) and customary law (*gewohnheitsrecht*). See Gewohnheitsrecht und Rechtsgewohnheiten im Mittelater (G. Dilcher ed.; Berlin: Duncker & Humbolt, 1992).
85. See Ullmann, supra note 63, at 20–21, 280–87.
86. See L. Mayali, La Coutume dans la Société Romaniste, in 2 La Coutume (Brussels: De Boeck-Wesmáel, 1990) (Recueils de la Société Jean Bodin, vols. 51 & 52); Walter Ullmann, Bartolus on Customary Law, 52 Juridical Review 265, 275 (1940).
87. See 2 E. Cortese, *La Norma Giuridica* 126–38 (Milan: Giuffrè, 1964).
88. See Berman, supra note 61 (ch. 1), at 472; Ian Maclean, Interpretation and Meaning in the Renaissance: The Case of Law 173–74 (Cambridge: Cambridge Univ. Press, 1992) (canvassing views of Bartolus and Baldus on custom); H. Pissard, Essai sur le Connaissance et la Preuve des Coutumes 98–159 (Paris: Rousseau, 1910).
89. See Ibbetson, supra note 11, at 158.
90. See Ibbetson, supra note 11, at 158–60. See also J. P. Dawson, A History of Lay Judges 94–102 (Cambridge, Mass.: Harvard Univ. Press, 1960); Gilissen, supra note 66, at 74–77; James Q. Whitman, Why Did the Revolutionary Lawyers Confuse Custom and Reason?, 58 UCLR 1321, 1330–33 (1991). For more on custom in Roman-Dutch law, see 1 Johannes Voet, The Selective Voet: Commentary on the Pandects 59–72 (Durban: Butterworth, 1955) (from the Paris ed. 1829).
91. See Ibbetson, supra note 11, at 159–60; Vinogradoff, supra note 2, at 31; Whitman, supra note 90, at 1333–38. See also 2 Paul Vinogradoff, The Collected Papers of Paul Vinogradoff: Jurisprudence 402 (Oxford: Clarendon Press, 1928).
92. See Ibbetson, supra note 11, at 160. See also H. F. Jolowicz, Roman Foundations of Modern Law 21–37 (Oxford: Clarendon Press, 1957); Peter Stein, The Civil Law

Doctrine of Custom and the Growth of Case Law, in 1 Scintillae Iuris: Studi in Memoria di Gino Gorla 371 (Milan: Giuffrè, 1994); Alan Watson, *The Evolution of Western Private Law* 96–109 (Baltimore: Johns Hopkins Press, 2001).

93. See 1 Philippe de Beaumanoir, *Coutumes de Beauvasis* § 683 (A. Salmon ed.; Paris, 1970). See also Whitman, supra note 90, at 1338–39.
94. See Whitman, supra note 90, at 1341–52 (discussing sixteenth- and seventeenth-century evidentiary developments for custom on the continent). See also Vinogradoff, supra note 2, at 32–34 (discussing German and Scandinavian practices).
95. See Chapter 1, text at notes 95–96.
96. See Peter Stein, Legal Evolution: The Story of an Idea ix (New York: Cambridge Univ. Press, 1980).
97. See George Friedrich Puchta, Das Gewohnheitsrecht (Erlangen: Palm, 1928). See also Christoph Kletzer, Custom and Positivity: An Examination of the Philosophic Ground of the Hegel-Savigny Controversy, in Nature of Customary Law, supra note 11, at 125, 130–36. For an extensive sociological critique of Savigny's and Puchta's views on custom, see Ehrlich, supra note 21, at 443–69.
98. Savigny, supra note 40, at § 12.
99. See Kletzer, supra note 97, at 136–37; Schiller, supra note 3, at 272.
100. See Mathias Reimann, Nineteenth Century German Legal Science, 31 B. C. L. Rev. 837, 853–54, 860–62 (1990).
101. See Allen, supra note 5 (ch. 1), at 92–93.
102. See id. at 96–101. See 1 Otto Friedrich von Gierke, Deutsches Privatrecht 125, 163 (Leipzig: Duncker & Humbolt, 1895).
103. See Allen, supra note 5 (ch. 1), at 112, 122 (discussing work of Ehrlich), 152–56 (discussing John Dewey, Book Review, 28 CLR 832 (1928) (reviewing an earlier edition of Allen's *Law in the Making*)).
104. Id. at 148; see also id. at 147–51.
105. Berman, supra note 61 (ch. 1), at 556. See also Vinogradoff, supra note, at 21 ("The historical development of law starts with custom. Rules are not imposed from above by legislative authorities but rise from below, from the society which comes to recognize them.").

3. HISTORY

1. For recent scholarship on this point, see William D. Bader, Some Thoughts on Blackstone, Precedent and Originalism, 19 Vt. L. Rev. 5 (1994); James Oldham, From Blackstone to Bentham: Common Law Versus Legislation in Eighteenth-Century Britain, 89 Mich. L. Rev. 1637 (1991); Alan Watson, The Structure of Blackstone's Commentaries, 97 YLJ 795 (1988).
2. See Helmholz, supra note 63 (ch. 2), at 45, 53, 60, 143–45, 158, 170, 225, 244.
3. See id. at 153–55.
4. See Alan Cromartie, The Idea of Common Law as Custom, in The Nature of Customary Law, supra note 11 (ch. 2), at 203, 204 (discussing the mid-twelfth-century work, *Leges Edwardi Confessoris*).
5. See Ibbetson, supra note 11 (ch. 2), at 164.

6. See Cromartie, supra note 4, at 205.
7. See Allen, supra note 5 (ch. 1), at 71–72 and n.3.
8. 2 Bracton, On the Laws and Customs of England 19 (G. E. Woodbine ed.; S. E. Thorne, transl.; Cambridge, Mass.: Harvard Univ. Press, 1968–78). See also K. E. Braybrooke, Custom as a Source of English Law, 50 Mich. L. Rev. 71, 72 (1951); Clark, supra note 55 (ch.2), at 377–413.
9. 2 Bracton, supra note 8, at 22 (citing Just. Inst. 1.2.9 and Just. Code 8.52.2).
10. See Ibbetson, supra note 11 (ch. 2), at 163–64.
11. See Greer, Custom in the Common Law, 9 L. Q. Rev. 153, 154 (1893); N. Neilson, Custom and the Common Law of Kent, 38 HLR 482, 483–84, 488–90 (1924). See also Thomas Usk, Testament of Love, bk. III, ch. 1, ll. 78–83 (R. Allen Shoaf ed., Medieval Inst. Pub. 1998) (c. 1380) ("But custome is a thyng that is accepted for right or for lawe, there as lawe and right faylen.... [C]ustome is of commen usage by length of tyme used, and custome nat writte is usage; and if it be writte, constitutyon it is ywritten and ycleped.").
12. See Ibbetson, supra note 11 (ch. 2), at 164–65.
13. See Sir John Fortescue, De Laudibus Legum Anglie 36–41 (S. E. Chrimes, ed. & transl.; Cambridge: Cambridge Univ. Press, 1949). See also Harold J. Berman, The Origins of Historical Jurisprudence: Coke, Selden, Hale, 103 YLJ 1651, 1658 (1994); Cromartie, supra note 4, at 208–09.
14. Cromartie, supra note 4, at 209.
15. Christopher St. German, Doctor and Student 45 (T. F. T. Plucknett & J. L. Barton, eds.; London: Selden Soc'y, 1974).
16. Id. at 47.
17. See Allen, supra note 5 (ch. 1), at 73; Cromartie, supra note 4, at 209–13. See also R. H. Helmholz, Christopher St. German and the Law of Custom, 70 UCLR 129 (2003).
18. See St. German, supra note 15, at 71. See also Andrea C. Loux, The Persistence of the Ancient Regime: Custom, Utility and the Common Law in the Nineteenth Century, 79 Cornell L. Rev. 183, 192 (1993); T. F. T. Plucknett, Concise History of the Common Law 310–13 (5th ed., Boston: Little Brown, 1956).
19. See Ibbetson, supra note 11 (ch. 2), at 167–71; Loux, supra note 18, at 190–91; Vinogradoff, supra note 2 (ch. 2), at 30.
20. See Braybrooke, supra note 8, at 82–87; Ibbetson, supra note 11 (ch. 2), at 170–71; Vinogradoff, supra note 2 (ch. 2), at 30.
21. See Braybrooke, supra note 8, at 88–89; Ibbetson, supra note 11 (ch. 2), at 172–75.
22. Plucknett, supra note 18, at 307. See also Antonin Scalia, A Matter of Interpretation: Federal Courts and the Law 4 (Princeton: Princeton Univ. Press, 1997) ("Perhaps in the very infancy of Anglo-Saxon law it could have been thought that the courts were mere expositors of generally accepted social practices.... But from an early time – as early as the Year Books... – any equivalence between custom and common law had ceased to exist.... The issue coming before the courts involved, more and more, refined questions to which customary practice provided no answer.").
23. 1 Sir Edward Coke, Institutes 110b.
24. 6 Co. Rep. 59b, 77 Eng. Rep. 355 (K. B. 1607). See also Loux, supra note 18, at 191–92.

25. Davis Rep. (Ireland) 28, 80 Eng. Rep. 516 (1608).

26. Id. at 32–33. See also Braybrooke, supra note 8, at 72–73; Whitman, supra note 90 (ch. 2), at 1355 and n.136.

27. Id. at 29. See also Plucknett, supra note 18, at 312–13.

28. See Whitman, supra note 90 (ch. 2), at 1352–55. See also Thomas Hedley's 1610 address to Parliament, reprinted in J. G. A. Pocock, The Ancient Constitution and the Feudal Law 272–73 (Cambridge: Cambridge Univ. Press, 2d ed., 1990) ("because I make custom a part of my definition of the common law [I would not] confound the common law with custom, which differ as much as artificial reason and bare precedents. Customs are confined to certain and particular places, triable by the country, but their reasonableness or unreasonableness by the judges, to be taken strictly according to letter and precedent....").

29. See Berman, Origins, supra note 13, at 1689, 1733; Cromartie, supra note 4, at 218–20.

30. See Cromartie, supra note 4, at 220–21; A. W. B. Simpson, Legal Theory and Legal History: Essays on the Common Law 376–77 (London: Hambledon Press, 1987) ("the common law system is properly located as a customary system of law [insofar as] it consists of a body of practices observed and ideas received by a caste of lawyers").

31. See id. at 221–22, 226. See also Berman, Origins, supra note 13, at 1699–1700 (for the even more populist views of John Selden); Postema, supra note 5 (ch. 1), at 6–9, 14; Whitman, supra note 90 (ch. 2), at 1360–61.

32. Thomas Hobbes, Dialogue between a Philosopher and Student of the Common Law 96 (c. 1666), reprinted in Postema, supra note 5 (ch. 1), at 47.

33. The treatment of custom in Scots law was analytically distinct from English law. See J. T. Cameron, Custom as a Source of Law in Scotland, 27 Mod. L. Rev. 306, 312 (1964); W. David H. Sellar, Custom in Scots Law, in 52 Recueils de la Société Jean Bodin pour L'Histoire Comparative des Institutions: Custom ["Jean Bodin Study on Custom"] 411 (1990); James Stair, The Institutions of the Law of Scotland 27, 84–95 (David M. Walker, ed.; Edinburgh: Univ. Presses of Edinburgh and Yale, 1981) (originally published 1693).

34. See 1 William Blackstone, Commentaries on the Laws of England *72–74 (1765–69) ["Blackstone"]. Where necessary, footnote and editorial material in Blackstone's *Commentaries* (as distinct from the original, starred pagination) will be cited to the 1908 American edition of the work, William Blackstone, Commentaries on the Laws of England: in four books, with an analysis of the work (Joseph Chitty, Edward Christian, John Eykyn Hovenden, Thomas Lee, Archer Ryland 1851) (Am. rev. ed. 1908).

35. See, e.g., Allen, supra note 5 (ch. 1), at 72; Buckland & McNair, supra note 12 (ch. 2), at 15 ("Our own common law is described by Blackstone as the general custom of the realm. It is notoriously, as a matter of history, nothing of the kind. The common law was brought into existence by the King's Justices, all over the country, precisely because there was no general custom of the realm."); Simpson, supra note 30, at 373–76.

36. See 1 Blackstone *63–67.

37. 1 Blackstone *67. See also id. at *68 ("SOME have divided the common law into two principal grounds or foundations: 1. established customs; such as that where

there are three brothers, the eldest brother shall be heir to the second, in exclusion of the youngest: and 2. established rules and maxims; as, "that the king can do no wrong," that no "man shall be bound to accuse himself," and the like. But I take there to be one and the same thing. For the authority of these maxims rests entirely upon general reception and usage; and the only method of proving, that this or that maxim is a rule of the common law, is by shewing that it hath been always the custom to observe it."). See also Simpson, *supra* note 30, at 373–76.

38. Id.

39. Id. at 73–74 (quoting Just. Dig. 1.3.32).

40. See Cromartie, *supra* note 4, at 222–25; Postema, *supra* note 5 (ch. 1), at 72–73.

41. 1 Blackstone *74. See also J. H. Balfour Browne, The Laws of Usages and Customs 5 (1875) ("Customs are said to be either 1, General, or those which prevail throughout the whole kingdom, or 2, Particular, those which for the most part affect only the inhabitants of a particular place, or the members of a particular class.").

42. 1 Blackstone *74. See also id. n.(z) (citing to various Acts of Parliament which recognized such privileges, including 9 Hen. 3, ch. 9; 1 Edw. 3, st. 2, ch. 9; 14 Edw. 3, st. i, ch. 1; 2 Hen. 4, ch. 1).

43. See 1 Blackstone *75. See also John H. Baker, An Introduction to English Legal History 31 (3d ed., London: Butterworths, 1990).

44. See Norman Doe, Fundamental Authority in Medieval English Law 20 (Cambridge: Cambridge Univ. Press, 1990); Albert Kiralfy, Custom in Mediaeval English Law, in 52 Jean Bodin Study on Custom, *supra* note 33, at 379, 389–98 (1990).

45. 1 Blackstone *75 (emphasis omitted).

46. Id. at *76. Blackstone went on to note that the customs of London can be proven upon a certificate from the Lord Mayor. See id. (citations omitted). See also Plummer v. Bentham, 1 Burr. 248, 97 Eng. Rep. 297 (K.B. 1757); Day v. Savadge, Hob. 85, 80 Eng. Rep. 235 (K. B. 1614). See also John Leybourn Goddard, A Treatise on the Law of Easements 19 (Edmund H. Bennett 2d Am. rev. ed., Boston: Houghton Mifflin, 1880); Kiralfy, *supra* note 44, at 397–98, 401.

47. See Hammerton v. Honey, 24 W. R. 603 (Ch. 1876) (Jessel, M. R.) ("A custom as I understand it is local common law. It is common law because it is not statute law, and it is local law because it is the law of a particular place as distinguished from the general common law.").

   Proof of a general custom, was considered in R. v. Lord Yarborough, 2 Bligh (n.s.) 147, 157, 4 Eng. Rep. 1087, 1091 (H. L. 1828) (Best, C.J.) ("General customs were, in ancient times, stated in the pleadings of those who claimed them.... But it has not been usual for a long time to allude to such customs in the pleadings, because no proof is required of their existence; they are considered as adopted into the common law, and as such are recognised by the Judges without any evidence.").

48. See The TWEE GEBROEDERS, 3 C. Rob. 336, 349–50, 165 Eng. Rep. 485, 490 (Adm. 1801) (Scott, J.) ("It is laid down by writers of the best authority that there must be at least two witnesses to prove a custom, and that they must assign the acts done as the ground of their belief.").

49. This method of making proof for a custom was quite different than that made for a usage of trade in the *lex mercatoria*:

   As regards the necessity of proof, [trade] usages ran through certain stages. There is the primary stage when the particular usage must be proved with certainty and precision; there is the secondary stage when the court has become to some degree familiar with the usage, and when slight evidence only is required to establish it; and there is the final stage when the court takes judicial notice of the usage, and evidence is not required.

12 Halsbury's Laws of England ¶ 479, at 49 (Lord Hailsham of St. Marylebone 4th ed. 1975).

50. 1 Blackstone *76 (original emphasis).

51. Blackstone's formulation refined earlier enunciations of the elements of custom in the treatise literature. Littleton had said merely that possession by custom must be long, continual, and peaceable. Thomas Coventry, A Readable Edition of Coke Upon Littleton § 110a (1830) [hereinafter "Coke on Littleton"]. See also S. C. Carter, Lex Costumaria: or, A Treatise of Copy-hold Estates (London 1696).

52. In an abundance of methodological caution, Blackstone insisted that questions as to "the *allowance* of special customs" were analytically distinct. Id. at *78 (original emphasis). Under this rubric, Blackstone prescribed a general rule of construction for local customs: "Customs, in derogation of the common law, must be construed narrowly." Id. See also Arthur v. Bokenham, 11 Mod. 148, 160, 88 Eng. Rep. 957. 962 (K. B. 1708) ("[A]ll customs which are against the common law of England, ought to be taken strictly, nay very strictly, even stricter than any Act of Parliament that alters the common law."). See also Loux, supra note 18, at 194.

53. But cf. Johnson v. Clark, [1908] 1 Ch. 303, 309 (Parker, J.) ("no custom bad in law is susceptible of proof.... It seems clear that a custom possible in law, because it is reasonable and fulfills the requisites of a good custom, may be established by very slender evidence.").

54. 1 Blackstone *76–77 (citations omitted).

55. Another point is that Blackstone's last observation – that a custom at variance with a statute must be bad – does not necessarily follow from the preceding conclusions. Obviously, it is within the power of any legislature to adopt a statute that changes the common law or any local custom. This would be an act of its sovereign prerogative. In such an instance, the enactment of a statute is an affirmative overruling of the contrary custom, and not necessarily a legislative finding that the contrary custom never existed.

Blackstone may have, instead, been suggesting that a statute could codify a custom. But then reliance on the custom would be unnecessary, and it would be inaccurate to say that the custom is being pled in a way to "prevail against an express act of parliament." But even in those cases, it would be wrong to say that the legislature was drafting on a blank slate, and that the statute was, therefore, evidence "of a time when such a custom did not exist." Codification suggests that a legal practice is being transcribed into written law. Compare New Windsor v. Taylor, 1899 App. Cas. 41, 49 (Davey, L. J.) ("Where an Act of Parliament ... has embraced and confirmed a right which previously existed by custom or prescription, such right becomes henceforth a statutory right, and the lower right by custom ... is merged in and extinguished by the higher title of the Act of Parliament"), with Truscott v. Merchant Tayors' Co., 11 Exch. 855, 866 (1856) (Compton, J.) ("It is said that the customs of London are parliamentary rights; but they are, nevertheless, customs. The only effect of sanctioning them by statute is, that they are to be treated as good customs.").

56. The selection of the year 1189 was originally historic serendipity, but later hardened into a clear vision of the idea of legal certainty. The reference to the coronation of Richard I was made in that part of the Statute of Westminster, ch. 39 (1275), concerning the starting date for a period of limitations of claims, and it was never revised. As one scholar has noted:

    Fixing an arbitrary limit for claims based on precedents was not a new device.... Up until the reign of Edward I the assumption seems to have been that memory extended back for a century at most, that is, to the earliest time which could be remembered by the oldest living persons; any period before that was considered "time out of mind." [T]he fixed limit of 3rd September, 1189, ... marked the formal beginning of the era of artificial memory.... [R]emembrance in litigation [thereafter] depended primarily upon documentary evidence and not on mortal memory.

    Michael T. Clanchy, From Memory to Written Record, England 1066–1307, at 123 (Cambridge, Mass.: Harvard Univ. Press, 1979). See also Allen, supra note 5 (ch. 1), at 133–34; Kiralfy, supra note 44, at 386–87. See also 3 William Cruise, A Digest of the Law of Real Property tit. 31, § 21, at 226–27 n.1 (Simon Greenleaf 2nd ed., Boston: Little Brown, 1856).

57. See also Plucknett, supra note 18, at 312. For an application of the rule of antiquity in disqualifying a custom, see Simpson v. Wells, 7 L.R.-Q.B. 214 (1872). For a sampling of cases affirming custom, see Wolstanton, Ltd. v. Newcastle-under-Lyme Corp., 1940 App. Cas. 860; Angus v. Dalton, 3 Q.B.D. 85, 104 (1877), rev'd on other grounds, 4 Q.B.D. 162 (C.A. 1878).

    In Scotland, the rule of proving the origin of custom as prior to 1189 has been rejected in favor of a more flexible standard. See Will's Trs. v. Cairngorm Canoeing & Sailing School, Ltd., 1976 Sess. Cas. 30 (H.L.) (appeal from Scotland) (40 years uninterrupted use of a river sufficient to prove custom).

58. 1 Blackstone *77 (original emphasis) (footnote omitted). See also Coke on Littleton, supra note 51, at § 114b ("Continua dico ita quod non fit legitime interupta.").

59. See Allen, supra note 5 (ch. 1), at 136.

60. See Busby v. Avgherino, 1928 App. Cas. 290, 294 (Sumner, J.) ("Proof [of custom] is required but it is hard to come by. The rules of evidence are liberal in matters of such antiquity, but they remain rules of evidence.... The party setting up the custom must have the benefit of all legal presumptions, but he can take nothing by any resort to mere surmise, however ingenious, and his proof, though scanty, must still be 'rational and solid'.").

61. See Hammerton v. Honey, 24 W.R. 603 (Ch. 1876).

62. See Scales v. Key, 11 Ad. & El. 819, 113 Eng. Rep. 625 (K.B. 1840).

63. 1 Blackstone *77 (original emphasis) (footnote omitted). See also Hall v. Hottingham, 1 Ex. D. 1 (1875).

64. See Allen, supra note 5 (ch. 1), at 136–37.

65. See Plucknett, supra note 18, at 312.

66. 1 Blackstone *78.

67. See id. (quoting the maxim, *id certum est, quod certum reddi potest*). To the same effect is Mercer v. Denne, [1904] 2 Ch. 534 (holding good a custom that allowed fishermen to dry their nets on the beach, even though erosion and tidal action could alter the configuration of the beach over time).

68. For more on the evolution of English custom in the period from 1500 – 1700, see Louis A. Knalfa, Law and Custom in Early Modern England, 52 Jean Bodin Study on Custom, supra note 33, at 403 (1990).

69. 6 Co. Rep. 59b, 77 Eng. Rep. 344 (K.B. 1608).

70. Specifically at issue in *Gateward's Case* was the right of the inhabitants-at-large to enter the lord's manor and to carry away dead and rotten trees and branches to burn as firewood. This the Court of King's Bench characterized as a *profit apprender*, 6 Co. Rep. at 60b, 77 Eng. Rep. at 345, which was not available by way of custom to the people of the district. It was, however, available to the copyholders, or tenants, on the lord's estate. See id.

71. See id. at 60b, 77 Eng. Rep. at 345. For more on the later English cases affirming the rule against the inhabitants of a district (as opposed to a smaller class of copyholders), see Loux, supra note 18, at 196 n.85.

72. Willes 360, 125 Eng. Rep. 1214 (C.P. 1742).

73. Id. at 361, 125 Eng. Rep. at 1215.

74. See Hammerton v. Honey, 24 W.R. 603 (1876) (Jessel, M.R.) ("when we are told that a custom must be certain – that relates to the evidence of a custom. There is no such thing as law which is uncertain – the notion of law means a certain rule of some kind."). See also Johnson v. Clark, [1908] 1 Ch. 303, 311; The Case of Tanistry, Dav. 28, 33, 80 Eng. Rep. 516, 521 (K.B. 1608) (reason for rule of certainty is that "it does not lie in prescription which lies in the will of man, for the will of man is uncertain.").

75. Selby v. Robinson, 2 Term Rep. 758, 100 Eng. Rep. 409 (K.B. 1788). See also Anonymous, Y.B. 12 and 13 Edw. 3 (r.s.) 236 (custom that allowed, in Hereford, a child to sell his own property as soon as he could count money, was held too uncertain).

76. Millechamp v. Johnson, Willes 205 n.(b), 125 Eng. Rep. 1133–34 n.(b) (C.P. 1746). See also Emory Washburn, A Treatise on the American Law of Easements and Servitudes 140 (4th ed., Boston: Little Brown, 1885).

77. Fitch v. Rawling, 2 H. Bl. 393, 126 Eng. Rep. 614 (C.P. 1795).

78. Id. at 398, 126 Eng. Rep. at 616–17 (Buller, J.). To the same effect is Earl of Coventry v. Willes, 12 W.R. 127, 128 (Q.B. 1863) (custom alleged was that general public could enter lord's manor to watch horse racing; held, a bad custom, because "the rights possessed by the Queen's subjects generally are part of the general law of the land, not the customs of a particular place"); Anonymous, Brook's New Cas. 56, 73 Eng. Rep. 871 (K.B. 1543).

79. See Coke on Littleton, supra note 51, at § 113b ("custom, which is local, is alleged in no person, but layd within some manor or other place."). See also Sowerby v. Coleman, 2 L.R.-Ex. 95, 100 (1867) (Channell, B.) (custom of inhabitants training their horses outside their parish on a neighboring manor was bad because the manor and parish were not co-extensive); H. E. Salt, The Local Ambit of Custom, in Cambridge Legal Essays Written in Honour of and Presented to Doctor Bond, Professor Buckland and Professor Kenny 279, 293 (G. G. Alexander et al., eds,; Cambridge, Mass.: Harvard University Press, 1926).

80. 1 Blackstone *78. Blackstone gives as an example of this that

    if one man prescribes that by custom he has a right to have windows looking into another's garden; the other cannot claim a right by custom to stop up or obstruct those windows: for these two contradictory customs cannot both be good, nor both stand together. He [the gardener] ought rather to deny the existence of the former custom.

Id. (citing to Aldred's Case, 9 Co. Rep. 57b, 77 Eng. Rep. 816 (K.B. 1610)).

81. Allen, supra note 5 (ch. 1), at 139.
82. 1 Blackstone *78 (original emphasis).
83. See Allen, supra note 5 (ch. 1), at 137.
84. See Kiralfy, supra note 44, at 385–86.
85. Mills v. Mayor of Colchester, 2 L.R.-C.P. 476, 486 (1867), aff'd 3 id. 575 (Exch. Ch. 1868).
86. 1 Blackstone *77 (original emphasis). The burden is, therefore, on the party that would seek to have the custom ruled bad to show that it is unreasonable. See Allen, supra note 5 (ch. 1), at 140.
87. 1 Blackstone *77 (citing 1 Sir Edward Coke, Systematic Arrangement of Lord Coke's First Institute of the Laws of England 1 (J. H. Thomas ed., Philadelphia, Alexander Towar 2d American ed. 1836). ("Reason is the life of the law.... [N]o man (out of his own private reason) ought to be wiser than the law, which is the perfection of reason.")).
88. 1 Blackstone *77. See also Hix v. Gardiner, 2 Bulst. 195, 196, 80 Eng. Rep. 1062, 1063 (K.B. 1614) ("you cannot imagine the reason of a custom, the custom of borough English and gravelkinde, are no reasonable customs, the reason to be shewed of the beginning of them is impossible.").
89. In these cases, the evidentiary overruling is virtually indistinguishable from the judges' application of reason. See Daun v. City of London Brewery Co., 8 L.R.-Eq. 155 (1869); Nelson v. Dahl, 12 Ch. D. 568 (1879); Gibbon v. Pease, [1905] 1 K.B. 810.
90. See Bryant v. Foot, 3 L.R.-Q.B. 497 (1868) (alleged custom that rector could claim 13 shillings stipend for celebrating a marriage was manifestly not of ancient origin since such a fee would have been grossly unreasonable in the reign of Richard I). But cf. Lawrence v. Hitch, 3 L.R.-Q.B. 521 (1868) (one shilling cartage fee on vegetables was "reasonable" under the standard of *Bryant*).
91. 7 East 121, 103 Eng. Rep. 46 (K.B. 1806) (Ellenborough, C. J.).
92. Id. at 121–25, 103 Eng. Rep. at 46–48.
93. Id. at 127–28, 103 Eng. Rep. at 49. See also, Steel v. Houghton, 126 Eng. Rep. 32 (C.P. 1788) (declaring invalid customary practice of gleaning leftover crops); Loux, supra note 18, at 199.
94. See Allen, supra note 5 (ch. 1), at 141 (citing Perry v. Barnett, 15 Q.B.D. 388 (1885)). But see Falmouth v. George, 5 Bing. 286, 293, 130 Eng. Rep. 1071, 1073–74 (C.P. 1828) (mere fact that custom conflicts with common law does not disqualify it). For more on that point, see A. E. Dick Howard, Magna Carta: Text and Commentary 39, 49 (Charlottesville: Univ. Press of Virginia, 1964).
95. Dav. 29, 80 Eng. Rep. 516 (K.B. 1608).
96. See Sir Henry Maine, Lectures on the Early History of Institutions 185–96 (lecture 7) (London: J. Murray, 1875); Gilbert T. Sadler, The Relation of Custom to Law 43–46 (London: Sweet & Maxwell, 1919) (for more on Brehon customs).
97. Dav. at 35–37, 80 Eng. Rep. at 523–24.
98. Maine, Institutions, supra note 96, at 186.

99. This may be in sharp contrast with the Scottish cases, which appear to more closely circumscribe judicial discretion in striking custom. See Bruce v. Smith, 17 R. 1000 (Sess. 1890) (Scot.). See also Dempster v. Cleghorn, 2 Dow. 40, 3 Eng. Rep. 780 (H.L. 1813) (appeal from Scotland) (customary right of people of St. Andrews to play at the St. Andrews Golf Club).

100. Produce Brokers' Co. v. Olympia Oil & Coke Co., [1916] 2 K.B. 296, 298.

101. See Allen, supra note 5 (ch. 1), at 140 n.3; Sadler, supra note 96, at 65–68.

102. Robinson v. Mollett, 7 L.R.-H.L. 802, 817 (1875) (Brett, L. J.).

103. See Hall v. Nottingham, 33 L.T.R. 697, 699 (Ex. D. 1876) (Kelly, C. B.) ("We are dealing, it must be remembered with a matter affecting an individual owner of a small piece of land on the one hand, and the rights and privileges of all the inhabitants of the entire parish on the other....").

104. Case of Tanistry, Dav. at 36, 80 Eng. Rep. at 524 (K.B. 1608). See also Tyson v. Smith, 9 Ad. & E. 406, 421–22, 112 Eng. Rep. 1265, 1271 (Exch. Ch. 1838); Geere v. Burkensham, 3 Lev. 85, 83 Eng. Rep. 589 (K.B. 1683) ("a lord of a manor shall have the best anchor and cable of any ship that strike upon a soil within his manor and perishes there, though it be not a wreck.").

105. See Barker v. Cocker, Hob. 329, 80 Eng. Rep. 471 (K.B. 1621) (tithe of sheep); Haspurt v. Wills, 1 Vent. 71, 86 Eng. Rep. 50 (K.B. 1671) (river toll). For more on utilitarian reasoning in nineteenth-century English custom cases, see Loux, supra note 18, at 203–04.

106. David Hume, Enquiry Concerning the Human Understanding 41 (L. A. Selby-Bigge & P. H. Nidditch, eds., 3d ed.; Oxford: Oxford Univ. Press, 1975) (London 1748).

107. 3 David Hume, The History of England from the Invasion of Julius Caesar to the Revolution of 1688, at 192 (Indianapolis, 1983) (Edinburgh, 1754 –).

108. See Postema, supra note 5 (ch. 1), at 98–99.

109. See Jeremy Bentham, A Comment on the Commentaries 182, 234–35, 308–09, 332–33 (J. H. Burns and H. L. A. Hart, eds.; London: Univ. of London Press, 1977).

110. Id. at 195–96.

111. See id. at 160 (discussing law of conveyances).

112. See id. at 234–35.

113. See id. at 218. See also Postema, supra note 5 (ch. 1), at 220–21.

114. Bentham, supra note 109, at 334.

115. See id. at 231–51.

116. Id. at 306 n.(c).

117. See id. at 234.

118. See supra notes 12–20 (ch. 1) and accompanying text.

119. See Chapter 1, text at notes 6–7. See also Loux, supra note 18, at 201–03; Postema, supra note 5 (ch. 1), at 254–62.

120. See Loux, supra note 18, at 203. See also 2 Matthew Bacon, A New Abridgment of the Law 567 (1798) (London, 1832) ("every custom which appears to have been unreasonable in itself, as being against the good of the commonwealth, or injurious to a multitude, though beneficial to a particular person, or owe its commencement to the arbitrary will and oppression of a powerful lord, and not the voluntary agreement of the parties, is void.").

121. 2 & 3 Will. 4, ch. 71 (1832).

122. Id.

123. By the Prescription Act, copyhold custom was declared nonrebuttable upon a showing of 30 years use, and "absolute and indefeasible" after 60 years. Id. But, it needs to be emphasized that the Act affected only customary rights as between manorial estates and their tenants, and not customs going to a wider community. See Mounsey v. Ismay, H. & C. 486, 159 Eng. Rep. 621 (Exch. 1865) (rejecting application of Prescription Act to claim of customary right by village to enter a property and race horses).

    For more on the effect of the Prescription Act, see Charles James Gale, A Treatise on the Law of Easements 166–69 (David Gibbons 5th ed., London: H. Sweet, 1876); Loux, supra note 18, at 204–06.

124. See Loux, supra note 18, at 204–06.

125. John Milton Goodenow, Historical Sketches of the Principles and Maxims of American Jurisprudence 40–41 (Steubenville, Ohio: Wilson, 1819) (rep. Buffalo: William S. Hein & Co., 1975).

126. [Justice] Joseph Story, Common Law, in 3 Encyclopedia Americana 394 (1830) (Francis Lieber, ed.).

127. [Justice] Joseph Story, Courts, in 3 Encyclopedia Americana 597 (1830) (Francis Lieber, ed.). See also [Justice] Joseph Story, Codification of the Common Law, in The Miscellaneous Writings of Joseph Story 701 (1851) (rep., New York: De Capo Press, 1972) ("local usages and principles… have the force of law, but which are not founded upon any local statutes. [They], indeed, are so few, and comparatively, in a general sense, so unimportant, that they may, for all our present purposes, be passed over without further observation or notice.").

128. Delaplane v. Crenshaw & Fisher, 56 Va. (15 Gratt.) 457, 475 (1860).

129. See Lewis A. Grossman, Langdell Upside-Down: James Coolidge Carter and the Anticlassical Jurisprudence of Anticodification, 19 Yale J. L. & Human. 149, 156–59 (2007); Kunal M. Parker, Context in History and Law: A Study of the Late Nineteenth-Century American Jurisprudence of Custom, 24 L. & Hist. Rev. 473, 499–500 (2006); Rutherglen, supra note 103 (ch. 1), at 955–56.

130. James Coolidge Carter, Law: Its Origin, Growth and Function 120 (New York: G. Putnam Sons, 1907).

131. Id.

132. Id. at 121.

133. Oliver Wendell Holmes, The Common Law 1–2 (Boston: Little Brown, 1881).

134. But see Rutherglen, supra note 103 (ch. 1), at 958 (for a different view of Holmes's customary law jurisprudence).

135. See John Chipman Gray, The Nature and Sources of the Law 297, 300–01 (2d ed.; New York: MacMillan, 1927). For more on Gray's influence, see Parker, supra note 129, at 513; Rutherglen, supra note 103 (ch. 1), at 957–58.

136. See Gray, supra note 135, at 282–84, 299–300.

137. See id. at 284. See also Parker, supra note 129, at 492–93 (discussing a similar trend in such treatises as John Lawson's *Law of Usage and Customs* (1881) and Balfour Browne's *Law of Usages and Customs* (1875)).

138. Gray, supra note 135, at 285 (original emphasis).

139. Id. at 291.

140. See id. at 291–94.

141. See id. at 296 (discussing Cal. Civil Practice Act § 621 (1851), reenacted Cal. Code of Civil Procedure § 748 (1872) ("in actions respecting 'mining claims,' proof shall be admitted of the customs, usages or regulations established and in force at the bar, or diggings, embracing such claim; and such customs, usages or regulations, when not in conflict with the constitution and laws of this State, shall govern the decision of the action.")). See also Parker, supra note 129, at 499–500; Vinogradoff, supra note 2 (ch. 2), at 72. But see Leonard v. Peeples, 30 Ga. 61, 63–64 (1860) (finding no proof of custom with respect to payment for mining claims in California and "[i]f there be such a custom, it is so unreasonable, that it was probably enforced by the bowie-knife.").

142. See Hans Kelsen, General Theory of Law and State 126 (Anders Wedberg transl.; Cambridge, Mass.: Harvard Univ. Press, 1945); Hans Kelsen, Principles of International Law 440–43 (2d ed.; Robert W. Tucker ed.; New York: Holt, Rinehart & Winston, 1966).

143. See Hull, supra note 29 (ch. 1), at 296–97 (discussing Llewellyn's memo to the drafting committee for the Uniform Commercial Code); Parker, supra note 129, at 515. See also David W. Carroll, Harpooning Whales, of Which Karl N. Llewellyn Is the Hero of the Piece; of Searching for More Expansion Joints in Karl's Crumbling Cathedral, 12 Boston College Indus. & Comm. L. Rev. 139 (1970).

144. 304 U.S. 64, 79 (1938) (quoting Black & White Taxicab Co. v. Brown & Yellow Taxicab Co., 276 U.S. 518, 533 34 (1928) (Holmes, J., dissenting)). See also Rutherglen, supra note 103 (ch. 1), at 962.

145. 1 Blackstone *78.

4. ECONOMICS, SOCIOBIOLOGY, AND PSYCHOLOGY

1. See Chapter 1, text at notes 12–28.

2. See Donald T. Campbell, On the Conflicts Between Biological and Social Evolution and Between Psychology and Moral Tradition, 30 Am. Psychologist 1103 (1975); System, Change, and Conflict: A Reader on Contemporary Sociological Theory and the Debate Over Functionalism (Nicholas J. Demerath & Richard A. Peterson eds.; New York: Free Press 1967).

3. Walter Bagheot, Physics and Politics (1872); William G. Sumner, Folkways (Boston: Ginn, 1906).

4. See Gabriel de Tarde, The Laws of Imitation (Elise Clews Parsons, transl.; New York: Henry Holt, 1903) (originally published 1890).

5. See Emile Durkheim, The Division of Labor in Society 49–229 (George Simpson transl.; New York: Free Press, 1933).

6. See Eugen Ehrlich, Fundamental Principles of the Sociology of Law (Walter L. Moll, transl.; Cambridge, Mass.: Harvard Univ. Press, 1936) (originally published 1913).

7. For more on Tarde's influence on theories of customary law, see Allen, supra note 5(ch. 1), at 103–05.

8. See Chapter 2, text at notes 95–105.

9. See Ehrlich, supra note 6, at 455–60.

10. Id. at 456.

11. See id. at 470–71.

12. See also Robert D. Cooter, Decentralized Law for a Complex Economy: The Structural Approach to Adjudicating the New Law Merchant, 144 U. Pa. L. Rev. 1643, 1661–64 (1996).

13. See George C. Homans, Coming to My Senses: The Autobiography of a Sociologist 154–57 (New Brunswick, N.J.: Transaction Books, 1984) (differentiating views of Malinowski and Alfred Radcliffe-Brown on this issue).

14. Robert C. Ellickson, Order Without Law: How Neighbors Settle Disputes 151–52 (Cambridge, Mass.: Harvard Univ. Press, 1991).

15. For some early examples, see George Edwin Pugh, The Biological Origin of Human Values (New York: Basic Books, 1977); Edward O. Wilson, Sociobiology: The New Synthesis 106–29 (Cambridge, Mass.: Belknap Press of Harvard Univ. Press, 1975); Jack Hirshleifer, Privacy: Its Origin, Function, and Future, 9 JLS 649 (1980); Paul H. Rubin, Evolved Ethics and Efficient Ethics, 3 J. Econ. Behav. & Org. 161 (1982).

16. See Howard S. Becker, Outsiders: Studies in the Sociology of Deviance 15–18, 147–63 (London: Free Press, 1963); Isaac D. Balbus, Commodity Form and Legal Form: An Essay on the 'Relative Autonomy' of Law, 11 L. & Soc'y Rev. 571 (1976).

17. See Max Weber, Max Weber on Law in Economy and Society 5 (Max Rheinstein ed., Cambridge, Mass.: Harvard Univ. Press, 1954); Anthony T. Kronman, Max Weber 28–31 (Stanford: Stanford Univ. Press, 1983).

18. For more on Llewellyn's contribution in this regard, see James Q. Whitman, Commercial Law and the American Volk: A Note on Llewellyn's German Sources for the Uniform Commercial Code, 97 YLJ 156 (1987); Zipporah B. Wiseman, The Limits of Vision: Karl Llewellyn and the Merchant Rules, 100 HLR 465 (1987).

19. See, e.g., Lon Fuller, Human Interaction, supra note 76 (ch. 1), at 2 (customary law "is not the product of official enactment, but owes its force to the fact that it has found direct expression in the conduct of men toward one another."); Lon Fuller, The Morality of Law (New Haven, Yale Univ. Press, 1964); Lon Fuller, American Legal Realism, 82 U. Pa. L. Rev. 429 (1934). See also Bruno Leoni, Freedom and the Law 216–18 (3d ed., Indianapolis: Liberty Fund, 1991); Anna di Robilant, Genealogies of Soft Law, 54 AJCL 499, 527–32 (2006).

20. Donald J. Boudreaux, Hayek's Relevance: A Comment on Richard A. Posner's Hayek, Law and Cognition, 2 N.Y.U. J. L. & Liberty, 157, 158 (2006).

21. See Chapter 3, text at notes 106–20. See also John Gray, Hayek on Liberty 31 (2d ed.; New York: Routledge, 1986); Richard A. Epstein, *International News Service v. Associated Press*: Custom and Law as Sources of Property Rights in News, 78 VLR 85, 88–89 (1992).

22. Hayek's theory of custom is also partially derivative of Hans Kelsen's work. See 2 F. A. Hayek, Law, Legislation and Liberty: The Mirage of Social Justice 49 & 171 (Chicago: Univ. of Chicago Press, 1976). See also Todd J. Zywicki & Anthony B. Sanders, Posner, Hayek, and the Economic Analysis of Law, 93 Iowa L. Rev. 559, 595–96 (2008).

23. 1 F. A. Hayek, Law, Legislation and Liberty: Rules and Order 43 (Chicago: Univ. of Chicago Press, 1973).

24. See id. at 45–46 ("Although undoubtedly an order originally formed itself sponta-
    neously because the individuals followed rules which had not been deliberately
    made but had arisen spontaneously, people gradually learned to improve those
    rules; and it is at least conceivable that the formation of a spontaneous order relies
    entirely on rules that were deliberately made. The spontaneous character of the
    resulting order must therefore be distinguished from the spontaneous origin of
    the rules on which it rests, and it is possible that an order which would still have to
    be described as spontaneous rests on rules which are entirely the result of deliber-
    ate design.").

25. See id. at 88, 95, 105.

26. See id. at 75 (citing John Rawls, Justice as Fairness, 67 Philosophical Review 195
    (1958)).

27. But see id. at 152 n.33, 155 n.4, 173 n.25 (for references to the work of Evans-
    Pritchard, Gluckman, and Malinowski).

28. Id. at 76.

29. Id. at 77. For a critique that Hayek's description of norm-creation with customs
    was incomplete, see John Hasnas, Hayek, The Common Law, and Fluid Drive, 1
    N.Y.U. J. L. & Liberty 79, 80 (2004).

30. See Chapter 3, text at note 141.

31. See Andrew P. Morriss, Miners, Vigilantes and Cattlemen: Overcoming Free
    Rider Problems in Private Provision of Law, 33 Land & Water L. Rev. 581, 592–625
    (1998).

32. See Andrew P. Morriss, Hayek and Cowboys, Customary Law in the American
    West, 1 N.Y.U. J. L. & Liberty 35, 42–47 (2005).

33. See Ghen v. Rich, 8 F. 159 (D. Mass. 1881) (custom that person who first lanced
    a whale took possession); Ellickson, supra note 14, at 191–206. See also Lisa
    Bernstein, Opting Out of the Legal System: Extralegal Contractual Relations in
    the Diamond Industry, 21 JLS 115 (1992) (discussing "private lawmaking" of New
    York diamond bourses); Eric A. Feldman, The Tuna Court: Laws and Norms in
    the World's Premier Fish Market, 94 Cal. L. Rev. 313 (2006) (institution of tuna
    courts in Tokyo).

34. See Epstein, supra note 21, at 89. See also Stewart Macaulay, Non-Contractual
    Relations in Business: A Preliminary Study, 28 Am. Soc. Rev. 55, 63 (1963); Carol
    Rose, The Comedy of the Commons: Custom, Commerce, and Inherently
    Public Property, 53 UCLR 711 (1986).

35. See H. Patrick Glenn, The Capture, Reconstruction and Marginalization of
    "Custom," 45 AJCL 613 (1997).

36. Hayek, supra note 23, at 94, 124.

37. Id. at 85.

38. Id. at 87.

39. See Friedrich A. Hayek, The Constitution of Liberty 151–54 (Chicago: Univ. of
    Chicago Press, 1960).

40. Id. at 100.

41. Id.

42. Richard A. Posner, Hayek, Law and Cognition, 1 N.Y.U. J. L. & Liberty 147, 151
    (2005).

43. See id. at 152.

44. Id. at 151.

45. See Hasnas, supra note 29, at 79, 80.

46. Hayek, supra note 23, at 73.

47. See Chapter 3, text at notes 86–105.

48. But see Hayek, supra note 23, at 163 n.5, 166 n.27, 167 n.32, 168 n.38, 174 n.1 (for citations to the works of Buckland, Holdsworth, Maitland, and Plucknett).

49. Compare Samuel T. Morison, Custom, Reason, and the Common Law: A Reply to Hasnas, 2 N.Y.U. J. L. & Liberty 209, 225–30 (2007); John Hasnas, Confusion About Hayek's Confusion: A Response to Morrison, 2 N.Y.U. J.L. & Liberty 241 (2007).

50. Posner, Hayek, supra note 42, at 151. For a response, see Donald J. Boudreaux, Hayek's Relevance: A Comment on Richard A. Posner's Hayek, Law, and Cognition, 2 N.Y.U. J. L. & Liberty 157 (2006).

51. Posner, Hayek, supra note 42, at 151.

52. See Gerald Postema, Nature as First Custom: Hayek on the Evolution of Social Rules, available at http://ssrn.com/abstract=1505430 (Nov. 23, 2009 revision); Zywicki & Sanders, supra note 22, at 595–96.

53. Lisa Bernstein, The Questionable Empirical Basis of Article 2's Incorporation Strategy: A Preliminary Study, 66 UCLR 710, 716–17 (1999).

54. Id. at 748. See also Richard Craswell, Do Trade Customs Exist?, in The Jurisprudential Foundations of Corporate and Commercial Law 118, 121, 125 (Jody S. Kraus Steven D. Walts, eds.; Cambridge: Cambridge Univ. Press, 2000).

55. Posner, Hayek, supra note 42, at 162.

56. See A. I. Ogus, Law and Spontaneous Order: Hayek's Contribution to Legal Theory, 6 J. L. & Soc'y 393 (1989).

57. Bernstein, supra note 53, at 754.

58. See Hayek, supra note 23, at 88 (recognizing that rules arising from an evolutionary process may "develop in very undesirable directions and that when this happens correction by deliberate legislation may … be the only practicable way out."). See also Richard A. Epstein, Confusion About Custom: Disentangling Informal Customs from Standard Contractual Provisions, 66 UCLR 821, 821–23 (1999).

59. For a general review of this literature, see Ekkehart Sclicht, On Custom, 149/1 J. Institutional & Theoretical Econ. 178 (1993).

60. 3 JLE 1 (1960).

61. See Robert Cooter, The Cost of Coase, 11 JLS 1 (1982); Donald Gjerdingen, The Coase Theorem and the Psychology of Common-Law Thought, 56 So. Cal. L. Rev. 711 (1983); Donald H. Regan, The Problem of Social Cost Revisited, 15 JLE 427 (1972).

62. William M. Landes & Richard A. Posner, The Economic Structure of Tort Law 132–33 (Cambridge, Mass.: Harvard Univ. Press, 1987).

63. See id. at 136.

64. Ellickson, supra note 14, at 2. See also Vincy Fon & Francesco Parisi, Customary Law and Articulation Theories: An Economic Analysis 4 (George Mason Univ. Sch. of Law, Law and Economics Working Papers Series, Paper No. 02–24, 2002), available at http://www.law.gmu.edu/faculty/papers/docs/02-24.pdf.; Francesco Parisi, The Formation of Customary Law 10 (George Mason Univ. Sch. of Law: Law and Econ. Research Paper Series, Paper No. 01–06, 2001), available at http://papers.ssrn.com/sol3/papers.cfm?abstract_id=262032 (Apr. 2, 2001 revision).

65. Epstein, INS, supra note 21, at 126.

66. See Stephen L. Carter, Custom, Adjudication, and Petrushevsky's Watch: Some Notes from the Intellectual Property Front, 78 VLR 129, 130 (1992).

67. Craswell, supra note 54, at 120.

68. Id. See also Cooter, supra note 12; Charles Goetz & Robert E. Scott, The Limits of Expanded Choice: An Analysis of the Interactions Between Express and Implied Contract Terms, 73 Calif. L. Rev. 261, 278 (1985) (who support this way to adopt custom).

69. See Jody S. Kraus, Legal Design and the Evolution of Commercial Norms, 26 JLS 377, 382–84 (1997) (citing and discussing the work of Savigny, Maine, Wigmore, and Robert Boyd & Peter Richerson). See also Clayton P. Gillette, The Law Merchant in the Modern Age: Institutional Design and International Usages Under the CISG, 5 Chi. J. Int'l L. 157 (2004).

70. See id. at 379. See also Lisa Bernstein, Merchant Law in a Merchant Court: Rethinking the Code's Search for Immanent Business Norms, 144 U. Pa. L. Rev. 1765, 1796–1802 (1996).

71. See Kraus, supra note 69, at 392–406.

72. Id. at 408–09.

73. See Chapter 3, text at notes 86–105.

74. See Jennifer E. Rothman, The Questionable Use of Custom in Intellectual Property, 93 VLR 1899, 1931–36 (2007).

75. Id. at 1954.

76. Id. at 1954–55.

77. Id. at 1955 (citing Sushil Bikchandani et al., A Theory of Fads, Fashion, Custom and Cultural Change as Informational Cascades, 100 J. Pol. Econ. 992, 994 (1992)).

78. Ellickson, supra note 14, at 137.

79. See Chapter 1, text at notes 29–62.

80. See Ellickson, supra note 14, at 147–55.

81. See id. at 147 (citing Arthur Allen Leff, Economic Analysis of Law: Some Realism About Nominalism, 60 VLR 451, 468 (1974)).

82. See Richard A. Posner, Frontiers of Legal Theory 288 (Cambridge, Mass.: Harvard Univ. Press, 2001).

83. See id. at 289–92.

84. Id. at 293.

85. Id. at 293–94.

86. Id. at 289.

87. See id. at 299–306. See also Richard H. McAdams, The Origin, Development, and Regulation of Norms, 96 Mich. L. Rev. 338 (1997).

88. See Ellickson, supra note 14, at 2.

89. Id. at 52–53.

90. See id. at 280–81.

91. See id. at 255.

5. FAMILY LAW

1. See A. N. Allott, What Is to Be Done with African Customary Law? The Experience of Problems and Reforms in Anglophone Africa from 1950, 28 JAL

56, 59 (1984). For parallels with French colonial practices, see Francis Snyder, Customary Law and the Economy, 28 JAL 34 (1984).

2. See D. J. Lewis, A Requiem for Chinese Customary Law in Hong Kong, 32 ICLQ 347 (1983); J. N. Matson, The Common Law Abroad: English and Indigenous Laws in the British Commonwealth, 42 ICLQ 753,762–66 (1993).

3. See John Y. Luluaki, Customary Marriage Laws in the Commonwealth: A Comparison Between Papua New Guineas and Anglophonic Africa, 11 Int'l J. Law, Policy and the Family 1 (1997); Leopold Popisil, Modern and Traditional Administration of Justice in New Guinea, 19 J. of Legal Pluralism 93 (1981); Jean G. Zorn & Jennifer Corrin Care, 'Barava Tru': Approaches to the Pleading and Proof of Custom in the South Pacific, 51 ICLQ 611, 611–12 (2002).

4. See Supreme Court Ordinance (Nigeria), No. 23, s. 17 (1943); Eshugbayi Eleko v. Nigerian Government, 1931 App. Cas. 662, 673 (P.C.) (appeal from Nigeria).

5. Re Southern Rhodesia, 1919 App. Cas. 211, 233–34 (P.C.) (appeal from South Africa).

6. See, e.g., Native Marriages Ordinance (Southern Rhodesia), No. 79 (1917); Native Marriages Act (Southern Rhodesia), No. 23 (1950); Marriage Ordinance (Ghana), ch. 127, s. 48. See also Luluaki, supra note 3, at 10 & n.12.

7. Compare T. O. Elias, The Nature of African Customary Law, supra note 59 (ch. 1); with J. F. Holleman, Shona Customary Law (Manchester: Manchester Univ. Press, 2d ed. 1969). See also Richard Abel, Custom, Rules, Administration, Community, 28 JAL 6, 13 (1984).

8. See Elias, supra note 59 (ch. 1), at 98–99.

9. See, e.g., Holleman, supra note 7, at 3–22 (describing for areas of Mashonaland in Southern Rhodesia in the period 1945–48 elaborate village (*musha*), tribal ward (*dunhu*), and tribe (*nyika*) institutions); T. W. Bennett, Customary Law in South Africa 101–11 (Cape Town: Juta, 2004) (discussing traditional leaders of South Africa).

10. See Holleman, supra note 7, at 23–71 (Shona genealogical and kinship group-ings); Gordon R. Woodman, Customary Land Law in the Ghanaian Courts 182–215 (Accra: Ghana Universities Press, 1996) (extended clan "stool" institutions in Ghana).

11. See Elias, supra note 59 (ch. 1), at 82–92 (discussing the work of Malinowski and Durkheim).

12. See id. at 33.

13. See id. at 177–86 (legal fictions), 191–207 (customary legislation).

14. See Peter Fitzpatrick, Law and State in Papua New Guinea 247–48 (New York: Academic Press, 1980); Francis G. Snyder, Capitalism and Legal Change: An African Transformation (New York: Academic Press, 1981).

15. See Martin Chanock, Law, Custom and Social Order: The Colonial Experience in Malawi and Zambia (Cambridge: Cambridge Univ. Press, 1985); M. Chanock, Neither Customary Nor Legal: African Customary Law in an Era of Family Law Reform, 3 Int'l J. L. & Family 72, 80 (1989).

16. See Simon Roberts, Some Notes on "African Customary Law," 28 JAL 1, 3 (1984) (citing *The Invention of Tradition* (E. J. Hobsbawm & T. O. Rangers, eds.; Cambridge: Cambridge Univ. Press, 1983)).

17. See id. at 3 (citing T. O. Rangers, The Invention of Tradition in Colonial Africa, in The Invention of Tradition 211, 250 (E. J. Hobsbawm & T. O. Rangers, eds.; Cambridge: Cambridge Univ. Press, 1983)).

18. See Peter Fitzpatrick, Traditionalism and Traditional Law, 28 JAL 20 (1984); T. Nhlapo, Cultural Diversity, Human Rights and the Family in Contemporary Africa: Lessons from the Southern Africa Constitutional Debate, 9 Int'l J. L. & Family 208, 217 (1995); Francis Snyder, Customary Law and the Economy, 28 JAL 34 (1984); Gordon Woodman, Some Realism about Customary Law: The West African Experience, 1969 Wisconsin L. Rev. 128; Zorn & Care, supra note 3, at 611–15. For a judicial recognition of this theory, see Bhe and Others v. Magistrate Khayelitsha and Others, 2005 (1) SA 580 (CC) at ¶ 89 (S. Af.) (Langa, DCJ). For an application of this theory to South Pacific jurisdictions, see Luluaki, supra note 3, at 5–8.

19. See T. W. Bennett, Re-Introducing African Customary Law to the South African Legal System, 57 AJCL 1, 8 (2009).

20. See Oyewumi v. Ogunesan, [1990] 3 N.W.L.R. (Pt. 137) 182, 207 (S.C.) (Nigeria) (Obaseki, JSC) ("Customary law is the organic or living law of the indigenous people of Nigeria regulating their lives and transactions. It is organic in that it is not static. It is regulatory in that it controls the lives and transactions of the Community subject to it. It is said that custom is a mirror of the culture of the people. I would say that Customary law goes further and imports justice to the lives of all those subject to it.").

21. See Allison D. Kent, Custody, Maintenance and Succession: The Internalization of Women's and Children's Rights Under Customary Law in Africa, 28 Michigan J. Int'l L. 507, 522 (2007).

22. See Lynn Berat, Customary Law in a New South Africa: A Proposal, 15 Fordham Int'l L. J. 92, 105, 110 (1991/1992) (Botswana and Lesotho).

23. See Luluaki, supra note 3; Zorn & Care, supra note 3.

24. See id.

25. See, e.g., Const. Fiji Islands (1997), s. 186(1); Papua New Guinea Const. (1975), sch. 2.1, para. (3); Const. Solomon Islands (1978), sch. 3, para. 3(2).

26. See, e.g., Customs Recognition Act (Papua New Guinea) (1963); Customs Recognition Act (Solomon Islands) (2000). But see Underlying Law Act (Papua New Guinea) (2000) (which treats custom as law). See generally Zorn & Care, supra note 3, at 620–21. In Africa, this followed from colonial precedents, see Angu v. Attah, [1916] Gold Coast Privy Counsel Judgments 1874–1928, 43, 44 (a rule of customary law "has to be proved in the first instance by calling witnesses acquainted with the native customs until the particular customs have, by frequent proof, become so notorious that the courts will take judicial notice of them"). See also Matson, supra note 2, at 768–73.

27. Evidence Act (Nigeria), s. 14(1) (1990). See also id. s. 58 (proof of custom can be adduced from "opinions of other persons having special knowledge of native law and custom," "opinions of native chiefs," and any "book" or "manuscript").

28. See id. s. 14(2).

29. See Olagbemiro v. Ajagungbade III, [1990] 3 N.W.L.R. (pt. 136) 37 (S.C.) (Nigeria) (ownership of chieftaincy lands); Onwuchekwa v. Onwuchekwa, [1991]

5 N.W.L.R. (pt. 194) 739 (C.A.) (Nigeria) (property rights of women in customary marriages).

30. See Bennett, supra note 9, at 48–49.

31. Law of Evidence Amendment Act (South Africa), no. 45, s. 1(1) (1988).

32. See id. s. 1(2). See Bennett, supra note 9, at 44–48; Jill Zimmerman, The Reconstitution of Customary Law in South Africa: Method and Discourse, 17 Harv. BlackLetter L.J. 197, 212–15 (2001). A similar transition occurred in postcolonial Ghana. See Courts Act (Ghana), ch. 372, s. 50(1) (1971) ("any question as to the existence or content of a rule of customary law is a question of law for the Court and not a question of fact."). See also Woodman, supra note 10, at 41–43.

33. See A. N. Allott, Customary Law in British Africa, 20 Mod. L. Rev. 244, 250 (1957); Zorn & Care, supra note 3, at 622–30.

34. See Matson, supra note 2, at 773–77; A. A. Oba, Islamic Law as Customary Law: The Changing Perspective in Nigeria, 51 ICLQ 817, 835–40 (2002) (noting judicial criticism of the characterization of Islamic personal law as customary, since Sharia law is not localized).

35. See A. A. Kolajo, Customary Law in Nigeria Through the Cases 128–55 (Ibadan: Spectrum Books, 2000) (discussing unique customary regime of succession and land acquisition for Benin).

36. See Nkeaka v. Nkeaka, [1994] 5 N.W.L.R. (pt. 346) 599 (C.A.) (Nigeria) (application of Ibusa custom regarding inheritance).

37. See Dawodu v. Damole, [1958] 3 F.S.C. 46 (S.C.) (Nigeria) (application of "Idi-igi" method of distribution of estate in Yoruba custom, as distinct from "Ori-ojori" method).

38. See Thibela v. Minister van Wet en Orde, 1995 (3) SA 147 (S. Afr.); Bennett, supra note 9, at 51–57, 69–70 (discussing Law of Evidence Amendment Act, 1988, provision on conflicts rules for customary law).

39. See Customary Law and Primary Courts Act, ch. 6, s. 3(2)(a) (1981) (Zimbabwe); Mokorosi v. Mokorosi & Others, [1967–1970] Lesotho L. Rep. 1; Hoohlo, [1967–1970] Lesotho L. Rep. 318.

40. See Edet v. Essien, 11 N.L.R. 47 (S.C. 1932) (Nigeria) (holding repugnant a custom that allowed a husband to claim the children of another man because that man had deprived him of his wife without paying dowry). See also Antony Allott, New Essays in African Law 158–71 (London: Butterworth, 1970); T. W. Bennett, Human Rights and African Customary Law Under the South African Constitution 20 (Cape Town: Juta, 1995).

41. See Chiduku v. Chidano, 1922 SR 55, 58 (S. Afr.).

42. See Bennett, supra note 9, at 68 (citing cases dealing with customs allowing marriage without consent, succession by illegitimate children, among others).

43. See Onwuchekwa v. Onwuchekwa, [1991] 5 N.W.L.R. (pt. 194) 739 (C.A.) (Nigeria); Local Court Act (Sierra Leone), s. 3 (1963). In Ghana, however, the caveat of repugnancy was eliminated. See Interpretation Act (Ghana), ch. 4, s. 18(I); 1992 Ghana Const. ch. 4, art. 11.

44. [1994] 9 N.W.L.R. (pt. 368) 301 (S.C.) (Nigeria).

45. Law of Evidence Amendment Act (South Africa), ch. 45, s. 1(1) (1988).

46. Id.

47. See Elias, supra note 59 (ch. 1), at 207–11; Holleman, supra note 7, at 369–77 (discussing Native Marriages Act (Rhodesia) (1950)).

48. See Ogunola v. Eiyekole, [1990] 4 N.W.L.R. (pt. 146) 632 (S.C.) (Nigeria) (Land Use Act, 1978, did not preempt custom); Amadi v. Nwosu, [1992] 5 N.W.L.R. (pt. 241) 273 (S.C.) (Nigeria) (Married Women's Property Act, 1881, did not preempt marriages under customary law); Idehen v. Idehen, [1991] 6 N.W.L.R. (pt. 198) 382 (S.C.) (Nigeria) (Wills Act, 1837, did preempt dispositions by testament under customary law).

49. Marriage Act (Nigeria), ch. 218, s. 35 (1990).

50. See Luluaki, supra note 3, at 8–9 (Papua New Guinea); Zorn & Care, supra note 3, at 620–21, 630–31 (discussing codification attempts in the Marshall Islands, Nauru, and Fiji).

51. Native Administration Act (South Africa), ch. 38, s. 11(1) (1927) (later renamed the Black Administration Act).

52. See Bennett, supra note 9, at 41–42, 141–47.

53. See id. at 46–49, 70–74.

54. Ch. 120 (1998) (S. Afr.).

55. See id. (Schedule).

56. See id. ss. 3–10.

57. See id. s. 11.

58. See Bennett, supra note 9, at 156–60 (South Africa); Kolajo, supra note 35 (Nigeria); Lewis, supra note 2, at 356–79 (Hong Kong); Matson, supra note 2, at 763–66; Woodman, supra note 10, at 44–45 (Ghana); Zorn & Care, supra note 3, at 631–37 (Solomon Islands and Vanuatu).

59. See Bennett, supra note 9, at 220–24; The Meaning of Marriage Payments 36–37 (J. L. Comaroff, ed.; London: Academic Press, 1980); Holleman, supra note 7, at 161–76, 265–317; African Systems of Kinship and Marriage 46 (A. R. Radcliffe-Brown & D. Forde, eds.; London: Oxford Univ. Press, 1950).

60. See Snyder, supra note 18, at 40–42 (discussing Senegambian practice of childwealth).

61. This has been implicitly the rule also in Nigeria. See Eze v. Omeke, [1977] 1 Anambra State L.R. 136 (H.C.) (Nigeria); Okpanum v. Okpanum & Another, [1972] 2 East Central State L.R. 561 (H.C.) (Nigeria).

62. See Bennett, supra note 9, at 232–33.

63. See id. at 277–78.

64. See Elias, supra note 59 (ch. 1), at 82–87, 163–66.

65. See Boateng v. Adjei, [1963] 1 Ghana L.R. 285, 296 (S.C.); Chieftaincy Act (Ghana), ch. 370, s. 36 (1971).

66. Id. s. 37; Woodman, supra note 10, at 199–215.

67. See, e.g., Tijani v. Secretary Southern Nigeria, [1921] 2 App. Cas. 399 (P.C.) (appeal from Nigeria) (family chief has usufructuary title); Alao & Others v. Alao & Others, [1989] 4 N.W.L.R. (pt. 113) 1 (S.C.) (Nigeria) (rules on alienation of family property in Yoruba custom); Adesanya v. Oyuewu, [1993] 1 N.W.L.R. (pt. 270) 414 (S.C.) (Nigeria) (under Yoruba custom, women can serve as family head).

68. See RCMA, supra note 54, s. 7(2).

69. See Bennett, supra note 9, at 235.

70. See Yusuff v. Dada, [1990] 4 N.W.L.R. (pt. 146) 657 (S.C.) (Nigeria) (under Yoruba custom, children of the deceased inherit in equal shares); Rabiu v. Abasi, [1996] 7 N.W.L.R. (pt. 462) 505 (S.C.) (Nigeria) (same); Idehen v. Idehen, [1991] 6 N.W.L.R.

(pt. 198) 382 (S.C.) (Nigeria) (under Benin custom, eldest son inherited); Akinnubi v. Akinnubi, [1997] 2 N.W.L.R. (pt. 486) 144 (S.C.) (Nigeria) (although wife cannot inherit, she can, under the Nigerian Constitution, sue as "next friend" on behalf of her children to lay claim to an estate). But see Mojekwu v. Mojekwu, [1997] 7 N.W.L.R. 283, 303–05 (C.A.) (Nigeria) (striking down Oli-ekpe custom as repugnant).

71. S. Afr. Const. 1996, s. 31(1) ("Persons belonging to a cultural, religious or linguistic community may not be denied the right, with other members of that community ... to enjoy their culture....").

72. See also id. s. 15(3) (allowing legislation recognizing "systems of personal and family law under any tradition"). See Bennett, supra note 9, at 78, 86–90.

73. S. Afr. Const. 1996, s. 31(2). By way of contrast, the Constitution of Zimbabwe inverted these constitutional values: the customary law of succession prevailed over gender equality. Zimbabwe Const. s. 23(3)(b). See also Magaya v. Magaya, 1999 (1) Zimb. L.R. 100, 109 (S).

74. See Bhe & Others v. Magistrate, Khayelitsha & Others, 2005 (1) B.C.L.R. 1 (CC), at ¶ 41 (S. Afr.). See also Bangindawo & Others v. Head of Nyande Regional Authority & Another, 1998 (3) SA 262 (Tk) (S. Afr.) (constitutionality of procedures in traditional courts).

75. In Mthembu v. Letsela & Another, 2000 (3) SA 867 (SCA), the South Africa Court of Appeal avoided a constitutional challenge to a custom in which property of decedent with no male children reverted back to the decedent's father, leaving the wife and female children with nothing. The Court concluded that there had been no valid customary marriage (for failure to pay full *lobolo*), and that any proposed reforms of the custom were best accomplished by the legislature or Law Commission. See also Jelil A. Omotola, Primogeniture and Illegitimacy in African Customary Law: The Battle for Survival of Culture, 15 Indiana Int'l & Comp. L. Rev. 115 (2004); Zimmerman, supra note 32, at 215–18.

76. See Promotion of Equality and Prevention of Unfair Discrimination Act, ch. 4, preamble, ch. 1 s. 1(viii) (2000) (S. Afr.) (including customary practices as within scope of the Act).

77. 2005 (1) B.C.L.R. 1 (CC) (S. Afr.).

78. See id. ¶¶ 80, 82.

79. See id. ¶¶ 117, 122–25.

80. Id. ¶¶ 139, 180–91 (Ngcobo, J.).

81. S. Afr. Const. 1996, s. 211(3).

82. Id. s. 39(2).

83. See Lewis, supra note 2, at 360–63 (institution of concubinage in Hong Kong and its statutory abolition).

84. See Holleman, supra note 7, at 322–23

85. See Kolajo, supra note 35, at 62.

86. See Bennett, supra note 9, at 243–45.

87. See Tracy E. Higgins, Jeanmarie Fenrich & Ziona Tanzer, Gender Equality and Customary Marriage: Bargaining in the Shadow of Post-Apartheid Legal Pluralism, 30 Fordham Int'l L.J. 1653, 1684–91 (2007) (for extensive empiric data on polygyny in South Africa).

88. See id. at 246–47.

89. See RCMA, supra note 54, s. 2(3). Interestingly, South Africa law does not sanction polygynous marriages under Islamic law, although equal succession rights for wives in such marriages are recognized. See Hassam v. No & Others, [2009] ZACC 19 (June 15, 2009) (Const. Ct. S. Afr.).

90. See RCMA, supra note 54, s. 2(4).

91. See id. ss. 7(6) & 7(7).

92. See Bennett, supra note 9, at 247–48.

93. See 2005 (1) B.C.L.R. 1 (CC), at ¶¶ 122–25 (Langa, DCJ) (S. Afr.).

94. See South Africa Law Commission Project 90: The Harmonisation of the Common Law and the Indigenous Law: Report on Customary Marriages (1998); Penelope E. Andrews, "Big Love": The Recognition of Customary Marriages in South Africa, 64 Wash. & Lee L. Rev. 1483 (2007).

6. PROPERTY

1. See, e.g., Jennifer E. Rothman, The Questionable Use of Custom in Intellectual Property, 93 VLR 1899 (2007).

2. See Carter, supra note 130 (ch. 3), at 120–21.

3. See Plucknett, supra note 18 (ch. 3), at 307–13.

4. See James Robert Arnett II, The American Legal System and Micronesian Customary Law: The Legal Legacy of the United States to the New Nations of the Trust Territory of the Pacific Islands, 4 Pacific Basin L. Rev. 161, 185 (1985) (statutory recognition of custom in Marshall Islands and Federated States of Micronesia).

5. In Canada, "aboriginal" rights are protected under its constitution. Canadian Charter of Rights and Duties, s. 35(1) (1982). This has been interpreted to include hunting and fishing practices. See R v. Van der Peet, [1996] 137 DLR (4th) 289, at ¶¶ 48 et seq. (S.C.) (Can.).

6. (1992) 175 C.L.R. 1, 61–65 (Austl.).

7. See s. 223(1) (Cth) (Austl.) ("The expression 'native title or native title rights and interests' means the communal, group or individual rights and interests of Aboriginal peoples or Torres Strait Islanders in relation to land or waters, where: (a) the rights and interests are possessed under the traditional laws acknowledged, and the traditional customs observed, by the Aboriginal peoples or Torres Strait Islanders; and (b) the Aboriginal peoples or Torres Strait Islanders, by those laws and customs, have a connection with the land or waters; and (c) the rights and interests are recognised by the common law of Australia.").

8. See id. ss. 10–199.

9. See Wik Peoples v. Queensland, (1996) 187 C.L.R. 1 (Austl.); Native Title Amendment Act 1998 (Cth) (Austl.).

10. See Yorta Yorta Aboriginal Cmty. v. Victoria, (2002) 214 C.L.R 422, 422–23, 492 (Austl.). See also Howard L. Highland, The Mote in the Common Law's Eye: Dislodging Eurocentric Barriers to Just Recognition of Native Title in the Wake of Yorta Yorta, 13 Wash. & Lee J. Civil Rights & Soc. Just. 349 (2007).

11. See Arnett, supra note 4, at 189–97 (evolution towards individual land ownership and hostility towards certain customary land-tenure rules).

12. I acknowledge that the newly sanctioned spelling of the state is Hawai`i, but that the former spelling will be used here, unless the context demands otherwise.

13. Unification of the islands was achieved by Kamehameha the Great between 1795 and 1810. See Ralph Simpson Kuykendall, The Hawaiian Kingdom 1778–1854 (Honolulu: Univ. of Hawaii Press, 1957). See also Native Hawaiian Rights Handbook 211–13, 223–25 (Melody Kapilialuha Mackenzie ed.; Honolulu: Univ. of Hawaii Press, 1991).

14. See Public Access Shoreline Hawaii v. Hawai`i County Planning Comm'n, 903 P.2d 1246, 1258 n.21 (Haw. 1995), cert. denied, 517 U.S. 1163 (1996) ["PASH"].

15. See Elizabeth Bentzel Buck, Paradise Remade: The Politics of Culture and History in Hawai`i (Philadelphia: Temple Univ. Press, 1993); Kuykendall, supra note 13.

16. See, e.g., City of Galveston v. Menard, 23 Tex. 349, 389–90 (1859); Knowles v. Dow, 22 N.H. 387, 404–06 (1851); Littlefield v. Maxwell, 31 Me. 134, 139 (1850).

17. See Oni v. Meek, 2 Haw. 87 (1858).

18. 1892 Haw. Sess. Laws ch. 57, § 5, codified at Haw. Rev. Stat. § 1–1 (1994). When this was later codified, the word "national" between "Hawaiian" and "usage" was dropped, a clear indication of the transition of Hawaii from an independent nation to a territory and then state of the United States. This provision was the subject of historical consideration in PASH, 903 P.2d at 1258 n.21.

19. See Pai` Ohana v. United States, 875 F. Supp. 680, 692 (D. Haw. 1995); State v. Zimring, 479 P.2d 202, 204 (Haw. 1970); De Freitas v. Trustees of Campbell Estate, 380 P.2d 762 (Haw. 1963).

20. See Kake v. Horton, 2 Haw. 209, 211 (1860) ("We do not regard the Common Law of England as being in force here *eo nomine* and as a whole.").

21. Branca v. Makuakane, 13 Haw. 499, 505 (1901).

22. County of Hawaii v. Sotomura, 517 P.2d 57, 62 (Haw. 1973) ("in the absence of … other evidence of Hawaiian custom to the question, we resort to common law principles.…").

23. 440 P.2d 76 (Haw. 1968).

24. As the court in *Ashford* explained, see id. at 77–78, a *kamaaina* was a person familiar with the locality from childhood, trained in the art of memorizing boundaries and titles. See also In re Boundaries of Pulehunui, 4 Haw. 239, 245 (1879); Kanaina v. Long, 3 Haw. 332 (1872).

25. Id. See also id. ("Hawaii's land laws are unique in that they are based on ancient tradition, custom, practice and usage.").

26. Id. at 80 (Marumoto, J., dissenting).

27. State v. Zimring, 479 P.2d 202, 203–04 (Haw. 1970).

28. See id. at 204.

29. See PASH, 903 P.2d at 1258–59 (Haw. 1995).

30. Haw. Const. art. XII, § 7.

31. 656 P.2d 745 (Haw. 1982).

32. The definition of a "native Hawaiian" was considered in Public Access Shoreline Hawaii, 903 P.2d at 1269–70 (Haw. 1995), where it was concluded that anyone who could trace a lineage back to someone who was an inhabitant of the island in 1778 could qualify. See id.

33. Haw. Civ. C. § 1477 (1859), codified at Haw. Rev. Stat. § 7–1 (1994) ("people… shall not be deprived of the right to take firewood, house-timber, aho cord,

thatch, or ki leaf, from the land on which they live, for their own private use. The people shall also have a right to drinking water, and running water, and the right of way."). The first sentence speaks to narrowly drawn gathering rights, while the second is more generally framed to cover access to water and rights-of-way.

This statute was described by the *Kalipi* court as being of "ancient origin initially passed when the concept of private property ownership of real property had first been introduced into these islands." 656 P.2d at 747. The phrase used in the statute – "from the land on which they live" – was held in *Kalipi* to refer to the *ahupua`a*. See id. See also those earlier cases that had so limited the application of § 7–1: Palama v. Sheehan, 440 P.2d 95 (Haw. 1986); Carter v. Territory, 24 Haw. 47, 67 (1917); Rogers v. Pedro, 642 P.2d 439 (Haw. App. 1982); Santos v. Perreira, 633 P.2d 1118 (Haw. App. 1981).

34. See Kalipi, 656 P.2d at 748.
35. See id. at 749 n.2.
36. Id. at 750–51 (some citations omitted).
37. Id. at 751.
38. Id. at 751–52.
39. 837 P.2d 1247 (Haw. 1992).
40. See id. at 1271.
41. See id. at 1272 ("We therefore hold that native Hawaiian rights protected by article XII, § 7 may extend beyond the ahupua`a in which a native Hawaiian resides where such rights have been customarily and traditionally exercised in this manner.").
42. See id. at 1247. See also Pai` Ohana v. United States, 875 F. Supp. 680, 692 (D. Haw. 1995).
43. 903 P.2d 1246 (Haw. 1995), aff'g, 900 P.2d 1313 (Haw. App. 1993) ["PASH"]. Certiorari was applied for in the U.S. Supreme Court and denied. See 517 U.S. 1163 (1996).
44. See id. at 1269.
45. Id. at 1268 n.39.
46. The court in PASH reaffirmed the ruling in *Pele Defense Fund* that people not of the ahupua`a could enjoy customary gatherings rights. This certainly compromises an element of certainty. The PASH court also emphasized that a customary right need not be exercised continuously to remain in force. PASH, 903 P.2d at 1270.
47. 1 William Blackstone, Commentaries, supra note 34 (ch. 3), at *78.
48. PASH, 903 P.2d at 1268.
49. 656 P.2d at 751.
50. PASH, 903 P.2d at 1271–72 (citations omitted).
51. Id.
52. 1986 Haw. Sess. Laws ch. 202, § 1, codified at Haw. Rev. Stat. § 5–7.5 (1994).
53. PASH, 903 P.2d at 1271 n.44 (quoting Haw. Rev. Stat. § 5–7.5(a)).
54. See Robert C. Ellickson, Property in Land, 102 YLJ 1315 (1993); Henry E. Smith, Community and Custom in Property, 10 Theoretical Inquiries in Law 5 (2009).
55. Customary norms may also influence other property doctrines like adverse possession or extinctive prescription. See, e.g., Nome 2000 v. Fagerstrom, 799 P.2d 304 (Alaska 1990).

56. See U.S. Const. amend. V ("[N]or shall private property be taken for public use, without just compensation.").
57. See Lucas v. South Carolina Coastal Council, 505 U.S. 1003 (1992).
58. Id. at 1027, 1030–31 (citations and footnotes omitted).
59. See Rutherglen, supra note 103 (ch. 1), at 970.
60. But see Sotomura v. County of Hawaii, 460 F. Supp. 473, 477 (D. Haw. 1978); Robinson v. Ariyoshi, 441 F. Supp. 559, 585 (D. Haw. 1977), aff'd, 753 F.2d 1468, 1475 (9th Cir. 1985) (holding that the recognition of a custom could constitute a taking of property or deprivation of due process).
61. PASH, 903 P.2d at 1272.
62. 462 P.2d 671, 676 (Or. 1969) ("Because many elements of prescription are present in this case, the state has relied upon the doctrine in support of the decree below. We believe, however, that there is a better legal basis for affirming the decree. The most cogent basis for the decision in this case is the English doctrine of custom. Strictly construed, prescription applies only to the specific tract of land before the court, and doubtful prescription cases could fill the courts for years with tract-by-tract litigation. An established custom, on the other hand, can be proven with reference to a larger region. Ocean-front lands from the northern to the southern border of the state ought to be treated uniformly.").
63. See id. at 677–78 ("The English law on customary rights grew up in a small island nation at a time when most inhabitants lived and died without travel-ing more than a day's walk from their birthplace. Most of the customary rights recorded in English cases are local in scope. The English had many cultural and language groups which eventually merged into a nation. After these groups developed their own unique customs, the unified nation recognized some of them as law. Some American scholars, looking at the vast geography of this conti-nent and the freshness of its civilization, have concluded that there is no need to look to English customary rights as a source of legal rights in this country. Some of the generalizations drawn by the text writers from English cases would tend to limit customary rights to specific usages in English towns and villages. But it does not follow that a custom, established in fact, cannot have regional application and be enjoyed by a larger public than the inhabitants of a single village.").
64. Id. at 678.
65. For more on the notion of judicial takings, see Barton H. Thompson, Jr., Judicial Takings, 76 VLR 1449 (1990). For U.S. Supreme Court cases considering the issue, see Muhlker v. New York & Harlem R.R., 197 U.S. 544 (1905); Hughes v. Washington, 389 U.S. 290, 296–98 (1967) (Stewart, J., concurring).
66. 760 P.2d 263, 268–70 (Or. Ct. App. 1988) (footnotes omitted), rev'd on other grounds, 780 P.2d 714 (Or. 1989).
67. 835 P.2d 940 (Or. 1992), aff'd, 854 P.2d 449 (Or. 1993), cert. denied, 510 U.S. 1207 (1994).
68. See Stevens, 835 P.2d at 942.
69. Id. at 452 n.9 (original emphasis).
70. 505 U.S. 1003 (1992).
71. Stevens, 854 P.2d at 456 (quoting Lucas, 505 U.S. at 1029).
72. Id.
73. Id. (quoting Lucas, 500 U.S. at 1029). See also Peter C. Meier, *Stevens v. City of Cannon Beach*, Taking Takings into the Post-*Lucas* Era, 22 Ecology L. Q.

413 (1995); Melody F. Havey, Comment, *Stevens v. City of Cannon Beach*: Does Oregon's Doctrine of Custom Find a Way Around *Lucas?*, 1 Ocean & Coastal L. J. 109, 121 (1994).

74. 510 U.S. 1207 (1994).
75. Id. at 1212 (Scalia, J., dissenting from denial of certiorari).
76. Stevens, 510 U.S. at 1212.
77. Id. at 1212 n.5.
78. Id. at 1211–12.
79. Id. at 1212–13. See also Lynda J. Oswald, Cornering the Quark: Investment-Backed Expectations and Economically Viable Uses in Takings Analysis, 70 Wash. L. Rev. 91, 151 & n.225 (1995).
80. For a very current case, see Stop the Beach Renourishment, Inc. v. Florida Dep't on Environmental Protection (U.S. S.Ct. Docket 08–1151) (argued Dec. 2, 2009).
81. See Hope M. Babcock, Has the U.S. Supreme Court Finally Drained the Swamp of Takings Jurisprudence?: The Impact of *Lucas v. South Carolina Coastal Council* on Wetlands and Coastal Barrier Beaches, 19 Harv. Envt'l L. Rev. 1, 30–31 (1995). See also Gregory M. Duhl, Property and Custom: Allocating Space in Public Places, 79 Temple L. Rev. 199, 239–41 (2006); Carol Rose, The Comedy of the Commons: Custom, Commerce and Inherently Public Property, 53 UCLR 711 (1986).
82. See Abbott v. Weekly, 1 Lev. 176, 83 Eng. Rep. 357 (K.B. 1665); Fitch v. Rawling, 2 H. Bl. 393, 126 Eng. Rep. 614 (C.P. 1795); Hall v. Nottingham, 33 L.T.R. 697 (Ex. D. 1876) (Eng.).
83. See Mercer v. Denne, [1904] 2 Ch. 534, aff'd, [1905] 2 Ch. 538 (C.A.) (Eng.).
84. See Delaplane v. Crenshaw & Fisher, 56 Va. (15 Gratt.) 457, 475 (1860) ("at this day and in this age, in a government like ours, there can be little need of resort to such a source as custom to form legal sanction"); John Chipman Gray, The Rule Against Perpetuities § 586, at 564 (Roland Gray ed., 4th ed.; Boston; Little Brown, 1942) ("in a country like most parts of America, where a population … has rapidly increased in density, such [customary] rights might become very oppressive. The clog that they would put on the use and transfer of land would far outweigh any advantage that could be acquired from them.").
85. Robinson v. Mollett, 7 L.R.-H.L. 802, 817 (1875) (Brett, L.J.) (Eng.).

7. CONTRACTS

1. See Amelia H. Boss. The Future of the Uniform Commercial Code Process in an Increasingly International World, 68 Ohio State L.J. 349 (2007).
2. See U.C.C. §§ 1–103, 1–205.
3. See 1 William Blackstone, Commentaries, supra note 34 (ch. 3), at *75.
4. See Moult v. Halliday, [1898] 1 Q.B. 125 (Eng.); Re Matthews ex parte Powell, [1875] 1 Ch.D. 501 (Eng.).
5. See Holderness v. Collinson, 7 B. & C. 212, 108 Eng. Rep. 702 (K.B. 1827) (Eng.).
6. The REESIDE, 20 F. Cas. 458, 459 (C.C. Mass. 1837) (No. 11,657) (Story, Circuit Justice). See also John D. Lawson, The Law of Usages and Customs 20 (St. Louis: F. H. Thomas & Co., 1881).
7. 11 Ad. & E. 589, 598, 113 Eng. Rep. 539, 543 (Q.B. 1840) (Eng.).

8. 16 U.S. (1 Pet.) 1 (1842). For more on *Swift's* invocation of customary commercial practices, see Rutherglen, supra note 103 (ch. 1), at 933–34.

9. The REESIDE, 20 F. Cas. 458, 459 (C.C. Mass. 1837) (No. 11,657) (Story, Circuit Justice). For similar language, see Barnard v. Kellogg, 77 U.S. (10 Wall.) 383, 390–91 (1870).

10. See Humfrey v. Dale, 7 El. & Bl. 266, 278, 119 Eng. Rep. 1246, 1250 (Q.B. 1857) (Campbell, C.J.) ("[Lawyers] desire certainty, and would have a contract express all its terms, and desire that no parol evidence beyond it should be receivable. But merchants and traders, with a multiplicity of transactions pressing on them, and moving in a narrow circle and meeting each other, desire to write little, and leave unwritten what they take for granted in every contract. In spite of the lamentations of judges they will continue to do so....").

11. Thomas Cooley, in his commentary on Blackstone, tended to minimize the role of commercial custom. See 1 William Blackstone, Commentaries 68 n.1 (Thomas M. Cooley & James DeWitt Andres eds., 4th ed.; Chicago: Callaghan, 1899). See also Rutherglen, supra note 103 (ch. 1), at 934–35. For a summary of proof of commercial custom in English law, see chapter 3, at note 49.

12. See, e.g.., Collings v. Hope, 6 F. Cas. 111, 111 (C.C.D. Pa. 1812) (No. 3,003) (Washington, Circuit Justice); In re Bowling Green Milling Co., 132 F.2d 279 (6th Cir. 1942); Shipley v. Pittsburgh & L.E.R. Co., 83 F. Supp. 722, 749 (W.D. Pa. 1949); Radio Station KFH Co. v. Musicians Ass'n Local No. 297, 220 P.2d 199 (Kan. 1950) (custom "must have been acquiesced in without contention or dispute so long and so continuously that contracting parties either had it in mind or ought to have had it in mind"); Mall Gift Cards, Inc. v. Wood, 261 So.2d 31 (Ala. 1972). See also Allen, supra note 5 (ch. 1), at 135 (reviewing English precedents); Lawson, supra note 6, at 36–37, 39–40; Joseph H. Levie, Trade Usage and Custom under the Common Law and the Uniform Commercial Code, 40 N.Y.U. L. Rev. 1101, 1103–06 (1965).

13. See Shipley v. Pittsburgh & L.E.R. Co., 83 F. Supp. 722, 750 (W.D. Pa. 1949); Parkway Baking Co. v. Freihofer Baking Co., 255 F.2d 641 (3d Cir. 1958). But see Lawson, supra note 6, at 58 (proof of custom by a single instance).

14. See, e.g., Energen Resources MAQ, Inc. v. Dalbosco, 23 S.W.3d 551, 554–56 (Tex. App. 1st Dist. 2000) (for detailed testimony); All Angles Constr. & Demolition, Inc. v. Metropolitan Atlanta Rapid Transit Authority, 539 S.E.2d 831, 833 (Ga. App. 2000) (proof of custom rejected when only evidence was testimony of the party asserting it); Sharple v. Airtouch Cellular of Georgia, Inc., 551 S.E.2d 87 (Ga. App. 2001) (burden of proving custom is on the party relying upon it). See also Lawson, supra note 6, at 99–104.

15. But see Note, Custom and Trade Usage: Its Application to Commercial Dealings and the Common Law, 55 CLR 1192, 1200 & n.31 (1955) (collecting cases). Curiously, though, a consistent thread in many of these "knowledge" cases is that when custom is used offensively by a party, they must show that they had actual knowledge of the practice. See id. at 1201–02; Lawson, supra note 6, at 58.

16. See Freeman & Co. v. Bolt, 968 P.2d 247, 252–53 (Idaho App. 1998).

17. See Elgin, J. & E. Ry Co. v. Burley, 327 U.S. 661, 664 (1946); Order of Ry. Conductors of Am. v. Pitney, 326 U.S. 561, 567 (1946); Frye v. State, 78 N.Y.S.2d 342, 347–48 (N.Y. Ct. Cl. 1948). See also Columbia Trade Usage Note, supra note 15, at 1200–02; Lawson, supra note 6, at 44–58.

18. See, e.g., Sickelco v. Union Pac. R. Co., 111 F.2d 746, 748 (9th Cir. 1940); In re Bowling Green Milling Co., 132 F.2d 279, 283 (6th Cir. 1942).

19. See, e.g., Sickelco v. Union Pac. R. Co., 111 F.2d 746, 748 (9th Cir. 1940); Shipley v. Pittsburgh & L.E.R. Co., 68 F. Supp. 395, 402–03 (W.D. Pa. 1946); Tennessee Enamel Mfg. Co. v. Stoves, Inc., 192 F.2d 863, 868 (6th Cir. 1951) (custom "must be imperative and compulsory in character."). See also Lawson, supra note 6, at 37–38.

20. See, e.g., AI R. Threadgill v. Peabody Coal Co., 526 P.2d 676, 678 (Colo. App. 1974) (citing 5 S. Williston, Contracts § 649 (3d ed. W. Jaeger; Mount Kisco, New York: Baker Voorhis, 1957)).

21. See Uniform Sales Act § 71 (1906) ("Where any right, duty, or liability would arise under a contract to sell or a sale by implication of law, it may be negatived or varied by express agreement or … by custom, if the custom be such as to bind both parties to the contract or the sale."); 25 Okl. Stat. Ann. § 19 ("Usage is a reasonable and lawful public custom concerning transactions of the same nature as those which are to be affected thereby, existing at the place where the obligation is to be performed, and either known to the parties, or so well established, general and uniform, that they must be presumed to have acted with reference thereto."). See also Jim C. Chen, Code, Custom, and Contract: The Uniform Commercial Code as Law Merchant, 27 Texas Int'l L.J. 91, 97 (1992).

22. Cutter v. Waddingham, 22 Mo. 206, 284 (1855). See also Oppenheimer Bros., Inc. v. Joyce & Co., 154 N.E.2d 856, 860 (Ill. App. 1st Dist. 1958); American Lead Pencil Co. v. Nashville C. & St. L. Ry., 134 S.W. 613, 615 (Tenn. 1911).

23. See, e.g., Rosenberg Bros. & Co. v. United States Shipping Bd., 7 F.2d 893, 896 (N.D. Cal. 1925).

24. Murray v. Albert Lea Home Inv. Co., 277 N.W. 424 (Minn. 1938).

25. 144 F.2d 759, 762 (2d Cir. 1944).

26. See Roger W. Kirst, Usage of Trade and Course of Dealing: Subversion of the UCC Theory, 1977 U. Chi. Law Forum 811, 828–32.

27. See Lawson, supra note 6, at 65–67 (collecting cases).

28. See, e.g., Metcalf v. Barnard-Curtiss Co., 180 P.2d 263 (Mont. 1947).

29. See Lichter v. Land Title Guar. & Trust Co., 150 N.E. 70, 75 (Ohio App. 1957).

30. Alden Sign Co. v. Roblee, 217 P.2d 867, 870 (Colo. 1950) ("custom" that salesman was not entitled to commissions on orders written before termination of employment held unreasonable); Beech Creek Coal Co. v. Jones, 262 S.W.2d 174, 177 (Ky. 1953). See also Allen, supra note 5 (ch. 1), at 136 (a custom cannot be "contrary to natural justice"); Lawson, supra note 6, at 69–78; Columbia Trade Usage Note, supra note 15, at 1198 & n.25 (collecting cases). But see Shipley, 83 F. Supp. at 751 ("I have not considered the reasonableness of the extra or additional day's pay for a few minutes' work since if the custom and usage should be read into the contracts, said factor is immaterial.").

31. See Wilty v. Jefferson Parish Democratic Exec. Comm., 157 So.2d 718, 725 (La. 1963); AI R. Threadgill v. Peabody Coal Co., 526 P.2d 676, 678 (Colo. App. 1974); Jones v. West Side Buick Co., 93 S.W.2d 1083 (1936) (practice by used car salesmen to roll back odometer on reconditioned cars held to be prejudicial to public good). See also Lawson, supra note 6, at 64–67.

32. Julius Cohen, Towards Realism in Legisprudence, 59 YLJ 886 (1950); Luc Wintgens, Legisprudence as a New Theory of Legislation, 19 Ratio Juris 1 (2006).

33. See Morris Plan Bank of Georgia v. Simmons, 39 S.E.2d 166 (Ga. 1946).
34. Commonwealth v. Welosky, 276 Mass. 398, 401 (1931).
35. See, e.g., Allen v. Mack, 28 A.2d 783 (Pa. 1942); Codd v. Westchester Fire Ins. Co.,
    128 P.2d 968 (Wash. 1942); Maddox v. Hunt, 202 So.2d 543 (Ala. 1967); Paulson v.
    Hardware Mutual Casualty Co., 85 N.W.2d 848 (Wisc. 1957). See also Lawson,
    supra note 6, at 453–62.
36. 15 Q.B.D. 388, 397 (C.A. 1885) (Bowen, L.J.) (Eng.).
37. See McKeen v. Delancy's Lessee, 9 U.S. (5 Cranch) 22, 29, 33 (1809);
    Commonwealth v. Welosky, 276 Mass. 398, 401 (1931) ("[s]tatutes are to be inter-
    preted … in connection with their development, their progression through the
    legislative body, the history of the times, prior legislation, contemporary customs
    and conditions and the system of positive law of which they are part.…"). See also
    Lawson, supra note 6, at 462–63.
38. See Levie, supra note 12, at 1116–17. But see La. Civ. C. Art. 3 (1987) (revising La.
    Civ. C. Art. 3 (1870)) (defining custom as to include *opinio juris* requirement).
39. See Wiseman, supra note 18 (ch. 4), at 466.
40. See id. at 505. See also Kirst, supra note 26, at 817–27.
41. See Wiseman, supra note 18 (ch. 4), at 528.
42. See Papke, supra note 102 (ch. 1), at 1461–62.
43. See Ger. Com. C. art. 346 (1897) ("All acts or omissions as between mercantile
    traders must be interpreted as regards their significance and effect with reference
    to mercantile usage and customs."). For more on Llewellyn's close ties of affinity
    to Germany (including his military service for that country during World War I),
    see Conley & O'Barr, supra note 31, at 182–83.
44. See Hull, supra note 29 (ch. 1), at 296–97. But see Rutherglen, supra note 103
    (ch. 1), at 960–61, 970 (for the view that Llewellyn sought to formalize merchant
    customs through "official endorsement").
45. See Chen, supra note 21, at 108; Allen R. Kamp, Between-the-Wars Social
    Thought: Karl Llewellyn, Legal Realism, and the Uniform Commercial Code in
    Context, 59 Alb. L. Rev. 325, 360 (1995).
46. See Kathleen Patchel, Interest Group Politics, Federalism, and the Uniform
    Laws Process: Some Lessons from the Uniform Commercial Code, 78 Minn. L.
    Rev. 83, 120–36 (1993).
47. See Richard Danzig, A Comment on the Jurisprudence of the Uniform Commercial
    Code, 27 Stan. L. Rev. 621, 622–23 (1975); Kamp, supra note 45, at 357.
48. U.C.C. § 1–103 (titled "Supplementary General Principles of Law Applicable").
    For a view that this section failed to revive the law merchant, see Peter Winship,
    Contemporary Commercial Law Literature in the United States, 43 Ohio St. L.J.
    643, 645 n.8 (1982).
49. U.C.C. § 1–205.
50. See id., cmt. 4.
51. Course of dealing is defined as "a sequence of previous conduct between the
    parties to a particular transaction which is fairly to be regarded as establishing
    a common basis of understanding for interpreting their expressions and other
    conduct." U.C.C. § 1–205(1).
52. UCC section 2–202's parol evidence rule only allows evidence of a usage of trade
    to "explain[]" or "supplement[]" the terms of an agreement, not contradict it.
    U.C.C. § 2–202(a).

53. See Fed. R. Civ. P. 44.1 ("A party who intends to raise an issue about a foreign country's law must give notice by a pleading or other writing.").
54. U.C.C. § 1–205, cmts. 5 & 7.
55. See Levie, supra note 12, at 1101, 1106–09.
56. See Chen, supra note 21, at 121.
57. U.C.C. § 1–205, cmt. 6.
58. See, e.g., Love v. Gamble, 448 S.E.2d 876, 880 (S.C. App. 1994).
59. See, e.g., Western Industries, Inc. v. Newcor Canada, Ltd., 739 F.2d 1198 (7th Cir. 1984). But see Posttape Assoc. v. Eastman Kodak Co., 537 F.2d 751 (3d Cir. 1976) (holding that proof of actual knowledge remains important for the party asserting reliance upon it).
60. See H & W Indus., Inc. v. Occidental Chem. Corp., 911 F.2d 1118 (5th Cir. 1990); Beachcomber Coins, Inc. v. Boskett, 400 A.2d 78 (N.J. Super. 1979).
61. U.C.C. § 1–205, cmt. 5.
62. U.C.C. § 1–205, cmt. 6.
63. See Chen, supra note 21, at 131.
64. See id. at 132–35; Danzig, supra note 47, at 629–35; Wiseman, supra note 18 (ch. 4), at 494–95, 505.
65. See Dana Backus & Henry Harfield, Custom and Letters of Credit: The *Dixon, Iramos* Case, 52 CLR 589 (1952); John Honnold, Letters of Credit, Custom, Missing Documents and the *Dixon* Case: A Reply to Backus and Harfield, 53 CLR 504 (1953).
66. See Levie, supra note 12, at 1110; Columbia Trade Usage Note, supra note 15, at 1195–96.
67. 451 F.2d 3 (4th Cir. 1971). See also Kirst, supra note 26, at 843–50 (for a detailed analysis of this case).
68. See Sunbeam Corp. v. Liberty Mutual Ins. Co., 781 A.2d 1189, 1193 (Pa. 2001) (citing Restatement (Second) of Contracts §§ 202(5) & 220 cmt. d (1981)); MPE Business Forms v. United States, 44 Fed. Cl. 421, 426 (1999). See also 12 Richard A. Lord, Williston on Contracts § 34:5 (4th ed.; Rochester, New York: Lawyers Cooperative, 2003).
69. 451 F.2d at 9; cf. Division of Triple T Serv. v. Mobil Oil Corp., 304 N.Y.S.2d 191, 203 (Sup. Ct. 1969) ("evidence of custom or usage in the trade is not admissible where *inconsistent* with the express terms of the contract") (emphasis added).
70. Southern Concrete Servs. Co. v. Mableton Contractors, Inc., 407 F. Supp. 581, 584 (N.D. Ga. 1975).
71. See Kirst, supra note 26, at 863–64 (quoting form contracts).
72. See, e.g., U.N. Convention on the International Sale of Goods (CISG), Apr. 11, 1980, art. 9(2), 1489 U.N.T.S. 3, 19 I.L.M. 671, 674 (1980) ("The parties are considered, unless otherwise agreed, to have impliedly made applicable to their contract or its formation a usage of which the parties knew or ought to have known and which in international trade is widely known to, and regularly observed by, parties to contracts of the type involved in the particular trade concerned.").
73. See Epstein, Confusion, supra note 58 (ch. 4).
74. U.C.C. § 1–102(2)(b).
75. Bernstein, Merchant Law, supra note 70 (ch. 4), at 1766.
76. See id. at 1805 n.154 (for a long list of U.S. trade associations that have recorded their trade usages).

77. See id. at 1771–80.
78. See id. at 1806–07. See also Omri Ben-Shahar, The Tentative Case Against Flexibility in Commercial Law, 66 UCLR 781 (1999).
79. See Bernstein, supra note 53 (ch. 4), at 778–79.
80. See Kraus, supra note 69 (ch. 4).
81. See Craswell, supra note 54 (ch. 4), at 139–42.
82. See Western Indus., Inc. v. Newcor Canada Ltd., 739 F.2d 1198, 1202–04 (7th Cir. 1984).
83. See U.C.C. 1–205, cmt. 6.

8. TORTS

1. There are obvious exceptions to this, as occurs with suits involving family, employer-employee, or doctor-patient relationships.
2. See McQuire v. W. Morning News Co., [1903] 2 K.B. 100, 109 (Eng.).
3. See Dorsey v. Clements, 44 S.E.2d 783 (Ga. 1947) (in a mixed contractual damages and trespass case, issue of sizing for pine trees used to make turpentine).
4. Roscoe Pound, Administrative Application of Legal Standards, 44 Reports of the American Bar Association 445, 456–57 (1919).
5. Trimarco v. Klein, 451 N.Y.S.2d 52, 55 (1982) (citing 2 Wigmore, Evidence (3d ed), § 461; and Prosser, Torts (4th ed), § 33).
6. Clarence Morris, Custom and Negligence, 42 CLR 1147, 1148 (1942). See also Kenneth S. Abraham, Custom, Non-Customary Practice, and Negligence, 109 CLR 1784 (2009); Steven Hetcher, The Jury's Out: Social Norms' Misunderstood Role in Negligence Law, 91 Geo. L.J. 633 (2003).
7. See Richard A. Epstein, The Path to *The T.J. Hooper*: The Theory and History of Custom in the Law of Tort, 21 JLS 1, 6–11 (1992); Morris, supra note 6, at 1153–55 (collecting cases).
8. Texas & Pac. R.R. v. Behymer, 189 U.S. 468, 470 (1903). For more on this decision, see Epstein, Hooper, supra note 7, at 30–31.
9. But see Fowler V. Harper, Fleming James, Jr. & Oscar S. Gray, The Law of Torts 581 (2d ed.; Boston: Little Brown, 1986) (which organizes cases on this topic not around the sword/shield typology, but, rather, in holding whether custom is conclusive of negligence, entirely inadmissible, or a middle position of being merely probative). See also Restatement (Third) of Torts: Liability for Physical Harms § 13, Reporters' Note, cmt. b (Proposed Final Draft No. 1, 2005) (discussing history of custom doctrine in tort); Restatement (Second) of Torts § 295A (1977) ("In determining whether conduct is negligent, the customs of the community, or of others under like circumstances, are factors to be taken into account, but are not controlling where a reasonable man would not follow them.").
10. See, e.g., Jones v. Jitney Jungle Stores of Am., Inc., 730 So.2d 555, 557 (Miss. 1998) (citations omitted).
11. See Morris, supra note 6, at 1151 & n.11.
12. See id. at 1152.
13. Cunningham v. Ft. Pitt Bridge Works, 47 A. 846, 847 (Pa. 1901).
14. See Morris, supra note 6, at 1161–63. See also Trimarco v. Klein, 451 N.Y.S.2d at 56.
15. Fonda v. St. Paul City Ry. Co., 74 N.W. 166, 169 (Minn. 1898).

16. Id. at 169–70.
17. See, e.g., Lucy Webb Hayes National Training School v. Perotti, 419 F.2d 704 (D.C. Cir. 1969); St. Louis-San Francisco R. Co. v. White, 369 So.2d 1007 (Fla. Dist. Ct. App. 1979).
18. See Epstein, Hooper, supra note 7, at 16–32; Morris, supra note 6, at 1147–51, 1155–61.
19. See 217 N.W. 16 (Mich. 1928). For more on this case, see Morris, supra note 6, at 1150–51, 1157 & n.23.
20. 20 A. 517, 518–19 (Pa. 1890). For more on this case, see Epstein, Hooper, supra note 7, at 21–25; Henry R. Miller, Jr., The So-called Unbending Test of Negligence, 3 VLR 537 (1915).
21. See Morris, supra note 6, at 1160–61 & n.36. See also Maynard v. Buck, 100 Mass. 40, 48 (1868); Sea Board Air Line Ry. Co. v. Watson, 113 So. 716, 718 (Fla. 1927).
22. Hibler v. McCartney, 31 Ala. 501, 508 (1858) (holding against practice of allowing lighted torch in proximity to combustible cotton).
23. See Smith v. Bradford, 512 So.2d 50, 52 (Ala. 1987).
24. See Epstein, Hooper, supra note 7, at 19–20 (discussing such cases as Bassett v. Shares, 27 A. 421 (Conn. 1893)).
25. Mayhew v. Sullivan Mining Co., 76 Me. 100, 112 (1884). For more on this case, see Epstein, Hooper, supra note 7, at 17–19.
26. Bimberg v. Northern Pacific Ry., 14 N.W.2d 410, 413 (Minn. 1944).
27. See, e.g., Complaint as to Porter, 890 P.2d 1377, 1385–86 (Or. 1995).
28. 451 N.Y.S. 2d at 56 (quoting Prosser, Torts (4th ed.) § 33, at 168; Restatement of Torts (Second), § 295A, at 62, cmt. a).
29. Sanders v. City of Chicago, 714 N.E.2d 547, 555 (Ill. App. 1st Dist. 1999).
30. 53 F.2d 107 (S.D.N.Y. 1931) (Coxe, J.), aff'd, 60 F.2d 737 (2d Cir. 1932) (Learned Hand, J.).
31. See 53 F.2d at 108–09; 60 F.2d at 737–39.
32. See 53 F.2d at 111 ("the use of the radio was shown to be so extensive as to amount almost to a universal practice in the navigation of coastwise tugs along the coast.").
33. 60 F.2d at 739.
34. See Landes & Posner, supra note 62 (ch. 4), at 134.
35. See Epstein, Hooper, supra note 7, at 32–36 (reviewing the bench memoranda prepared by the other appeals judges on the panel: Judge Thomas Swan and Judge Augustus Hand (Learned's first cousin)).
36. 60 F.2d at 740 (citations omitted).
37. Although not cited by Judge Hand, this was consistent with earlier rulings in admiralty cases (where a judge, not a jury, typically serves as trier of fact). See, e.g., Lamb v. Parkman, 14 F. Cas. 1019, 1023 (D. Mass. 1857) (No. 8020) (holding a usage of Calcutta traders in loading cargoes to be amply proven, but still could be struck if found "so unreasonable and so injurious to the shipper, that he ought not to be bound by it.").
38. See Murray v. Albert Lea Home Inv. Co., 277 N.W. 424, 426 (Minn. 1938) ("a custom, however well established, will not be recognized if it is contrary to common sense").
39. 451 N.Y.S.2d at 56.
40. See Morris, supra note 6, at 1164.

41. See 53 F.2d at 111.
42. See 451 N.Y.S.2d at 56–57.
43. See Trimarco, 451 N.Y.S.2d at 55–56; Lamb, 14 F. Cas. at 1023 ("The merchants and ship-owners engaged in the Calcutta trade are second to none in intelligence and integrity, and it would be not a little surprising, if they had for many years acquiesced in, and established a usage so injurious to one party....[W]ould the expense to the shipper of such mode exceed the benefit?"). See also Epstein, Hooper, supra note 7, at 1.
44. Petition of Oskar Tiedemann & Co., 179 F. Supp. 227, 238–39 (D.D.C. 1959) (citing *The T.J. HOOPER*).
45. Guido Calabresi, Views and Overviews, 1967 U. Ill. L. Forum 600, 600.
46. See Chapter 4, text with notes 62–77.
47. See James A. Henderson & John A. Siliciano, Universal Health Care and the Continued Reliance on Custom in Determining Medical Malpractice, 79 Cornell L. Rev. 1382, 1384–89 (1994).
48. See Landes & Posner, supra note 62 (ch. 4), at 136.
49. Id. at 133.
50. Id.
51. United States v. Carroll Towing Co., 159 F. 2d 169, 173 (2d Cir. 1947) ("[I]f the probability is called P; the injury, L; and the burden, B; liability depends upon whether B is less than L multiplied by P: i.e., whether B < PL.").
52. Epstein, Hooper, supra note 7, at 13.
53. See id. at 15.
54. Id. at 14.
55. See Richard A. Epstein, Cases and Materials on Torts 175 (5th ed.; Boston: Little Brown, 1990) (quoting unpublished lecture by Morton J. Horwitz).
56. Porter, 890 P.2d at 1385 (In construing Oregon Bar Rule 7–106(c)(5)'s reference to "known local customs of courtesy or practice" the Oregon Supreme Court noted that "The practice of law is a professional calling," and that charging constructive knowledge of such customs on lawyers is fair, otherwise it would "plac[e] a premium on studied stupidity by practitioners who assiduously avoid learning about the community in which they practice.").
57. 519 P.2d 981 (Wash. 1974).
58. See 519 P.2d at 982.
59. Id. at 982–83.
60. See, e.g., Brune v. Belinkoff, 235 N.E.2d 793 (Mass. 1968).
61. Landes & Posner, supra note 62 (ch. 4), at 137.
62. See, e.g., Barton v. Owen, 139 Cal. Rptr. 494 (1977).
63. See Wash. Rev. Code § 4.24.290 (1988).
64. See Richard A. Epstein, Medical Malpractice, Imperfect Information, and the Contractual Foundation for Medical Services, 49 L. & Contemp. Probs. 201, 203–05 (1986); Henderson & Siliciano, supra note 47, at 1389–95.

9. CONSTITUTIONAL LAW

1. See Chapter 1, text at note 103; Chapter 6, text at notes 2 & 3.
2. See Chapter 3, text at notes 5–18.

3. For the Germanic volk custom tradition, see Chapter 1, text at notes 95–101. See also Pocock, supra note 28 (ch. 3), at 19–20.

4. See S. B. Chrimes, English Constitutional History 73–74 (London: Oxford Univ. Press, 1965).

5. See id. at 74–76.

6. See Chapter 2, text at note 67.

7. Coronation Charter, 1100, 1 Hen. 1, ch. 1, reprinted in Sources of English Constitutional History: A Selection of Documents from AD 600 to the Present 46 (Carl Stephenson & Frederick George Marcham, eds.; New York: Harper & Bros., 1937) ["English Constitutional Sources"].

8. See id., ch. 2 ("If any one of my barons, earls, or other men who hold of me dies, his heir shall not redeem his land as he did in the time of my brother, but he shall relieve it by a just and legitimate relief. In the same way, furthermore, the men of my barons shall relieve their lands from their lords by just and legitimate reliefs."), 6 ("If any one of my barons or men commits an offence, he shall not [be declared] in mercy [and required to] give a pledge from his chattels, as he was in the time of my father and my brother; but he shall pay compensation according to the measure of the offence, as was done before the time of my father, in the time of my other predecessors.").

9. See J. C. Holt, Magna Carta 32 (Cambridge: Cambridge Univ. Press, 1965); Pocock, supra note 28 (ch. 3), at 44–45.

10. See Holt, supra note 9, at 78–79.

11. See id. at 81–82.

12. See id. at 94–96.

13. See Chapter 2, text at notes 27–31.

14. See Chrimes, supra note 4, at 97.

15. See id. at 99; Holt, supra note 9, at 98–103.

16. See Magna Carta, 1215, 16 John, chs. 2, 4, reprinted in English Constitutional Sources, supra note 7, at 116.

17. See id. at ch. 23, reprinted in id. at 119 ("Neither vill nor man shall be distrained to make bridges on river-banks, except such as by right and ancient custom ought to do so.").

18. Id ch. 13, reprinted at id. at 118.

19. Id. ch. 41, reprinted at id. at 121 ("All merchants may safely and securely go away from England, come to England, stay in and go through England, by land or by water, for buying and selling under right and ancient customs and without any evil exactions").

20. See id. ch. 54 (second reissue of the Charter), reprinted at id. at 123 n.45 ("Henceforth no county [court] shall be held oftener than once a month; and wherever a longer time [between sessions] has been customary, let it be longer. Nor shall any sheriff or his bailiff make his tour through a hundred more often than twice a year; and [then he shall hold the court] only at the due and accustomed place [and time], namely, once after Easter and again after Michaelmas. And view of frankpledge shall without excuse be made then, at that Michaelmas term; and in such a way that every one shall enjoy the liberties which he was accustomed to have in the time of King Henry, our grandfather, or which he has subsequently acquired.").

21. Id. ch. 48, reprinted at id. at 122. For more on this provision, see Holt, supra note 9, at 205–06, 236–38.
22. Id. ch. 60, reprinted at id. at 125.
23. Chrimes, supra note 4, at 121.
24. See Pocock, supra note 28 (ch. 3), at 32–33, 44–51.
25. Case of the Five Knights – Darnel's Case, 3 How. St. Tr. 1 (K.B. 1627). For more on this case, see J. A. Guy, The Origins of the Petition of Right Reconsidered, 25 Hist. J. 289 (1982); Mark Kishlansky, Tyranny Denied: Charles I, Attorney General Heath, and the Five Knights' Case, 42 Hist. J. 53 (1999).
26. 3 How. St. Tr. at 51–59, reprinted in English Constitutional Sources, supra note 7, at 458.
27. See English Constitutional Sources, supra note 7, at 450.
28. Petition of Right, reprinted at id. at 451, paraphrasing, Magna Carta, ch. 39, reprinted at id. 121.
29. Id. at 453 (proceedings in Parliament of June 2, 1628).
30. See Pocock, supra note 28 (ch. 3), at 229–35.
31. Coronation Oath of George VI, 1937, reprinted in English Constitutional Sources, supra note 7, at 891. See also Coronation Oath Act, 1688, 1 Will. & Mar., c. 6.
32. See Walter Bagheot, The English Constitution 214 (Ithaca, New York: Cornell Univ. Press, 1963).
33. I speak here of the United Kingdom's "structural constitution," the allocation of power among government entities. Arguably, the United Kingdom's "rights constitution" is now embodied through its adherence to the guarantees of the European Convention on Human Rights. See Human Rights Act (U.K.), 1998, c. 42.
34. One contemporary debate involves whether certain punishments have, because of historical practice and usage, become "cruel and unusual" and thus proscribed by the U.S. Constitution's Eighth Amendment. See John F. Stinneford, The Original Meaning of "Unusual": The Eighth Amendment as a Bar to Cruel Innovation, 102 Nw. U. L. Rev. 739, 1768–1800 (2008).
35. Rutherglen, supra note 103 (ch. 1), at 970.
36. See United States v. Arredondo, 31 U.S. (6 Pet.) 691, 715 (1832) ("The court not only may, but are bound to notice and respect general customs and usage as the law of the land, equally with the written law, and, when clearly proved, they will control the general law; this necessarily follows from its presumed origin, – an act of parliament or a legislative act.").
37. Weidler v. Arizona Power Co., 7 P.2d 241, 244 (Ariz. 1932).
38. See State v. Standard Oil Co. of Louisiana, 178 So. 601 (La. 1937); Mic-Central Fish Co. v. United States, 112 F. Supp. 792 (W.D. Mo. 1953).
39. See Beneficial Finance Co. v. Administrator of Loan Laws, 272 A.2d 649, 654 (Md. App. 1971) (collecting cases).
40. See Barland v. Eau Claire County, 575 N.W.2d 691, 704 (Wis. 1998).
41. See id. at 707–08 ("vague references to 'custom' are not determinative of this constitutional question.") (Geske, J., dissenting) (citing Justice Scalia's critique of custom in Stevens v. City of Cannon Beach, 510 U.S. 1207, 1212 (1994), discussed in chapter 6, at notes 67–80 with text).

42. Act of Apr. 20, 1871, ch. 22, 17 Stat. 13, codified at 42 U.S.C. §§ 1981, 1983.
43. See Rutherglen, supra note 103 (ch. 1), at 940–41.
44. Act of Apr. 20, 1871, ch. 22, 17 Stat. 13, codified at 42 U.S.C. § 1983.
45. See Rutherglen, supra note 103 (ch. 1), at 930–31, 950; Steven L. Winter, The Meaning of "Under Color of" Law, 91 Mich. L. Rev. 323, 325 (1992).
46. 165 U.S. 275 (1897).
47. Id. at 282.
48. Id. at 293–94, 301 (Harlan, J., dissenting).
49. 163 U.S. 537, 550 (1896).
50. 365 U.S. 167 (1961).
51. See id. at 235–36, 258–59 (Frankfurter, J., dissenting).
52. 398 U.S. 144, 166–68 (1970).
53. Id. at 171–72.
54. Id. at 171.
55. See Chapter 1, at note 57 with text.
56. 398 U.S. at 224–25 (Brennan, J., dissenting) (omitting citations and footnotes) (citing, inter alia, "B. Cardozo, The Nature of the Judicial Process 58–64 (1921)").
57. See id. at 181–82 (citing "B. Malinowski, Crime and Custom in Savage Society 66–67 (1962).").
58. See id. at 178 & n.1 (Douglas, J., dissenting) (quoting The Federalist, No. 15 (Hamilton) ("It is essential to the idea of a law, that it be attended with a sanction; or, in other words, a penalty or punishment for disobedience. If there be no penalty annexed to disobedience, the resolutions or commands which pretend to be laws will, in fact, amount to nothing more than advice or recommendation. This penalty, whatever it may be, can only be inflicted in two ways: by the agency of the courts and ministers of justice, or by military force; by the COERCION of the magistracy, or by the COERCION of arms.") (Hamilton's original emphasis).
59. Id. at 179.
60. Id. at 181.
61. See Rutherglen, supra note 103 (ch. 1), at 966–67.
62. Marsh v. Chambers, 463 U.S. 783, 786–91 (1983).
63. Stuart v. Laird, 5 U.S. (1 Cranch) 299, 309 (1803).
64. Fairbank v. United States, 181 U.S. 283, 306 (1901).
65. 5 U.S. (1 Cranch) at 309.
66. See, e.g., United States v. Midwest Oil Co., 236 U.S. 458, 473 (1914); Indian Tribes of Washington v. United States (Pocket Veto Case), 279 U.S. 655, 690 (1929).
67. See, e.g., Jason T. Burnette, Eyes on Their Own Paper: Practical Construction in Constitutional Interpretation, 39 Ga. L. Rev. 1065 (2005); Robert J. Delahunty & John C. Yoo, The President's Constitutional Authority to Conduct Military Operations Against Terrorist Organizations and the Nations that Harbor or Support Them, 25 Harv. J. L. & Pub. Pol'y 488, 502–03 (2002); Michael J. Glennon, The Use of Custom in Resolving Separation of Powers Disputes, 64 B.U. L. Rev. 109, 115 (1984); Harold Hongju Koh, The National Security Constitution: Sharing Power After the Iran-Contra Affair 70–71 (New Haven: Yale Univ. Press, 1990); John Houston Pope, The Pocket Veto Reconsidered, 72 Iowa L. Rev. 163, 174–75 (1986).
68. See 5 U.S. (1 Cranch) at 303–06 (argument of counsel). See also Mistretta v. United States, 488 U.S. 361, 400–01 (1989) (constitutionality of service by federal

judges on U.S. sentencing commission and postfounding period examples of extrajudicial service).

69. See, e.g., Eldred v. Ashcroft, 537 U.S. 186, 200–02 (2003) (reviewing early congressional action with respect to copyrights in order to determine the meaning of the constitutional grant of power); Printz v. United States, 521 U.S. 898, 905–07 (1997) (examining early congressional statutes as to limits on the power to commandeer state officials); Myers v. United States, 272 U.S. 52, 136 (1926) (whether Congress can block the removal from office of presidential appointees).

70. See Glennon, supra note 67, at 111.

71. See Chapter 2, text at notes 47–55; Chapter 4, text at note 11.

72. 236 U.S. at 469–72.

73. Id. at 472–73.

74. See, e.g., United States v. Curtiss-Wright Export Corp., 299 U.S. 304, 324 (1936) (president's unilateral imposition of embargoes); Dames & Moore v. Regan, 453 U.S. 654, 678–84 (1981) (president's power to conclude claims settlement agreements with foreign nations); Am. Ins. Ass'n v. Garamendi, 539 U.S. 396, 416 (2003) (same).

75. See 272 U.S. at 150 (citing historical precedents for unilateral presidential removal), 170–71.

76. See 181 U.S. at 306–07.

77. See Inland Waterways Corp. v. Young, 309 U.S. 517, 525 (1940) ("Even constitutional power, when the text is doubtful, may be established by usage.").

78. See 181 U.S. at 308, 311–12.

79. 462 U.S. 919 (1983).

80. See id. at 942 n.13 (noting that presidents have signed bills containing such legislative vetoes, even as they protested their constitutionality), 967–74 (White, J., dissenting) (narrating history of over 200 statutes containing legislative veto provisions).

81. See Youngstown Sheet & Tube Co. v. Sawyer, 343 U.S. 579, 610 (1952) (Frankfurter, J., concurring) (holding that a constitutional customary norm must be "systematic," "unbroken," and "long pursued").

82. See 453 U.S. at 679 n.8.

83. See Curtiss-Wright, 299 U.S. at 328 (practice over 140 years); Ex Parte Grossman, 267 U.S. 87, 118–19 (1925) (85 years of presidents pardoning criminal contempts); The LAURA, 114 U.S. 411, 415–17 (1885) (pardons of lesser executive officials over the past 100 years).

84. Midwest Oil, 236 U.S. at 469.

85. See also Zemel v. Rusk, 381 U.S. 1, 8–9 (1965) (affirming secretary of state's authority to impose area restrictions on travel with passports).

86. See, e.g., Springer v. Government of the Philippine Islands, 277 U.S. 189, 205 (1928) (rejecting assertion as being based on a "limited number" of incidents).

87. See Myers, 272 U.S. at 170–71.

88. See Helen Silving, "Customary Law": Continuity in Municipal and International Law, 31 Iowa L. Rev. 616, 622–23 (1946).

89. See Stuart, 5 U.S. (1 Cranch) at 309 ("practice and acquiescence under it for a period of several years … affords an irresistible answer, and has indeed fixed the construction.").

90. 343 U.S. at 610 (1952) (Frankfurter, J., concurring).
91. This occurred with the enactment of the War Powers Resolution of 1973, Pub. L. No. 93–148, 87 Stat. 555 (1998).
92. See Dames & Moore, 453 U.S. at 669 (support for, or objection to, executive action may range from "explicit congressional authorization to explicit congressional prohibition"). See also Glennon, supra note 67, at 139–41.
93. See, e.g., Kent v. Dulles, 357 U.S. 116, 125 (1958) (rejecting executive branch assertion of a customary practice, because it was stated as a mere policy); Haig v. Agee, 453 U.S. 280, 315–16 (1981) (Brennan, J., dissenting).
94. See, e.g., Dames & Moore, 453 U.S. at 686 (executive agreements settling international claims communicated to congress); Midwest Oil, 236 U.S. at 475, 481 (withdrawals of public lands communicated to Congress 92 times).
95. See 462 U.S. at 942 n.13.
96. See 453 U.S. at 317 n.7 (Brennan, J., dissenting).
97. See id. at 307–10.
98. See Matthew Baker, The Sound of Congressional Silence: Judicial Distortion of the Legislative-Executive Balance of Power, 2009 B.Y.U. L. Rev. 225, 231–43; Henry P. Monaghan, The Protective Power of the Presidency, 93 CLR 1, 45, 61–74 (1993); Jane E. Stromseth, Understanding Constitutional War Powers Today: Why Methodology Matters, 106 YLJ 845, 872–86 (1996) (reviewing Louis Fisher, Presidential War Power (1995)).
99. Dames & Moore, 453 U.S. at 680.
100. See Michael J. Gerhardt, Non-Judicial Precedent, 61 Vand. L. Rev. 713, 733–36 (2008); Stromseth, supra note 98, at 882–86.
101. See Goldwater v. Carter, 444 U.S. 996 (1979) (leaving open the question of the president's power to unilaterally terminate treaties that had earlier received advice and consent by the senate).
102. See Glennon, supra note 67, at 140–42; Stromseth, supra note 98, at 881 and n.187.
103. See Cass R. Sunstein, Burkean Minimalism, 105 Mich. L. Rev. 353, 375 (2006); Congressional Restrictions on the President's Appointment Power and the Role of Longstanding Practice in Constitutional Interpretation, 120 HLR 1914, 1929–31 (2007). For more on Edmund Burke's vision of custom, see Chapter 2, text at note 96; Chapter 4, text at note 56.
104. Youngstown Steel, 343 U.S. at 610 (Frankfurter, J., concurring).
105. Inland Waterways Corp. v. Young, 309 U.S. 517, 525 (1940).
106. Saint Cyprian, Epistola ad Pompeium in 3 Patrologia Latina 1127, 1154 (J. P. Migne ed.) (photo. rep. Turnhout, Belgium: Brepols 1985) (1844) (unofficial translation from Latin).
107. See La. Civ. Code Ann. art. 1 (1999) ("The sources of law are legislation and custom."). See also John Henry Merryman, The Civil Law Tradition: An Introduction to the Legal Systems of Western Europe and Latin America 23 (Stanford: Stanford Univ. Press, 1985).
108. In physics, the observer effect refers to changes that the act of observation will make on the phenomenon being observed. It is related to the Heisenberg Uncertainty Principle. Gerard Folland & Alladi Sitaram, The Uncertainty Principle: A Mathematical Survey, 3(3) J. Fourier Analysis and Applications 207

(May 1997). In psychology, a related idea is the Hawthorne effect, a form of reactivity whereby subjects improve an aspect of their behavior being experimentally measured simply in response to the fact that they are being studied, not in response to any particular experimental manipulation. Stephen R. G. Jones, Was There a Hawthorne Effect?, 98(3) Am. J. Sociology 451 (Nov. 1992).

10. PRIVATE INTERNATIONAL LAW

1. See Leon E. Trakman, The Law Merchant: The Evolution of Commercial Law 7 (Littleton, Colo.: Rothman, 1983) ("Custom, not law, has been the fulcrum of commerce since the origins of exchange.").

2. See Gesa Baron, Do the UNIDROIT Principles of International Contracts Form a New Lex Mercatoria?, available at http://www.cisg.law.pace.edu/cisg/biblio/baron.html#b1; Stephen E. Sachs, From St. Ives to Cyberspace: The Modern Distortion of the Medieval "Law Merchant," 21 Am. U. Int'l L. Rev. 685, 688–89 (2006) (characterizing a "'Romantic' vision of a universal law merchant – produced, interpreted, and enforced by a legally autonomous merchant class").

3. See Maine, supra note 4 (ch. 1), at 86; see also Sir Henry Sumner Maine, Village Communities in the East and West 193–94 (London: John Murray, 1871). Maine's discussion of *ius gentium* was intended primarily as a rebuttal to the notion that it was later transformed into the modern law of nations. See Maine, Ancient Law, supra, at 43–44, 80–83. For the same view, see Henry Wheaton, History of the Law of Nations in Europe and America 26 (New York: Gould Banks & Co., 1845).

4. See 1 F. C. von Savigny, System de Heutigen Römischen Rechts 105–22 (Berlin: Veitund Comp., 1840).

5. See 1 Coleman Phillipson, The International Law and Custom of Ancient Greece and Rome 72–76 (London: Macmillan, 1911).

6. See Dig. 1.3.35 (Hermogenian, Epitome of the Law 1) (Theodor Mommsen & Paul Krueger eds., Alan Watson trans., 1985); Dig. 50.7.18(17) (Pomponius, Quintus Mucius 37); see also Alan Watson, International Law in Archaic Rome: War and Religion 87–88 n.12 (Baltimore: Johns Hopkins Univ. Press, 1993).

7. See 3 Marcus Tullius Cicero, De Officiis 339, at xvii (Walter Miller trans., rev. ed.; Cambridge, Mass.: Harvard Univ. Press, 1990).

8. See Berman, Law and Revolution I, supra note (ch. 1), at 339–41. But see the vigorous critique of Berman's views on lex mercatoria, in Sachs, supra note 2, at 686 ("the traditional [Berman's] view is deeply flawed"); Emily Kadens, Order Within Law, Variety Within Custom: The Character of the Medieval Merchant Law, 5 Chi. J. Int'l L. 39 (2004).

9. See Robert D. Benedict, The Historical Position of the Rhodian Law, 18 YLJ 223 (1909); Harold J. Berman, The Law of International Commercial Transactions (Lex Mercatoria), 2 Emory J. Int'l Dispute Resolution 235, 239–40 (1988) ["Berman, Lex"]; William Tetley, The General Maritime Law – The Lex Maritima, 20 Syracuse J. Int'l L. & Com. 105 (1994).

10. See Thomas E. Carbonneau & Marc S. Firestone, Transnational Law-Making: Assessing the Impact of the Vienna Convention and the Viability of

Arbitral Adjudication, 1 Emory J. Int'l Dispute Resolution 51, 58–59 (1986). For a detailed history of the fair at St. Ives, England, from 1270 to 1350, see Sachs, supra note 2, at 690–93.

11. Magna Carta, 17 John c. 41 (1215).

12. See Francis Marion Burdick, Contributions of the Law Merchant to the Common Law, in 3 Select Essays in Anglo-American Legal History 34, 50 (Boston: Little Brown, 1909).

13. See Berman, Law and Revolution I, supra note 61 (ch. 1), at 336–48; see also 1 William Blackstone, Commentaries, supra note 34 (ch. 3), at *273; William Mitchell, An Essay on the Early History of the Law Merchant (Cambridge: Cambridge Univ. Press, 1904).

14. See Anon. v. Sheriff of London (The Carriers' Case), Y.B. East. 13 Edw. 4, fol. 9, pl. 5 (Exch. Ch. 1473) (foreign merchants must not be judged according to English law, but rather according to "the law of nature which by some is called the law merchant, which is law universal throughout the world"). See also Mary Elizabeth Basile, Jane Fair Bestor, Daniel R. Coquillette, and Charles Donahue, transl. & eds., Lex Mercatoria and Legal Pluralism: A Late Thirteenth Century Treatise and Its Afterlife (Cambridge, Mass.: Ames Foundation, 1998); Louise Hertwig Hayes, A Modern Lex Mercatoria: Political Rhetoric or Substantive Progress?, 3 Brook. J. Int'l L. 210, 212–14 (1976–77).

15. Gerard Malynes, Consuetudo, vel, Lex mercatoria, or the ancient law-merchant, at a (3d ed. 1686) (Abingdon, England: Professional Books, 1981).

16. See Berman, Law and Revolution I, supra note 61 (ch. 1), at 344.

17. See id. at 349–54.

18. See Alan Watson, Legal Transplants: An Approach to Comparative Law (2nd ed.; Athens, Ga.: Univ. of Georgia Press, 1993).

19. See John Henry Merryman, On the Convergence (and Divergence) of the Civil Law and the Common Law, 17 Stan. J. Int'l L. 357, 359–61 (1991).

20. See Sir Paul Vinogradoff, supra note 95 (ch. 1), at 157–59. But see Jean-Louis Halpérin, L'approche Historique et la Problématique du Jus Commune, 52 Revue Internationale de Droit Compare 717 (2000) (criticizing "romantic" notions of the *ius commune*); Marie-France Renoux-Zagame, Le Droit Commun European Entre Histoire et Raison, 14 Droits: Revue Francaise de Theorie Juridique 27 (1991) (same).

21. Edward G. Hinkelman, A Short Course in International Trade Documentation, at v (Novato, Calif.: World Trade Press, 2002) (discussing discovery, at Ur, of tokens in hollow clay balls, known as *bullas*, containing bills of lading and documentary transactions).

22. See 2 Hubert Hall, Select Cases Concerning the Law Merchant 79–80 (London: Selden Soc'y (vol. 46), 1930); James Steven Rogers, The Early History of the Law of Bills and Notes: A Study of the Origins of Anglo-American Commercial Law 45–48, 173–74 (Cambridge: Cambridge Univ. Press, 1995) (discussing a 1309 dispute in England concerning payment on an ostensible bearer note from Italy).

23. See Wyndham Anstis Bewes, The Romance of the Law Merchant 28–62, 77–79 (London: Sweet & Maxwell, 1923).

24. See Berman, Law and Revolution I, supra note 61 (ch. 1), at 347–48.

25. See James Oldham, The Origins of the Special Jury, 50 CLR 137, 167–68 (1983); Penny Tucker, Law Courts and Lawyers in the City of London, 1300–1550, at 34–35 (Cambridge: Cambridge Univ. Press, 2007).
26. 31 Edw. 1, ch. 11 (Feb. 1, 1303).
27. 11 Edw. I (1283).
28. See T. F. T. Plucknett, Legislation of Edward I, at 136–41 (Oxford: Clarendon Press, 1949).
29. See Bewes, supra note 23; Sachs, supra note 2, at 688 n.5 (collecting sources espousing the "romantic" view).
30. See Filip De Ly, International Business Law and Lex Mercatoria 8–9, 18 (Amsterdam: North Holland, 1992).
31. See Kadens, supra note 8, at 40 ("The evidence strongly suggests that Berman's classic account is at least partially inaccurate in almost every respect.").
32. See Bruce L. Benson, Justice Without Government: The Merchant Courts of Medieval England and Their Modern Counterparts, in The Voluntary City: Choice, Community and Civil Society 127, 128 (David T. Beito, Peter Gordon & Alexander Tabarrok, eds.; Ann Arbor: Univ. of Michigan Press, 2002).
33. See Sachs, supra note 2, at 737–38 (describing incident at the St. Ives Fair with Robert Pole in 1287).
34. See id. at 694.
35. Kadens, supra note 8, at 42. See also Charles Donahue, Jr., Medieval and Modern Lex Mercatoria: An Attempt at the Probatio Diabolica, 5 Chi. J. Int'l L. 21 (2004); Oliver Volckart & Antje Mangels, Are the Roots of the Modern Lex Mercatoria Really Medieval?, 65 S. Econ. J. 427 (1999).
36. See Kadens, supra note 8, at 56–63.
37. See id. at 56–57, 62–63.
38. Harold J. Berman & Felix J. Dasser, The "New" Law Merchant and the "Old": Sources, Content, and Legitimacy, in Lex Mercatoria and Arbitration: A Discussion of the New Law Merchant 53, 55 (Thomas E. Carbonneau, ed.; Cambridge, Mass.: Kluwer, rev. ed. 1998) (different strands of thought regarding autonomous character of lex mercatoria).
39. See Plucknett, supra note 18 (ch. 3), at 660.
40. See C. H. S. Fifoot, English Law and Its Background 105 (London: G. Bell & Sons, 1932).
41. 3 Burr. 1663, 97 Eng. Rep. 1035 (K.B. 1765) (Eng.).
42. See Vanheath v. Turner, Winch. 24, 25, 120 Eng. Rep. 20, 21 (1621) (Hobart, C. J.) ("the custom of merchants is part of the common law of this kingdom"). But see Luke v. Lyde, 2 Burr. 882, 887, 97 Eng. Rep. 614, 617 (1759) (Mansfield, J.) ("the Maritime Law is not the Law of a particular Country, but the general Law of Nations"). For further criticism of this incorporation theory, see Rogers, supra note 22.
43. See Ernst Von Caemmerer, The Influence of the Law of International Trade on the Development and Character of the Commercial Law in the Civil Law Countries, in Clive M. Schmitthoff, The Sources of the Law of International Trade 88, 90 (London: Stevens & Sons, 1964).
44. See James Whitman, Volk, supra note 18 (ch. 4), at 158–65 (glossing Levin Goldshmidt, Handbuch des Handelsrechts (Stuttgart & Erlangen: F. Enke, 1864 & 1875)). See also Mitchell, supra note 13, at 10 (discussing Goldschmidt).

45. See J. H. Dalhuisen, Custom and Its Revival in Transnational Private Law, 18 Duke J. Comp. & Int'l L. 339, 344–46 (2008) (discussing decline of custom in civil law jurisdictions in nineteenth century, as reflected in the 1804 French and 1900 German civil codes); Merryman, supra note 107 (ch. 9), at 23 (noting that customary law's importance in civil law is "slight and decreasing").

46. John Austin, The Province of Jurisprudence Determined (1832), in The Great Legal Philosophers: Selected Readings in Jurisprudence 342 (Clarence Morris, ed.; Philadelphia: Univ. of Pennsylvania Press, 1959).

47. Hart, supra note 1 (ch. 1), at 26.

48. Berman & Dasser, supra note 38, at 64 (citing Allen, supra note 5 (ch. 1), at 65–66)).

49. See Berman, Lex, supra note 9, at 276–89 (offering a catalog of transnational commercial norms).

50. 41 U.S. (16 Pet.) 1, 2 (1842).

51. Id. at 19 (citing Cicero's maxim "Non erit alia lex Romae, alia Athenis; alia nunc, alia posthac; sed et apud omnes gentes, et omni tempore una eademque lex obtinebit").

52. The CHINA, 74 U.S. 53, 67 (1868). See also Insurance Co. v. Dunham, 78 U.S. 1, 23 (1870) ("venerable law of the sea which reaches back to sources long anterior even to those of the civil law itself; which Lord Mansfield says is not the law of any particular country, but the general law of nations") (citing Luke v. Lyde, supra note 42).

53. See Friedrich K. Juenger, The Lex Mercatoria and the Conflict of Laws, in Carbonneau, supra note 38, at 265, 268–69 (for Justice Holmes's influence on the *Erie* decision).

54. See The SCOTIA, 81 U.S. 170, 187–88 (1871) ("Whatever may have been its origin, whether in the usages of navigation or in the ordinances of maritime states, or in both, it has become the law of the sea only by the concurrent sanction of those nations who may be said to constitute the commercial world. Many of the usages which prevail, and which have the force of law, doubtless originated in the positive prescriptions of some single state, which were at first of limited effect, but which when generally accepted became of universal obligation").

55. [1911] 1 K.B. 214, 16 Com. Cas. 8; rev'd, [1911] 1 K.B. 934, 16 Com. Cas. 197 (C.A.); restored, 1912 App. Cas. 18, 17 Com. Cas. 55 (H.L.) (Eng.).

56. [1911] 1 K.B. at 934.

57. Id. at 935.

58. See id. at 944 ("I gather from the words of the learned judge when dealing with the plaintiffs' case 'A judge, at any rate when he takes the commercial list, aspires to be both a man of business and a lawyer, but, if he cannot be both, he must be content to be as nearly a lawyer as he can, and I think the law is as I have laid it down with regard to the plaintiffs' claim,' that his decision is based upon his personal knowledge in the Commercial Court. This, of course, is a statement of great weight which must impress every one, but I do not think we ought to allow this to be the basis of a decision between litigants in an action in a case where there is no evidence whatsoever either as to local usage in England or as to such general usage in England or foreign countries as is a condition of the admission and adoption as part of the law merchant of England of any legal proposition outside the common law.").

59. See id. at 952 (Kennedy, L. J., dissenting).
60. See Karl N. Llewellyn, Paul Gewirtz & Michael Ansaldi, The Case Law System in America, 88 CLR 989, 1004 n.3 (1988) (Llewellyn 1929 manuscript on "Separate Opinions: Their Legal, Political and Social Value").
61. Comptoir d'Achat et de Vente du Boerenbond Belge S/A v Luis de Ridder, [1949] App. Cas. 293, [1949] 1 All E.R. 269, 275–76 (H.L.) (Eng.).
62. See Berman, Lex, supra note 9, at 282–83.
63. [1957] 2 Q.B. 621, [1957] 2 Lloyd's List L.R. 1 (C.A.) (Eng.).
64. For more on customary practices for bills of lading, see Daniel E. Murray, History and Development of the Bill of Lading, 27 U. Miami L. Rev. 689, 693, 709 (1983); William Tetley, Marine Cargo Claims 291, 851 n.55 (3d ed.; Montréal: Y. Blais, 1988).
65. [1957] 2 Lloyd's List L.R. at 13. See also Berman, Lex, supra note 9, at 288–89.
66. See Fr. Com. Code (1807); An act to codify the Law of Marine Insurance, 6 Edw. 7, ch. 41 (1906).
67. [1921] 3 K.B. 443 (K.B.D.) (Eng.).
68. See, e.g., The "Marlborough Hill" v. Cowan & Sons, [1921] 1 App. Cas. 444, 452 (P.C. 1920) (Phillimore, L. J.) ("If this document is a bill of lading, it is a negotiable instrument. Money can be advanced upon it, and business can be done in the way that maritime commerce has been carried out for at least half a century, throughout the civilized world.").
69. [1921] 3 K.B. at 457.
70. Id. at 458.
71. See id. (citing Manbre Saccharine Case, [1919] 1 K. B. 198. 206 (Eng.); Wilson v. Holgate & Co.'s Case, [1920] 2 K. B. 1, 8 (Eng.)).
72. 299 F. 991 (S.D.N.Y. 1924).
73. Id. at 991.
74. See id. at 993 (citing Diamond Alkali, among other recent English decisions).
75. Id. at 994 (quoting Justice Holt in Humfrey v. Dale, 7 E. & B. 266, 278 (1857) (Eng.) ("It is the business of courts reasonably so to shape their rules of evidence as to make them suitable to the habits of mankind.")).
76. See id. at 994–95.
77. Id.
78. U.C.C. § 2–320(2)(c).
79. See Chapter 8, text at notes 48–56.
80. See, e.g., Nat'l Am. Ins. Co. of Calif. v. Certain Underwriters at Lloyd's London, 93 F.3d 529, 536–37 (9th Cir. 1995).
81. See Chapter 7, text at notes 25–26, 65.
82. See Dixon, Irmaos, & Cia LTDA v. Chase National Bank, 53 F. Supp. 933 (S.D.N.Y. 1943).
83. See 144 F.2d 759, 762 (2d Cir. 1944) ("Numerous witnesses, experts in the fields of banking and of commerce, testified to the existence of the custom; not one testified to a single instance where a tender such as was here made had been rejected and the draft dishonored solely on the ground that the set of bills of lading was incomplete.").
84. Berman, Lex, supra note 9, at 285.

85. ICC Doc. 500, available at http://www.remburskonsulenten.com/NewFiles/
   UCP500.pdf. A new version of this document, UCP 600, entered into force in
   July 2007.
86. 288 F.3d 262, 265 (5th Cir. 2002).
87. Id.
88. See id. at 266, 267.
89. July 1, 1964, 3 I.L.M. 855 (1964) ["ULISG"].
90. July 1, 1964, 3 I.L.M. 864 (1964) ["ULFC"].
91. ULSIG, supra note 89, Annex I, art. 9.
92. See Chapter 7, text at note 49.
93. ULFC, supra note 90, Annex I, art. 13 (same general definition of a usage as in
   ULISG art. 9: "Usage means any practice or method of dealing, which reasonable persons in the same situation as the parties usually consider to be applicable
   to the formation of their contract.").
94. See id. arts. 2(1), 4(2), 5(3), 6(2) & 11.
95. Apr. 11, 1980, 1489 U.N.T.S. 3, 19 I.L.M. 671, 674 (1980) ["CISG"].
96. See John O. Honnold, Uniform Law for International Sales Under the 1980
   United Nations Convention 165 n.8, 176 (2d ed.; Boston: Kluwer, 1991).
97. See CISG, supra note 95, art. 9(2).
98. See id. art. 8(3).
99. See id. art. 18(3).
100. See Berman & Dasser, supra note 38, at 65.
101. ULSIG, supra note 89, Annex I, art. 9.
102. See Berman, Lex, supra note 9, at 296.
103. Id.
104. Michael J. Bonnell, Article 9 – Usages and Practices, in Cesare M. Bianca & M.
   J. Bonnell, Commentary on the International Sales Law: The 1980 Vienna Sales
   Convention 103, 108–09 (Milan: Giuffrè, 1987).
105. See John Honnold, Documentary History of the Uniform Law for International
   Sales: The Studies, Deliberations, and Decisions That Led to the 1980 United
   Nations Convention with Introductions and Explanations 484 (Deventer: Kluwer,
   1989).
106. See CISG, supra note 95, art. 4(a) ("This Convention governs only the formation of the contract of sale and the rights and obligations of the seller and the
   buyer arising from such a contract. In particular, except as otherwise expressly
   provided in this Convention, it is not concerned with: (a) the validity of the
   contract or of any of its provisions or of any usage...."). See also Raj Bhala,
   Self-Regulation in Global Electronic Markets Through Reinvigorated Trade
   Usages, 31 Idaho L. Rev. 863, 897 n.95 (1995); J. H. Dalhuisen, Custom and
   Its Revival in Transnational Private Law, 18 Duke J. Comp. & Int'l L. 339,
   359 (2008); Michael P. Van Altsine, Consensus, Dissensus and Contractual
   Obligations through the Prism of Uniform International Sales Law, 37 VJIL 1,
   46–48 (1996).
107. See Berman, Lex, supra note 9, at 97; Chen, supra note 21 (ch. 7), at 103–04; Note,
   Unification and Certainty: The United Nations Convention on Contracts for the
   International Sale of Goods, 97 HLR 1984, 1989–91 (1984).

108. See Bernard Audit, The Vienna Sales Convention and the Lex Mercatoria, in Carbonneau, supra note 38, at 173, 176; Chen, supra note 21 (ch. 7), at 104; Isaak I. Dore & James E. DeFranco, A Comparison of the Non-Substantive Provisions of the UNCITRAL Convention on the International Sale of Goods and the Uniform Commercial Code, 23 Harv. Int'l L.J. 49, 59 (1982); Muna Ndulo, The Vienna Sales Convention 1980 and the Hague Uniform Laws on International Sale of Goods 1964: A Comparative Analysis, 38 ICLQ 1, 9–10 (1989).

109. ULSIG, supra note 89, Annex I, art. 9(2).

110. See Allen, supra note 5 (ch. 1), at 134 & n.3, 135 & n.1 (noting practice of English courts to strike repugnant commercial customs).

111. See Gillette, supra note 69 (ch. 4), at 172.

112. See Maria del Pilar Perales Viscasillas, UNIDROIT Principles of International Commercial Contracts: Sphere of Application and General Provisions, 13 Ariz. J. Int'l & Comp. L. 381, 434–35 (1996).

113. 34 I.L.M. 1067 (1995). These have been slightly updated in 2004, see http://www.unidroit.org/english/principles/contracts/principles2004/blackletter2004.pdf.

114. Id. ¶ 1.8 (¶ 1.9 in the 2004 version).

115. See id. ¶ 2.6(3) (¶ 2.1.6(3) in the 2004 version).

116. See id. ¶ 4.3.

117. See id. ¶ 5.2 (¶ 5.1.2 in the 2004 version).

118. See Michael Joachim Bonnell, The UNIDROIT Principles on International Commercial Contracts: Why? What? How?, 69 Tul. L. Rev. 1121, 1135–36 (1995).

119. This categorization tends to exclude investor-state arbitration, typically featuring a private claimant and sovereign respondent. Ironically, investor-state cases are often publicly reported, and thus can serve as a stronger empiric database for conclusions about the role of custom in transnational commercial disputes. See William Tetley, The Lex Maritima, in Carbonneau, supra note 38, at 43, 49.

120. See, e.g., Grant Hanessian, "General Principles of Law" in the Iran-U.S. Claims Tribunal, 27 Colum. J. Transnat'l L. 309 (1989).

121. Declarations of the Government of the Democratic and Popular Republic of Algeria, Jan. 19, 1981, Claims Settlement Declaration, art. V, Iran-U.S., 20 I.L.M. 224 (1981).

122. UNCITRAL Arbitration Rules, G.A. Res. 31/98 U.N. GAOR, 31st Sess., Supp. No. 17, U.N. Doc. A/31/17, art. 33(3) (Dec. 15, 1976), available at http://www.unci-tral.org/pdf/english/texts/arbitration/arb-rules/arb-rules.pdf, 15 I.L.M. 701 (1976). For the background of this provision, see U.N. Doc. A/CN.9/9/C.2/SR.14, at ¶¶ 35–54 (23 April 1976).

123. See Berman & Dasser, supra note 38, at 67–68.

124. See Christopher R. Drahozal, Busting Arbitration Myths, 56 Kan. L. Rev. 663, 672–73 (2008) (reviewing ICC and SEC filings and concluding that barely 20 percent of all arbitral clauses included a provision for recourse to a body of non-national law); Christopher R. Drahozal, Private Ordering and International Commercial Arbitration, 113 Penn. State L. Rev. 1031, 1038–39 (2009) (extending empirical research); Rt. Hon. Lord Justice Mustill, The New Lex Mercatoria: The First Twenty-Five Years, 4 Arb. Int'l 86, 114 (1988).

125. See Bruce L. Benson, The Spontaneous Evolution of Commercial Law, 55 S. Econ. J. 644, 644 (1989).

126. See id. at 673; Gillette, supra note 69 (ch. 4), at 173–79 (reviewing cases where INCOTERMS and UCP were applied).
127. See Felix Dasser, Mouse or Monster? Some Facts and Figures on the Lex Mercatoria, in Globalisierung und Enstaatlichung des Rechts 129, 144–45, 157 (Annex) (Reinhard Zimmermann ed.; Tübingen: Mohr Siebeck, 2008) (finding, over a 50-year period, only 38 awards in which the lex mercatoria was applied in the absence of party agreement); Drahozal, Private Ordering, supra note 124, at 1039.
128. See Bhala, supra note 106, at 906–12 (discussing trade usages for currency "switches" as a device to hedge risk).
129. See Janet Koven Levit, A Bottom-Up Approach to International Law-Making: The Tale of Three Trade Finance Instruments, 30 Yale J. Int'l L. 125, 144–67 (2005).
130. See Sachs, supra note 2, at 807–12.
131. See Janet Koven Levit, Bottom-Up Lawmaking Through a Pluralist Lens: The ICC Banking Commission and the Transnational Regulation of Letters of Credit, 57 Emory L.J. 1147 (2008).
132. See id. at 1159–65 (collecting sources).
133. See Chapter 5, text at notes 51–94; Chapter 6, text at notes 11–54.
134. See Levitt, Bottom-Up, supra note 129, at 126–67.
135. See id. at 194–209.
136. Better known as the "Berne Union." See id. at 146–49.
137. See David J. Bederman, The Spirit of International Law 150–54 (Athens, Ga.: Univ. of Georgia Press, 2002).
138. See Levitt, Bottom-Up, supra note 129, at 192.

11. PUBLIC INTERNATIONAL LAW

1. Statute of the International Court of Justice, art. 38, para. 1, June 26, 1945, 59 Stat. 1055, 1066.
2. See Chapter 7, text at note 49.
3. See Chapter 5, text at notes 28 (Nigeria), 54 & 72–73 (South Africa).
4. See, e.g., Arrest Warrant Case, 2002 I.C.J. 3, 21 (para. 52); Ahmadou Sadio Diallo, Republic of Guinea v. Democratic Republic of Congo (Preliminary Objections), para. 39 (I.C.J. May 24, 2007).
5. See, e.g., Nicaragua Case, 1986 I.C.J. 14, 98–10 (paras. 187–90) (prohibition on the use of nondefensive force), 145 (para. 290) (peaceful settlement of disputes); Wall Advisory Opinion, 2004 I.C.J. 136, 182 (para. 117) (impermissibility of the acquisition of territory through warfare); Oil Platforms Case, 2003 I.C.J. 161, 186–87 (para. 51) (right of self-defense after armed attack); Nuclear Weapons Advisory Opinion, 1996 I.C.J. 226, 245 (para. 41) (necessity and proportionality requirements for use of force).
6. See, e.g., Nuclear Weapons Advisory Opinion, 1996 I.C.J. 226, 241–42 (para. 29) (obligation to prevent extraterritorial environmental harms); Maritime Delimitation Case (Qatar v. Bahrain), 2001 I.C.J. 40, 110 (para. 223) (right of innocent passage in territorial seas); Continental Shelf Case (Tunisia v. Libya), 1982 I.C.J. 18, 74 (para. 100) (continental shelf regime).

7. See, e.g., Nicaragua Case, 1986 I.C.J. 14, 113–14 (para. 218); Nuclear Weapons Advisory Opinion, 1996 I.C.J. 226, 256–60 (paras. 74–87) (international humanitarian law).

8. See, e.g., Land and Maritime Boundary (Cameroon v. Nigeria), 2002 I.C.J. 303, 429–30 (paras. 263–64); Wall Advisory Opinion, 2004 I.C.J. 136, 174 (para. 94); Gabčikovo-Nagymaros Project Case (Slovakia v. Hungary), 1997 I.C.J. 7, 38 (para. 46).

9. See, e.g., Immunity of Special Rapporteur Advisory Opinion, 1999 I.C.J. 62, 87 (para. 62); Genocide Convention Case (Bosnia v. Serbia), at paras. 385, 398, 419–20 (I.C.J. Feb. 26, 2007); Elletronica Sicula Case (U.S. v. Italy), 1989 I.C.J. 15, 42 (para. 50).

10. See Chapter 1, text at note 103.

11. See Kelsen, supra note 142 (ch. 3), at 440–41. See also Michael Byers, Custom, Power and the Power of Rules: International Relations and Customary International Law 124–26 (Cambridge: Cambridge Univ. Press, 1999).

12. See J. Patrick Kelly, The Twilight of Customary International Law, 40 VJIL 449, 459–65, 497–98 (2000); Eugene Kontorovich, Inefficient Customs in International Law, 48 Wm. & Mary L. Rev. 859, 877–84 (2006); Francesco Parisi, Spontaneous Emergence of Law: Customary Law, 5 Encyclopedia L. & Econ. 603, 612–14 (2000) (No. 9500).

13. See, e.g., La. Civ. C. Art. 3 (1999) ("Custom results from practice repeated for a long time and generally accepted as having acquired the force of law."); id. rev. comm. (b) ("According to civilian theory, the two elements of custom are long practice (*longa consuetudo*) and the conviction that the practice has the force of law (*opinio necessitatis* or *opinio juris*).").

14. See Chapter 2, text at notes 38–39.

15. See James Brown Scott, The Spanish Conception of International Law (Washington, D.C.: Georgetown Univ. Press, 1934); J. Kosters, Les Fondements du Droit des Gens, in 4 Bibliotheca Visseriana Dissertationum Ius Internationale Illustrantium (part 9), at 115–18 (The Hague: Brill, 1925).

16. See Brian Tierney, Vitoria and Suárez on *Ius Gentium*, Natural Law, and Custom, in Nature of Customary Law, supra note 11 (ch. 2), at 101, 119–21.

17. 2 Francisco Suárez, Selections from three works of Francisco Suárez, S. J.; De legibus, ac Deo legislatore 326, 341–42 (Gwladys L. Williams, Ammi Brown & John Waldron, transl.; James Brown Scott, ed.; Oxford: Clarendon Press, 1944) (passages 2.17.2 & 2.19.1).

18. Id. at 345–46 (passage 2.19.6).

19. Id. (passage 6.7.1.1).

20. See id. 545, 564–65 (passages 7.12.1, 7.14.5).

21. See id. at 442. But see Raphael M. Walden, The Subjective Element in the Formation of Customary International Law, 12 Israel L. Rev. 344, 345–46 (1977) (who argues that Suárez imposed an *opinio juris* requirement on CIL).

22. Just. Dig. 1.3.32.1 (Julian, Digest 84). See Chapter 2, text at note 39.

23. Suárez, supra note 17, at 565–66, 573 (passages 7.14.7 & 7.15.10).

24. Id. at 562–63 (passage 7.14.3).

25. Id. at 348–49 (passage 2.19.9).

26. Id. at 347–48 (passage 2.19.8).

27. Id. at 351 (passage 2.20.1). For a modern take on the *"inter se"* and *"intra se"* distinction, see IIT v. Vencamp, Ltd., 519 F.2d 1001, 1015 (2d Cir. 1975) (Friendly, J.) (CIL are those "standards, rules or customs (a) affecting the relationship between states or between an individual and a foreign state, and (b) used by those states for their common good and/or in dealings *inter se*").

28. See Tierney, supra note 16, at 123.

29. Suárez, supra note 17, at 465–66 (passage 7.4.6).

30. See id. at 466–67 (passage 7.4.7).

31. Id. at 459–60 (passage 7.3.7).

32. See Paul Guggenheim, Contribution a L'Histoire des Sources du Droit des Gens, 94 RCADI 1, 41 (1958 – II). But see Gerald J. Postema, Custom in International Law: A Normative Practice Account, in The Nature of Customary Law, supra note 11 (ch. 2), at 279, 280 (disputing whether Suárez endorsed an *opinio juris* requirement).

33. See Walden, supra note 21, at 347–49.

34. See Alf Ross, A Text-Book of International Law 94 (London: Longmans Green, 1947). See also Maurice H. Mendelson, The Formation of Customary International Law, 272 RCADI 155 (1998 – II); S.S. Lotus Case, 1927 P.C.I.J. (Ser. A) No. 10, at 18 ("The rules binding upon states therefore emanate from their own free will....").

35. See 3 E[mmerich] de Vattel, Les Droit des Gens [Law of Nations] 9 (1758) (intro; § 27) (Charles G. Fenwick transl., Washington, D.C.: Carnegie Foundation, 1916); Cornelius van Bynkershoek, Quaestiones Juris Publici [On Questions of Public Law] (1737) (Tenney Frank., transl.; Oxford: Clarendon Press, 1930).

36. Charles G. Fenwick, International Law 36 (4th ed.; New York: Appleton-Century-Crofts, 1965).

37. See James L. Brierly, The Law of Nations 51–52 (Sir Humphrey Waldock ed., 6th ed.; Oxford: Oxford Univ. Press, 1963). Cf. Brigitte Stern, Custom at the Heart of International Law, 11 Duke J. Comp. & Int'l L. 89, 98 (2001) ("Within the framework of a strict voluntarism, it is unreasonable to claim that once custom has been formed it must govern all the states that are part of the international community, independently of their will.").

38. See Manley O. Hudson, The Permanent Court of Justice, 1920–42, at 142–44, 194–95 (New York: MacMillan, 1943); Mohamed Shahabuddeen, Precedent in the World Court 52–53 (Cambridge: Cambridge Univ. Press, 1996).

39. See, e.g., Permanent Court of International Justice, Advisory Committee of Jurists, Documents Presented to the Committee, Plan of the Five Neutral Powers, Annex 11, at 301, art. 2(1); Bevilaqua Draft, Annex 15, at 353, art. 24 (1920). See also Karol Wolfke, Custom in Present International Law 3–5 (2nd rev. ed.; Dordrecht: Martinus Nijhoff, 1993).

40. Permanent Court of International Justice, Advisory Committee of Jurists, Procès-Verbaux of the Committee, June 16th–July 24th 1920, at 293–95 (13th Meeting) (The Hague: van Langenhuysen Bros., 1920).

41. Id. at 306 (13th Meeting; Annex No. 3).

42. Id. at 322 (14th Meeting; Annex No. 1).

43. Id. at 286–87, 293 (13th Meeting).

44. See id. at 547–48 (24th Meeting; Annex No. 3) (Root-Phillimore plan).

45. League of Nations, Permanent Court of International Justice, Documents concerning the action taken by the Council of the League of Nations, and the adoption by the Assembly, of the Statute of the Permanent Court, at 58, 219 (1921).

46. See Josef L. Kunz, The Nature of Customary International Law, 47 AJIL 662, 664 (1953) ("This untenable theory is also responsible for the extremely bad drafting of Article 38(1)....").

47. See Chapter 2, text at notes 95–105.

48. See Anthony D'Amato, The Concept of Custom in International Law 47–49 (Ithaca, N.Y.: Cornell Univ. Press, 1971); Walden, supra note 21, at 357–62.

49. François Gény, Méthode d'interprétation et sources en droit privé positif; Essai critique 319–24, 360 (§§ 110, 118) (Paris: Chevalier-Marescq, 1899) (*opinio juris* means that the "usage must reflect the "exercise of a [subjective] right of those who practice it"). See also Peter E. Benson, Francois Geny's Doctrine on Customary Law, 20 Can. Y.B. Int'l L. 267 (1983); Guggenheim, supra note 32, at 52; 1 Alphonse Rivier, Principes du droit des gens 35 (Paris: A. Rousseau, 1896).

50. See G. M. Danilenko, Law-Making in the International Community 76–77 (Dordrecht: Martinus Nijhoff, 1993); Peter Haggenmacher, La doctrine des deux éléments du droit coutumier dans la pratique de la Cour internationale, 90 Revue Générale de Droit International Public 5, 27–28 (1986).

51. See Hersch Lauterpacht, Règles générales du droit de la paix, 62 RCADI 95, 158 (1937 – IV); J.-P.-A. François, Règles générales du droit de la paix, 66 RCADI 1, 173 (1938 – IV) ("La coutume ne crée pas le droit, elle est l'expression d'une norme de droit, une mode de constatation du droit.").

52. See Alexander Orakhelashvili, Natural Law and Customary Law, 68 Zeitschrift für Ausländisches Öffentliches Recht und Völkerrecht 69 (2008); Amanda Perreau-Saussine, Three Ways of Writing a Treatise on Public International Law: Textbooks and the Nature of Customary International Law, in Nature of Customary Law, supra note 11 (ch. 2), at 228, 235–40 (reviewing such writers as Brierly and Phillimore (a member of the Advisory Committee of Jurists)). For Lord Phillimore's contribution to commercial custom jurisprudence, see Chapter 10, at note 68.

53. See Wolfke, supra note 39, at 5–8 (discussing work of de Visscher, Haggenmacher, Meijers, and Tunkin).

54. See Postema, supra note 32, at 281; Charles Rousseau, Principes généraux du droit international public 825 (Paris: A. Pedone, 1944).

55. See Continental Shelf Case (Libya v. Malta), 1985 I.C.J. 13, 29–30 (para. 27) (CIL's substance must be "looked for primarily in the actual practice and *opinio juris* of States"); Nicaragua Case, 1986 I.C.J. 14, 97 (para. 183) (the Court "directs its intention to the practice and *opinio juris* of States").

56. Article 24 of the Statute of the International Law Commission, [1950] 2 Y.B. Int'l L. Comm'n 25, 26.

57. Id. (quoting James Brierly, The Law of Nations: An Introduction to the Law of Peace 62 (4th ed.; Oxford: Clarendon Press, 1953)).

58. For the ILC debate, see [1950] 1 Y.B. Int'l L. Comm'n 4–6; see also Wolfke, supra note 39, at 29–35.

59. See Heinrich Triepel, Les Rapports entre le Droit Interne et la Droit International, 1 RCADI 73, 82–83 (1923 – I); Karl Strupp, Les Règles Générales du Droit de la

Paix, 47 RCADI 259, 302–04 (1934 – I). See also Walden, supra note 21, at 349–55. See also Jurisdiction of the European Commission of the Danube, 1927 P.C.I.J. Ser. B (No. 14) 17 ("In this usage [Rumania] tacitly but formally acquiesced....").

60. See Kelsen, supra note 142 (ch. 3), at 312–13. See also Kunz, supra note 46, at 663–64.

61. See Walden, supra note 21, at 355–5; Wolfke, supra note 39, at 164–68.

62. See Paul Guggenheim, Traité de Droit International Public 46–48 (Geneva: Georg, 1953).

63. Anthea Elizabeth Roberts, Traditional and Modern Approaches to Customary International Law: A Reconciliation, 95 AJIL 757, 758 (2001) (original emphasis; citations omitted).

64. Id. (original emphasis; citations omitted).

65. See, e.g., Jonathan I. Charney, Universal International Law, 87 AJIL 529, 544–45 (1993); David Fidler, Challenging the Classical Concept of Custom, 1996 Ger. Y.B. Int'l L. 198, 216–31; Richard B. Lillich, The Growing Importance of Customary International Human Rights Law, 25 Ga. J. Int'l & Comp. L. 1, 8 (1995/1996); Hugh Thirlway, The Sources of International Law, in International Law 115, 123 (Malcolm D. Evans, ed., 2nd ed.; Oxford: Oxford Univ. Press, 2006).

66. See W. Michael Reisman, The Cult of Custom in the Late 20th Century, 17 Cal. W. Int'l L.J. 133, 135 (1987).

67. See Anthony A. D'Amato, Trashing Customary International Law, 81 AJIL 101 (1987); Robert Y. Jennings, The Identification of International Law, in International Law: Teaching and Practice 3, 5 (Bin Cheng, ed.; London: Stevens, 1982); Kelly, supra note 12, at 451; Arthur A. Weisburd, Customary International Law: The Problem of Treaties, 21 Vand. J. Transnat'l L. 1 (1988).

68. For a handy summary, see Roberts, supra note 63, at 767–70.

69. See H. Meijers, How Is International Law Made? – The Stages of Growth of International Law and the Use of Its Customary Rules, 9 Neth. Y.B. Int'l L. 3 (1978); G. J. H. van Hoof, Rethinking the Sources of International Law 91–106 (Deventer: Kluwer, 1983).

70. See Frederic L. Kirgis, Custom on a Sliding Scale, 81 AJIL 146 (1987); John Tasioulas, In Defense of Relative Normativity: Communitarian Values and the *Nicaragua* Case, 16 Oxford J. Legal Stud. 85 (1996). For a criticism of this theory, see Bruno Simma & Philip Alston, The Sources of Human Rights Law: Custom, Jus Cogens, and General Principles, 1988–89 Austl. Y.B. Int'l L. 82, 83.

71. See 1 Pitt Cobbett, Leading Cases on International Law 5 (4th ed.; London: Sweet & Maxwell, 1922) ("usage" becomes "custom" just as footsteps across a common eventually become a "path" habitually followed by all).

72. See [1950] 2 Y.B. Int'l L. Comm'n at 29–30 (for a review of the availability of such sources).

73. See Wolfke, supra note 39, at 41–44, 58–61, 150–51.

74. See Fisheries Case (U.K. v. Nor.), 1951 I.C.J. 116, 191 (Read, J., dissenting) ("[c]laims may be important as starting points, which, if not challenged, may ripen into historic title.... The only convincing evidence of State practice is to be found in seizures, where the coastal State asserts its sovereignty over the water in question by arresting a foreign ship."); Jack L. Goldsmith & Eric A. Posner, The Limits of International Law 53 (Oxford: Oxford Univ. Press, 2005) (questioning

this assumption in the context of the "free ships, free goods" doctrine); H. W. A. Thirlway, International Customary Law and Codification 58 (Leiden: Sijthoff, 1972).

75.   See D'Amato, supra note 48, at 87–98 (referring to an "act" or "commitment" in support of a CIL norm); Wolfke, supra note 39, at 84 (verbal acts "do not constitute acts of conduct, nor, even multiplied, any conclusive evidence of state practice"). Contra Michael Akehurst, Custom as a Source of International Law, 47 BYBIL 1, 1–8 (1974–75) (characterizing D'Amato's theory as "very restrictive" and "a minority view"); Byers, supra note 11, at 133–35 (offering a "compromise position"); Andrew T. Guzman, Saving Customary International Law, 27 Mich. J. Int'l L. 115, 151–53 (2005).

76.   See Danilenko, supra note 50, at 87–94; Eric Suy, Les Actes Juridiques Unilatéraux en Droit International Public 215–67 (Paris: Pichon & Durand-Auzias, 1962).

77.   See [1950] 2 Y.B. Int'l L. Comm'n at 28–29; Akehurst, supra note 75, at 8–10; Lazare Kopelmanas, Custom as a Means of the Creation of International Law, 18 BYBIL 127, 148–49 (1937); Max Sørensen, Les Sources du Droit International 90–94 (Copenhagen: Einar Munksgaard, 1946).

78.   See Akehurst, supra note 75, at 10–11; Byers, supra note 11, at 142–45; I. C. MacGibbon, Customary International Law and Acquiescence, 33 BYBIL 115 (1957); Mark E. Villiger, Customary International Law and Treaties 37–42 (rev. 2nd ed.; The Hague: Kluwer, 1997).

79.   See North Sea Continental Shelf Cases, 1969 I.C.J. at 42 (para. 73); 227 (Lachs, J., dissenting) (searching for evidence of practice from States "with different political, economic and legal systems" and from "all continents"). See also Akehurst, supra note 75, at 22–23; Danilenko, supra note 50, at 95–96; Villiger, supra note 78, at 30–33.

80.   See Charney, supra note 65, at 537; Hiram Chodosh, Neither Treaty Nor Custom: The Emergence of Declarative International Law, 26 Tex. Int'l L.J. 87, 102 (1991).

81.   See Villiger, supra note 78, at 32–33.

82.   175 U.S. 677 (1990). For the background of this case, see William S. Dodge, *The Paquete Habana*: Customary International Law as Part of Our Law, in International Law Stories 175 (John E. Noyes, Laura A. Dickinson & Mark W. Janis, eds.; New York: Foundation Press, 2007).

83.   See 175 U.S. at 686–707.

84.   1 C. Rob. 20, 165 Eng. Rep. 81 (Adm. 1798) (Eng.).

85.   See Brian D. Lepard, Customary International Law: A New Theory with Practical Applications 15–16 (Cambridge: Cambridge Univ. Press, 2010).

86.   But see Goldsmith & Posner, supra note 74, at 66–78 (disputing whether the practice of immunizing small fishing vessels from capture was as well observed as claimed by Justice Gray).

87.   See Military and Paramilitary Activities (Nicar. v. U.S.) (Merits), 1986 I.C.J. 14, 98 (para. 184). See also Gulf of Maine Case (U.S. v. Can.), 1984 I.C.J. 246, 299 (para. 111).

88.   But see European Commission of the Danube Case, 1927 P.C.I.J. Ser. B (No. 14) 105 (Negulesco, J., dissenting) (indicating that CIL required immemorial usage).

89. See Akehurst, supra note 75, at 12–16; Marten Bos, The Identification of Custom in International Law, 25 Ger. Y.B. Int'l L. 9, 25–28 (1982); Bin Cheng, United Nations Resolutions on Outer Space: "Instant" International Customary Law?, 5 Indian J. Int'l L. 23, 35–48 (1965); Jorg Kammerhofer, Uncertainty in the Formal Sources of International Law: Customary International Law and Some of Its Problems, 15 Eur. J. Int'l L. 523, 530–31 (2004); Michael P. Scharf, Seizing the "Grotian Moment": Accelerated Formation of Customary International Law in Times of Fundamental Change, available at http://ssvn.com/abstract=1588283(version of April 2010).

90. See North Sea Continental Shelf Cases (F.R.G. v. Neth./Den.), 1969 I.C.J. 3, 43.

91. See Right of Passage Case (Port. v. India), 1960 I.C.J. 6, 40. See also Akehurst, supra note 75, at 20.

92. 1927 P.C.I.J. (Ser. A) No. 10 (Fr. v. Tur.).

93. See id. at 18 (referring to "usages generally accepted as expressing principles of law").

94. See id. at 22, 31. See also Wolfke, supra note 39, at 119–20.

95. See 1927 P.C.I.J. (Ser. A) No. 10, at 23, 28–29. See also D'Amato, supra note 48, at 82–83.

96. See 1927 P.C.I.J. (Ser. A) No. 10, at 28. See also Sir Hersch Lauterpacht, The Development of International Law by the International Court 384–88 (New York: Praeger, 1958); Lepard, supra note 85, at 188–89.

97. See Wolfke, supra note 39, at 10–11.

98. 630 F.2d 876 (2d Cir. 1980). For more on this case, see Harold Hongju Koh, *Filártiga v. Peña-Irala*, Judicial Internalization into Domestic Law of the Customary International Law Norm Against Torture, in International Law Stories, supra note 82, at 45. The Alien Tort Claims Act allows suits brought in the United States for torts committed in violation of the law of nations. 28 U.S.C. § 1350.

99. See Lepard, supra note 85, at 35, 208–17; Mendelson, supra note 34, at 382–90 (for a more nuanced view).

100. See Fidler, supra note 65, at 203 & n.21; Goldsmith & Posner, supra note 74, at 132–33; Arthur Weisburd, supra note 67, at 23–29.

101. See Lepard, supra note 85, at 20–23, 112; John Tasioulas, Customary International Law and the Quest for Global Justice, in The Nature of Customary Law, supra note 11 (ch. 2), at 307, 320–21.

102. Thirlway, supra note 74, at 48.

103. See, e.g., International Law Association, Committee on Formation of Customary International Law, Statement of Principles Applicable to the Formation of General Customary International Law: Report of the Sixty-Ninth Conference, London, at 712, 713, 743–53 (2000). Contra Sienho Yee, The News That Opinio Juris "Is Not a Necessary Element of Customary [International] Law" Is Greatly Exaggerated, 2000 German Y.B. Int'l L. 227.

104. Compare North Sea Continental Shelf Cases, 1969 I.C.J. 3, 44 ("Not only must the acts concerned amount to a settled practice, but they must also be... carried out in such a way[] as to be evidence of a belief that this practice is rendered obligatory by the existence of a rule requiring it"); and Gulf of Maine Case (U.S. v. Can.), 1984 I.C.J. 246, 293–94 (both rejecting rule of equidistance as not supported by *opinio juris*); with Military and Paramilitary Activities (Nicar. v. U.S.) (Merits), 1986 I.C.J. 14, 108–09 (accepting as CIL norms against use of force).

105. For a discussion of these decisions, see Kirgis, supra note 70, at 149; Mendelson, supra note 34, at 275–77; Wolfke, supra note 39, at 15–23.
106. See Fidler, supra note 65, at 206–07.
107. Fisheries Jurisdiction Case (U.K. v. Ice.), 1974 I.C.J. 3, 23 (para. 53) (characterizing such rights as "aspirations, rather than as expressing principles of existing law").
108. Southwest Africa Cases, 1966 I.C.J. 6, 48 (para. 91) ("Rights cannot be presumed to exist merely because it might seem desirable that they should.").
109. Barcelona Traction (Belg. v. Sp.), 1970 I.C.J. 3, 40 (para. 61) (characterizing bilateral treaties on nationality of claims as "[f]ar from evidencing any norm" are "*sui generis* and provide no guide in the present case").
110. Nuclear Weapons Advisory Opinion, 1996 I.C.J. 226, 255 (para. 73) ("The emergence, as *lex lata*, of a customary rule specifically prohibiting the use of nuclear weapons as such is hampered by the continuing tensions between the nascent *opinio juris* on the one hand, and the still strong adherence to the practice of deterrence on the other.").
111. See Danilenko, supra note 50, at 103–06; Lepard, supra note 85, at 113–17.
112. Gulf of Maine Case, 1984 I.C.J. 246, 299 (para. 111). See also Kelly, supra note 12, at 469–79 (arguing that *opinio juris* is indeterminate and tribunals should declare a *non liquet* when it is not evident that a usage has achieved CIL status).
113. Nicaragua Case, 1986 I.C.J. 14, 98 (para. 184), 108 (para. 206). See also Bos, supra note 89, at 32–37.
114. See, e.g., Nottebohm Case, 1955 I.C.J. 4, 22 (looking at national laws for "genuine link" theory of nationality); Arrest Warrant Case, 2002 I.C.J. 3, 24 (para. 58) (examining national legislation and decisions on immunities afforded sitting ministers of foreign affairs).
115. See, e.g., Nuclear Weapons Advisory Opinion, 1996 I.C.J. 226, 258 (para. 81); Prosecutor v. Tadic, Decision on the Defense Motion for Interlocutory Appeal on Jurisdiction, at para. 133 (Int'l Crim. Trib. Yugo. Appeals Chamber) (October 2, 1995), 35 ILM 32 (1996). See also Danilenko, supra note 50, at 121–22; Lepard, supra note 85, at 180–85, 191–207 (considering the relative weight to be accorded multilateral, as opposed to bilateral, treaties).
116. See Stephen McCaffrey, Is Codification in Decline?, 20 Hastings Int'l & Comp. L. Rev. 639 (1997); Myres S. McDougal, The Hydrogen Bomb Tests and the International Law of the Sea, 49 AJIL 356, 359, 361 (1955); John Fischer Williams, Some Aspects of Modern International Law 44–46 (London: Oxford Univ. Press, 1939).
117. See Vattel, supra note 35, at § 26 ("if that custom … be useful and reasonable, it becomes obligatory on all the nations in question"). See also Akehurst, supra note 75, at 34–35 (*opinio juris* as the consciousness of moral or social needs).
118. See MacGibbon, supra note 78, at 133–35; Orakhelashvili, supra note 52, at 100–01.
119. North Sea Continental Shelf Cases, 1969 I.C.J. at 23 (paras. 22–23). See also Diallo Case, at paras. 88–90 (Preliminary Objections) (Judgment of May 24, 2007) (for a similar ruling).
120. See Danilenko, supra note 50, at 102–09; Olufemi Elias, The Nature of the Subjective Element in Customary International Law, 44 ICLQ 501 (1995); Mendelson, supra note 34, at 264–67.

121. See North Sea Continental Shelf Cases, 1969 I.C.J. at 28; but see id. at 231 (Lachs, J., dissenting) ("to postulate that all states, even those that initiate a given practice, believe themselves to be acting under a legal obligation is to resort to a fiction.... For the path may indeed start from voluntary, unilateral acts relying on the confident expectation that they will find acquiescence or be emulated.").
122. North Sea Continental Shelf Cases, 1969 I.C.J. at 44. See also Jurisdiction of the European Commission of the Danube, 1927 P.C.I.J. Ser. B (No. 14), at 105 (Negulesco, J., dissenting) (CIL can only be "based upon the mutual conviction that the recurrence of the [usage was] the result of a compulsory rule").
123. See Guzman, supra note 75, at 143–44 (noting, however, that it is difficult to infer implied consent to CIL norms for newly independent states); Kelsen, supra note 142 (ch. 3), at 444–45. But see G. I. Tunkin, Remarks on the Juridical Nature of Customary Norms of International Law, 49 Cal. L. Rev. 419, 423 (1961).
124. See Byers, supra note 11, at 147–51.
125. 1950 I.C.J. 266 (Colom. v. Peru).
126. See Herbert W. Briggs, The Colombian-Peruvian Case and Proof of Customary International Law, 45 AJIL 728 (1951); D'Amato, supra note 48, at 246–48; Lauterpacht, supra note 96, at 374–76, 380; Thirlway, supra note 74, at 100–03, 136–37.
127. 1960 I.C.J. 6 (Port. v. India).
128. See D'Amato, supra note 48, at 256–58; Thirlway, supra note 74, at 138–39.
129. Right of Nationals of the United States in Morocco (U.S. v. Mor.), 1952 I.C.J. 176, 199–200 (specifically referring to "local custom"). See also D'Amato, supra note 48, at 254–55; Lauterpacht, supra note 96, at 388–92; Thirlway, supra note 74, at 92–94.
130. For the connection between special customs in CIL and these domestic-law analogies, see D'Amato, supra note 48, at 234–46.
131. 1951 I.C.J. 116 (U.K. v. Nor.).
132. See D'Amato, supra note 48, at 258–62; Lauterpacht, supra note 96, at 368–70; MacGibbon, supra note 78, at 134.
133. See Akehurst, supra note 75, at 28–31; Guzman, supra note 75, at 159–61.
134. Compare Jonathan I. Charney, The Persistent Objector Rule and the Development of Customary International Law, 56 BYBIL 1, 21 (1986) ("the persistent objector rule has no legitimate basis in the international legal system"); with Mendelson, supra note 34, at 227–44 (arguing that the persistent objector rule has substantial authority from international precedents); and Ted L. Stein, The Approach of the Different Drummer: The Principle of Persistent Objection in International Law, 26 Harv. Int'l L.J. 457 (1985). See also Lepard, supra note 85, at 229–42.For the origins of the persistent objector rule in academic literature, see Olufemi Elias, Some Remarks on the Persistent Objector Rule in Customary International Law, 1991 Denning L.J. 37 (tracing it to the writings of Ian Brownlie).See also Curtis A. Bradley & Mitu Gulati, Withdrawing from International Custom, 119 YLJ – (2010) (forthcoming) (for a superb review of this issue).
135. See North Sea Continental Shelf Cases, 1969 I.C.J. at 38 (para. 63) (CIL "cannot ... be the subject of any right of unilateral exclusion exercisable at will by any [state] in its own favour."). See also Guzman, supra note 75, at 170–71; Villiger, supra note 78, at 36–37.
136. See Chapter 9, text at notes 89–106.

137. See also Kelly, supra note 12, at 511–12.
138. See D'Amato, supra note 48, at 99–102.
139. See Guzman, supra note 75, at 164–71 (arguing that the persistent objector rule is an artifact of state-consent theories for CIL, but suggesting it has utility from a rational choice perspective). See also Vincy Fon & Francesco Parisi, Stability and Change in International Customary Law, available at http://papers.ssrn.com/sol3/papers.cfm?abstract_id=399960.
140. See Wolfke, supra note 39, at 66–67.
141. ILA Report, supra note 103, at section II.C.15, cmt. c.
142. See Anglo-Norwegian Fisheries, 1951 I.C.J. at 131 (the delimitation rule "would appear to be inapplicable as against Norway, in as much as she has always opposed any attempt to apply it to the Norwegian coast"). See also Akehurst, supra note 75, at 23–27; Danilenko, supra note 50, at 109–13.
143. See Advisory Committee of Jurists, supra note 40, at 332–38 (conflicting debate as to whether the sources of international law mentioned in Article 38 should be followed in the order listed, or, rather "simultaneously"). See also Gary L. Scott & Craig L. Carr, Multilateral Treaties and the Formation of Customary International Law, 25 Denver J. Int'l L. & Pol'y 71 (1996); Villiger, supra note 78, at 57–59.
144. See Mendelson, supra note 34, at 295–301.
145. 1969 I.C.J. 3 (F.R.G. v. Den./Neth.).
146. See Meijers, supra note 69, at 17 (for the *opinio juris* aspects of this decision).
147. See D'Amato, supra note 48, at 109–12, 120–21; Thirlway, supra note 74, at 80–91, 105.
148. See The MARIA, 1 C. Rob. 340, 360, 165 Eng. Rep. 199, 206 (Adm. 1799) (Scott, J.) (Eng.) (right of search of merchant vessels "is equally clear in practice; for practice is uniform and universal upon the subject. The many European treaties which refer to this right, refer to it as preexisting, and merely regulate the exercise of it.").
149. But see R. R. Baxter, Treaties and Custom, 129 RCADI 25, 73 (1970 – I) ("As the express acceptance of the treaty increases, the number of States whose practice is relevant diminishes. There will be less scope for the development of international law dehors the treaty, particularly if the non-parties include many States with relatively few international links.").
150. See 5 Iran-U.S. Claims Trib. Rep. 251 (1984).
151. Jan. 19, 1981, Iran-U.S., 1 id. 3; 20 I.L.M. 224 (1981).
152. Nottebohm Case (Second Phase) (Liecht. v. Guat.), 1955 I.C.J. 4, 21–23. See also D'Amato, supra note 48, at 113–16.
153. See 1986 I.C.J. at 108–09 (paras. 206–08). See also Vienna Convention on the Law of Treaties (VCLT), art. 38, 1155 U.N.T.S. 331 ("Nothing in articles 34 to 37 precludes a rule set forth in a treaty from becoming binding upon a third State as a customary rule of international law, recognized as such."); art. 43 ("The invalidity, termination or denunciation of a treaty, the withdrawal of a party from it, or the suspension of its operation, as a result of the application of the present Convention or of the provisions of the treaty, shall not in any way impair the duty of any State to fulfil any obligation embodied in the treaty to which it would be subject under international law independently of the treaty."); Fred L. Morrison, Legal Issues in the *Nicaragua* Opinion, 81 AJIL 160, 160–62 (1987); Villiger, supra note 78, at 169–72.

154. See Lepard, supra note 85, at 40–41, 270–76 (providing a detailed schematic for different sorts of treaty-CIL conflicts).
155. The S.S. China Incident, [1916] For. Relations of the U.S. Supp. 667.
156. 1921 P.C.I.J. Ser. A (No. 1) (Fr./U.K./It./Jap. v. Ger.).
157. See 1 J.H.W. Verzijl, The Jurisprudence of the World Court 41–45(Leyden: Sijthoff, 1965); Sheila Weinberger, The Wimbledon Paradox and the World Court: Confronting Inevitable Conflicts between Conventional and Customary International Law, 10 Emory Int'l L. Rev. 397 (1996); Ernst Wolgast, Der Wimbledonprozess vor dem Völkerbundsgerichtshof (Berlin: Verlag Rothschild, 1926).
158. The State (Duggan) v. Tapley, 18 I.L.R. 336, 338–39 (Ir. S.Ct. 1951).
159. West Rand Central Gold Mining Co. v. The King, [1905] 2 K.B. 391, 402, 405 (Alverstone, L.J.).
160. See Thirlway, supra note 74, at 95–108 (distinguishing custom *contra legem* and custom *praeter legem*).
161. VCLT, supra note 153, art. 31(3)(c).
162. See [1964] 2 Y.B. Int'l L. Comm'n 198 (proposing, in draft article 68, which provided that "The operation of a treaty may also be modified: ... (c) by the subsequent emergence of a new rule of customary international law relating to matters dealt with in the treaty and binding upon all the parties."); [1966] 2 Y.B. Int'l L. Comm'n 236 (proposing, in draft article 38: "A treaty may be modified by subsequent practice in the application of the treaty establishing the agreement of the parties to modify its provisions."). See also Nancy Kontou, The Termination and Revision of Treaties in the Light of New Customary International Law 135–39 (Oxford: Clarendon Press, 1994).
163. See Kontou, supra note 162, at 37–71 (examples from the law of the sea), 72–108 (examples from other fields, including extradition, capitulation, diplomatic, and common spaces regimes).
164. See, e.g., Fisheries Jurisdiction (Merits) (U.K. v. Ice.), 1974 I.C.J. 3, 23 (para. 52); A.-G. v. Burgoa, 1980 Eur. Ct. Justice 2787, 2798 (both concerning the extent of fishing zones and holding that CIL had supervened earlier fishing treaty regimes).
165. Aug. 15, 1955, Iran-U.S., 284 U.N.T.S. 93.
166. See Sedco, Inc. v. National Iranian Oil Co., 10 Iran-U.S. Claims Trib. Rep. 180, 184–89 (March 27, 1986). But see Phillips Petroleum Co. v. National Iranian Oil Co., 21 Iran-U.S. Claims Trib. Rep. 79, 120–21 (para. 107) (June 29, 1989) (expressly rejecting the supervening custom theory). See also George H. Aldrich, The Jurisprudence of the Iran-United States Claims Tribunal 218–26 (Oxford: Clarendon Press, 1996).
167. See Chapter 9, text at notes 62–106.
168. 1971 I.C.J. 16, 22 (para. 22).
169. 1962 I.C.J. 151, 160–61, 175, 178.
170. See VCLT, supra note 153, arts. 53 & 64; [1976] 2 Y.B. Int'l L. Comm'n 95, 121. See also Lauri Hannikainen, Peremptory Norms (Jus Cogens) in International Law: Historical Development, Criteria, Present Status (Helsinki: Finnish Lawyers Pub. Co., 1988); Christos L. Rozakis, The Concept of Jus Cogens in the Law of Treaties (Amsterdam: North Holland Pub. Co., 1976).

171. VCLT, supra note 153, art. 53.
172. See Military and Paramilitary Activities Case (Nicar. v. U.S.) (Merits), 1986 I.C.J. 14, 100–01 (para. 190).
173. VCLT, supra note 153, art. 64 ("If a new peremptory norm of general international law emerges, any existing treaty which is in conflict with that norm becomes void and terminates."), art. 71 (provision on the "Consequences of the invalidity of a treaty which conflicts with a peremptory norm of general international law").
174. See Fidler, supra note 65, at 210.
175. See Chapter 2, text at notes 47–55; Chapter 4, text at note 11.
176. See Chapter 7, text at note 36 (English commercial case of *Perry v. Barnett*); Chapter 9, text at notes 71–73 (*Midwest Oil* decision in the U.S. Supreme Court).
177. See Barcelona Traction Case, 1970 I.C.J. at 32 (para. 33); [2001] 2 Y.B. Int'l L. Comm'n at 110–12. See also Maurizio Ragazzi, The Concept of International Obligations *Erga Omnes* (Oxford: Oxford Univ. Press, 1997).
178. See Byers, supra note 11, at 198–201.
179. See, e.g., East Timor Case (Port. v. Austl.), 1995 I.C.J. 90, 102 (para. 29) (indicating that "the right of peoples to self-determination … has an *erga omnes* character" but not indicating that it is *jus cogens*). See also Lepard, supra note 85, at 261–69.
180. See Lepard, supra note 85, at 251–52.
181. See id. at 243–69 (offering a coherent theory for recognizing *jus cogens* norms).
182. See, e.g., Georg Schwarzenberger, International Law and Order 39–40, 50–53 (London: Stevens & Sons, 1971); Ian Sinclair, The Vienna Convention on the Law of Treaties 24 (Manchester: Manchester Univ. Press, 1984); A. Mark Weisburd, The Emptiness of the Concept of *Jus Cogens*, as Illustrated by the War in Bosnia-Herzegovina, 17 Mich. J. Int'l L. 1, 19, 28 (1995); Wolfke, supra note 39, at 92. For a bibliography of scholars supporting jus cogens, see Byers, supra note 11, at 184 n.91.
183. For France's position, see Olivier Deleau, Les positions françaises à la Conférence de Vienne sur le droits des traités, 15 Annuaire Françaises de droit international 7, 14–17, 23 (1969).
184. See Oscar Chinn Case, 1934 P.C.I.J. Ser. A (No. 23) 148, 150 (Schücking, J., sep. op.) (the "Court would never … apply a convention the terms of which were contrary to public morality"); G. G. Fitzmaurice, Law of Treaties, [1958] 2 Y.B. Int'l L. Comm'n 20, 40–41 (para. 76) (*jus cogens* norms involve "considerations of morals and of international good order"); Alfred von Verdross, Forbidden Treaties in International Law, 31 AJIL 571, 574 (1937) (*jus cogens* norms should "correspond to the universal ethics of the international community"). But see Byers, supra note 11, at 189 (disputing whether *jus cogens* incorporates natural law); Michael Byers, Conceptualising the Relationship Between Jus Cogens and *Erga Omnes* Rules, 66 Nordic J. Int'l L. 211, 213–14 (1997).
185. Rosalyn Higgins, Problems and Process: International Law and How We Use It 21–22 (Oxford: Clarendon Press, 1994).
186. Nicaragua Case, 1986 I.C.J. at 100 (para. 190).
187. See VCLT, supra note 153, art. 53; [1963] 2 Y.B. Int'l L. Comm'n 187, 199 (para. 4) (jus cogens norms could be altered by a general multilateral treaty).
188. See E. Jiménez de Aréchega, International Law in the Past Third of a Century, 159 RCADI 1, 21 (1978- I); D'Amato, supra note 48, at 239–40.

189. See Chapter 2, text at note 46.
190. See van Hoof, supra note 69, at 99.
191. Kammerhofer, supra note 89, at 531.
192. Id. at 97–98.
193. 1986 I.C.J. at 98.
194. See Wolfke, supra note 39, at 65–66.
195. See Akehurst, supra note 75, at 8.
196. See Villiger, supra note 78, at 55.
197. 1986 I.C.J. at 109.
198. Lepard, supra note 85, at 279 (original emphasis).
199. See Krzysztof Skubiszewski, Elements of Custom and the Hague Court, 31 Zeitschrift für Ausländisches Öffentliches Recht und Völkerrecht 810, 846 (1971).
200. Aréchega, supra note 188, at 21. See also Anglo-Norwegian Fisheries Case, 1951 I.C.J. at 148 (Alvarez, J., sep. op.) ("a new case strongly stated may be sufficient to render obsolete an ancient custom").
201. Wolfke, supra note 39, at 65.
202. See Akehurst, supra note 75, at 8 (CIL can be altered simply "by repeatedly declaring that the old rule no longer exists").
203. 1982 I.C.J. at 115.
204. See Kelsen, supra note 142 (ch. 3), at 454.
205. But see van Hoof, supra note 69, at 101 (who argues that only changes in *opinio juris* can effectuate modifications of CIL).
206. See Goldsmith & Posner, supra note 74, at 21–78.
207. For an intellectual history, see D'Amato, supra note 48, at 23–29; Lepard, supra note 85, at 14–15, 99–100.
208. See Hart, supra note 1 (ch. 1), at 44–47; Kelsen, supra note 142 (ch. 3), at 440–43.
209. See Hart, supra note 1 (ch. 1), at 219–26; Kelsen, supra note 142 (ch. 3), at 444–45.
210. Hart, supra note 1 (ch. 1), at 44.
211. See Goldsmith & Posner, supra note 74, at 225–26.
212. See id. at 26–27. See also Edward T. Swaine, Rational Custom, 52 Duke L.J. 559, 560–67 (2002).
213. See Goldsmith & Posner, supra note 74, at 27–28.
214. See id. at 28–29.
215. See id. at 29–35 (where the authors distinguish "cooperation" as a bilateral, "single-play" Prisoners' Dilemma, while "coordination" is multilateral, "repeated-play" scenarios).
216. See id. at 39.
217. For a review of the game-theoretic implications of Goldsmith's and Posner's work, see George Norman & Joel P. Trachtman, The Customary International Law Game, 99 AJIL 541 (2005); Swaine, supra note 212, at 573–88.
218. See Harold Hongju Koh, Why Do Nations Obey International Law?, 106 YLJ 2599 (1997) (review essay of Abram Chayes & Antonia Handler Chayes, The New Sovereignty: Compliance with International Regulatory Agreements (1995); and Thomas M. Franck, Fairness in International Law and Institutions (1995)); Swaine, supra note 212, at 588–92.
219. See Andrew T. Guzman, A Compliance-Based Theory of International Law, 90 Cal. L. Rev. 1823, 1875–76 (2002).

220. Goldsmith & Posner, supra note 74, at 38.
221. See Chapter 1, text at notes 14–28.
222. For more on these phenomena, see David J. Bederman, Globalization and International Law (New York: Palgrave-MacMillan, 2008).
223. Goldsmith and Posner refer to their's as an "instrumental theory." See Goldsmith & Posner, supra note 74, at 185.
224. See Bederman, supra note 137 (ch. 10), at 94–95; A. I. L. Campbell, International Law and Primitive Law, 8 Oxford J. Leg. Stud. 169 (1988); Yoram Dinstein, International Law as a Primitive Legal System, 19 NYU J. Int'l L. & Pol. 1 (1986).
225. See Baxter, supra note 149, at 42, 96; Fidler, supra note 65, at 220–24 (describing CIL as a "dynamo"); Lepard, supra note 85, at 371–79; Julius Stone, On the Vocation of the International Law Commission, 57 CLR 16, 21, 32 (1957) (CIL superior to codification).
226. For the development of CIL by individuals, NGOs, and members of international "civil society," see Christiana Ochoa, The Individual and Customary International Law Formation, 48 VJIL 119 (2007).
227. See Advisory Committee of Jurists, supra note 40, at 322 (14th Meeting; July 2, 1920) (Annex 1) (Speech by Baron Descamps).
228. See Francesco Parisi & Nita Ghei, The Role of Reciprocity in International Law, 36 Corn. Int'l L. J. 93, 122–23 (2003); Norman & Trachtman, supra note 217, at 554–55.
229. See this chapter, text at notes 118–19.
230. See Kontorovich, supra note 12, at 877–94, 895–96.
231. See Chapter 3, text at notes 86–105 (English common law); Chapter 5, text at notes 76–82 (family law; *Bhe* case); Chapter 8, text at notes 22–39 (torts; *The T.J. HOOPER*); Chapter 9, text at notes 95–105 (constitutional law; *Chadha* case).
232. See Bernstein, supra note 53 (ch. 4), at 714 & n.14.
233. Some factors are present, such as the (relatively) small number of states (about 190 today), and the likelihood (at least for some issues) of a high number of repeat transactions. See Ellickson, supra note 14 (ch. 4), at 84, 178–81.
234. See Ellickson, supra note 14 (ch. 4), at 54; Kontorovich, supra note 12, at 893–94.
235. See Kontorovich, supra note 12, at 916–17 (discussing CIL of diplomatic privileges and immunities as being paradigmatic of this phenomenon), 917–20 (examining laws of war and human rights, and concluding that these realms are unlikely to find equilibrium with efficient customs because of a lack of reciprocity and mutuality). See also Clayton P. Gillette, The Exercise of Trumps by Decentralized Governments, 83 VLR 1347, 1373–74 (1997) (homogenous groups use custom as a way to avoid hold-out problems by individuals).
236. Goldsmith & Posner, supra note 74, at 37.
237. See Christopher J. Borgen, Resolving Treaty Conflicts, 37 Geo. Wash. Int'l L. Rev. 573 (2005); Bethany Lukitsch Hicks, Treaty Congestion in International Environmental Law: The Need for Greater International Coordination, 32 U. Rich. L. Rev. 1643 (1999); Edith Brown Weiss, Symposium, International Environmental Law: Contemporary Issues and the Emergence of a New World Order, 81 Geo. L.J. 675, 697–702 (1993).
238. See N. C. H. Dunbar, The Myth of Customary International Law, 8 Austl. Y.B. Int'l L. 1 (1983); Jack L. Goldsmith & Eric A. Posner, A Theory of Customary International Law, 66 UCLR 1113, 1120–39 (1999).

239. See Fidler, supra note 65, at 234–48; Tasioulas, supra note 101, at 313–20.
240. For the academic literature on custom's "stickiness" or lack of responsiveness of new norms, see Omri Ben-Shahar & John A. E. Pottow, On the Stickiness of Default Rules, 33 Fla. St. U. L. Rev. 651 (2006); Victor Flesicher, The Missing Preferred Return, 31 J. Corp. L. 77, 91–92 (2005).
241. D'Amato, supra note 48, at 12.
242. Id.
243. Thomas M. Franck, Legitimacy in the International System, 82 AJIL 705, 706 (1988). See also David Dyzenhaus, Legality and Legitimacy 1–37 (Oxford: Clarendon Press, 1997).
244. See Ben Chigara, Legitimacy Deficit in Custom: A Deconstructionist Critique 146–56 (Aldershot: Ashgate Dartmouth, 2001) (explaining a deconstruction of CIL's legitimacy).
245. See id. at 107–9, 111–13.
246. See Franck, supra note 243, at 725, 735. See also Thomas M. Franck, The Power of Legitimacy Among Nations 92–96 (Oxford: Oxford Univ. Press, 1990).
247. Franck, supra note 243, at 725.
248. See Kelly, supra note 12, at 518–26 (also discussing the problem of extending the application of CIL norms to newly independent states); Lepard, supra note 85, at 26–28.
249. See this chapter, supra text at notes 79–81. Compare 1 Georg Schwarzenberger, International Law as Applied by International Courts and Tribunals 35 (3d ed.; London: Stevens & Sons, 1957) (arguing that all states count equally in the process of CIL formation); with Wolfke, supra note 39, at 78–79 ("Practice being the nucleus of custom, those states are the most important which have the greatest share and interests in such practice – that is, in most cases the great powers.").
250. See Goldsmith & Posner, supra note 74, at 205–24. See also John O. McGinnis, The Comparative Disadvantage of Customary International Law, 30 Harv. J. L. & Pub. Pol'y 7 (2006).
251. See Robert Jennings, International Courts and International Politics 65–67 (Hull: Hull Univ. Press, 1986); Kelly, supra note 12, at 537 (any "perceived advantages [of retaining CIL] are not only illusory, but are more than offset by significant disadvantages."); van Hoof, supra note 69, at 114–16; Charles de Visscher, Theory and Reality in Public International Law 156 (P. E. Corbett transl.; Princeton: Princeton Univ. Press, 1957).
252. See Kelly, supra note 12, at 538–42 (arguing that treaties provide a complete alternative to CIL).
253. See Fidler, supra note 65, at 220–24; Roozbeh (Rudy) B. Baker, Customary International Law in the 21st Century: Old Challenges and New Debates, 21 Eur. J. Int. Law 173 (2010).

CONCLUSION

1. See Bederman, supra note 137 (ch. 10), at 140–54.
2. See Chapter 9, text at notes 62–105.
3. See Chapter 5, text at notes 71–94.
4. See Chapter 6, text at notes 43–79.

5. See Chapter 2, text at notes 27–31.
6. See Chapter 2, text at note 84; Chapter 3, text at note 30; Chapter 9, text at note 13.
7. See Chapter 3, text at notes 5–18.
8. See Chapter 6, text at notes 62–79.
9. See Chapter 8, text at notes 27–64.
10. See Chapter 9, text at note 58.
11. See Chapter 10, text at note 46.
12. See Chapter 11, text at notes 207–210.
13. See Chapter 1, text at note 6.
14. See Frederick Schauer, Positivism Before Hart, available at http://papers.ssrn.com/sol3/papers.cfm?abstract_id=1512646 (version of Nov. 24, 2009).
15. See Chapter 7, text at notes 75–79 (Lisa Bernstein); Chapter 9, text at note 35 (George Rutherglen); Chapter 11, text at notes 206–23 (Jack Goldsmith and Eric Posner).
16. See Chapter 10, text at note 47.
17. See, e.g., Chapter 2, text at notes 40–45.
18. See Chapter 2, text at notes 95–105.
19. See Chapter 7, text at notes 75–79.
20. See Chapter 10, text at note 47.
21. See Chapter 10, text at notes 119–27.
22. See Chapter 2, text at notes 32–36, 85–86.
23. See Chapter 3, text at note 23.
24. See Chapter 3, text at notes 54–62.
25. See Chapter 7, text at note 12.
26. See Chapter 9, text at notes 81–87.
27. See Chapter 11, text at notes 89–90.
28. See Chapter 11, text at notes 136–37.
29. This may help to explain why under the Uniform Commercial Code, courses of dealing are given more probative weight than industry usages. See U.C.C. § 205(4). See Chapter 7, text at note 49.
30. See Chapter 2, text at notes 6, 37–39.
31. See Chapter 2, text at notes 79–82.
32. See Chapter 3, text at notes 82–105.
33. See Chapter 1, text at notes 84–88.
34. Agreement for the Prosecution and Punishment of the Major War Criminals of the European Axis, Aug. 8, 1945, art. 6, 59 Stat. 1544, 1548, 82 U.N.T.S. 279, 288 ("London Charter").
35. See In re Goering, 13 Ann. Dig. of Public Int'l L. Cases 203, 208 (Int'l Mil. Trib. 1946); In re Ohlendorf, 15 I.L.R. 656 (U.S. Mil. Trib. 1948).
36. See Tadic, 35 I.L.M. 32 (Int'l Crim. Trib. Former Yugo. 1996). See also Theodor Meron, The Continuing Role of Custom in the Formation of International Humanitarian Law, 90 AJIL 238 (1996); Baker, supra note 253 (Ch. 11), at 184–209.
37. See Chapter 4, text at notes 44, 55 84–85.
38. See Chapter 5, text at notes 40–57, 71–94.
39. See Chapter 7, text at notes 23–31, 61–64; Chapter 10, text at notes 63–65.
40. See Chapter 8, text at notes 30–55.
41. See Chapter 1, at note 80.

42. See Chapter 8, text at notes 10–17 (issues in tort law).
43. See Chapter 3, text at notes 5–18; Chapter 9, text at notes 3–31.
44. See Chapter 4, text at notes 22–49.
45. See Chapter 4, text at note 85.
46. See Chapter 6, text at notes 80–84 (property rights and takings); Chapter 9, text at notes 42–62 (civil liberties and section 1983).
47. See Chapter 1, text at note 5; Chapter 4, text at note 21 (for Hayek's position).
48. See Chapter 5, text at notes 1–20.
49. See Chapter 7, text at notes 10, 79; Chapter 8, text at 40–64.
50. See Chapter 11, text at note 250.
51. See Chapter 11, text at notes 242–51.
52. See Chapter 5 (Nigeria and South Africa); Chapter 6 (Australia, Hawaii, and Oregon), Chapters 8 and 9 (United States).
53. But see Chapter 7, text at note 43; Chapter 10, text at note 44 (for material on custom in German commercial law).
54. See Chapter 7, text at notes 38–71; Chapter 10, text at notes 89–118.
55. See Chapter 5, text at notes 58–94.
56. See Chapter 7, text at note 49.
57. See Chapter 10, text at notes 89–118.
58. See Chapter 3, text at notes 121–24; Chapter 5, text at notes 54–57.
59. See Chapter 3, at note 55 (in English common law); Chapter 10, text at note 66 (international commercial usages).
60. See Chapter 11, text at notes 143–69, 251–52.
61. Just. Dig. 1.3.37 (Paul, Questions 1). See also Chapter, at note 26.
62. See Chapter 2, text at notes 53–55.
63. See Chapter 7, text at note 36.
64. See Chapter 9, text at notes 72–73.
65. See Chapter 11, text at notes 160–84.
66. Hart, supra note 1 (ch. 1), at 44.
67. See Chapter 1, text at notes 14–28; Chapter 3, text at notes 106–20.
68. See Chapter 1, text at notes 73–80.
69. See Chapter 4, text at notes 57–77.
70. See Chapter 4, text at note 64.
71. See Chapter 8, text at notes 46–47.
72. See Chapter 9, text at notes 62–105.
73. See Chapter 11, text at notes 134–42.
74. See Chapter 11, text at notes 124 & 245.
75. See Chapter 1, text at notes 29–52; Chapter 3, text at notes 129–32; Chapter 4, text at notes 78–90.
76. Charles Davenant, Circe: A Tragedy (act II; scene 3) (London: Richard Tonson, 1677).
77. Hume, supra note 106 (ch. 3), at § 5, pt. 1, at 36.
78. William Shakespeare, Hamlet, in The Complete Works 940 (Alfred Harbage gen. ed.; New York: Viking Press, 1969) (act I, scene 4, line 16) (c. 1599).

Index

positivism (*Cont.*)
    medieval *ius commune*, 22–25
    overview, 16
    Roman law, 17–22
    of Suárez, and customary international
        law, 138–40
Posner, Richard
    critique of Hayek, 47–48
    customary international law, 161–62, 163
    evolution of customs, 46–47
    implications of Coase theorem, 48–49
    insidious practices in customary regimes,
        47
    laws versus norms, 51–52
    The T.J. HOOPER, 98
    trade usages, 89
Pound, Roscoe, 91
"practical construction" of constitutional
        provisions, 108–12
practices
    international customs as general, 144,
        145–49
    versus rules, 45
    versus standards, 9
pre-Blackstonian epoch, 27, 28–30
pre-literate societies
    applications of custom, 11–14
    evolutions of custom, 11–14
    overview, 3–4
    proof of custom, 11–14
    theories of custom in law of, 4–11
    top-down custom creation in, 45
    transitions to literate legal cultures, 14–15
Prescription Act, 38
presidency, and separation-of-powers
        disputes, 108–12
primary rules of obligation, 5
primitive law, 3. *See also* pre-literate societies
Primitive Law Past and Present (Diamond),
        10
primogeniture, 65–66
Principles of International Commercial
        Contracts ("UNIDROIT Principles"),
        130–131
private international law
    in Anglo-American case-law, 124–29
    historical roots of, 118–21
    international codifications, 129–31
    modern *lex mercatoria*, 131–34
    overview, 117–18
    positivist revolution and cross-border trade
        usages, 121–24

private law, 18, 168–69. *See also* contracts;
        family law; property law; torts
private rules of conduct, in tort, 93
The Problem of Social Cost (Coase), 48
proof of customs
    Blackstone, 32
    in canon law, 23–24
    commercial, 82–83
    constitutional, 110–11
    in Hawaii, 71
    in *ius commune*, 24
    overview, 172–73, 200
    in pluralistic legal systems, 61–62
    pre-literate, 11–14
    probative of standard of care, 95–97
    in Roman law, 19
    unallowable as evidence in tort, 94–95
property law
    amongst Trobriand Islanders, 12
    customary easements and judicial
        takings, 75–79
    indigenous custom, 69–75
    overview, 68–69
provincial customs in Roman law, 18–19
psychology
    anti-law, custom as, 51–52
    efficient custom, 48–51
    functional component, custom as, 42–44
    overview, 42
    social control, custom as, 44–48
*Public Access Shoreline Hawaii v. Hawai`i
        County Planning Commission*
        ("PASH"), 72–75, 76
public beach access, 76–78
public international law
    change and death for, 159–61
    and commercial norms, 133–34
    evolution of CIL, 138–43
    formation of CIL, 144–51
    new synthesis for, 161–67
    overview, 135–138
    regional and special customs, 151–55
    and treaties, 155–59
public law, 168–69. *See also* constitutional law
public policy, and torts, 97–100
pupillary inheritance, 18

R
Rawls, John, 45
reasonableness of customs, 35–37, 83–84,
        87, 89, 163
reciprocity, 6, 13